PINDAR

II

LCL 485

PINDAR

NEMEAN ODES
ISTHMIAN ODES
FRAGMENTS

EDITED AND TRANSLATED BY

WILLIAM H. RACE

HARVARD UNIVERSITY PRESS

CAMBRIDGE, MASSACHUSETTS
LONDON, ENGLAND

First published 1997
Revised 2012

Library of Congress Control Number 95-42927
CIP data available from the Library of Congress

ISBN 978-0-674-99534-5

Composed in ZephGreek and ZephText by
Technologies 'N Typography, Merrimac, Massachusetts.
Printed on acid-free paper and bound by
The Maple-Vail Book Manufacturing Group

CONTENTS

NEMEONIKAI

NEMEAN ODES

NEMEAN 1

Pindar composed two odes for Chromius (*Nem.* 1 and 9), Hieron's powerful and wealthy general. In his previous service as a military commander for Hippocrates, tyrant of Gela (498–491), Chromius had distinguished himself in the battle at the Helorus River in 492 (cf. *Nem.* 9.40) against the Syracusans. He then joined Hippocrates' successor, Gelon, who became tyrant of Syracuse, and upon Gelon's death in 478, he served Hieron, who had succeeded his older brother. Chromius was probably sent to protect Western Locri from Anaxilas of Rhegium in 477 and according to the scholia was appointed governor of Aetna after its foundation in 476. The inscriptions of two MSS designate the victor as Chromius "of Aetna" (cf. "Zeus of Aetna" at 6). If they are correct, the ode was composed after 476.

This is one of two epinicia—the other is *Nem.* 10—whose central narrative extends to the end of the poem. The account of Heracles' prodigious infancy is probably meant to reflect Chromius' own divinely inspired beginnings (8–9), while the concluding depiction of the apotheosis Heracles earned by his arduous service to the gods perhaps hints at the posthumous fame Chromius may win by his own career.

The opening address names Ortygia, the eponymous

nymph of the island enclosing Syracuse's harbor, as the source of this poem celebrating Chromius' Nemean chariot victory (1–7). After reflections on the divine basis of Chromius' talents and the glorification of success in poetry, Pindar praises Sicily for its fertility, fine cities, and success in war and athletics (8–18).

He then praises Chromius for his generous hospitality, which wins him friends to defend against detractors, and for his combination of strength and wisdom (19–30). The poet personally endorses the use of wealth to help friends and gain praise because all men hope for relief from hardship and fame for achievements (31–33). The poet declares his eagerness to sing of Heracles when he is treating great achievements, and begins by recounting how, when Heracles and his twin brother Iphicles were born, Hera sent two snakes to kill them in their crib (33–43), but Heracles grasped one in each hand and strangled them (43–47). Alcmene jumped up from her bed in panic to protect her son, while Amphitryon came with a band of warriors (48–53). His fearful expectations, however, turned to relief and awe when he saw the wondrous power of his son (54–59).

Teiresias, summoned to interpret the events, prophesied Heracles' future career (60–61), telling that after slaying numerous beasts on land and sea, and vanquishing savage men, he would help the gods defeat the Giants at Phlegra, and that in reward for his labors he would find peace with the gods on Olympus, with Hebe as his wife (62–72).

1. ΧΡΟΜΙΩΙ ΑΙΤΝΑΙΩΙ

ΙΠΠΟΙΣ

Α΄ Ἄμπνευμα σεμνὸν Ἀλφεοῦ,
κλεινᾶν Συρακοσσᾶν θάλος Ὀρτυγία,
δέμνιον Ἀρτέμιδος,
Δάλου κασιγνήτα, σέθεν ἁδυεπής
5 ὕμνος ὁρμᾶται θέμεν
αἶνον ἀελλοπόδων
μέγαν ἵππων Ζηνὸς Αἰτναίου χάριν·
ἅρμα δ᾽ ὀτρύνει Χρομίου Νεμέα
τ᾽ ἔργμασιν νικαφόροις ἐγκώμιον ζεῦξαι μέλος.

ἀρχαὶ δὲ βέβληνται θεῶν
κείνου σὺν ἀνδρὸς δαιμονίαις ἀρεταῖς·
10 ἔστι δ᾽ ἐν εὐτυχίᾳ
πανδοξίας ἄκρον· μεγάλων δ᾽ ἀέθλων
Μοῖσα μεμνᾶσθαι φιλεῖ.

inscr. αἰτναίῳ ἵπποις UV²: om. BV¹D: συρακουσίῳ ἵπποις
Schroeder

---

[1] Or *resting place*. The river Alpheus fell in love with the
nymph Arethusa and pursued her under the sea until she came to

4

1. FOR CHROMIUS OF AETNA

WINNER, CHARIOT RACE, post 476 B.C.

Hallowed spout[1] of Alpheus,   Str. 1
Ortygia, offspring of famous Syracuse,
couch of Artemis,
and sister of Delos,[2] from you a sweetly worded
hymn issues forth to render   5
mighty praise for storm-footed
    horses in honor of Zeus of Aetna;
and the chariot of Chromius and Nemea urge me
    to yoke a song of celebration for victorious deeds.

The beginnings have been laid by the gods   Ant. 1
with that man's divine abilities,
but in success is   10
the summit of absolute glory, and the Muse
loves to recall great contests.

the island of Ortygia, where her fountain was located and from
which his waters were believed to re-issue.
  [2] A cult center for Artemis (cf. *Pyth.* 2.7), Ortygia is called
sister of Delos (the birthplace of Artemis), one of whose names is
also Ortygia (cf. Verg. *Aen.* 3.124).

σπεῖρέ νυν ἀγλαΐαν
   τινὰ νάσῳ, τὰν Ὀλύμπου δεσπότας
Ζεὺς ἔδωκεν Φερσεφόνᾳ, κατένευ-
   σέν τέ οἱ χαίταις ἀριστεύοισαν εὐκάρπου χθονός

15 Σικελίαν πίειραν ὀρθώ-
   σειν κορυφαῖς πολίων ἀφνεαῖς·
ὤπασε δὲ Κρονίων πολέμου
   μναστῆρά οἱ χαλκεντέος
λαὸν ἵππαιχμον, θαμὰ δὴ καὶ Ὀλυμ-
   πιάδων φύλλοις ἐλαιᾶν χρυσέοις
μιχθέντα. πολλῶν ἐπέβαν
   καιρὸν οὐ ψεύδει βαλών.

Β΄ ἔσταν δ᾽ ἐπ᾽ αὐλείαις θύραις
20 ἀνδρὸς φιλοξείνου καλὰ μελπόμενος,
ἔνθα μοι ἁρμόδιον
   δεῖπνον κεκόσμηται, θαμὰ δ᾽ ἀλλοδαπῶν
οὐκ ἀπείρατοι δόμοι
   ἐντί· λέλογχε δὲ μεμ-
φομένοις ἐσλοὺς ὕδωρ καπνῷ φέρειν
25 ἀντίον. τέχναι δ᾽ ἑτέρων ἕτεραι·
   χρὴ δ᾽ ἐν εὐθείαις ὁδοῖς στείχοντα μάρνασθαι
   φυᾷ.

13 σπεῖρέ νυν Beck e schol.: ἔγειρε νῦν codd.
24 ἐσλοὺς Aristarchus: ἐσλὸς codd.

6

Sow, then, some splendor
    on the island, which Zeus, the master of Olympus,
gave to Persephone, and with a nod of his locks
    assured her that he would exalt

fertile Sicily to be the best of the fruitful earth   Ep. 1
    with her lofty and prosperous cities;
and Cronus' son granted to her[3] a people   16
    of cavalrymen enamored of bronze-armored war
and often indeed crowned
    with golden olive leaves
from Olympic festivals.[4] I have embarked on an occasion
    for many topics without casting any falsehood.

And I have taken my stand at the courtyard gates   Str. 2
of a generous host as I sing of noble deeds,   20
where a fitting feast
has been arranged for me, for this home
is not unfamiliar with frequent visitors
from abroad. It is his lot to bring
    good men against his detractors as water
against smoke. Various men have various skills,   25
    but one must travel in straight paths and strive by
        means of natural talent.

[3] Persephone, or perhaps Sicily.
[4] Since Chromius has no Olympic victories, this refers generally to Sicilian success at Olympia and perhaps as well to Gelon's and Hieron's victories there.

7

πράσσει γὰρ ἔργῳ μὲν σθένος,
βουλαῖσι δὲ φρήν, ἐσσόμενον προϊδεῖν
συγγενὲς οἷς ἕπεται.
Ἀγησιδάμου παῖ, σέο δ᾽ ἀμφὶ τρόπῳ
30 τῶν τε καὶ τῶν χρήσιες.
οὐκ ἔραμαι πολὺν ἐν
    μεγάρῳ πλοῦτον κατακρύψαις ἔχειν,
ἀλλ᾽ ἐόντων εὖ τε παθεῖν καὶ ἀκοῦ-
    σαι φίλοις ἐξαρκέων. κοιναὶ γὰρ ἔρχοντ᾽ ἐλπίδες

πολυπόνων ἀνδρῶν. ἐγὼ δ᾽ Ἡ-
    ρακλέος ἀντέχομαι προφρόνως
ἐν κορυφαῖς ἀρετᾶν μεγάλαις,
    ἀρχαῖον ὀτρύνων λόγον,
35 ὡς, ἐπεὶ σπλάγχνων ὕπο ματέρος αὐ-
    τίκα θαητὰν ἐς αἴγλαν παῖς Διός
ὠδῖνα φεύγων διδύμῳ
    σὺν κασιγνήτῳ μόλεν,

Γ´ ὡς οὐ λαθὼν χρυσόθρονον
    Ἥραν κροκωτὸν σπάργανον ἐγκατέβα·
ἀλλὰ θεῶν βασίλεα
40 σπερχθεῖσα θυμῷ πέμπε δράκοντας ἄφαρ.

37 ὥς Hermann: ὥς τ᾽ codd.
39 βασίλεα Heyne: βασιλέα Boeckh: βασίλεια codd.

8

For strength achieves its result through action,   Ant. 2
and wisdom through the counsels of those attended by
inborn ability to foresee what will happen.
But, son of Hagesidamus, by virtue of your character
there are uses for both of them.   30
I do not desire to keep great wealth
    hidden away in a palace,
but to succeed with what I have and be praised for
    helping friends, because to all alike come the hopes

of much-toiling men.[5] For my part, I gladly   Ep. 2
    embrace Heracles
when my theme is achievements' great heights,
    and rouse up the old tale,
how, as soon as Zeus' son came down from his mother's   35
    womb into the wondrous brightness of day,
fleeing her birth pains
    with his twin brother,[6]

he did not escape the notice of Hera on her golden   Str. 3
    throne
when he lay down in his yellow swaddling clothes,
but the queen of the gods
with anger in her heart immediately sent snakes.   40

---

[5] ἐλπίδες may be negative and imply "expectations" of trouble
or death (cf. *Nem.* 7.30–31) or positive and imply "hopes" for fame
after death. As E. L. Bundy (*Studia Pindarica* 87) points out, the
forthcoming narrative culminating in Heracles' apotheosis em-
phasizes the latter.

[6] Iphicles, Heracles' half-brother and son of the mortal Am-
phitryon.

τοὶ μὲν οἰχθεισᾶν πυλᾶν
ἐς θαλάμου μυχὸν εὐ-
    ρὺν ἔβαν, τέκνοισιν ὠκείας γνάθους
ἀμφελίξασθαι μεμαῶτες· ὁ δ' ὀρ-
    θὸν μὲν ἄντεινεν κάρα, πειρᾶτο δὲ πρῶτον
        μάχας,

διссαῖσι δοιοὺς αὐχένων
45 μάρψαις ἀφύκτοις χερσὶν ἑαῖς ὄφιας·
ἀγχομένοις δὲ χρόνος
ψυχὰς ἀπέπνευσεν μελέων ἀφάτων.
ἐκ δ' ἄρ' ἄτλατον δέος
πλᾶξε γυναῖκας, ὅσαι
    τύχον Ἀλκμήνας ἀρήγοισαι λέχει·
50 καὶ γὰρ αὐτὰ ποσσὶν ἄπεπλος ὀρού-
    σαισ' ἀπὸ στρωμνᾶς ὅμως ἄμυνεν ὕβριν
        κνωδάλων.

ταχὺ δὲ Καδμείων ἀγοὶ χαλ-
    κέοις σὺν ὅπλοις ἔδραμον ἀθρόοι,
ἐν χερὶ δ' Ἀμφιτρύων κολεοῦ
    γυμνὸν τινάσσων ⟨φάσγανον⟩
ἵκετ', ὀξείαις ἀνίαισι τυπείς.
    τὸ γὰρ οἰκεῖον πιέζει πάνθ' ὁμῶς·
εὐθὺς δ' ἀπήμων κραδία
    κᾶδος ἀμφ' ἀλλότριον.

Δ′ ἔστα δὲ θάμβει δυσφόρῳ
56 τερπνῷ τε μιχθείς. εἶδε γὰρ ἐκνόμιον

10

When the doors had been opened
they went into the deep recess of the bedroom,
    eager to wrap their darting jaws
around the babies. But the boy lifted
    his head straight up and engaged in his first battle,

grasping the two snakes by their necks   Ant. 3
in his two inescapable hands,   45
and as they were being strangled, the passage of time
exhaled the life from their monstrous bodies.
Unbearable fear
struck all the women who at the time
    were attending Alcmene's bed,
and even in her condition she sprang from her couch   50
    to her feet without any robe and began warding off
        the beasts' attack.

And swiftly the Cadmean chieftains came running   Ep. 3
    in a group with their bronze arms,
and Amphitryon arrived brandishing his unsheathed
    sword in his hand,
stricken with piercing anguish
    (for one's own sorrow oppresses every man alike,
whereas the heart is soon free from pain
    at someone else's trouble).

He stood there, stunned with wonder both painful   Str. 4
and joyous, for he saw the extraordinary   56

---

52 ⟨φάσγανον⟩ suppl. Moschopulus

PINDAR

λῆμά τε καὶ δύναμιν
υἱοῦ· παλίγγλωσσον δέ οἱ ἀθάνατοι
ἀγγέλων ῥῆσιν θέσαν.
60 γείτονα δ᾽ ἐκκάλεσεν
    Διὸς ὑψίστου προφάταν ἔξοχον,
    ὀρθόμαντιν Τειρεσίαν· ὁ δέ οἱ
    φράζε καὶ παντὶ στρατῷ, ποίαις ὁμιλήσει τύχαις,

    ὅσσους μὲν ἐν χέρσῳ κτανών,
    ὅσσους δὲ πόντῳ θῆρας ἀιδροδίκας·
    καί τινα σὺν πλαγίῳ
65 ἀνδρῶν κόρῳ στείχοντα τὸν ἐχθρότατον
    φᾶσέ νιν δώσειν μόρον.
    καὶ γὰρ ὅταν θεοὶ ἐν
    πεδίῳ Φλέγρας Γιγάντεσσιν μάχαν
    ἀντιάζωσιν, βελέων ὑπὸ ῥι-
    παῖσι κείνου φαιδίμαν γαίᾳ πεφύρσεσθαι κόμαν

    ἔνεπεν· αὐτὸν μὰν ἐν εἰρή-
    νᾳ τὸν ἄπαντα χρόνον ⟨ἐν⟩ σχερῷ

60 ἐκκάλεσεν Triclinius: ἐκκάλεσαν BᵖᶜDVl: ἐκάλεσαν
BᵃᶜUV
64–65 τινα . . . στείχοντα codd.: τινι . . . στείχοντι
Hermann
66 φᾶσέ νιν δώσειν codd.: φᾶ ἓ δωάσειν Snell praeeuntibus
Wilamowitz et Theiler | μόρῳ Beck
69 ⟨ἐν⟩ suppl. Hermann

12

determination and power
of his son, since the immortal gods had
reversed the messengers' report to him.[7]
He summoned his neighbor,   60
    the foremost prophet of highest Zeus,
the straight-speaking seer Teiresias, who declared to him
    and to all the people what fortunes he[8] would
        encounter:

all the lawless beasts he would slay on land,   Ant. 4
and all those in the sea;
and to many a man[9] who traveled
in crooked excess he said that   65
he[10] would give the most hateful doom.
And furthermore, when the gods would meet the Giants
    in battle on the plain of Phlegra,
he said that beneath a volley of his arrows
    their bright hair would be fouled

with earth, but that he himself   Ep. 4
    in continual peace for all time

[7] I.e. Heracles had killed the snakes, not the reverse (schol.).
[8] Heracles.
[9] Or *a certain man*: a scholion suggests Busiris and Antaeus
(cf. *Isth.* 4.52–55).
[10] Heracles.

70 ἡσυχίαν καμάτων μεγάλων
      ποινὰν λαχόντ᾽ ἐξαίρετον
    ὀλβίοις ἐν δώμασι, δεξάμενον
      θαλερὰν Ἥβαν ἄκοιτιν καὶ γάμον
    δαίσαντα πὰρ Δὶ Κρονίδᾳ,
      σεμνὸν αἰνήσειν νόμον.

72 *νόμον* Pauw e schol.: δόμον B^iDU: γάμον B^sV

would be allotted tranquillity as the choicest   70
    recompense for his great labors
in a blissful home, and, after receiving
    flourishing Hebe as his wife
and celebrating his wedding feast with Cronus' son Zeus,
    would praise his[11] hallowed rule.

[11] Zeus'.

NEMEAN 2

Timodemus, the namesake of his clan, the Timodemidae from Acharnae (an Athenian deme), has increased their impressive list of successes by his Nemean victory in the pancratium. The poet surmises that this is but the prelude (or down payment) to future victories in the crown games, and suggests, by the analogy of Orion following close behind the Pleiades, that an Olympic victory, conspicuously absent from the family's list, may come in due course. This optimism is bolstered by the example of Ajax from nearby Salamis (where the scholia claim Timodemus was raised) and by the proven success of the Timodemidae in athletics.

Because the poem is monostrophic and at the end calls on the citizens to lead off in song, some have suggested that it was a processional song intended for *da capo* repetition. There is, however, no external evidence for such a practice.

Just as rhapsodes begin their performances with a prelude to Zeus, Timodemus has made a beginning with his victory at Zeus' Nemean games (1–5), and if he continues in the tradition of his fathers, he is likely to win many more times at the Isthmus, Delphi, and (it is implied) at Olympia (6–12). Salamis raised a great fighter in Ajax, and Timodemus is exalted by his victory in the pancratium

(13–15). Among the brave Acharnians the Timodemidae are the foremost in athletics (16–18). They have won four Pythian crowns, eight Isthmian, seven Nemean, and many local ones (19–24). The citizens are called upon to sing praises of Zeus as Timodemus returns in glory (24–25).

2. ΤΙΜΟΔΗΜΩΙ
ΑΧΑΡΝΕΙ
ΠΑΓΚΡΑΤΕΙ

A΄ Ὅθεν περ καὶ Ὁμηρίδαι
ῥαπτῶν ἐπέων τὰ πόλλ᾽ ἀοιδοί
ἄρχονται, Διὸς ἐκ προοιμίου, καὶ ὅδ᾽ ἀνήρ
καταβολὰν ἱερῶν ἀγώ-
νων νικαφορίας δέδεκται πρῶτον Νεμεαίου
5 ἐν πολυυμνήτῳ Διὸς ἄλσει.

B΄ ὀφείλει δ᾽ ἔτι, πατρίαν
εἴπερ καθ᾽ ὁδόν νιν εὐθυπομπός
αἰὼν ταῖς μεγάλαις δέδωκε κόσμον Ἀθάναις,
θαμὰ μὲν Ἰσθμιάδων δρέπε-
σθαι κάλλιστον ἄωτον ἐν Πυθίοισί τε νικᾶν
10 Τιμονόου παῖδ᾽· ἔστι δ᾽ ἐοικός

inscr. παγκρατεῖ D: παγκράτιον TU: παγκρατιαστῇ
Moschopulus: om. BV

18

2. FOR TIMODEMUS OF ACHARNAE

WINNER, PANCRATIUM

Just as the sons of Homer, those singers   Str. 1
of verses stitched together,[1] most often begin
with a prelude to Zeus, so has this man
received his first installment of victory
    in the sacred games at the much-hymned
sanctuary of Nemean Zeus.   5

But Timonoös' son is still indebted—if indeed his life,   Str. 2
while guiding him straight on the path of his fathers,
has given him as an adornment for great Athens—
to pluck again and again the fairest prize
    of the Isthmian festivals and to be victorious
in the Pythian games; and it is likely   10

---

[1] Composers and reciters of Homeric poems were called "sons of Homer" or "rhapsodes" (literally "singers of stitched-together verses"). Their independent compositions, like the Homeric Hymns, were commonly called "preludes."

Γ'   ὀρειᾶν γε Πελειάδων
     μὴ τηλόθεν Ὠαρίωνα νεῖσθαι.
     καὶ μὰν ἁ Σαλαμίς γε θρέψαι φῶτα μαχατάν
     δυνατός. ἐν Τροΐᾳ μὲν Ἕ-
        κτωρ Αἴαντος ἄκουσεν· ὦ Τιμόδημε, σὲ δ' ἀλκά
15   παγκρατίου τλάθυμος ἀέξει.

Δ'   Ἀχάρναι δὲ παλαίφατον
     εὐάνορες· ὅσσα δ' ἀμφ' ἀέθλοις,
     Τιμοδημίδαι ἐξοχώτατοι προλέγονται.
     παρὰ μὲν ὑψιμέδοντι Παρ-
        νασσῷ τέσσαρας ἐξ ἀέθλων νίκας ἐκόμιξαν·
20   ἀλλὰ Κορινθίων ὑπὸ φωτῶν

Ε'   ἐν ἐσλοῦ Πέλοπος πτυχαῖς
     ὀκτὼ στεφάνοις ἔμιχθεν ἤδη·
     ἑπτὰ δ' ἐν Νεμέᾳ, τὰ δ' οἴκοι μάσσον' ἀριθμοῦ,
     Διὸς ἀγῶνι. τόν, ὦ πολῖ-
        ται, κωμάξατε Τιμοδήμῳ σὺν εὐκλέι νόστῳ·
25   ἁδυμελεῖ δ' ἐξάρχετε φωνᾷ.

     14 μὲν Byz.: μὰν vett.

that Orion is traveling not far behind   Str. 3
the mountain Pleiades.[2]
And indeed Salamis is certainly capable of rearing
a fighter. At Troy Hector heard
    from Ajax;[3] but you, O Timodemus, the stout-hearted
strength of the pancratium exalts.   15

Acharnae is famous of old   Str. 4
for brave men, and in all that pertains to athletic games
the Timodemidae are proclaimed foremost.
From the games beside lofty-ruling Parnassus
    they have carried off four victories,
whereas by the men of Corinth   20

in the valleys of noble Pelops[4]   Str. 5
they have so far been joined to eight crowns;
there are seven at Nemea in Zeus' contest, and at home
too many to count. Celebrate him,[5] O citizens,
    in honor of Timodemus upon his glorious return,
and lead off with a sweetly melodious voice.   25

  [2] As constellations the Pleiades rise about the middle of May,
Orion a week later. Given the rising prestige of the envisioned
victories—(Nemean), Isthmian, Pythian—the presence of Orion
probably hints at an Olympic victory to follow.
  [3] Cf. *Il.* 7.181–272 and 14.402–420.
  [4] In the Peloponnesus.
  [5] Zeus.

NEMEAN 3

At the beginning of the poem the chorus of young men is eagerly waiting on Aegina to receive the song from the Muse, and at the end we are told that the ode was late in coming. The poet, however, provides no explanation for the delay. The central portion of the ode sketches the principal exploits of three Aeginetan heroes, Peleus, Telamon, and Achilles. In particular, Achilles' youthful prowess exemplifies the inborn greatness of the Aeacidae.

The poet summons the Muse to Aegina, where the chorus is awaiting her voice (1–5). A summary priamel emphasizes victory's love of song (6–8). The Muse is requested to begin a hymn to Zeus for the poet to impart to the singers and the lyre (9–12). He is pleased to praise this island, home of the Myrmidons, and Aristocleides, who has won the pancratium at Nemea (12–18).

The assertion that Aristocleides has reached the limit of human success, symbolized by the Pillars of Heracles, prompts a brief digression on Heracles' exploration of the western Mediterranean (19–26). Implying that his enthusiasm has carried him away, the poet redirects his praise to the Aeacidae, a more relevant theme (26–32).

Peleus single-handedly subdued the city of Iolcus and captured Thetis for his wife (32–36); Telamon and Iolaus sacked Laomedon's Troy and fought against the Amazons

(36–39). A gnomic statement praising inborn ability and declaring that mere learning lacks clear purpose and proves ineffective (40–42) leads to extended praise of Achilles, whose prodigious hunting prowess at age six amazed even Artemis and Athena (43–52). A brief priamel listing Chiron's pupils culminates in his preparation of Achilles for the expedition against Troy, where he fought against Memnon (52–63).

After addressing Zeus as progenitor of the Aeacidae and patron of Nemea, the poet praises Aristocleides for the glory he brings to Aegina and for the hopeful expectations he inspires in the official delegation to Delphi (64–70). But it is through trial that merit is revealed at each stage of a man's life (70–74). We mortals are guided by four virtues and must live in the present (74–75). The poet states that the victor possesses these virtues and, in imitation of hymnal style, bids him farewell (76).

He sends the victor this draught of song and admits that it is late (76–80). By implicitly comparing himself to an eagle swooping on its prey, Pindar implies that he has nobly fulfilled his duty to praise Aristocleides (80–82) and assures him that his victories at Nemea, Epidaurus, and Megara have achieved recognition in poetry (83–84).

3. ΑΡΙΣΤΟΚΛΕΙΔΗΙ
ΑΙΓΙΝΗΤΗΙ
ΠΑΓΚΡΑΤΙΑΣΤΗΙ

Α΄   Ὦ πότνια Μοῖσα, μᾶτερ ἁμετέρα, λίσσομαι,
   τὰν πολυξέναν ἐν ἱερομηνίᾳ Νεμεάδι
   ἵκεο Δωρίδα νᾶσον Αἴγιναν· ὕδατι γάρ
   μένοντ᾽ ἐπ᾽ Ἀσωπίῳ μελιγαρύων τέκτονες
5   κώμων νεανίαι, σέθεν ὄπα μαιόμενοι.
   διψῇ δὲ πρᾶγος ἄλλο μὲν ἄλλου,
   ἀεθλονικία δὲ μάλιστ᾽ ἀοιδὰν φιλεῖ,
   στεφάνων ἀρετᾶν τε δεξιωτάταν ὀπαδόν·

   τᾶς ἀφθονίαν ὄπαζε μήτιος ἁμᾶς ἄπο·
10 ἄρχε δ᾽ οὐρανοῦ πολυνεφέλα κρέοντι, θύγατερ,
   δόκιμον ὕμνον· ἐγὼ δὲ κείνων τέ νιν ὀάροις
   λύρᾳ τε κοινάσομαι. χαρίεντα δ᾽ ἕξει πόνον
   χώρας ἄγαλμα, Μυρμιδόνες ἵνα πρότεροι

inscr. αἰγινήτῃ παγκρατιαστῇ D: om. BV

---

[1] The main river Asopus runs through Boeotia, south of
Thebes; an Asopus also ran near Sicyon. Following a citation of

24

3. FOR ARISTOCLEIDES OF AEGINA

WINNER, PANCRATIUM

O mistress Muse, our mother, I beg of you,	Str. 1
come in the Nemean sacred month to this	
much-visited Dorian island of Aegina, for by the water	
of Asopus[1] are waiting the builders of honey-sounding	
revels, young men who seek your voice.	5
Different deeds thirst for different rewards,	
but victory in the games loves song most of all,	
the fittest companion for crowned achievements.	

Grant from my skill an abundance of such song,	Ant. 1
but begin for the ruler of the cloud-covered sky,	10
daughter,[2]	
a proper hymn, and I shall impart it to their voices	
and the lyre. It will be a joyous task to glorify	
this land, where the Myrmidons of old	

Callistratus (2nd cent. B.C.) in the scholia, G. A. Privitera, in *Quaderni Urbinati di Cultura Classica* 29 (1988) 63–70, has shown the likelihood of a fountain called Asopus on Aegina connected with local athletic contests in honor of Apollo Delphinius.

[2] The Muses were daughters of Zeus by Mnemosyne (cf. Hes. *Th.* 53–55).

PINDAR

ᾤκησαν, ὧν παλαίφατον ἀγοράν
15 οὐκ ἐλεγχέεσσιν Ἀριστοκλείδας τεάν
ἐμίανε κατ' αἶσαν ἐν περισθενεῖ μαλαχθείς

παγκρατίου στόλῳ· καματωδέων δὲ πλαγᾶν
ἄκος ὑγιηρὸν ἐν βαθυπεδίῳ Νεμέᾳ
τὸ καλλίνικον φέρει.
εἰ δ' ἐὼν καλὸς ἔρδων τ' ἐοικότα μορφᾷ
20 ἀνορέαις ὑπερτάταις ἐπέβα
παῖς Ἀριστοφάνεος, οὐκέτι πρόσω
ἀβάταν ἅλα κιόνων ὕπερ Ἡρακλέος περᾶν εὐμαρές,

Β' ἥρως θεὸς ἃς ἔθηκε ναυτιλίας ἐσχάτας
μάρτυρας κλυτάς· δάμασε δὲ θῆρας ἐν πελάγει
ὑπερόχους, ἰδίᾳ τ' ἐρεύνασε τεναγέων
25 ῥοάς, ὁπᾷ πόμπιμον κατέβαινε νόστου τέλος,
καὶ γᾶν φράδασε. θυμέ, τίνα πρὸς ἀλλοδαπάν
ἄκραν ἐμὸν πλόον παραμείβεαι;
Αἰακῷ σε φαμὶ γένει τε Μοῖσαν φέρειν.
ἕπεται δὲ λόγῳ δίκας ἄωτος, "ἐσλὸν αἰνεῖν,"

30 οὐδ' ἀλλοτρίων ἔρωτες ἀνδρὶ φέρειν κρέσσονες·
οἴκοθεν μάτευε. ποτίφορον δὲ κόσμον ἔλαχες

29 ἐσλὸν BVˢVˡ: ἐσλὸς VˡBˡDᶜˡ
31 ἔλαχες Bergk e schol.: ἔλαβες codd.

26

dwelled, whose long-famed assembly place
Aristocleides did not stain with dishonor,   15
thanks to your favor, by weakening in the mighty

course of the pancratium. And for his fatiguing blows   Ep. 1
in Nemea's deep plain he earns as a healing remedy
   his victory.[3]
If, being fair and performing deeds to match his form,
the son of Aristophanes has embarked on utmost   20
   deeds of manhood, it is no easy task to go yet further
across the untracked sea beyond the pillars of Heracles,

which that hero-god established as famed witnesses   Str. 2
of his furthermost voyage. He subdued monstrous beasts
in the sea, and on his own explored the streams of the
   shallows,[4]
where he reached the limit that sent him back home,   25
and he made known the land. My heart, to what alien
headland are you turning aside my ship's course?
To Aeacus and his race I bid you bring the Muse.
The essence of justice attends the precept "praise the
   good,"

but longings for foreign themes are not better for a man   Ant. 2
   to bear.
Search at home, for you have been granted a fitting   31
   adornment

[3] Or *this victory song*.
[4] Probably the currents in the Straits of Gibraltar, where the
so-called pillars of Heracles (Mt. Atlas and the Rock of Gibraltar)
marked the limits of the known world.

γλυκύ τι γαρυέμεν. παλαιαῖσι δ᾽ ἐν ἀρεταῖς
γέγαθε Πηλεὺς ἄναξ, ὑπέραλλον αἰχμὰν ταμών·
ὃς καὶ Ἰαολκὸν εἷλε μόνος ἄνευ στρατιᾶς,
35 καὶ ποντίαν Θέτιν κατέμαρψεν
ἐγκονητί. Λαομέδοντα δ᾽ εὐρυσθενής
Τελαμὼν Ἰόλᾳ παραστάτας ἐὼν ἔπερσεν

καί ποτε χαλκότοξον Ἀμαζόνων μετ᾽ ἀλκάν
ἕπετό οἱ, οὐδέ νίν ποτε φόβος ἀνδροδάμας
    ἔπαυσεν ἀκμὰν φρενῶν.
40 συγγενεῖ δέ τις εὐδοξίᾳ μέγα βρίθει.
ὃς δὲ διδάκτ᾽ ἔχει, ψεφεννὸς ἀνὴρ
    ἄλλοτ᾽ ἄλλα πνέων οὔ ποτ᾽ ἀτρεκεῖ
κατέβα ποδί, μυριᾶν δ᾽ ἀρετᾶν ἀτελεῖ νόῳ γεύεται.

Γ´ ξανθὸς δ᾽ Ἀχιλεὺς τὰ μὲν μένων Φιλύρας ἐν δόμοις,
παῖς ἐὼν ἄθυρε μεγάλα ἔργα· χερσὶ θαμινά
45 βραχυσίδαρον ἄκοντα πάλλων ἴσα τ᾽ ἀνέμοις,
μάχᾳ λεόντεσσιν ἀγροτέροις ἔπρασσεν φόνον,
κάπρους τ᾽ ἔναιρε· σώματα δὲ παρὰ Κρονίδαν
Κένταυρον ἀσθμαίνοντα κόμιζεν,
ἑξέτης τὸ πρῶτον, ὅλον δ᾽ ἔπειτ᾽ ἂν χρόνον·
50 τὸν ἐθάμβεον Ἄρτεμίς τε καὶ θρασεῖ Ἀθάνα,

38 χαλκότοξον V: χαλκοτόξων BD
39 ἀκμὰν V: ἀλκὰν BD
45 ἴσα τ᾽ Moschopulus: ἶσον τ᾽ codd.
46 μάχᾳ Triclinius: ἐν μάχᾳ codd.

to laud in sweet song. In achievements of long ago
lord Peleus took delight, after cutting his matchless
    spear;[5]
he took Iolcus all alone without an army
and captured the sea nymph Thetis   35
with great effort. And mighty Telamon,
fighting beside Iolaus, destroyed Laomedon[6]

and once joined him in pursuit of the brave Amazons   Ep. 2
with bronze bows, and never did man-crushing fear
    check the sharpness of his mind.
One with inborn glory carries great weight,   40
but he who has mere learning is a shadowy man;
    ever changing his purpose, he never takes a precise
step,[7] but attempts innumerable feats with an ineffectual
    mind.

But fair-haired Achilles, while living in Philyra's[8] home,   Str. 3
even as a child at play would perform great deeds; often
did he brandish in his hands his short iron-tipped javelin   45
and, swiftly as the winds, deal death in battle to wild
    lions
and kill boars. He would bring their gasping bodies
to the Centaur, Cronus' son,
beginning at age six and for all time thereafter.
Artemis and bold Athena marveled to see him   50

    [5] Peleus' ashen spear from Mt. Pelion (cf. *Il.* 16.143–144). For
Peleus' exploits, see *Nem.* 4.54–65.
    [6] In the first sack of Troy with Heracles and Iolaus.
    [7] Or *never enters the contest with a sure foot.*
    [8] Chiron's mother.

κτείνοντ᾽ ἐλάφους ἄνευ κυνῶν δολίων θ᾽ ἑρκέων·
ποσσὶ γὰρ κράτεσκε. λεγόμενον δὲ τοῦτο προτέρων
ἔπος ἔχω· βαθυμῆτα Χείρων τράφε λιθίνῳ
Ἰάσον᾽ ἔνδον τέγει, καὶ ἔπειτεν Ἀσκλαπιόν,
55 τὸν φαρμάκων δίδαξε μαλακόχειρα νόμον·
νύμφευσε δ᾽ αὖτις ἀγλαόκολπον
Νηρέος θύγατρα, γόνον τέ οἱ φέρτατον
ἀτίταλλεν ⟨ἐν⟩ ἁρμένοισι πᾶσι θυμὸν αὔξων,

ὄφρα θαλασσίαις ἀνέμων ῥιπαῖσι πεμφθείς
60 ὑπὸ Τροΐαν δορίκτυπον ἀλαλὰν Λυκίων
τε προσμένοι καὶ Φρυγῶν
Δαρδάνων τε, καὶ ἐγχεσφόροις ἐπιμείξαις
Αἰθιόπεσσι χεῖρας ἐν φρασὶ πά-
ξαιθ᾽, ὅπως σφίσι μὴ κοίρανος ὀπίσω
πάλιν οἴκαδ᾽ ἀνεψιὸς ζαμενὴς Ἑλένοιο Μέμνων
μόλοι.

Δ΄ τηλαυγὲς ἄραρε φέγγος Αἰακιδᾶν αὐτόθεν·
65 Ζεῦ, τεὸν γὰρ αἷμα, σέο δ᾽ ἀγών, τὸν ὕμνος ἔβαλεν
ὀπὶ νέων ἐπιχώριον χάρμα κελαδέων.
βοὰ δὲ νικαφόρῳ σὺν Ἀριστοκλείδᾳ πρέπει,
ὃς τάνδε νᾶσον εὐκλέι προσέθηκε λόγῳ
καὶ σεμνὸν ἀγλααῖσι μερίμναις

52 προτέρων B^{s}V^s: πρότερον B^{i}DV^i
56 ἀγλαόκολπον B^i(V^s): ἀγλαόκαρπον B^s: ἀγλαόκαρνον V^i:
ἀγλαόκρανον D^{lit}
58 ⟨ἐν⟩ suppl. E. Schmid | πᾶσι Mingarelli: πάντα codd.

slaying deer without dogs or deceitful nets,   Ant. 3
for he overtook them on foot. The story I have to tell
was told by former poets: deep-devising Chiron raised
Jason in his rocky dwelling and then Asclepius,
whom he taught the gentle-handed province of   55
    medicines.
Then too he betrothed the splendid-breasted
daughter of Nereus,[9] and fostered her matchless
    offspring,
making his spirit great in all things fitting,

so that, when sent by the blasts of the winds at sea   Ep. 3
to the foot of Troy, he would withstand the spear-   60
    clashing
    battle cry of the Lycians and Phrygians
and Dardanians, and when grappling with spear-bearing
Ethiopians he would fix it in his mind
    that their leader Memnon,
Helenus' fierce cousin, would not go back home again.

The far-shining light of the Aeacidae is fixed from here.   Str. 4
Zeus, yours is the blood,[10] and yours the contest, which   65
    this hymn has struck
with young men's voices as it celebrates this land's joy.
Loud acclaim is in order for victorious Aristocleides,
who has linked this island to glorious praise
and the hallowed Delegation of the Pythian god

[9] Chiron performed the marriage of Thetis and Peleus and tutored their son Achilles (cf. *Isth.* 8.41–42).
[10] Aeacus was Zeus' son by Aegina (cf. *Nem.* 8.6–8).

70　Πυθίου Θεάριον. ἐν δὲ πείρᾳ τέλος
　　διαφαίνεται, ὧν τις ἐξοχώτερος γένηται,

　　ἐν παισὶ νέοισι παῖς, ἐν ἀνδράσιν ἀνήρ, τρίτον
　　ἐν παλαιτέροισι, μέρος ἕκαστον οἷον ἔχομεν
　　βρότεον ἔθνος· ἐλᾷ δὲ καὶ τέσσαρας ἀρετάς
75　⟨ὁ⟩ θνατὸς αἰών, φρονεῖν δ' ἐνέπει τὸ παρκείμενον.
　　τῶν οὐκ ἄπεσσι· χαῖρε, φίλος· ἐγὼ τόδε τοι
　　πέμπω μεμιγμένον μέλι λευκῷ
　　σὺν γάλακτι, κιρναμένα δ' ἔερσ' ἀμφέπει,
　　πόμ' ἀοίδιμον Αἰολίσσιν ἐν πνοαῖσιν αὐλῶν,

80　ὀψέ περ. ἔστι δ' αἰετὸς ὠκὺς ἐν ποτανοῖς,
　　ὃς ἔλαβεν αἶψα, τηλόθε μεταμαιόμενος,
　　　δαφοινὸν ἄγραν ποσίν·
　　κραγέται δὲ κολοιοὶ ταπεινὰ νέμονται.
　　τίν γε μέν, εὐθρόνου Κλεοῦς ἐθελοί-
　　　σας, ἀεθλοφόρου λήματος ἕνεκεν
　　Νεμέας Ἐπιδαυρόθεν τ' ἄπο καὶ Μεγάρων δέδορκεν
　　　φάος.

72 ἐν ἀνδράσιν Hermann: ἐν δ' ἀνδράσιν codd.
75 ⟨ὁ⟩ suppl. Triclinius | θνατὸς B, Aristarchus: μακρὸς VD
76 ἄπεσσι Bergk: ἄπεστι codd.

32

to splendid ambitions.[11] But in the test the result   70
shines clear, in what ways someone proves superior,

as a child among young children, man among men, and   Ant. 4
        thirdly
among elders—such is each stage that our human race
attains. Then too, our mortal life drives a team of
four virtues,[12] and it bids us heed what is at hand.   75
Of these you have no lack. Farewell, friend. I send you
this mixture of honey with white
milk, which the stirred foam crowns,
a drink of song accompanied by the Aeolian breaths of
        pipes,

late though it be. Swift is the eagle among birds,   Ep. 4
which suddenly seizes, as it searches from afar,   81
        the bloodied prey in its talons,
while the cawing jackdaws range down below.
But for you, through the favor of fair-throned Cleo[13]
        and because of your determination for victory,
from Nemea, Epidaurus, and Megara has shone the light
        of glory.

[11] Sacred Delegations (*theoroi*) were sent from various cities
to Delphi. Pindar seems to imply that Aristocleides' victory gives
the Aeginetan delegation hopes that he will be victorious in the
Pythian games.

[12] The exact meaning of the four virtues is much disputed;
Pindar seems to adumbrate the canonical four virtues (wisdom,
self-control, courage, and justice) at *Pyth.* 6.47–51 and *Isth.* 8.24–
26.

[13] One of the Muses (whose name means "Fame").

NEMEAN 4

This poem in celebration of Timasarchus, a victorious boy wrestler, reflects upon the interrelationship of song, struggle, suffering, and death. The ode opens with an image of limbs tired from the contest for which song provides the most soothing remedy; we soon learn that the boy's father, a musician, is dead; the brief account of Heracles' fight with the giant Alcyoneus stresses the suffering that victory entails; and we are told that the boy's uncle, also a victorious athlete, has died. Although poetry provides consolation for suffering and death, it too requires struggle, and in a digression (33–43) on how best to execute his poem, the poet portrays himself in contention with rival poets. He concludes by comparing himself to a wrestler as he praises the trainer Melesias.

Songs of praise are more relaxing even than warm water after hard toil, for well-executed poetry survives after deeds are completed (1–8). The poet hopes that he can fittingly praise Timasarchus and find favor with Aegina, hospitable to foreigners (9–13). If Timocritus were still alive, he would be performing this song in celebration of his son's victories at Nemea, Athens, and Thebes (13–24). Mention of Thebes prompts a digression on the achievements of Telamon and Heracles, culminating in their battle against Alcyoneus (25–32).

The poet announces that he will resist the constraints of the genre, the pressure of time, and his own desire to celebrate the new-moon festival, and by not curtailing his narrative will prove victorious over rival poets who would begrudge full praise to those who deserve it (33–41). He then confidently strikes up a song for Aegina's heroes (41–46). A geographical survey of lands ruled by the Aeacidae culminates in the exploits of Peleus, including his capture of Iolcus after overcoming the treachery of Acastus and Hippolyta, his struggle to win Thetis, and their wedding attended by the gods (46–68).

The poet turns his ship of song from the inexhaustible glory of the Aeacidae to Timasarchus' clan, the Theandridae, who have commissioned him to announce their athletic victories in song (69–79). He politely declines, however, to sing the full praises of Timasarchus' dead uncle, a former victor at the Isthmus, on the grounds that Timasarchus' grandfather, who possesses firsthand knowledge, is better qualified to eulogize him (79–92). But were he to praise the trainer Melesias, Pindar imagines how formidable a competitor he would be (93–96).

4. ΤΙΜΑΣΑΡΧΩΙ
ΑΙΓΙΝΗΤΗΙ

ΠΑΙΔΙ ΠΑΛΑΙΣΤΗΙ

Α΄ Ἄριστος εὐφροσύνα πόνων κεκριμένων
ἰατρός· αἱ δὲ σοφαί
Μοισᾶν θύγατρες ἀοιδαὶ θέλξαν νιν ἁπτόμεναι.
οὐδὲ θερμὸν ὕδωρ τόσον γε μαλθακὰ τεύχει
5 γυῖα, τόσσον εὐλογία φόρμιγγι συνάορος.
ῥῆμα δ᾽ ἐργμάτων χρονιώτερον βιοτεύει,
ὅ τι κε σὺν Χαρίτων τύχᾳ
γλῶσσα φρενὸς ἐξέλοι βαθείας.

Β΄ τό μοι θέμεν Κρονίδᾳ τε Δὶ καὶ Νεμέᾳ
10 Τιμασάρχου τε πάλᾳ
ὕμνου προκώμιον εἴη· δέξαιτο δ᾽ Αἰακιδᾶν
ἠύπυργον ἕδος, δίκᾳ ξεναρκέι κοινόν
φέγγος. εἰ δ᾽ ἔτι ζαμενεῖ Τιμόκριτος ἁλίῳ
σὸς πατὴρ ἐθάλπετο, ποικίλον κιθαρίζων
15 θαμά κε, τῷδε μέλει κλιθείς,
υἱὸν κελάδησε καλλίνικον

inscr. αἰγινήτῃ παλαιστῇ D: om. B: παιδὶ add. Boeckh
16 υἱὸν Bergk: ὕμνον codd.

36

4. FOR TIMASARCHUS
OF AEGINA

WINNER, BOYS' WRESTLING

The best healer for toils judged successful   Str. 1
is joyous revelry, but songs too, those wise
daughters of the Muses, soothe them[1] with their touch.
Not even warm water relaxes the limbs as much
as praise, the companion of the lyre.   5
For the word lives longer than deeds,
which, with the Graces' blessing,
the tongue draws from the depths of the mind.

May I set forth such a word for Cronus' son Zeus and   Str. 2
     Nemea,
and for Timasarchus' wrestling,   10
as my hymn's prelude; and may it find welcome in the
Aeacidae's high-towered domain, that beacon of justice
protecting all foreigners. And if your father Timocritus
were still warmed by the blazing sun, often would he
     have
played an elaborate tune on the lyre, and, relying on   15
this song, would have celebrated his triumphant son

---

[1] I.e. the painful toils; others understand "him," the victor.

PINDAR

Γʹ   Κλεωναίου τ᾽ ἀπ᾽ ἀγῶνος ὅρμον στεφάνων
    πέμψαντα καὶ λιπαρᾶν
    εὐωνύμων ἀπ᾽ Ἀθανᾶν, Θήβαις τ᾽ ἐν ἑπταπύλοις
20 οὕνεκ᾽ Ἀμφιτρύωνος ἀγλαὸν παρὰ τύμβον
    Καδμεῖοί νιν οὐκ ἀέκοντες ἄνθεσι μείγνυον,
    Αἰγίνας ἕκατι. φίλοισι γὰρ φίλος ἐλθὼν
    ξένιον ἄστυ κατέδρακεν
    Ἡρακλέος ὀλβίαν πρὸς αὐλάν.

Δʹ   σὺν ᾧ ποτε Τροΐαν κραταιὸς Τελαμών
26 πόρθησε καὶ Μέροπας
    καὶ τὸν μέγαν πολεμιστὰν ἔκπαγλον Ἀλκυονῆ,
    οὐ τετραορίας γε πρὶν δυώδεκα πέτρῳ
    ἥροάς τ᾽ ἐπεμβεβαῶτας ἱπποδάμους ἕλεν
30 δὶς τόσους. ἀπειρομάχας ἐών κε φανείη
    λόγον ὁ μὴ συνιείς· ἐπεὶ
    ῥέζοντά τι καὶ παθεῖν ἔοικεν.

Εʹ   τὰ μακρὰ δ᾽ ἐξενέπειν ἐρύκει με τεθμός
    ὧραί τ᾽ ἐπειγόμεναι·
35 ἴυγγι δ᾽ ἕλκομαι ἦτορ νεομηνίᾳ θιγέμεν.
    ἔμπα, καίπερ ἔχει βαθεῖα ποντιὰς ἅλμα

---

² The Nemean games, overseen by Cleonae, a nearby town.

³ For the close relationship between Aegina and Thebes, see *Isth.* 8.16–18.

⁴ Presumably the Heracleion above the Electran gates in Thebes (cf. *Isth.* 4.61–62 and Paus. 9.11.4, 7).

38

for bringing a wreath of crowns from Cleonae's games[2]   Str. 3
and from shining,
famous Athens, and because in seven-gated Thebes
beside the glorious tomb of Amphitryon   20
the Cadmeans gladly crowned him with flowers,
on account of Aegina.[3] For, coming as a friend to
    friends,
he beheld the welcoming city
on his way to the blessed hall of Heracles,[4]

with whom mighty Telamon once destroyed Troy   Str. 4
and the Meropes   26
and that giant warrior, awesome Alcyoneus,[5]
but not before he dashed twelve chariots with a boulder
and killed the horse-taming heroes riding in them—
two in each. One would show himself inexperienced   30
in battle if he did not understand this story, since
it is fitting for one who achieves something to suffer as
    well.

But the law of song keeps me from telling the long tale,   Str. 5
and the pressing hours;
and by a love charm I am drawn in my heart to touch   35
    upon the new-moon festival.[6]
Nevertheless, although the deep salt sea holds you

---

[5] For these exploits of Heracles and Telamon, see *Isth.* 6.31–35.   [6] Presumably the festival at which this ode was performed. The poet implies that he is eager to treat Timasarchus' victory, but in the following lines exhorts himself to resist that temptation and not stint the Aeacidae of their just praises, as an inferior eulogist might do.

PINDAR

μέσσον, ἀντίτειν' ἐπιβουλίᾳ· σφόδρα δόξομεν
δαΐων ὑπέρτεροι ἐν φάει καταβαίνειν·
φθονερὰ δ' ἄλλος ἀνὴρ βλέπων
40 γνώμαν κενεὰν σκότῳ κυλίνδει

ϝ΄ χαμαὶ πετοῖσαν. ἐμοὶ δ' ὁποίαν ἀρετάν
ἔδωκε Πότμος ἄναξ,
εὖ οἶδ' ὅτι χρόνος ἕρπων πεπρωμέναν τελέσει.
ἐξύφαινε, γλυκεῖα, καὶ τόδ' αὐτίκα, φόρμιγξ,
45 Λυδίᾳ σὺν ἁρμονίᾳ μέλος πεφιλημένον
Οἰνώνᾳ τε καὶ Κύπρῳ, ἔνθα Τεῦκρος ἀπάρχει
ὁ Τελαμωνιάδας· ἀτὰρ
Αἴας Σαλαμῖν' ἔχει πατρῴαν·

ζ΄ ἐν δ' Εὐξείνῳ πελάγει φαεννὰν Ἀχιλεύς
50 νᾶσον· Θέτις δὲ κρατεῖ
Φθίᾳ· Νεοπτόλεμος δ' ἀπείρῳ διαπρυσίᾳ,
βουβόται τόθι πρῶνες ἔξοχοι κατάκεινται
Δωδώναθεν ἀρχόμενοι πρὸς Ἰόνιον πόρον.
Παλίου δὲ πὰρ ποδὶ λατρίαν Ἰαολκόν
55 πολεμίᾳ χερὶ προστραπών
Πηλεὺς παρέδωκεν Αἱμόνεσσιν

> 37 ἐπιβουλίᾳ BD: ἐπιβουλίαις V
> 39 ἄλλος codd.: ἆλλος (= ἠλεός) Lobel

---

[7] The ancient name for Aegina.
[8] After returning to Salamis from Troy, Teucer was exiled for

by the waist, resist its treachery; we shall be seen
to enter the contest in the light, far superior to our foes.
Another man, with envy in his eye,
rolls an empty thought in the dark   40

that falls to the ground. But whatever kind of excellence   Str. 6
lord Destiny has given me,
well I know that coming time will accomplish its fated
        end.
Quickly now, sweet lyre, weave out this song too
in Lydian harmony, one beloved   45
by Oenona[7] and Cyprus, where Teucer rules in exile,[8]
the son of Telamon, but
Ajax holds the paternal home of Salamis;

and in the Euxine Sea Achilles holds the shining   Str. 7
island.[9] Thetis rules   50
over Phthia, Neoptolemus over the far-reaching
        mainland
where high cattle-grazing forelands descend,
beginning from Dodona, to the Ionian Sea.[10]
But at the foot of Pelion, Peleus subdued Iolcus
with hostile hand,   55
and gave it over in bondage to the Haemones,[11]

not having saved his half-brother Ajax; he founded a new Salamis
in Cyprus.

[9] Leuce, in the Black Sea, where the shade of Achilles was be-
lieved to dwell (cf. Eur. *Andr.* 1260–1262 and Paus. 3.19.11).

[10] I.e. in Epirus (cf. *Nem.* 7.37–38).

[11] Local Thessalian peoples.

PINDAR

Η΄ δάμαρτος Ἱππολύτας Ἀκάστου δολίαις
    τέχναισι χρησάμενος·
    τᾷ Δαιδάλου δὲ μαχαίρᾳ φύτευέ οἱ θάνατον
60 ἐκ λόχου Πελίαο παῖς· ἄλαλκε δὲ Χείρων,
    καὶ τὸ μόρσιμον Διόθεν πεπρωμένον ἔκφερεν·
    πῦρ δὲ παγκρατὲς θρασυμαχάνων τε λεόντων
    ὄνυχας ὀξυτάτους ἀκμάν
    καὶ δεινοτάτων σχάσαις ὀδόντων

Θ΄ ἔγαμεν ὑψιθρόνων μίαν Νηρεΐδων.
66 εἶδεν δ᾽ εὔκυκλον ἕδραν,
    τᾶς οὐρανοῦ βασιλῆες πόντου τ᾽ ἐφεζόμενοι
    δῶρα καὶ κράτος ἐξέφαναν ἐγγενὲς αὐτῷ.
    Γαδείρων τὸ πρὸς ζόφον οὐ περατόν· ἀπότρεπε
70 αὖτις Εὐρώπαν ποτὶ χέρσον ἔντεα ναός·
    ἄπορα γὰρ λόγον Αἰακοῦ
    παίδων τὸν ἅπαντά μοι διελθεῖν.

Ι΄   Θεανδρίδαισι δ᾽ ἀεξιγυίων ἀέθλων
    κάρυξ ἑτοῖμος ἔβαν
75 Οὐλυμπίᾳ τε καὶ Ἰσθμοῖ Νεμέᾳ τε συνθέμενος,
    ἔνθα πεῖραν ἔχοντες οἴκαδε κλυτοκάρπων

        62 θρασυμαχάνων Hermann: θρασυμαχᾶν codd.
        64 καὶ Ahlwardt: τε codd.
        67 τᾶς codd.: τὰν Herwerden
        68 ἐγγενὲς Rittershusius e schol.: ἐς γενεὰς codd.

    [12] Acastus. After Peleus spurned Hippolyta's advances (cf.

42

after he had experienced the treacherous wiles	Str. 8
of Acastus' wife Hippolyta.	
Using the sword of Daedalus, Pelias' son[12] was plotting	
death for him from ambush, but Chiron averted it,	60
and he[13] carried out the destiny fated by Zeus.	
After thwarting the all-powerful fire,	
the razor-sharp claws of boldly devising lions	
and the points of fiercest teeth,	

he married one of the lofty-throned Nereids.[14]	Str. 9
He beheld the fine circle of seats	66
on which the lords of the sky and sea sat	
and revealed to him their gifts and his race's power.	
That which lies to the west of Gadira cannot be crossed;	
turn back	
again the ship's tackle to the mainland of Europe,	70
because it is impossible for me to go through	
the whole account of Aeacus' descendants.	

It is for the Theandridae that I contracted to come	Str. 10
as a ready herald of their limb-strengthening contests	
at Olympia and the Isthmus, and at Nemea.	75
From there, when they compete, they do not return	
without the fruit	

Nem. 5.26–34), she convinced Acastus to kill him. He stole Peleus' sword made by Daedalus (or Hephaestus) and set the Centaurs to ambush him as he searched for it, but Chiron returned the sword to Peleus, who defeated them and captured Iolcus (cf. Hes. *Cat. fr.* 209, quoted by the schol.). [13] Peleus; others take Chiron as subject. [14] In order to win Thetis, Peleus had to hold on to her as she assumed fearsome forms.

PINDAR

οὐ νέοντ᾽ ἄνευ στεφάνων, πάτραν ἵν᾽ ἀκούομεν,
Τιμάσαρχε, τεὰν ἐπινικίοισιν ἀοιδαῖς
πρόπολον ἔμμεναι. εἰ δέ τοι
80 μάτρῳ μ᾽ ἔτι Καλλικλεῖ κελεύεις

ΙΑ΄ στάλαν θέμεν Παρίου λίθου λευκοτέραν·
ὁ χρυσὸς ἑψόμενος
αὐγὰς ἔδειξεν ἁπάσας, ὕμνος δὲ τῶν ἀγαθῶν
ἐργμάτων βασιλεῦσιν ἰσοδαίμονα τεύχει
85 φῶτα· κεῖνος ἀμφ᾽ Ἀχέροντι ναιετάων ἐμάν
γλῶσσαν εὑρέτω κελαδῆτιν, Ὀρσοτριαίνα
ἵν᾽ ἐν ἀγῶνι βαρυκτύπου
θάλησε Κορινθίοις σελίνοις·

ΙΒ΄ τὸν Εὐφάνης ἐθέλων γεραιὸς προπάτωρ
90 ἀείσεται, παῖ, ὁ σός.
ἄλλοισι δ᾽ ἅλικες ἄλλοι· τὰ δ᾽ αὐτὸς ἀντιτύχῃ,
ἔλπεταί τις ἕκαστος ἐξοχώτατα φάσθαι.
οἷον αἰνέων κε Μελησίαν ἔριδα στρέφοι,
ῥήματα πλέκων, ἀπάλαιστος ἐν λόγῳ ἕλκειν,
95 μαλακὰ μὲν φρονέων ἐσλοῖς,
τραχὺς δὲ παλιγκότοις ἔφεδρος.

77 ἵν᾽ Hermann: νιν BDᵖᶜ
90 ἀείσεται, παῖ, ὁ σός Mommsen: ὁ σὸς ἀείσεται, παῖ
codd.: σὸς ἄεισέν ποτε, παῖ Boeckh Hermanno praeeunte

15 That is, to compose a memorial song. The sentence is inter-
rupted by a statement implying a comparison ("*as* gold . . . *so* a
hymn").　　16 Callicles.

44

of glorious crowns to their home, where we hear,
Timasarchus, that your clan is devoted
to victory songs. But if indeed
you bid me yet to erect for your maternal uncle Callicles   80

a stele whiter than Parian marble[15]—   Str. 11
refined gold
displays all its radiance, and a hymn
of noble deeds makes a man equal in fortune
to kings—let him[16] who dwells by the Acheron   85
find my voice ringing out, where, in the games
of the deep-thundering Wielder of the Trident,
he blossomed with Corinthian parsley.

Him will your aged grandfather Euphanes gladly   Str. 12
celebrate in song, my boy.[17]   90
For people belong to different generations, and each
    man
hopes to express best what he has himself encountered.
But a praiser of Melesias,[18] how he would twist in a
    match
as he wove his words, an unthrowable wrestler in
    speech,
with gentle thoughts for good men,   95
but a rough backup[19] against resentful adversaries.

[17] Boeckh's emendation (σὸς ἄεισέν ποτε, παῖ: "your grand-
father once celebrated him, my boy") assumes that Euphanes is
dead.
[18] The boy's trainer (cf. Ol. 8.54–66). The poet has witnessed
his work and could compete with anyone in praising him.
[19] The *ephedros* waited to take on the winner of the current
round.

NEMEAN 5

This is one of four extant epinicia by Pindar and Bac-
chylides praising the two sons of Lampon, members of
an Aeginetan family expert in the pancratium. Pindar and
Bacchylides (13) both composed odes in celebration of this
Nemean victory won by Pytheas, probably in 485 or 483.
Pindar subsequently composed *Isth.* 6 for Pytheas' youn-
ger brother Phylacidas, a boy victor at the Isthmus, and
Isth. 5, also for Phylacidas after he had won a Nemean
and second Isthmian victory. The boys' maternal uncle
Euthymenes and grandfather Themistius were also vic-
tors. All four odes are composed of dactylo-epitritic triads
and feature episodes from the sagas of the Aeacidae.

Contrasting his ode with statues that rest on their bases,
Pindar bids his song travel forth on all boats, large and
small, from the island of Aegina to announce the Nemean
victory of young Pytheas, who brings glory to the Aeacidae
and to Aegina, hospitable to foreigners (1–8). The poet
abruptly adds that Peleus, Telamon, and their half-brother
Phocus prayed to Zeus Hellanius that Aegina would be a
land of brave sailors (9–13), but refrains from stating what
subsequently caused the two brothers to be driven from
Aegina, on the grounds that not everything true needs to
be said (14–18).

Eager to praise success, he turns instead to the wedding of Peleus and Thetis on Pelion, at which the Muses sang of how Hippolyta, the wife of Acastus, attempted to seduce Peleus, her guest. When he rejected her advances, she falsely told her husband that he had attempted to rape her (19–34). In appreciation of his virtue, Zeus rewarded him with the sea nymph Thetis for a bride (34–39).

A gnomic reflection on the importance of inherited ability introduces Pytheas' uncle, twice victorious—perhaps at the Isthmus—and at Nemea, Aegina, and Megara (40–46). After expressing his pleasure at the whole city's enthusiasm for athletics, the poet reminds Pytheas that he owes his victory to his trainer Menander from Athens (46–49). He concludes with praise of Themistius, the victor's grandfather, who had won a double victory at Epidaurus in boxing and the pancratium (50–54).

5. ΠΥΘΕΑΙ ⟨ΑΙΓΙΝΗΤΗΙ

ΑΓΕΝΕΙΩΙ⟩ ΠΑΓΚΡΑΤΙΑΣΤΗΙ

Α΄ Οὐκ ἀνδριαντοποιός εἰμ᾽, ὥστ᾽ ἐλινύσοντα ἐργά-
    ζεσθαι ἀγάλματ᾽ ἐπ᾽ αὐτᾶς βαθμίδος
    ἑσταότ᾽· ἀλλ᾽ ἐπὶ πάσας
    ὁλκάδος ἔν τ᾽ ἀκάτῳ, γλυκεῖ᾽ ἀοιδά,
    στεῖχ᾽ ἀπ᾽ Αἰγίνας διαγγέλλοισ᾽, ὅτι
    Λάμπωνος υἱὸς Πυθέας εὐρυσθενής
5   νίκη Νεμείοις παγκρατίου στέφανον,
    οὔπω γένυσι φαίνων τερείνας
    ματέρ᾽ οἰνάνθας ὀπώραν,

    ἐκ δὲ Κρόνου καὶ Ζηνὸς ἥρωας αἰχματὰς φυτευθέν-
    τας καὶ ἀπὸ χρυσεᾶν Νηρηΐδων
    Αἰακίδας ἐγέραιρεν
    ματρόπολίν τε, φίλαν ξένων ἄρουραν·
    τάν ποτ᾽ εὔανδρόν τε καὶ ναυσικλυτάν

inscr. suppl. Boeckh et Blass
6 τερείνας Dreykorn: τέρειναν BD | οἰνάνθαν ὀπώρας Pauw

48

5. FOR PYTHEAS OF AEGINA

WINNER, YOUTHS' PANCRATIUM

I am not a sculptor, so as to fashion stationary   Str. 1
    statues that stand on their same base.
Rather, on board every ship
    and in every boat, sweet song,
go forth from Aegina and spread the news that
Lampon's mighty son Pytheas
has won the crown for the pancratium in Nemea's   5
        games,
not yet showing on his cheeks late summer,
    the mother of the grape's soft bloom,[1]

and he has glorified the Aeacidae, heroic warriors   Ant. 1
    born of Cronus and Zeus and from
the golden Nereids, and his
    mother city, a land welcoming to foreigners,
which Endais' illustrious sons[2] and mighty prince

---

[1] This elaborate periphrasis probably indicates that he won in
the division of the beardless (ἀγένειοι) youths. Blass emended
the inscription to reflect this.

[2] Peleus and Telamon, whose mother Endais was Chiron's
daughter.

PINDAR

10 θέσσαντο, πὰρ βωμὸν πατέρος Ἑλλανίου
στάντες, πίτναν τ᾽ ἐς αἰθέρα χεῖρας ἁμᾶ
Ἐνδαΐδος ἀριγνῶτες υἱοὶ
    καὶ βία Φώκου κρέοντος,

ὁ τᾶς θεοῦ, ὃν Ψαμάθεια τίκτ᾽ ἐπὶ ῥηγμῖνι πόντου.
αἰδέομαι μέγα εἰπεῖν
    ἐν δίκᾳ τε μὴ κεκινδυνευμένον,
15 πῶς δὴ λίπον εὐκλέα νᾶσον,
    καὶ τίς ἄνδρας ἀλκίμους
δαίμων ἀπ᾽ Οἰνώνας ἔλασεν.
    στάσομαι· οὔ τοι ἅπασα κερδίων
φαίνοισα πρόσωπον ἀλάθει᾽ ἀτρεκής·
    καὶ τὸ σιγᾶν πολλάκις ἐστὶ σοφώ-
    τατον ἀνθρώπῳ νοῆσαι.

Β΄ εἰ δ᾽ ὄλβον ἢ χειρῶν βίαν ἢ σιδαρίταν ἐπαινῆ-
    σαι πόλεμον δεδόκηται, μακρά μοι
20 αὐτόθεν ἅλμαθ᾽ ὑποσκά-
    πτοι τις· ἔχω γονάτων ὁρμὰν ἐλαφράν·
καὶ πέραν πόντοιο πάλλοντ᾽ αἰετοί.
πρόφρων δὲ καὶ κείνοις ἄειδ᾽ ἐν Παλίῳ

17 ἀτρεκής B, ἀτερκής D: ἀτρεκές Stobaeus
20 ὁρμὰν ἐλαφράν Turyn: ἐλαφρὰν ὁρμάν BD
22 ἄειδ᾽ ἐν Pauw: ἀείδει BD

3 Psamatheia ("Sandy") bore Phocus ("Seal") upon the sea-shore of the island.

50

Phocus, son of the goddess Psamatheia who bore him on   10
    the seashore,[3]
prayed would one day be a land of brave men
and renowned for sailing,
    as they stood by the altar of father Hellanius[4]

and together stretched their hands toward the sky.   Ep. 1
I shrink from telling of a mighty deed,
    one ventured not in accord with justice,[5]
how in fact they left the glorious island   15
    and what fortune drove the brave men
from Oenona.[6]
    I will halt, for not every exact truth
is better for showing its face,[7]
and silence is often the wisest thing
    for a man to observe.

But if it is decided to praise happiness, strength of   Str. 2
    hands,
    or steel-clad war, let someone dig for me
a jumping pit far from this point,   20
    for I have a light spring in my knees,
and eagles leap even beyond the sea.
Gladly did that fairest chorus of the Muses

[4] Zeus of Hellas, worshiped at Aegina from the time of the Myrmidons (cf. *Pae.* 6.125).

[5] The murder of their half-brother Phocus by Peleus and Telamon, for which they were exiled from Aegina, Telamon going to Salamis, Peleus to Iolcus.

[6] The ancient name for Aegina.   [7] Or (reading ἀτρεκές) *not every truth is better for showing its exact face.*

PINDAR

Μοισᾶν ὁ κάλλιστος χορός, ἐν δὲ μέσαις
φόρμιγγ᾽ Ἀπόλλων ἑπτάγλωσσον
χρυσέῳ πλάκτρῳ διώκων

25 ἀγεῖτο παντοίων νόμων· αἱ δὲ πρώτιστον μὲν ὕμνη-
σαν Διὸς ἀρχόμεναι σεμνὰν Θέτιν
Πηλέα θ᾽, ὥς τέ νιν ἁβρὰ
Κρηθεῒς Ἱππολύτα δόλῳ πεδᾶσαι
ἤθελε ξυνᾶνα Μαγνήτων σκοπόν
πείσαισ᾽ ἀκοίταν ποικίλοις βουλεύμασιν,
ψεύσταν δὲ ποιητὸν συνέπαξε λόγον,
30 ὡς ἦρα νυμφείας ἐπείρα
κεῖνος ἐν λέκτροις Ἀκάστου

εὐνᾶς· τὸ δ᾽ ἐναντίον ἔσκεν· πολλὰ γάρ νιν παντὶ
θυμῷ
παρφαμένα λιτάνευεν.
τοῖο δ᾽ ὀργὰν κνίζον αἰπεινοὶ λόγοι·
εὐθὺς δ᾽ ἀπανάνατο νύμφαν,
ξεινίου πατρὸς χόλον
δείσαις· ὁ δ᾽ εὖ φράσθη κατένευ-
σέν τέ οἱ ὀρσινεφὴς ἐξ οὐρανοῦ
35 Ζεὺς ἀθανάτων βασιλεύς, ὥστ᾽ ἐν τάχει
ποντίαν χρυσαλακάτων τινὰ Νη-
ρεΐδων πράξειν ἄκοιτιν,

29 συνέπαξε B: συνέπλεξε D

52

sing for those men on Pelion,[8] while in their midst
Apollo swept his seven-tongued lyre
   with a golden plectrum,

and led them in tunes of all kinds. And, after a prelude   Ant. 2
   to Zeus, they first sang of august Thetis
and Peleus, telling how elegant Hippolyta, Cretheus'   26
   daughter, sought to snare him by a trick, after she
persuaded her husband,[9] overseer of the Magnesians,
to be an accomplice through her elaborate designs:
she put together a falsely fabricated tale,
claiming that in Acastus' own marriage bed   30
   he[10] was trying to gain her wifely

love. But the opposite was true, for again and again   Ep. 2
with all her heart she begged him beguilingly.
   But her precipitous words provoked his anger,
and he immediately rejected the wife,
   for he feared the wrath of the father who protects
hospitality.[11] And cloud-driving Zeus,
   king of the immortals, observed it well
and promised to him from heaven that he would soon   35
make a sea nymph, one of the Nereids
   of the golden distaffs, to be his bride,

[8] I.e. for the Aeacidae at the wedding of Peleus and Thetis (cf. *Pyth.* 3.88–92).

[9] Acastus. For his attempt to kill Peleus in ambush, see *Nem.* 4.59–60.

[10] Peleus.

[11] Zeus, "god of guests."

PINDAR

Γ´   γαμβρὸν Ποσειδάωνα πείσαις, ὃς Αἰγᾶθεν ποτὶ
      κλει-
      τὰν θαμὰ νίσεται Ἰσθμὸν Δωρίαν·
    ἔνθα νιν εὔφρονες ἶλαι
      σὺν καλάμοιο βοᾷ θεὸν δέκονται,
    καὶ σθένει γυίων ἐρίζοντι θρασεῖ.
40 Πότμος δὲ κρίνει συγγενὴς ἔργων πέρι
    πάντων. τὺ δ᾽ Αἰγίναθε δίς, Εὐθύμενες,
      Νίκας ἐν ἀγκώνεσσι πίτνων
      ποικίλων ἔψαυσας ὕμνων.

    ἤτοι μεταΐξαις σὲ καὶ νῦν τεὸς μάτρως ἀγάλλει
      κείνου ὁμόσπορον ἔθνος, Πυθέα.
    ἁ Νεμέα μὲν ἄραρεν
      μείς τ᾽ ἐπιχώριος, ὃν φίλησ᾽ Ἀπόλλων·
45 ἅλικας δ᾽ ἐλθόντας οἴκοι τ᾽ ἐκράτει
    Νίσου τ᾽ ἐν εὐαγκεῖ λόφῳ. χαίρω δ᾽ ὅτι
    ἐσλοῖσι μάρναται πέρι πᾶσα πόλις.
    ἴσθι, γλυκεῖάν τοι Μενάνδρου
      σὺν τύχᾳ μόχθων ἀμοιβάν

      41 Αἰγίναθε δίς Ed. Schwartz: αἰγιναθεας BD
      43 μεταΐξαις σὲ Byz., Wilamowitz, Turyn: μεταΐξαντα BD |
Πυθέα Mingarelli e schol.: Πυθέας BD
      45 ἐκράτεις Kayser

after persuading their kinsman, Poseidon, who often   Str. 3
    goes from Aegae[12] to the famous Dorian Isthmus,
where joyous crowds receive the god
    to the sound of the pipe
and compete with the bold strength of their limbs.
Inherited Destiny decides the outcome   40
of all deeds. Euthymenes, twice from Aegina
did you fall into Victory's arms
    and enjoy elaborate hymns.

Indeed, Pytheas, now too your maternal uncle, following   Ant. 3
    in your footsteps, glorifies that hero's[13] kindred race.
Nemea stands firm for him,
    as well as the local month that Apollo loved.[14]
He defeated those of his age who came to compete at   45
    home
and at Nisus' hill with its lovely glens.[15] I rejoice
that the entire city strives for noble prizes.
Remember that it was truly through Menander's[16] good
    fortune that you won that sweet reward

[12] A cult center of Poseidon in Achaea (cf. *Il.* 8.203).

[13] Peleus'; Euthymenes had also won at Nemea.

[14] The Aeginetan month of Delphinius, sacred to Apollo, in whose honor the local games (the Delphinia) were held.

[15] At Megara.

[16] His trainer.

ἐπαύρεο. χρὴ δ᾽ ἀπ᾽ Ἀθανᾶν τέκτον᾽ ἀεθληταῖσιν
    ἔμμεν.
50 εἰ δὲ Θεμίστιον ἵκεις
    ὥστ᾽ ἀείδειν, μηκέτι ῥίγει· δίδοι
φωνάν, ἀνὰ δ᾽ ἱστία τεῖνον
    πρὸς ζυγὸν καρχασίου,
πύκταν τέ νιν καὶ παγκρατίου
    φθέγξαι ἑλεῖν Ἐπιδαύρῳ διπλόαν
νικῶντ᾽ ἀρετάν, προθύροισιν δ᾽ Αἰακοῦ
ἀνθέων ποιάεντα φέρε στεφανώ-
    ματα σὺν ξανθαῖς Χάρισσιν.

52 παγκρατίου D: παγκρατίῳ B | διπλόαν B¹D: τριπλόαν B
54 ἀνθέων Hermann: ἄνθεα BD | φέρε Wilamowitz: φέρειν
BD

for your toils. A fashioner of athletes ought to be from   Ep. 3
     Athens.[17]
But if it is Themistius[18] you have come   50
    to sing, hold back no longer: give forth
your voice, hoist the sails to the
     topmost yard,
proclaim that as a boxer and in the pancratium
    he won at Epidaurus a double
victory, and to the portals of Aeacus' temple
bring the leafy crowns of flowers
    in the company of the fair-haired Graces.

[17] Pindar plays on the similarity of sound in *ath-letai* and *Ath-anai.*

[18] Pytheas' maternal grandfather (schol.).

NEMEAN 6

The victory of Alcimidas in boys' wrestling marks the twenty-fifth won in the crown games by his clan the Bassidae. A remarkable feature of the victor's own family, which Pindar declares holds more boxing crowns than any other in Greece, is its athletic success in alternate generations. Alcimidas' father is not even named, but his grandfather, Praxidamas, was extremely successful, with three victories at Nemea, five at the Isthmus, and one at Olympia. His great-grandfather, Socleides, was not distinguished, but his great-great-grandfather, Hagesimachus, apparently was. Two other family members, Callias and Creontidas (whose relationship to the victor is not clear), were also successful athletes.

Although we share the same mother (Earth) with the gods and resemble them in mind and body, our mortality and inability to foresee the future make us as nothing in comparison to them (1–7). Alcimidas' inherited destiny has been like the fields, alternately productive and fallow, for having won the boys' wrestling at Nemea he emulates his successful grandfather, Praxidamas (8–20), whose own father, Socleides, derived his fame from his three successful sons (20–24).

The poet declares that no other house has won more boxing crowns than theirs, and expresses the hope that his bold claim is accurate (24–28). He summons the Muse to sing of the Bassidae, whose achievements provide the Muses' plowmen with much work (28–34). He adds that other members of the family, Callias and Creontidas, had been victorious at Delphi and Nemea (34–44).

Eulogists have many ways to praise Aegina, because the achievements of the Aeacidae are known far and wide (45–49), even to the Ethiopians, whose leader Memnon was killed by Achilles at Troy (49–53). Former poets had much to say about the exploits of the Aeacidae, and the poet, too, has followed their lead, but he now turns to the occasion of his ode (53–57). His task is to announce that Alcimidas has won his family's twenty-fifth crown victory (57–61). He mentions in passing that two Olympic victories were denied Alcimidas and Polytimidas because of an unlucky draw (61–63). The poem concludes with brief praise of the trainer Melesias (64–66).

6. ΑΛΚΙΜΙΔΑΙ ΑΙΓΙΝΗΤΗΙ
ΠΑΙΔΙ ΠΑΛΑΙΣΤΗΙ

Α΄　Ἓν ἀνδρῶν, ἓν θεῶν γένος· ἐκ μιᾶς δὲ πνέομεν
　　ματρὸς ἀμφότεροι· διείργει δὲ πᾶσα κεκριμένα
　　δύναμις, ὡς τὸ μὲν οὐδέν, ὁ δὲ
　　　　χάλκεος ἀσφαλὲς αἰὲν ἕδος
　　μένει οὐρανός. ἀλλά τι προσφέρομεν ἔμπαν ἢ
　　　　μέγαν
　5　νόον ἤτοι φύσιν ἀθανάτοις,
　　καίπερ ἐφαμερίαν οὐκ
　　　　εἰδότες οὐδὲ μετὰ νύκτας
　6b　ἄμμε πότμος
　　ἅντιν᾽ ἔγραψε δραμεῖν ποτὶ στάθμαν.

　　τεκμαίρει καί νυν Ἀλκιμίδας τὸ συγγενὲς ἰδεῖν
　　ἄγχι καρποφόροις ἀρούραισιν, αἵτ᾽ ἀμειβόμεναι
　10　τόκα μὲν ὦν βίον ἀνδράσιν ἐπ-
　　　　ηετανὸν ἐκ πεδίων ἔδοσαν,

　　inscr. affert D: om. B
　　8 τεκμαίρει E. Schmid: τεκμαίρει δὲ BD

6. FOR ALCIMIDAS OF AEGINA

WINNER, BOYS' WRESTLING

There is one race of men, another of gods; but from one   Str. 1
    mother[1]
we both draw our breath. Yet the allotment of a wholly
different power separates us, for the one race is nothing,
    whereas the bronze heaven remains a secure abode
forever. Nevertheless, we do somewhat resemble
the immortals, either in greatness of mind or bodily   5
    nature,
although we do not know
    by day or in the night
to what goal destiny   6b
has marked for us to run.

And now Alcimidas makes it clear to see that his   Ant. 1
    inherited
nature is like crop-bearing fields, which alternate
and at one time give men abundant sustenance   10
    from the plains,

[1] I.e. Gaea, Earth.

τόκα δ' αὖτ' ἀναπαυσάμεναι σθένος ἔμαρψαν. ἦλθέ
    τοι
Νεμέας ἐξ ἐρατῶν ἀέθλων
παῖς ἐναγώνιος, ὃς ταύ-
    ταν μεθέπων Διόθεν αἶσαν
13b νῦν πέφανται
οὐκ ἄμμορος ἀμφὶ πάλᾳ κυναγέτας,

15 ἴχνεσιν ἐν Πραξιδάμαντος ἑὸν πόδα νέμων
πατροπάτορος ὁμαιμίου.
κεῖνος γὰρ Ὀλυμπιόνικος ἐὼν Αἰακίδαις
ἔρνεα πρῶτος ⟨ἔνεικεν⟩ ἀπ' Ἀλφεοῦ,
καὶ πεντάκις Ἰσθμοῖ στεφανωσάμενος,
20 Νεμέᾳ δὲ τρεῖς, ἔπαυσε λάθαν
Σαοκλείδα', ὃς ὑπέρτατος
Ἁγησιμάχοι' υἱέων γένετο·

Β΄ ἐπεί οἱ τρεῖς ἀεθλοφόροι πρὸς ἄκρον ἀρετᾶς
ἦλθον, οἵ τε πόνων ἐγεύσαντο. σὺν θεοῦ δὲ τύχᾳ
25 ἕτερον οὔ τινα οἶκον ἀπε-
    φάνατο πυγμαχία ⟨πλεόνων⟩

13b νῦν Triclinius: νῦν τε BD
16 ὁμαιμίοις Schroeder   18 ⟨ἔνεικεν⟩ suppl. Bergk
20 τρεῖς Hermann: τρίς BD
21 Σαοκλείδα' Wilamowitz: σωκλείδα BD
22 Ἁγησιμάχοι' Maas: ἀγησιμάχῳ BD | υἱέων Wilhelm
Schulze: υἱῶν BD: υἱέων Triclinius | γένετο Triclinius: ἐγένετο
BD   25 ⟨πλεόνων⟩ suppl. E. Schmid e schol.

but at another rest to gather strength.
For from the lovely games of Nemea
has come that boy competitor, who, following
    such a fortune from Zeus,
has now shown himself   13b
to be no empty-handed hunter at wrestling,

as he plants his step in the tracks   Ep. 1
of his own true grandfather Praxidamas.[2]   16
For he was the first Olympic victor to bring garlands
from the Alpheus to the Aeacidae,
and by winning crowns five times at the Isthmus
and three at Nemea, he ended the oblivion   20
of Socleides, who became the greatest[3]
of Hagesimachus' sons,

since for him three victors[4] who tasted of toils   Str. 2
reached the summit of excellence. By the god's grace
the art of boxing has revealed   25
    no other house to be the steward of more crowns

[2] Or (reading ὁμαιμίοις) *in the kindred tracks of his grand-father.*

[3] Or *was the eldest* (schol.). Presumably he was greatest by having three victorious sons. See Appendix for a possible reconstruction of the family genealogy.

[4] His three sons: Praxidamas and perhaps the Callias and Creontidas mentioned in 34–44.

ταμίαν στεφάνων μυχῷ Ἑλλάδος ἁπάσας. ἔλπομαι
μέγα εἰπὼν σκοποῦ ἄντα τυχεῖν
ὤτ᾽ ἀπὸ τόξου ἱείς· εὔ-
θυν᾽ ἐπὶ τοῦτον, ἄγε, Μοῖσα,
28b   οὖρον ἐπέων
εὐκλέα· παροιχομένων γὰρ ἀνέρων

30   ἀοιδαὶ καὶ λόγοι τὰ καλά σφιν ἔργ᾽ ἐκόμισαν,
Βασσίδαισιν ἅ τ᾽ οὐ σπανίζει· παλαίφατος γενεά,
ἴδια ναυστολέοντες ἐπι-
κώμια, Πιερίδων ἀρόταις
δυνατοὶ παρέχειν πολὺν ὕμνον ἀγερώχων ἐργμάτων
ἕνεκεν. καὶ γὰρ ἐν ἀγαθέᾳ
35   χεῖρας ἱμάντι δεθεὶς Πυ-
θῶνι κράτησεν ἀπὸ ταύτας
35b   αἷμα πάτρας
χρυσαλακάτου ποτὲ Καλλίας ἁδών

ἔρνεσι Λατοῦς, παρὰ Κασταλίαν τε Χαρίτων
ἑσπέριος ὁμάδῳ φλέγεν·
πόντου τε γέφυρ᾽ ἀκάμαντος ἐν ἀμφικτιόνων

27 εἰπὼν σκοποῦ ἄντα Mingarelli: ει]πων σκο[που Π⁴¹: εἰ-
πὼν ἄντα σκοποῦ BD | τυχεῖν D: τετυχεῖν B
28 ὤτ᾽ edd.: ὥ τ᾽ B: ᾧ τ᾽ D: ωστ απο Π⁴¹
30 ἀοιδαὶ καὶ λόγοι Pauw: ἀοιδοὶ καὶ λόγιοι (αοιδοι και
λο[Π⁴¹) BD   37 κασταλίαν V: κασταλία BD

in the heart of all Hellas.[5] I hope,
in making this great claim, to hit the mark head on,
shooting, like an archer, from my bow.
    Come, Muse, direct to that house
a glorious wind   28b
of verses, because when men are dead and gone,

songs and words preserve for them their noble deeds,   Ant. 2
and of these the Bassidae have no lack; a family famed of 31
       old,
they carry their own shipload of victory songs
    and can supply the Pierians' plowmen[6]
much to sing about because of their proud
accomplishments. For indeed, once in holy Pytho
Callias, a blood relative   35
    of that clan, bound his hands
with thongs[7] and was victorious,   35b
having found favor with the offspring[8] of golden-
       spindled

Leto, and in the evening by the Castalian spring   Ep. 2
he was ablaze with the clamor of the Graces;
and the bridge of the unwearied sea[9] honored
       Creontidas

  [5] It is unclear whether this refers only to the Isthmus or to all
Greece (schol.).
  [6] I.e. poets.
  [7] Boxers bound their hands with leather straps (*himantes*) to
protect their knuckles.
  [8] Apollo and Artemis.
  [9] The Isthmus of Corinth.

40 ταυροφόνῳ τριετηρίδι Κρεοντίδαν
τίμασε Ποσειδάνιον ἂν τέμενος·
βοτάνα τέ νίν ποθ᾽ ἁ λέοντος
νικάσαντ᾽ ἤρεφε δασκίοις
Φλειοῦντος ὑπ᾽ ὠγυγίοις ὄρεσιν.

Γ΄ πλατεῖαι πάντοθεν λογίοισιν ἐντὶ πρόσοδοι
46 νᾶσον εὐκλέα τάνδε κοσμεῖν· ἐπεί σφιν Αἰακίδαι
ἔπορον ἔξοχον αἶσαν ἀρε-
    τὰς ἀποδεικνύμενοι μεγάλας,
πέταται δ᾽ ἐπί τε χθόνα καὶ διὰ θαλάσσας τηλόθεν
ὄνυμ᾽ αὐτῶν· καὶ ἐς Αἰθίοπας
50 Μέμνονος οὐκ ἀπονοστή-
    σαντος ἔπαλτο· βαρὺ δέ σφιν
50b νεῖκος Ἀχιλεύς
ἔμπεσε χαμαὶ καταβὰς ἀφ᾽ ἁρμάτων,

φαεννᾶς υἱὸν εὖτ᾽ ἐνάριξεν Ἀόος ἀκμᾷ
ἔγχεος ζακότοιο. καὶ ταῦτα μὲν παλαιότεροι
ὁδὸν ἀμαξιτὸν εὖρον· ἕπο-
    μαι δὲ καὶ αὐτὸς ἔχων μελέταν·
55 τὸ δὲ πὰρ ποδὶ ναὸς ἑλισσόμενον αἰεὶ κυμάτων
λέγεται παντὶ μάλιστα δονεῖν

43 ἤρεφε Hermann: ἔρεψε BDV
50 οὐκ Triclinius: οὐκ ἂν BD   52 ἐνάριξεν Triclinius:
ἐνάριζεν BD | ἀκμᾷ E. Schmid e schol.: αἰχμᾷ BD
53 ταῦτα Pauw: ταύταν BD

at the biennial sacrifice of oxen by the neighboring   40
    peoples
in the precinct of Poseidon;
and the lion's herb[10] once crowned him
when he was victorious beneath the ancient
shadowy hills of Phleius.

Wide are the avenues from every direction for eulogists   Str. 3
to adorn this famous island, because the Aeacidae   46
have given them[11] a distinguished fortune
    by displaying great achievements,
and their name flies far away over the land
and through the sea, and it leapt even to the Ethiopians,
when Memnon did not return.[12]   50
    Upon them fell
a heavy opponent, Achilles,   50b
after stepping down from his chariot onto the ground,

when he slew the son of shining Dawn with the point   Ant. 3
of his raging spear. The older poets found in such deeds
as those a highway of song,
    and I myself follow along, making it my concern.
But the wave that rolls in the path of the ship   55
is said to disturb every man's heart

---

[10] Parsley from which the crowns at Nemea were made.

[11] Either the Aeginetans or the eulogists (schol.); if $a\hat{\iota}\sigma a$ means fortune (rather than portion), the former is more likely.

[12] He was slain by Achilles (cf. *Nem.* 3.61–63, *Isth.* 5.40–41, and *Isth.* 8.54).

PINDAR

θυμόν. ἑκόντι δ' ἐγὼ νώ-
τῳ μεθέπων δίδυμον ἄχθος
57b ἄγγελος ἔβαν,
πέμπτον ἐπὶ εἴκοσι τοῦτο γαρύων

εὖχος ἀγώνων ἄπο, τοὺς ἐνέποισιν ἱερούς,
60 Ἀλκίμιδα, σέ γ' ἐπαρκέσαι
κλειτᾷ γενεᾷ· δύο μὲν Κρονίου πὰρ τεμένει,
παῖ, σέ τ' ἐνόσφισε καὶ Πολυτιμίδαν
κλᾶρος προπετὴς ἄνθε' Ὀλυμπιάδος.
δελφῖνι καὶ τάχος δι' ἅλμας
65 ἶσον ‹κ'› εἴποιμι Μελησίαν
χειρῶν τε καὶ ἰσχύος ἀνίοχον.

60 Ἀλκίμιδα Hartung: ἀλκιμίδας BD | σέ γ' ἐπαρκέσαι
Turyn: τό γ' ἐπάρκεσε BD
64 καὶ Schroeder e schol.: κε BD: κεν Triclinius
65 ‹κ'› suppl. Wilamowitz

68

the most. On my willing back I accept
    a double burden,[13]
and have come as a messenger,   57b
proclaiming that this is the twenty-fifth

triumph won from the games that men call sacred   Ep. 3
which you, Alcimidas, have provided   60
for your illustrious family—although a random[14] lot
robbed you, my boy, and Polytimidas of two wreaths
from the Olympic festival by the precinct of Cronus' son.
As swift as a dolphin through the sea
would I say that Melesias[15] is,   65
that charioteer of hands and strength.

[13] I.e. praise for both the victor and his family; his victory is
their twenty-fifth.

[14] Presumably an unlucky draw of opponents prevented Alci-
midas and Polytimidas (a relative according to the scholion) from
winning.

[15] The trainer.

NEMEAN 7

This ode, which Gildersleeve called "the touchstone of Pindaric interpretation," is one of the most difficult to understand. There are a number of textual problems, most importantly at 33–34; in several places the tone becomes very defensive without any indication of what is at issue (e.g., 64–69, 75–76, and 102–105); one topic often follows another without a clear transition; and finally the meaning or point of several passages is doubtful (e.g., 17–20, 31, 70–73, 77–79, and 102–105). Many scholars follow remarks in the scholia asserting that Pindar is apologizing for his supposedly unflattering treatment of Neoptolemus in *Pae.* 6, but neither poem can be dated and such speculation has proved of little assistance in interpreting *Nem.* 7. What is remarkable is that such a long, complex, and often beautiful poem should have been written for a boy athlete.

A hymn to Eleithyia, goddess of childbirth, leads to an announcement of Sogenes' victory in the pentathlon (1–8). His city Aegina, home of the Aeacidae, fosters athletics and song (9–10). Poetry serves as a mirror to reflect and hold the memory of successful deeds (11–16). Wise men, recognizing that death is inevitable, do not hoard their wealth (17–20).

Pindar claims that Homer has exaggerated Odysseus' real experiences through his deceptive poetic craft (20–

23), and that if the majority of men had not been blind to the fact that Ajax was the best fighter after Achilles, Ajax would not have killed himself in anger over the decision of the arms (23–30). Although all men must die, some are honored in posthumous song by a god's grace (30–32).

The poet brings his helping song to Delphi, where Neoptolemus is buried (33–36). After reigning briefly in Molossia, Neoptolemus brought spoils from Troy to Delphi, where he was killed in a quarrel (36–42), but he fulfilled his fate and now presides over festival processions (43–47). No lengthy proof is required: Apollo is the witness for Neoptolemus' greatness (48–49). The poet could say much more about Aegina and her heroes, but declines to do so (50–53).

Gnomic reflections echoing those in the opening hymn conclude with the observation that no one enjoys perfect happiness (53–58). The poet praises his host Thearion for wise use of his good fortune (58–63), and calls a descendant of Neoptolemus to witness that his praise is just (64–69). Turning to Sogenes, he compares his own poetic efforts to those required in the pentathlon, and strikes up a new prelude, celebrating Zeus, Nemea, Aegina, and Aeacus and ending with Heracles (70–86), upon whom Sogenes can rely as a neighbor because his home is located between two of Heracles' sanctuaries (86–94). The poet prays that Heracles may grant the victor, his father, and their descendants a happy life (94–101), and concludes by declaring that he has praised Neoptolemus with fitting words and that there is no need to repeat what is obvious (102–105).

7. ΣΩΓΕΝΕΙ ΑΙΓΙΝΗΤΗΙ

ΠΑΙΔΙ ΠΕΝΤΑΘΛΩΙ

Α΄ Ἐλείθυια, πάρεδρε Μοιρᾶν βαθυφρόνων,
παῖ μεγαλοσθενέος, ἄκου-
σον, Ἥρας, γενέτειρα τέκνων· ἄνευ σέθεν
οὐ φάος, οὐ μέλαιναν δρακέντες εὐφρόναν
τεὰν ἀδελφεὰν ἐλάχομεν ἀγλαόγυιον Ἥβαν.
5 ἀναπνέομεν δ᾽ οὐχ ἅπαντες ἐπὶ ἴσα·
εἴργει δὲ πότμῳ ζυγένθ᾽ ἕτερον ἕτερα. σὺν δὲ τίν
καὶ παῖς ὁ Θεαρίωνος ἀρετᾷ κριθείς
εὔδοξος ἀείδεται Σω-
γένης μετὰ πενταέθλοις.

πόλιν γὰρ φιλόμολπον οἰκεῖ δορικτύπων
10 Αἰακιδᾶν· μάλα δ᾽ ἐθέλον-
τι σύμπειρον ἀγωνίᾳ θυμὸν ἀμφέπειν.
εἰ δὲ τύχῃ τις ἔρδων, μελίφρον᾽ αἰτίαν

inscr. σωγένι αἰγινήτῳ πεντάθλῳ παιδί D: corr. Triclinius:
om. B
6 πότμῳ B: πότμος D | ζυγένθ᾽ E. Schmid: ζυγόν θ᾽ BD
8 εὔδοξος B: ἔνδοξος D(schol.)
9 δορικτύπων Bˢ: δορίκτυπον Bⁱ: δορύκτυπον D

72

7. FOR SOGENES OF AEGINA

WINNER, BOYS' PENTATHLON

Eleithyia, enthroned beside the deep-thinking Fates,   Str. 1
daughter of mighty Hera, hear me,
   giver of birth to children. Without you
we behold neither light nor the darkness of night,
nor are we allotted your sister, splendid-limbed Hebe.[1]
Yet we do not all draw breath for equal ends,   5
for different things constrain each man in destiny's yoke.
      But by your grace
Thearion's son, Sogenes, is made famous in song
because he was distinguished for his excellence
   among pentathletes.

For he lives in the song-loving city of the spear-clashing   Ant. 1
Aeacidae,[2] and they most eagerly cherish a spirit   10
   that has been tested in competition.
If a man succeeds in an exploit, he casts a honey-minded

[1] Goddess of Youth.
[2] Aegina.

73

ῥοαῖσι Μοισᾶν ἐνέβαλε· ταὶ μεγάλαι γὰρ ἀλκαί
σκότον πολὺν ὕμνων ἔχοντι δεόμεναι·
ἔργοις δὲ καλοῖς ἔσοπτρον ἴσαμεν ἑνὶ σὺν τρόπῳ,
15 εἰ Μναμοσύνας ἔκατι λιπαράμπυκος
εὕρηται ἄποινα μόχθων
κλυταῖς ἐπέων ἀοιδαῖς.

σοφοὶ δὲ μέλλοντα τριταῖον ἄνεμον
ἔμαθον, οὐδ᾽ ὑπὸ κέρδει βλάβεν·
ἀφνεὸς πενιχρός τε θανάτου παρά
20 σᾶμα νέονται. ἐγὼ δὲ πλέον᾽ ἔλπομαι
λόγον Ὀδυσσέος ἢ πάθαν
διὰ τὸν ἁδυεπῆ γενέσθ᾽ Ὅμηρον·

Β΄ ἐπεὶ ψεύδεσί οἱ ποτανᾷ ⟨τε⟩ μαχανᾷ
σεμνὸν ἔπεστί τι· σοφία
δὲ κλέπτει παράγοισα μύθοις. τυφλὸν δ᾽ ἔχει
ἦτορ ὅμιλος ἀνδρῶν ὁ πλεῖστος. εἰ γὰρ ἦν
25 ἓ τὰν ἀλάθειαν ἰδέμεν, οὔ κεν ὅπλων χολωθείς
ὁ καρτερὸς Αἴας ἔπαξε διὰ φρενῶν
λευρὸν ξίφος· ὃν κράτιστον Ἀχιλέος ἄτερ μάχᾳ
ξανθῷ Μενέλᾳ δάμαρτα κομίσαι θοαῖς

16 εὕρηται Hermann: εὕρηταί τις BD
19 ἀφνεὸς Triclinius: ἀφνεός τε BD
19–20 παρὰ σᾶμα BD: πέρας ἅμα Wieseler
22 ⟨τε⟩ suppl. Hermann
25 ἓ τὰν Boeckh: ἐὰν BDΣᵍʳ: ἐὰν schol. Dionysius Char-
midis filius

74

cause[3] into the Muses' streams, for great deeds of valor
remain in deep darkness when they lack hymns.
We know of a mirror for noble deeds in only one way,
if, by the grace of Mnemosyne with the shining crown,   15
one finds a recompense for his labors
    in poetry's famous songs.

Wise men know well the wind to come   Ep. 1
on the third day[4] and are not harmed by greed for gain,
for rich and poor travel to the tomb[5]
of death. I believe that Odysseus' story   20
has become greater than his actual suffering
    because of Homer's sweet verse,

for upon his fictions and soaring craft   Str. 2
rests great majesty, and his skill
    deceives with misleading tales. The great majority
of men have a blind heart, for if they could have seen
the truth, mighty Ajax, in anger over the arms,   25
would not have planted in his chest
the smooth sword. Except for Achilles, in battle he was
      the best
whom the favoring breezes of the straight-blowing

[3] I.e. a pleasing theme for song.
[4] Wise men recognize the uncertainty of the future (i.e. the third day's wind), which eventually ends in death, and do not hoard their gain (cf. *Ol.* 2.56, *Nem.* 1.31–33, and *Isth.* 1.67–68).
[5] Or (reading πέρας ἅμα) *travel together to the boundary of death.*

ἂν ναυσὶ πόρευσαν εὐθυ-
πνόου Ζεφύροιο πομπαί

30 πρὸς Ἴλου πόλιν. ἀλλὰ κοινὸν γὰρ ἔρχεται
κῦμ’ Ἀίδα, πέσε δ’ ἀδόκη-
τον ἐν καὶ δοκέοντα· τιμὰ δὲ γίνεται
ὧν θεὸς ἁβρὸν αὔξει λόγον τεθνακότων.
βοαθῶν τοι παρὰ μέγαν ὀμφαλὸν εὐρυκόλπου
μόλον χθονός. ἐν Πυθίοισι δὲ δαπέδοις
35 κεῖται Πριάμου πόλιν Νεοπτόλεμος ἐπεὶ πράθεν,
τᾷ καὶ Δαναοὶ πόνησαν· ὁ δ’ ἀποπλέων
Σκύρου μὲν ἅμαρτε, πλαγχθέν-
τες δ’ εἰς Ἐφύραν ἵκοντο.

Μολοσσίᾳ δ’ ἐμβασίλευεν ὀλίγον
χρόνον· ἀτὰρ γένος αἰεὶ φέρει
40 τοῦτό οἱ γέρας. ᾤχετο δὲ πρὸς θεόν,
κτέατ’ ἄγων Τροΐαθεν ἀκροθινίων·
ἵνα κρεῶν νιν ὕπερ μάχας
ἔλασεν ἀντιτυχόντ’ ἀνὴρ μαχαίρᾳ.

Γ´ βάρυνθεν δὲ περισσὰ Δελφοὶ ξεναγέται.
ἀλλὰ τὸ μόρσιμον ἀπέδω-
κεν· ἐχρῆν δέ τιν’ ἔνδον ἄλσει παλαιτάτῳ

29 εὐθυπνόου D: εὐθυπόρου B | πομπαί BγρD: πνοαί B
33 βοαθῶν Farnell: βοαθόων BD | παρὰ Hermann e schol.:
γὰρ BD   34 μόλον Hermann: ἔμολε(ν) BD, Didymus:
ἔμολον Σγρ: μόλε Bundy   39 φέρει D: φέρεν B

76

Zephyr conducted to the city of Ilus
   in swift ships, to return his wife

to fair-haired Menelaus. But to all alike comes   Ant. 2
the wave of Hades, and it falls upon the obscure   31
   and the famous;[6] yet honor belongs to those
whose fair story a god exalts after they die.
As a helper, then, I have come to the great navel
of the broad-bosomed earth. For in Pytho's holy ground
lies Neoptolemus, after he sacked Priam's city,   35
where the Danaans also toiled. When he sailed away,
he missed Scyros,[7] but, after wandering,
   he and his men reached Ephyra.[8]

In Molossia[9] he was king for a short   Ep. 2
time, but his offspring have forever held
that privilege of his. He then went to visit the god,[10]   40
bringing with him items from the finest spoils of Troy.
There, when he became involved in a quarrel over
   sacrificial meats, a man struck him with a sword.

The hospitable Delphians were exceedingly grieved,   Str. 3
but he had paid his debt to destiny, for it was necessary
   that within that most ancient precinct

---

[6] Or *upon the unexpecting and expecting.*
[7] The island where he was raised.
[8] The capital of Thesprotia, a district of Epirus.
[9] A district of Epirus.
[10] Apollo.

45 Αἰακιδᾶν κρεόντων τὸ λοιπὸν ἔμμεναι
θεοῦ παρ᾽ εὐτειχέα δόμον, ἡρῴαις δὲ πομπαῖς
θεμισκόπον οἰκεῖν ἐόντα πολυθύτοις.
εὐώνυμον ἐς δίκαν τρία ἔπεα διαρκέσει·
οὐ ψεῦδις ὁ μάρτυς ἔργμασιν ἐπιστατεῖ.
50 Αἴγινα, τεῶν Διός τ᾽ ἐκ-
γόνων θρασύ μοι τόδ᾽ εἰπεῖν

φαενναῖς ἀρεταῖς ὁδὸν κυρίαν λόγων
οἴκοθεν· ἀλλὰ γὰρ ἀνάπαυ-
σις ἐν παντὶ γλυκεῖα ἔργῳ· κόρον δ᾽ ἔχει
καὶ μέλι καὶ τὰ τέρπν᾽ ἄνθε᾽ Ἀφροδίσια.
φυᾷ δ᾽ ἕκαστος διαφέρομεν βιοτὰν λαχόντες
55 ὁ μὲν τά, τὰ δ᾽ ἄλλοι· τυχεῖν δ᾽ ἕν᾽ ἀδύνατον
εὐδαιμονίαν ἅπασαν ἀνελόμενον· οὐκ ἔχω
εἰπεῖν, τίνι τοῦτο Μοῖρα τέλος ἔμπεδον
ὤρεξε. Θεαρίων, τὶν δ᾽
ἐοικότα καιρὸν ὄλβου

δίδωσι, τόλμαν τε καλῶν ἀρομένῳ
60 σύνεσιν οὐκ ἀποβλάπτει φρενῶν.
ξεινός εἰμι· σκοτεινὸν ἀπέχων ψόγον,
ὕδατος ὥτε ῥοὰς φίλον ἐς ἄνδρ᾽ ἄγων
κλέος ἐτήτυμον αἰνέσω·
ποτίφορος δ᾽ ἀγαθοῖσι μισθὸς οὗτος.

51 μυρίαν Janko
59–60 ἀρομένῳ σύνεσιν Hermann: ἀραμένῳ σύνεσις BD

78

one of the royal Aeacidae remain ever after   45
beside the god's well-walled temple, to dwell there
as a rightful overseer of processions honoring heroes
    with many sacrifices.
When it comes to his just renown, three words will
    suffice:
no lying witness presides over his accomplishments.[11]
Aegina, I am emboldened to say   50
    that for the splendid achievements

of your offspring and Zeus' there is a royal road of words   Ant. 3
stretching from your home; but rest is sweet
    in every endeavor and even honey
and Aphrodite's delightful flowers can be cloying.
By nature each of us is allotted a life that sets him apart:
one person has this, others that, and it is impossible   55
for one man to succeed in winning complete happiness:
I cannot name any to whom Fate has given such a prize
that lasts. But, Thearion,[12] to you
    she gives fitting measure of prosperity,

and although you have won boldness for noble deeds,   Ep. 3
she does not harm your mind's understanding.   60
I am a guest-friend. Keeping away dark blame,
like streams of water I shall bring genuine fame
with my praises to the man who is my friend,
    for that is the proper reward for good men.

[11] I.e. Apollo's favor testifies to Neoptolemus' greatness. Others punctuate this sentence to read: *no lying witness presides over the accomplishments, Aegina, of your offspring and Zeus'*.
[12] The victor's father.

Δ´ ἐὼν δ᾽ ἐγγὺς Ἀχαιὸς οὐ μέμψεταί μ᾽ ἀνήρ
65 Ἰονίας ὑπὲρ ἁλὸς οἰ-
κέων, καὶ προξενίᾳ πέποιθ᾽, ἔν τε δαμόταις
ὄμματι δέρκομαι λαμπρόν, οὐχ ὑπερβαλών,
βίαια πάντ᾽ ἐκ ποδὸς ἐρύσαις· ὁ δὲ λοιπὸς εὔφρων
ποτὶ χρόνος ἕρποι. μαθὼν δέ τις ἀνερεῖ,
εἰ πὰρ μέλος ἔρχομαι ψάγιον ὄαρον ἐννέπων.
70 Εὐξένιδα πάτραθε Σώγενες, ἀπομνύω
μὴ τέρμα προβαὶς ἄκονθ᾽ ὥ-
τε χαλκοπάραον ὄρσαι

θοὰν γλῶσσαν, ὃς ἐξέπεμψεν παλαισμάτων
αὐχένα καὶ σθένος ἀδίαν-
τον, αἴθωνι πρὶν ἁλίῳ γυῖον ἐμπεσεῖν.
εἰ πόνος ἦν, τὸ τερπνὸν πλέον πεδέρχεται.
75 ἔα με· νικῶντί γε χάριν, εἴ τι πέραν ἀερθεὶς
ἀνέκραγον, οὐ τραχύς εἰμι καταθέμεν.
εἴρειν στεφάνους ἐλαφρόν, ἀναβάλεο· Μοῖσά τοι
κολλᾷ χρυσὸν ἔν τε λευκὸν ἐλέφανθ᾽ ἁμᾶ
καὶ λείριον ἄνθεμον πον-
τίας ὑφελοῖσ᾽ ἐέρσας.

66 ὑπερβαλών E. Schmid: ὑπερβάλλων BD
68 ἀνερεῖ Gildersleeve: ἂν ἐρεῖ BD
72 ἐξέπεμψεν Boeckh: ἐξέπεμψε D: ἐξέπεμψας B

---

13 I.e. a descendant of Neoptolemus in Molossia.
14 I interpret this to mean that his praise of Thearion and
Neoptolemus has not been exaggerated or forced.

80

If any Achaean man is nearby, one dwelling beyond   Str. 4
the Ionian Sea,[13] he will not blame me; I also trust   65
    in my host's hospitality, and among his townsmen
my gaze is bright, since I have not been excessive,
but have removed everything forced from my path.[14]
      May time to come
approach favorably. One who knows me will proclaim
if I come saying a crooked utterance out of tune.
Sogenes from the clan of the Euxenidae, I swear   70
that I have not stepped up to the line
    and sent my tongue

speeding like a bronze-cheeked javelin, which releases   Ant. 4
the strong neck from wrestling without sweat,
    before the body falls under the blazing sun.[15]
If there was hard work, greater is the delight that
      follows.
Forgive me. If in excessive elation I cried out, to a   75
      victor,
at least, I am not averse to paying a debt of honor.
Weaving crowns is easy. Strike up the prelude. The
      Muse,
you know, binds together gold and white ivory
with the lily flower[16] she has taken
    from under the dew of the sea.

[15] The pentathlon could be won with enough victories in ear-
lier events such as the javelin throw, thereby obviating the decid-
ing wrestling match in the heat of the day. The implication is that
Pindar will spare no effort in praising the victor.
[16] Coral.

80 Διὸς δὲ μεμναμένος ἀμφὶ Νεμέᾳ
πολύφατον θρόον ὕμνων δόνει
ἡσυχᾷ. βασιλῆα δὲ θεῶν πρέπει
δάπεδον ἂν τόδε γαρυέμεν ἡμέρᾳ
ὀπί· λέγοντι γὰρ Αἰακόν
νιν ὑπὸ ματροδόκοις γοναῖς φυτεῦσαι,

Ε΄ ἐμᾷ μὲν πολίαρχον εὐωνύμῳ πάτρᾳ,
86 Ἡράκλεες, σέο δὲ προπράον᾽
ἔμμεν ξεῖνον ἀδελφεόν τ᾽. εἰ δὲ γεύεται
ἀνδρὸς ἀνήρ τι, φαῖμέν κε γείτον᾽ ἔμμεναι
νόῳ φιλήσαντ᾽ ἀτενέι γείτονι χάρμα πάντων
ἐπάξιον· εἰ δ᾽ αὐτὸ καὶ θεὸς ἀνέχοι,
90 ἐν τίν κ᾽ ἐθέλοι, Γίγαντας ὃς ἐδάμασας, εὐτυχῶς
ναίειν πατρὶ Σωγένης ἀταλὸν ἀμφέπων
θυμὸν προγόνων εὐκτή-
μονα ζαθέαν ἄγυιαν·

ἐπεὶ τετραόροισιν ὥθ᾽ ἁρμάτων ζυγοῖς
ἐν τεμένεσσι δόμον ἔχει
τεοῖς, ἀμφοτέρας ἰὼν χειρός. ὦ μάκαρ,

83 ἡμέρᾳ Benedictus (invit. schol. metr.): θαμερᾶ B: θεμερᾶ
D
85 ἑᾷ Hermann
86 προπράον᾽ ἔμμεν Schroeder, Jurenka, Turyn: προπρεῶνα
μὲν BD | γεύεται BsD, Aristarchus: δεύεται Bi(schol.)

But, after mentioning Zeus, set in motion[17] Ep. 4
the famous sound of hymns for Nemea, 81
softly. It is fitting to sing of the king of the gods
on this holy ground[18] with a gentle
voice, for they say that through the mother[19]
    who received his seed he begat Aeacus

to be ruler of cities in my[20] illustrious land, Str. 5
and, Heracles, to be your kindly guest-friend 86
    and brother. If man has any enjoyment
of his fellow man, I would say that a neighbor who loved
his neighbor with fixed purpose is a joy to him worth
everything. And if a god[21] should also uphold this
        principle,
then with your help, subduer of the Giants, 90
Sogenes might wish, as he cherishes a spirit of
        tenderness
for his father, to live joyfully on the well-built
    sacred street of his forefathers;

for, like the yokes of a four-horse chariot, Ant. 5
he has his home in your precincts
    on either hand as he goes forth.[22] Blessed one,

[17] The poet is addressing himself (or the chorus leader).
[18] In Aegina.   [19] The nymph Aegina.
[20] The first person implies that the poet is speaking for the chorus or the Aeginetans; many editors adopt Hermann's emendation ἑᾷ ("his own").   [21] For Heracles as a god, see *Nem.* 3.22; for his part in slaying the Giants, see *Nem.* 1.67–69.
[22] Sogenes had his home between two precincts dedicated to Heracles, like the pole that runs between the yokes on a four-horse chariot (schol.).

PINDAR

95　τὶν δ' ἐπέοικεν Ἥρας πόσιν τε πειθέμεν
　　κόραν τε γλαυκώπιδα· δύνασαι δὲ βροτοῖσιν ἀλκάν
　　ἀμαχανιᾶν δυσβάτων θαμὰ διδόμεν.
　　εἰ γάρ σφισιν ἐμπεδοσθενέα βίοτον ἁρμόσαις
　　ἥβᾳ λιπαρῷ τε γήραϊ διαπλέκοις
100　εὐδαίμον' ἐόντα, παίδων
　　　δὲ παῖδες ἔχοιεν αἰεί

　　γέρας τό περ νῦν καὶ ἄρειον ὄπιθεν.
　　τὸ δ' ἐμὸν οὔ ποτε φάσει κέαρ
　　ἀτρόποισι Νεοπτόλεμον ἑλκύσαι
　　ἔπεσι· ταὐτὰ δὲ τρὶς τετράκι τ' ἀμπολεῖν
105　ἀπορία τελέθει, τέκνοι-
　　　σιν ἅτε μαψυλάκας "Διὸς Κόρινθος."

　　　95 Ἥρας Bothe: ἥραν BD
　　　98 σφισιν Triclinius: σφιν BD: σύ ἰν Maas
　　　104 ταὐτὰ Boeckh e schol.: ταῦτα BD

84

it is fitting for you to win over Hera's husband   95
and the gray-eyed virgin,[23] for you are often able to give
mortals defense against desperate difficulties.
I pray that you may match a steadfast life
to their[24] youth and splendid old age and weave it
to a happy end, and that   100
    their children's children may always have such

honor as they now enjoy and even greater hereafter.   Ep. 5
My heart will never say
that it has treated Neoptolemus with unyielding
words, but to plow the same ruts three and four times
is pointless, like someone yapping at children,   105
    "Corinth belongs to Zeus."

[23] Athena.
[24] Sogenes and Thearion. Or (reading σύ ἱν) *his*.

NEMEAN 8

Since the ode lacks a title in the MSS, the event must be conjectured from the ambiguous notices in lines 16 and 47–48. Some editors argue that the victories were in the stadion, but most follow Didymus and the scholia in assigning them to the diaulos, the double stadion. The victor's deceased father Megas had won the same event at Nemea. The main narrative, introduced as an illustration of the power of envy to obscure true greatness, tells of Odysseus' use of deceptive speech to win the arms of Achilles, an episode also treated in *Nem.* 7 and *Isth.* 4.

The opening hymn to Hora, the goddess of adolescence, emphasizes that her treatment of the young can be mild or harsh (1–3). A gnomic statement recommending noble love is illustrated by that of Zeus and Aegina, which produced Aeacus, renowned for his just rule (4–12). The poet comes as a suppliant of Aeacus bringing this tribute for the racing victories of Deinias and his father Megas (13–16).

A gnomic reflection on the longevity of god-given prosperity is briefly illustrated by the example of Cinyras (17–18). As if standing at the starting line of a race, the poet draws breath before continuing because, he avows, new words of praise are exposed to envy, which delights in assailing good men, as when it caused Ajax's suicide (19–23).

Because that hero was unable to speak for himself, the prize of the armor was awarded in a secret vote to Odysseus (24–27). In fact, however, Ajax had proven himself a much more effective fighter, but malicious misrepresentation existed even then to abase good men and raise up unworthy ones (28–34).

The poet prays that he may never be guilty of misrepresenting true worth, but instead be forthright and leave behind a good name for his children (35–37). In a brief priamel he states his desire to bestow praise and blame where it is due (37–39). The wise and just poet nurtures excellence (40–42). Although friends are most needed during times of trial, they are also sought out in times of joy (42–44). The poet cannot bring Megas back to life, but he can, in song, honor his homeland, his clan, and his victories, and thereby provide consolation for pain (44–50). The hymn of celebration predates the war of the Seven against Thebes (50–51).

8. ⟨ΔΕΙΝΙΑΙ ΑΙΓΙΝΗΤΗΙ
ΔΙΑΥΛΟΔΡΟΜΩΙ⟩

Α΄ ῟Ωρα πότνια, κάρυξ Ἀφροδίτας
   ἀμβροσιᾶν φιλοτάτων,
ἅ τε παρθενηίοις παί-
   δων τ᾽ ἐφίζοισα γλεφάροις,
τὸν μὲν ἡμέροις ἀνάγκας χερσὶ βαστά-
   ζεις, ἕτερον δ᾽ ἑτέραις.
ἀγαπατὰ δὲ καιροῦ μὴ πλανα-
   θέντα πρὸς ἔργον ἕκαστον
5 τῶν ἀρειόνων ἐρώτων ἐπικρατεῖν δύνασθαι.

οἷοι καὶ Διὸς Αἰγίνας τε λέκτρον
   ποιμένες ἀμφεπόλησαν
Κυπρίας δώρων· ἔβλαστεν δ᾽
   υἱὸς Οἰνώνας βασιλεύς
χειρὶ καὶ βουλαῖς ἄριστος. πολλά νιν πολ-
   λοὶ λιτάνευον ἰδεῖν·
ἀβοατὶ γὰρ ἡρώων ἄω-
   τοι περιναιεταόντων
10 ἤθελον κείνου γε πείθεσθ᾽ ἀναξίαις ἑκόντες,

inscr. suppl. Schroeder e schol.: om. BD

88

8. FOR DEINIAS OF AEGINA

WINNER, DIAULOS

Queen Hora,[1] herald of Aphrodite's Str. 1
  ambrosial acts of love,
settling upon the eyes
  of unwed girls and of boys,
you hold one person with gentle hands of necessity,
  but another with hands of a different kind.[2]
Pleasant it is not to stray from due measure
  in each endeavor
and be able to win the loves that are more noble. 5

Such were the loves, shepherds of Cypris'[3] gifts, Ant. 1
  that attended the bed of Zeus
and Aegina. A son[4] was born
  as king of Oenona,[5]
preeminent in strength of hand and counsels. Many men
  often begged to see him,
for without summons the best
  of the neighboring heroes
were willing and eager to submit to that man's kingship, 10

[1] The personification of youthful beauty (cf. *Ol.* 10.104).
[2] I.e. rough ones.
[3] Aphrodite's.   [4] Aeacus.
[5] The ancient name for Aegina.

οἵ τε κρανααῖς ἐν Ἀθάναισιν ἅρμοζον στρατόν,
οἵ τ' ἀνὰ Σπάρταν Πελοπηιάδαι.
ἱκέτας Αἰακοῦ
  σεμνῶν γονάτων πόλιός θ' ὑπὲρ φίλας
  ἀστῶν θ' ὑπὲρ τῶνδ' ἅπτομαι φέρων
15 Λυδίαν μίτραν καναχηδὰ πεποικιλμέναν,
Δείνιος δισσῶν σταδίων
  καὶ πατρὸς Μέγα Νεμεαῖον ἄγαλμα.
  σὺν θεῷ γάρ τοι φυτευθεὶς
  ὄλβος ἀνθρώποισι παρμονώτερος·

Β΄ ὅσπερ καὶ Κινύραν ἔβρισε πλούτῳ
  ποντίᾳ ἔν ποτε Κύπρῳ.
ἵσταμαι δὴ ποσσὶ κούφοις,
  ἀμπνέων τε πρίν τι φάμεν.
20 πολλὰ γὰρ πολλᾷ λέλεκται, νεαρὰ δ' ἐξευ-
    ρόντα δόμεν βασάνῳ
ἐς ἔλεγχον, ἅπας κίνδυνος· ὄ-
    ψον δὲ λόγοι φθονεροῖσιν,
  ἅπτεται δ' ἐσλῶν ἀεί, χειρόνεσσι δ' οὐκ ἐρίζει.

κεῖνος καὶ Τελαμῶνος δάψεν υἱόν,
  φασγάνῳ ἀμφικυλίσαις.
ἦ τιν' ἄγλωσσον μέν, ἦτορ δ'
  ἄλκιμον, λάθα κατέχει
25 ἐν λυγρῷ νείκει· μέγιστον δ' αἰόλῳ ψεύ-
    δει γέρας ἀντέταται.

90

both those who marshaled the host in rocky Athens   Ep. 1
and the descendants of Pelops in Sparta.
As a suppliant I am clasping the hallowed knees
    of Aeacus, and on behalf of his beloved city
and of these citizens I am bringing
a Lydian fillet embellished with ringing notes,[6]   15
a Nemean ornament for the double stadion races[7]
    of Deinias and his father Megas.
For truly, when it is planted with a god's blessing,
    happiness lasts longer for men;

such happiness long ago loaded Cinyras   Str. 2
    with wealth on sea-washed Cyprus.
But here I stand on light feet
    and draw breath before uttering a word.
For many things have been said in many ways, but   20
    to discover new ones and put them to the touchstone
for testing is sheer danger, since words are dessert
    to the envious, and envy fastens
always on the good, but has no quarrel with lesser men.

It was that which feasted on the son of Telamon   Ant. 2
    when it rolled him onto his sword.
Truly, oblivion overwhelms many a man whose tongue
    is speechless, but heart is bold,
in a grievous quarrel; and the greatest prize   25
    has been offered up to shifty falsehood.

───────

[6] I.e. this poem in Lydian mode accompanied by pipes. Victors
wore woolen ribbons around their heads.

[7] It is unclear whether they won two victories in the stadion or
in the double-stadion (diaulos) as a scholion claims.

κρυφίαισι γὰρ ἐν ψάφοις Ὀδυσ-
σῆ Δαναοὶ θεράπευσαν·
χρυσέων δ' Αἴας στερηθεὶς ὅπλων φόνῳ πάλαισεν.

ἦ μὰν ἀνόμοιά γε δάοισιν ἐν θερμῷ χροΐ
ἕλκεα ῥῆξαν πελεμιζόμενοι
30 ὑπ' ἀλεξιμβρότῳ
λόγχᾳ, τὰ μὲν ἀμφ' Ἀχιλεῖ νεοκτόνῳ,
ἄλλων τε μόχθων ἐν πολυφθόροις
ἀμέραις. ἐχθρὰ δ' ἄρα πάρφασις ἦν καὶ πάλαι,
αἱμύλων μύθων ὁμόφοι-
τος, δολοφραδής, κακοποιὸν ὄνειδος·
ἃ τὸ μὲν λαμπρὸν βιᾶται,
τῶν δ' ἀφάντων κῦδος ἀντείνει σαθρόν.

Γ΄ εἴη μή ποτέ μοι τοιοῦτον ἦθος,
Ζεῦ πάτερ, ἀλλὰ κελεύθοις
36 ἁπλόαις ζωᾶς ἐφαπτοί-
μαν, θανὼν ὡς παισὶ κλέος
μὴ τὸ δύσφαμον προσάψω. χρυσὸν εὔχον-
ται, πεδίον δ' ἕτεροι
ἀπέραντον, ἐγὼ δ' ἀστοῖς ἁδὼν
καὶ χθονὶ γυῖα καλύψαι,
αἰνέων αἰνητά, μομφὰν δ' ἐπισπείρων ἀλιτροῖς.

29 πελεμιζόμενοι Wakefield e schol.: πολεμιζόμενοι BD
38 καλύψαι Wackernagel: καλύψαιμ' BD

92

For with secret votes
　　the Danaans favored Odysseus, while Ajax,
stripped of the golden armor, wrestled with a gory death.

In truth, unequal indeed were the wounds they tore　　Ep. 2
in the warm flesh of their foes
with succoring spears when they were hard pressed,　　30
　　both in fighting over Achilles newly slain
and in the murderous days of their other
labors. Yes, hateful deception existed even long ago,
the companion of flattering tales,
　　guileful contriver, evil-working disgrace,
which represses what is illustrious,
　　but holds up for obscure men a glory that is rotten.

May I never have such a disposition,　　Str. 3
　　father Zeus, but let me travel
the straightforward paths of life,　　36
　　so that when I die I may leave my children
no such disreputable fame. Some pray for gold,
　　others for land
without end, but I pray to find favor with my townsmen
　　until I cover my limbs with earth,
praising things praiseworthy, but casting blame on
　　　　evildoers.

40 αὔξεται δ᾽ ἀρετά, χλωραῖς ἐέρσαις
    ὡς ὅτε δένδρεον ᾄσσει,
    ⟨ἐν⟩ σοφοῖς ἀνδρῶν ἀερθεῖσ᾽
    ἐν δικαίοις τε πρὸς ὑγρόν
    αἰθέρα. χρεῖαι δὲ παντοῖαι φίλων ἀν-
      δρῶν· τὰ μὲν ἀμφὶ πόνοις
    ὑπερώτατα, μαστεύει δὲ καὶ
      τέρψις ἐν ὄμμασι θέσθαι
    πιστόν. ὦ Μέγα, τὸ δ᾽ αὖτις τεὰν ψυχὰν κομίξαι

45 οὔ μοι δυνατόν· κενεᾶν δ᾽ ἐλπίδων χαῦνον τέλος·
    σεῦ δὲ πάτρᾳ Χαριάδαις τε λάβρον
    ὑπερεῖσαι λίθον
    Μοισαῖον ἕκατι ποδῶν εὐωνύμων
    δὶς δὴ δυοῖν. χαίρω δὲ πρόσφορον
    ἐν μὲν ἔργῳ κόμπον ἱείς, ἐπαοιδαῖς δ᾽ ἀνήρ
50 νώδυνον καί τις κάματον.
      θῆκεν· ἦν γε μὰν ἐπικώμιος ὕμνος
    δὴ πάλαι καὶ πρὶν γενέσθαι
      τὰν Ἀδράστου τάν τε Καδμείων ἔριν.

40–41 αὔξεται BD: αὔξηται (perfect.) Turyn: ἀίσσει huc e
fine versus transp. F. Vogt et Snell | ᾄσσει ⟨ἐν⟩ σοφοῖς Boeckh:
ᾄσσει σοφοῖς BD: lacunam post δένδρεον statuerunt F. Vogt et
Snell.
    44 πιστόν Mommsen e paraphr.: πιστά B: πίσταν D
    46 τ᾽ ἐλαφρόν Sandys praeeuntibus Bergk et Cookesley

Excellence grows like a tree	Ant. 3
that springs up to fresh dew,	
when lifted among wise	41
and just men to liquid	
heaven. There are all sorts of needs for friends,	
and while help amid toils	
is greatest, joy too seeks	
to set in view	
what is trustworthy.[8] O Megas, to bring back your life	

is impossible for me: that is the vain goal of empty	Ep. 3
hopes.	
But for your homeland and the Chariadae, I can erect	46
a loud-sounding stone[9]	
of the Muses in honor of those twice famous	
pairs of feet.[10] I am glad to cast a fitting vaunt	
upon your accomplishment, and many a man has	
with healing songs made even hard toil painless.	50
Yes, truly the hymn of victory	
existed long ago, even before that strife arose	
between Adrastus and the Cadmeans.[11]	

[8] I.e. celebratory poetry, which serves as a faithful pledge of noble deeds (cf. *Ol.* 11.6).

[9] Or (reading τ᾽ ἐλαφρόν) *it is easy to erect a stone of the Muses.* Pindar compares his poem to a commemorative stele.

[10] The two running victories of Deinias and Megas.

[11] That is, there were encomia before the Nemean games were founded by Adrastus and his army on their way to Thebes (schol.).

NEMEAN 9

The last three odes in the Nemean collection do not celebrate victories in the Nemean games. This poem, like *Nem.* 1, is dedicated to Chromius, Hieron's eminent commander, but was placed here at the end of the roll because it celebrates a victory in the Sicyonian games. Since Aetna, its place of performance, is called "newly founded" (2), the victory was probably won in 474 or soon thereafter. In contrast to *Nem.* 1, which praises Chromius in general terms (and by implicit comparison with Heracles), this poem concentrates on his martial successes. It is not certain which ode was composed first.

The games celebrated at Sicyon in Pindar's time had been instituted by Cleisthenes in honor of Pythian Apollo (Hdt. 5.67), but the poet attributes their founding to Adrastus during his exile there from Argos before his first expedition against Thebes. By placing a prayer that battle with the Carthaginians may be long postponed immediately after a narration of the disastrous expedition of the Seven against Thebes, Pindar seems to imply that an invasion by them would entail the same consequences.

The poem opens with a summons to the Muses to proceed from Sicyon to Aetna and to Chromius' home swamped with guests, where Chromius in his chariot calls for a song to honor Leto and her twins (1–5). A gnomic statement on the need to praise achievement prompts the poet to celebrate the equestrian contests instituted by Adrastus at Sicyon, where he reigned after his expulsion from Argos by Amphiaraus (6–14). Adrastus ended their quarrel by marrying his sister Eriphyle to Amphiaraus (15–17). Subsequently, Adrastus disregarded Zeus' unfavorable omens and led an expedition against Thebes that resulted in disaster for the army and death for Amphiaraus (18–27).

The poet prays that Zeus may avert any such confrontation with the Carthaginians as long as possible, provide good governance for generations within Aetna, and foster festivals (28–32). He praises the Aetnaeans for their horsemanship and uncorrupted sense of honor, and Chromius for his courage in many battles on land and sea, beginning with his early victory at the Helorus River (32–43). The poet assures Chromius that the gods have granted him a happy life; when one is prosperous and famous, he has reached the limit of success (44–47).

The poet calls for wine to be served in the silver bowls that Chromius and his horses won at Sicyon, and concludes by praying that he may surpass other eulogists in praising such achievement (48–55).

9. ⟨ΧΡΟΜΙΩΙ ΑΙΤΝΑΙΩΙ

ΑΡΜΑΤΙ⟩

Α΄ Κωμάσομεν παρ' Ἀπόλλωνος Σικυωνόθε, Μοῖσαι,
τὰν νεοκτίσταν ἐς Αἴτναν, ἔνθ' ἀναπεπταμέναι
  ξείνων νενίκανται θύραι,
ὄλβιον ἐς Χρομίου
    δῶμ'. ἀλλ' ἐπέων γλυκὺν ὕμνον πράσσετε.
τὸ κρατήσιππον γὰρ ἐς ἄρμ' ἀναβαίνων
  ματέρι καὶ διδύμοις παίδεσσιν αὐδὰν μανύει
5 Πυθῶνος αἰπεινᾶς ὁμοκλάροις ἐπόπταις.

Β΄ ἔστι δέ τις λόγος ἀνθρώπων, τετελεσμένον ἐσλόν
μὴ χαμαὶ σιγᾷ καλύψαι· θεσπεσία δ' ἐπέων
  καύχας ἀοιδὰ πρόσφορος.
ἀλλ' ἀνὰ μὲν βρομίαν
    φόρμιγγ', ἀνὰ δ' αὐλὸν ἐπ' αὐτὰν ὄρσομεν
ἱππίων ἀέθλων κορυφάν, ἅ τε Φοίβῳ
  θῆκεν Ἄδραστος ἐπ' Ἀσωποῦ ῥεέθροις· ὧν ἐγὼ
10 μνασθεὶς ἐπασκήσω κλυταῖς ἥρωα τιμαῖς,

inscr. suppl. Triclinius: om. BD
7 καύχαις Benedictus

98

9. FOR CHROMIUS OF AETNA

WINNER, CHARIOT RACE

Let us go in revelry from Apollo at Sicyon, Muses,   Str. 1
to the newly founded Aetna, where the wide-open gates
   are overwhelmed by guests,
to Chromius' blessed
   home. Come, make a sweet hymn of verses.
For, mounting his chariot of victorious horses,
   he signals for a song to honor the mother and twin
children,[1] who keep joint watch over steep Pytho.   5

Men have a saying: do not hide a noble accomplishment   Str. 2
on the ground in silence. Rather, a divine song
   with verses of acclaim is called for.
Let us rouse up, then, the resounding lyre
   and rouse the pipe for the very apex of contests
for horses, which Adrastus established for Phoebus
   by the streams of Asopus. Having mentioned them,
I shall exalt the hero with fame-bringing honors,   10

---

[1] Leto and her children Apollo and Artemis.

---

8 αὐτὰν Ceporinus: αὐτὸν BD

PINDAR

Γ´ ὃς τότε μὲν βασιλεύων κεῖθι νέαισί θ' ἑορταῖς
ἰσχύος τ' ἀνδρῶν ἁμίλλαις ἅρμασί τε γλαφυροῖς
   ἄμφαινε κυδαίνων πόλιν.
φεῦγε γὰρ Ἀμφιαρῆ
   ποτε θρασυμήδεα καὶ δεινὰν στάσιν
πατρίων οἴκων ἀπό τ' Ἄργεος· ἀρχοὶ
   δ' οὐκ ἔτ' ἔσαν Ταλαοῦ παῖδες, βιασθέντες λύᾳ.
15 κρέσσων δὲ καππαύει δίκαν τὰν πρόσθεν ἀνήρ.

Δ´ ἀνδροδάμαντ' Ἐριφύλαν, ὅρκιον ὡς ὅτε πιστόν,
δόντες Οἰκλείδᾳ γυναῖκα, ξανθοκομᾶν Δαναῶν
   ἦσαν μέγιστοι <–∪–>
καί ποτ' ἐς ἑπταπύλους
   Θήβας ἄγαγον στρατὸν ἀνδρῶν αἰσιᾶν
οὐ κατ' ὀρνίχων ὁδόν· οὐδὲ Κρονίων
   ἀστεροπὰν ἐλελίξαις οἴκοθεν μαργουμένους
20 στείχειν ἐπώτρυν', ἀλλὰ φείσασθαι κελεύθου.

Ε´ φαινομέναν δ' ἄρ' ἐς ἄταν σπεῦδεν ὅμιλος ἱκέσθαι
χαλκέοις ὅπλοισιν ἱππείοις τε σὺν ἔντεσιν· Ἰσ-
   μηνοῦ δ' ἐπ' ὄχθαισι γλυκύν

17–18 ⟨λαγέται⟩ Bergk: ⟨δεσπόται⟩ Mair: μέγιστοι καί
ποτε / ἐς⟨λὸν ἐς⟩ ἑπταπύλους Boehmer
18 αἰσιᾶν Triclinius: αἰσιῶν B: om. D

---

[2] Talaus was Adrastus' father.   [3] I.e. Adrastus put an
end to the quarrel by giving his sister Eriphyle in marriage to
Amphiaraus. Others take it to refer to Amphiaraus: *the stronger*

100

who, reigning there at that time, made the city famous   Str. 3
by glorifying it with new festivals and contests
     for men's strength and with polished chariots.
For in time past, to escape bold-counseling Amphiaraus
     and terrible civil strife, he had fled
from his ancestral home and Argos. No longer were
     Talaus'[2] sons rulers; they had been overpowered by
          discord.
But the stronger man puts an end to a former dispute.[3]   15

After giving man-subduing Eriphyle as a faithful pledge   Str. 4
to Oecles' son[4] for a wife, they[5] became the greatest
     of the fair-haired Danaans . . .
and later they led an army of men
     to seven-gated Thebes
on a journey with no favorable omens, and Cronus' son
     brandished his lightning and urged them not to set
          out
recklessly from home, but to forgo the expedition.[6]   20

But after all, the host was eager to march, with bronze   Str. 5
weapons and cavalry gear, into obvious disaster,
     and on the banks of the Ismenus[7]

man puts an end to what was just before. The scholia support both
interpretations.   [4] Amphiaraus. Eriphyle persuaded him to
embark on the expedition against his better judgment.
     [5] The sons of Talaus. No convincing supplement has been pro-
posed for the lacuna at the end of the verse.
     [6] For lightning as a warning to hold back, see *Od.* 24.539–544.
If οὐδέ is taken with both ἐλελίξαις and ἐπώτρυν', the passage
means: *and by not brandishing his lightning Cronus' son did not
urge them to set out.*   [7] A river near Thebes.

PINDAR

νόστον ἐρεισάμενοι
  λευκανθέα σώμασι πίαναν καπνόν·
ἑπτὰ γὰρ δαίσαντο πυραὶ νεογυίους
  φῶτας· ὁ δ' Ἀμφιαρεῖ σχίσσεν κεραυνῷ παμβίᾳ
25 Ζεὺς τὰν βαθύστερνον χθόνα, κρύψεν δ' ἅμ' ἵπποις,

F´ δουρὶ Περικλυμένου πρὶν νῶτα τυπέντα μαχατάν
  θυμὸν αἰσχυνθῆμεν. ἐν γὰρ δαιμονίοισι φόβοις
    φεύγοντι καὶ παῖδες θεῶν.
  εἰ δυνατόν, Κρονίων,
    πεῖραν μὲν ἀγάνορα Φοινικοστόλων
  ἐγχέων ταύταν θανάτου πέρι καὶ ζω-
    ᾶς ἀναβάλλομαι ὡς πόρσιστα, μοῖραν δ' εὔνομον
30 αἰτέω σε παισὶν δαρὸν Αἰτναίων ὀπάζειν,

Z´ Ζεῦ πάτερ, ἀγλαΐαισιν δ' ἀστυνόμοις ἐπιμεῖξαι
  λαόν. ἐντί τοι φίλιπποί τ' αὐτόθι καὶ κτεάνων
    ψυχὰς ἔχοντες κρέσσονας
  ἄνδρες. ἄπιστον ἔειπ'·
    αἰδὼς γὰρ ὑπὸ κρύφα κέρδει κλέπτεται,
  ἃ φέρει δόξαν. Χρομίῳ κεν ὑπασπί-
    ζων παρὰ πεζοβόαις ἵπποις τε ναῶν τ' ἐν μάχαις
35 ἔκρινας, ἂν κίνδυνον ὀξείας ἀυτᾶς,

---

8 There was a pyre for each contingent of the Seven.

9 A Theban defender, son of Poseidon and Chloris (Teiresias' daughter), with the same name as the son of Neleus at *Pyth.* 4.175 (schol.).

102

they laid down their sweet homecoming
    and fed the white-flowering smoke with their bodies,
for seven pyres feasted on the men's young limbs.[8] But
    for Amphiaraus' sake Zeus split the deep-bosomed
earth with his almighty thunderbolt and buried him with   25
       his team,

before being struck in the back by Periclymenus'[9] spear   Str. 6
and suffering disgrace in his warrior spirit. For in panics
    sent from heaven, even the gods' sons take flight.
If possible, son of Cronus,
    I would put off as long as can be such a lordly trial
of life and death against the spears of a Phoenician host;
    and I beg you to grant the dispensation of good rule
long hereafter to the descendants of Aetna's men,   30

father Zeus, and to bring its people together in   Str. 7
public celebrations. For they are lovers of horses here
    and men who have souls superior to
possessions. My words are hard to believe, for the sense
    of honor[10] that brings fame is secretly stolen by
greed for gain. Had you carried Chromius' shield among
    the shouting infantry and cavalry and in sea battles,
you would have judged, during the danger of the fierce   35
       battle cry,

[10] Aidos, the sense of honor and self-respect that gives one the courage to keep his place in a hoplite formation and turn the tide of battle against the opposing army.

PINDAR

Η΄ οὕνεκεν ἐν πολέμῳ κείνα θεὸς ἔντυεν αὐτοῦ
    θυμὸν αἰχματὰν ἀμύνειν λοιγὸν Ἐνναλίου.
      παῦροι δὲ βουλεῦσαι φόνου
    παρποδίου νεφέλαν
      τρέψαι ποτὶ δυσμενέων ἀνδρῶν στίχας
    χερσὶ καὶ ψυχᾷ δυνατοί· λέγεται μὰν
      Ἕκτορι μὲν κλέος ἀνθῆσαι Σκαμάνδρου
        χεύμασιν
40 ἀγχοῦ, βαθυκρήμνοισι δ' ἀμφ' ἀκταῖς Ἑλώρου,

Θ΄ ἔνθ' Ἀρείας πόρον ἄνθρωποι καλέοισι, δέδορκεν
    παιδὶ τοῦθ' Ἁγησιδάμου φέγγος ἐν ἁλικίᾳ
      πρώτᾳ· τὰ δ' ἄλλαις ἁμέραις
    πολλὰ μὲν ἐν κονίᾳ
      χέρσῳ, τὰ δὲ γείτονι πόντῳ φάσομαι.
    ἐκ πόνων δ', οἳ σὺν νεότατι γένωνται
      σύν τε δίκᾳ, τελέθει πρὸς γῆρας αἰὼν ἡμέρα.
45 ἴστω λαχὼν πρὸς δαιμόνων θαυμαστὸν ὄλβον.

Ι΄ εἰ γὰρ ἅμα κτεάνοις πολλοῖς ἐπίδοξον ἄρηται
    κῦδος, οὐκ ἔστι πρόσωθεν θνατὸν ἔτι σκοπιᾶς
      ἄλλας ἐφάψασθαι ποδοῖν.

    41 ἔνθ' Ἀρείας BD: ἔνθ' Ἀρέας Bothe: ἔνθα Ῥέας Boeckh
    (schol. inter Ἀρείας et Ῥείας fluctuat)
    47 οὐκ ἔστι πρόσωθεν Boehmer: οὐκέτι πόρσω B: οὐκ ἔστι
    πρόσω D

104

that in war that goddess[11] was urging on   Str. 8
his martial spirit to ward off the onslaught of Enyalius.[12]
    Few are able to counsel how,
with hands and soul, to turn the storm cloud
    of imminent slaughter toward
the ranks of the enemy. Truly they say that Hector's
    fame blossomed close by Scamander's streams,
but beside the steep and rugged banks of the Helorus,   40

at the place men call Areia's Ford,[13] such a beacon   Str. 9
has shone forth for the son of Hagesidamus in his
    earliest youth. I shall tell of his deeds on other days,
many on the dusty land
    and others on the neighboring sea.
From labors which are borne in youth and with justice
    life becomes gentle toward old age.
Let him know that he has received marvelous happiness   45
      from the gods.

For if along with many possessions one wins famous   Str. 10
glory, there is no further promontory
    upon which a mortal may set his feet.

[11] I.e. Aidos.
[12] An epithet of Ares.
[13] The battle of Helorus in 492, where Chromius fought for Hippocrates of Gela against the Syracusans. From the time of the scholia the specific location and the text have been in doubt. Some editors read ἔνθα ῾Ρέας πόρον, "the passage of Rhea," meaning the Ionian Sea (cf. Aesch. PV 837).

ἡσυχία δὲ φιλεῖ
  μὲν συμπόσιον· νεοθαλὴς δ' αὔξεται
μαλθακᾷ νικαφορία σὺν ἀοιδᾷ·
  θαρσαλέα δὲ παρὰ κρατῆρα φωνὰ γίνεται.
50 ἐγκιρνάτω τίς νιν, γλυκὺν κώμου προφάταν,

ΙΑ΄ ἀργυρέαισι δὲ νωμάτω φιάλαισι βιατάν
  ἀμπέλου παῖδ', ἅς ποθ' ἵπποι κτησάμεναι Χρομίῳ
    πέμψαν θεμιπλέκτοις ἁμᾶ
  Λατοΐδα στεφάνοις
    ἐκ τᾶς ἱερᾶς Σικυῶνος. Ζεῦ πάτερ,
εὔχομαι ταύταν ἀρετὰν κελαδῆσαι
    σὺν Χαρίτεσσιν, ὑπὲρ πολλῶν τε τιμαλφεῖν
      λόγοις
55 νίκαν, ἀκοντίζων σκοποῖ ἄγχιστα Μοισᾶν.

52 ἁμᾶ F. Vogt: ἀμφὶ (scil. ex AMAI corruptum) BD: ἅμα
schol.

Peace loves
    the symposium, but victory increases
with new bloom to the accompaniment of gentle song,
    and the voice becomes confident beside the
        winebowl.
Let someone mix that sweet prompter of the revel,   50

and let him serve the powerful child of the vine in the   Str. 11
silver bowls which his horses once won for Chromius
    and brought to him along with the duly woven
crowns of Leto's son[14]
    from holy Sicyon. Father Zeus,
I pray that with the Graces' aid I may celebrate that
    achievement and surpass many in honoring victory
in words, casting my javelin nearest the target of the   55
        Muses.

[14] Apollo, patron of the games at Sicyon.

NEMEAN 10

Although Theaeus had previously been victorious in wrestling at Nemea, this poem was placed with the other two anomalous odes at the end of the Nemean roll because it celebrates his victory in the Argive Heraea (or Hecatombaea). The first triad contains an impressive catalog of Argive heroes that culminates in Heracles, Hebe, and Hera on Olympus. Mirroring his city's abundance of distinctions, Theaeus has won at all the major games, but lacks an Olympic victory to become a *periodonikēs*. The poet tactfully portrays this veteran wrestler as too modest to voice his hope for an Olympic crown.

This is the only epinician besides *Nem.* 1 in which the main narrative continues to the very end of the poem. It is one of the most impressive narratives in the corpus; its long dactylo-epitritic periods, alternating speeches, martial subject, and concentration on one moment of choice give it a decidedly Iliadic character.

The Graces are summoned to sing of Hera's Argos, a city with countless claims to fame (1–3). A catalog of Argive heroes (Perseus, Epaphus, Hypermestra, Diomedes, Amphiaraus, Alcmene, Danaë, Talaus, Lynceus, Amphitryon, and Heracles) is rounded off with an allusion to Hera (4–18).

The poet curtails his praise of Argos' past achievements

by expressing his inability to recount (and his listeners to endure) all its glories (19–20). Turning his attention to wrestling, he lists Theaeus' achievements, beginning with his two victories in the local games dedicated to Hera (21–24), followed by his Panhellenic crowns: one at Pytho and three each at the Isthmus and Nemea (25–28). The poet prays to Zeus for an Olympic victory to follow and cites as harbingers two previous successes in the Athenian Panathenaea (29–36).

Theaeus' maternal relatives are praised for their victories in horse racing at the Isthmus and Nemea, and numerous victories are mentioned at other games in the Peloponnesus (37–48). The poet attributes the family's athletic success to the favor of the Tyndaridae, who were hosted by an ancestor named Pamphaës and have faithfully watched over the family ever since (49–54).

A brief summary of the forthcoming narrative tells that after Castor was killed Polydeuces chose to share his lot by spending every other day in the underworld (55–59). The ensuing account describes how Idas and Lynceus quarreled with the Tyndaridae and fatally wounded Castor. After Polydeuces and Zeus killed the two sons of Aphareus, Polydeuces returned to his dying brother and prayed to Zeus that he might die as well (60–79). Zeus granted him the choice of remaining immortal himself or sharing with his brother a daily alternation between the underworld and Olympus (80–88). Without hesitation Polydeuces chose to revive his brother Castor (89–90).

10. <ΘΕΑΙΩΙ ΑΡΓΕΙΩΙ

ΠΑΛΑΙΣΤΗΙ>

Α΄ Δαναοῦ πόλιν ἀγλαοθρό-
  νων τε πεντήκοντα κορᾶν, Χάριτες,
Ἄργος Ἥρας δῶμα θεοπρεπὲς ὑμνεῖ-
  τε· φλέγεται δ᾽ ἀρεταῖς
μυρίαις ἔργων θρασέων ἕνεκεν.
μακρὰ μὲν τὰ Περσέος ἀμφὶ Μεδοίσας Γοργόνος,
5 πολλὰ δ᾽ Αἰγύπτῳ καταοίκισεν ἄστη
  ταῖς Ἐπάφου παλάμαις·
οὐδ᾽ Ὑπερμήστρα παρεπλάγχθη, μονό-
  ψαφον ἐν κολεῷ κατασχοῖσα ξίφος.

Διομήδεα δ᾽ ἄμβροτον ξαν-
  θά ποτε Γλαυκῶπις ἔθηκε θεόν·

inscr. suppl. Boeckh: om. BD
5 καταοίκισεν Maas: κατῴκισθεν BD

---

[1] Danaus and his fifty daughters fled from their Egyptian cous-
ins and were received in Argos.

[2] For Hera's preference for Argos, see *Il.* 4.52.

[3] For Perseus' exploits, see *Pyth.* 10.46–48 and *Pyth.* 12.6–17.

110

10. FOR THEAEUS OF ARGOS

WINNER, WRESTLING

Sing, Graces, a hymn to Argos, the city of Danaus	Str. 1

Sing, Graces, a hymn to Argos, the city of Danaus
    and of his fifty daughters on their splendid thrones,[1]
Hera's home, fit for a goddess.[2]
    It is ablaze with achievements
beyond number because of its valiant deeds.
Lengthy to tell are Perseus' dealings with the Gorgon
      Medusa;[3]
many the cities it established in Egypt   5
    through the efforts of Epaphus;[4]
nor did Hypermestra go astray, when she kept
    her sole-dissenting sword in its scabbard.[5]

The fair-haired Gray-Eyed Goddess long ago made   Ant. 1
    Diomedes an immortal god,[6]

Medusa's head was supposedly buried under a mound near the marketplace of Argos (Paus. 2.21.6).

[4] Son of Zeus and Argive Io (cf. Aesch. *PV* 846–852).

[5] When the Danaids murdered their Egyptian husbands, Hypermestra alone spared Lynceus, who succeeded her father Danaus as king of Argos.

[6] The Argive hero Diomedes received from Athene the gift of immortality which she had intended to confer on his father Tydeus (schol.).

γαῖα δ' ἐν Θήβαις ὑπέδεκτο κεραυνω-
θεῖσα Διὸς βέλεσιν
μάντιν Οἰκλείδαν, πολέμοιο νέφος·
10 καὶ γυναιξὶν καλλικόμοισιν ἀριστεύει πάλαι·
Ζεὺς ἐπ' Ἀλκμήναν Δανάαν τε μολὼν τοῦ-
τον κατέφανε λόγον·
πατρὶ δ' Ἀδράστοιο Λυγκεῖ τε φρενῶν
καρπὸν εὐθείᾳ συνάρμοξεν δίκᾳ·

θρέψε δ' αἰχμὰν Ἀμφιτρύωνος. ὁ δ' ὄλβῳ φέρτατος
ἵκετ' ἐς κείνου γενεάν, ἐπεὶ ἐν χαλκέοις ὅπλοις
15 Τηλεβόας ἔναρεν· τῷ ὄψιν ἐειδόμενος
ἀθανάτων βασιλεὺς αὐλὰν ἐσῆλθεν,
σπέρμ' ἀδείμαντον φέρων Ἡρακλέος· οὗ κατ'
Ὄλυμπον
ἄλοχος Ἥβα τελείᾳ παρὰ ματέρι βαίνοισ'
ἔστι, καλλίστα θεῶν.

Β΄ βραχύ μοι στόμα πάντ' ἀναγή-
σασθ', ὅσων Ἀργεῖον ἔχει τέμενος
20 μοῖραν ἐσλῶν· ἔστι δὲ καὶ κόρος ἀνθρώ-
πων βαρὺς ἀντιάσαι·

12 πατρὶ δ' D¹: πατρί τ' BD
15 ἔναρεν· τῷ Mingarelli: ἔναιρεν. τί οἱ B: ἔναρε. τί οἱ D

---

7 Amphiaraus, one of the Argive chieftains who attacked
Thebes, was swallowed up in the earth near Thebes (cf. *Nem.*
9.24–27).

112

and at Thebes the earth, blasted with Zeus'
    thunderbolts, received beneath her
Oecles' son the seer, a storm cloud of war.[7]
And of old has the city excelled in lovely-haired women.   10
Zeus, in coming to Alcmene and Danaë,
    clearly proved that claim,
and in Adrastus' father and in Lynceus it[8] coupled
    the fruit of judgment with unswerving justice,

and it raised the spearman Amphitryon. He had the   Ep. 1
        supreme good fortune
to become that god's[9] kin, when, in his bronze armor,
he had slain the Teleboae; for, taking on his likeness,   15
the king of the immortals entered his hall,
bearing the fearless seed of Heracles, whose bride
        Hebe,
most beautiful of goddesses, walks on Olympus
    beside her mother, the Fulfiller.[10]

My mouth is too small to recount all the things   Str. 2
    that the holy precinct of Argos holds as its
portion of blessings; furthermore, men's satiety   20
    is grievous to encounter.

[8] I.e. Argos; some take Zeus as subject. Adrastus' father was
Talaus, whose tomb stood beside Lynceus' on the acropolis of
Argos (Paus. 2.21.2).

[9] Zeus'.

[10] Hera, Fulfiller of marriage; for Heracles as Hebe's husband,
see *Nem.* 1.71–72 and *Isth.* 4.58–60.

ἀλλ' ὅμως εὔχορδον ἔγειρε λύραν,
καὶ παλαισμάτων λάβε φροντίδ'· ἀγών τοι χάλκεος
δᾶμον ὀτρύνει ποτὶ βουθυσίαν Ἥ-
ρας ἀέθλων τε κρίσιν·
Οὐλία παῖς ἔνθα νικάσαις δὶς ἔ-
σχεν Θεαῖος εὐφόρων λάθαν πόνων.

25 ἐκράτησε δὲ καί ποθ' Ἕλλα-
να στρατὸν Πυθῶνι, τύχᾳ τε μολών
καὶ τὸν Ἰσθμοῖ καὶ Νεμέᾳ στέφανον, Μοί-
σαισί τ' ἔδωκ' ἀρόσαι,
τρὶς μὲν ἐν πόντοιο πύλαισι λαχών,
τρὶς δὲ καὶ σεμνοῖς δαπέδοις ἐν Ἀδραστείῳ νόμῳ.
Ζεῦ πάτερ, τῶν μὰν ἔραται φρενί, σιγᾷ
οἱ στόμα· πᾶν δὲ τέλος
30 ἐν τὶν ἔργων· οὐδ' ἀμόχθῳ καρδίᾳ
προσφέρων τόλμαν παραιτεῖται χάριν.

γνώτ' ἀείδω θεῷ τε καὶ ὅστις ἁμιλλᾶται περὶ
ἐσχάτων ἀέθλων κορυφαῖς· ὕπατον δ' ἔσχεν Πίσα
Ἡρακλέος τεθμόν. ἁδείαί γε μὲν ἀμβολάδαν
ἐν τελεταῖς δὶς Ἀθαναίων νιν ὀμφαί
35 κώμασαν· γαίᾳ δὲ καυθείσᾳ πυρὶ καρπὸς ἐλαίας

29 μὰν E. Schmid e schol.: μὲν BD
31 θεῷ BD: οἷ Kayser

114

Nevertheless, wake the well strung lyre
and take thought of wrestling, since the contest for
    bronze[11]
calls forth the people to the sacrifice of oxen
    for Hera and to the judging of the games,
in which Ulias' son, Theaeus, was twice victorious
    and won forgetfulness of his bravely borne labors.

Before that, he also defeated the host of Hellenes   Ant. 2
    at Pytho, and coming with good fortune
won the crown at both the Isthmus and Nemea   26
    and gave the Muses work for their plow,
by thrice winning crowns at the gates to the sea,[12]
and thrice on the hallowed ground in Adrastus'
    institution.[13]
Father Zeus, what in truth his mind desires
    his mouth holds in silence, for fulfillment of all deeds
lies with you; but in asking for this favor, he offers   30
    courage with a heart not unused to labor.

The god knows of what I sing, as does anyone who   Ep. 2
    strives
for the summits of the ultimate games: Pisa holds
the highest ordinance of Heracles. Yet, as a prelude,
twice in the rites of the Athenians did sweet voices
celebrate him, and in earth baked by fire came fruit   35

[11] The prize at the Argive Heraea (or Hecatombaea) was a
bronze shield (schol.).
[12] I.e. at the Isthmus.
[13] Adrastus instituted the Nemean games on his way to
Thebes (cf. *Nem.* 8.51).

ἔμολεν Ἥρας τὸν εὐάνορα λαὸν ἐν ἀγγέων
    ἔρκεσιν παμποικίλοις.

Γ΄ ἔπεται δέ, Θεαῖε, ματρώ-
        ων πολύγνωτον γένος ὑμετέρων
    εὐάγων τιμᾷ Χαρίτεσσί τε καὶ σὺν
        Τυνδαρίδαις θαμάκις.
    ἀξιωθείην κεν, ἐὼν Θρασύκλου
40 Ἀντία τε σύγγονος, Ἄργεϊ μὴ κρύπτειν φάος
    ὀμμάτων. νικαφορίαις γὰρ ὅσαις Προί-
        τοιο τόδ᾽ ἱπποτρόφον
    ἄστυ θάλησεν Κορίνθου τ᾽ ἐν μυχοῖς,
        καὶ Κλεωναίων πρὸς ἀνδρῶν τετράκις·

    Σικυωνόθε δ᾽ ἀργυρωθέν-
        τες σὺν οἰνηραῖς φιάλαις ἀπέβαν,
    ἐκ δὲ Πελλάνας ἐπιεσσάμενοι νῶ-
        τον μαλακαῖσι κρόκαις·
45 ἀλλὰ χαλκὸν μυρίον οὐ δυνατὸν
    ἐξελέγχειν—μακροτέρας γὰρ ἀριθμῆσαι σχολᾶς—
    ὅν τε Κλείτωρ καὶ Τεγέα καὶ Ἀχαιῶν
        ὑψίβατοι πόλιες

37 ἔπεται BD: ἐπέβα Wilamowitz
38 σὺν suppl. E. Schmid e schol.: om. BD
41–42 Προίτοιο τόδ᾽ ἱπποτρόφον ἄστυ Boeckh: ἱπποτρό-
φον ἄστυ τὸ Προίτοιο BD

116

of the olive to that brave people of Hera
  in the richly ornamented walls of jars.[14]

Theaeus, honor for athletic success often attends   Str. 3
  the famous race of your mother's ancestors
with the help of the Graces
  and the Tyndaridae.
Were I a relative of Thrasyclus and Antias,[15]
I would think it proper not to hide the light of my eyes   40
in Argos, for with how many victories
  has this horse-raising city of Proetus[16]
flourished in the glens of Corinth;
  and four times from the men of Cleonae[17]

and from Sicyon they departed laden   Ant. 3
  with silver wine bowls
and from Pellana wearing softest woolens
  on their backs.
But it is not possible to reckon the vast amount   45
of bronze (there is too little leisure to count it),
which Cleitor, Tegea,
  the lofty cities of the Achaeans,

14 Amphoras containing olive oil were prizes at the Panathenaic games.
15 Ancestors on his mother's side, whose fame came from horse racing.
16 Proetus and his twin brother Acrisius contended for the kingdom of Argos and divided it between them.
17 The site of the Nemean games lay between Phlius and Cleonae; the management of the games at this time was in the hands of Cleonae (cf. *Nem.* 4.17).

PINDAR

καὶ Λύκαιον πὰρ Διὸς θῆκε δρόμῳ,
σὺν ποδῶν χειρῶν τε νικᾶσαι σθένει.

Κάστορος δ᾽ ἐλθόντος ἐπὶ ξενίαν πὰρ Παμφάη
50 καὶ κασιγνήτου Πολυδεύκεος, οὐ θαῦμα σφίσιν
ἐγγενὲς ἔμμεν ἀεθληταῖς ἀγαθοῖσιν· ἐπεί
εὐρυχόρου ταμίαι Σπάρτας ἀγώνων
μοῖραν Ἑρμᾷ καὶ σὺν Ἡρακλεῖ διέποντι θάλειαν,
μάλα μὲν ἀνδρῶν δικαίων περικαδόμενοι. καί
μὰν θεῶν πιστὸν γένος.

Δ´ μεταμειβόμενοι δ᾽ ἐναλλὰξ
ἀμέραν τὰν μὲν παρὰ πατρὶ φίλῳ
56 Δὶ νέμονται, τὰν δ᾽ ὑπὸ κεύθεσι γαίας
ἐν γυάλοις Θεράπνας,
πότμον ἀμπιπλάντες ὁμοῖον· ἐπεί
τοῦτον, ἢ πάμπαν θεὸς ἔμμεναι οἰκεῖν τ᾽ οὐρανῷ,
εἵλετ᾽ αἰῶνα φθιμένου Πολυδεύκης
Κάστορος ἐν πολέμῳ.
60 τὸν γὰρ Ἴδας ἀμφὶ βουσίν πως χολω-
θεὶς ἔτρωσεν χαλκέας λόγχας ἀκμᾷ.

48 νικᾶσαι BD: νικῶντι Snell
60 ἀκμᾷ Pauw: αἰχμᾷ BD

---

[18] The games at Cleitor were in honor of Persephone and Demeter, those at Tegea in honor of Athena Aleaea (Paus. 8.21.2 and 47.3). Achaean cities are named in Il. 2.573–575, but which

118

and Lycaeon[18] set beside the racecourse of Zeus
    for men to win with strength of feet and hands.

But given that Castor and his brother Polydeuces came   Ep. 3
for hospitality to the home of Pamphaës,[19] it is no   50
    wonder
that they have inborn ability to be good athletes, because
those stewards of spacious Sparta, along with Hermes
    and Heracles,
administer their flourishing allotment of the games
and are very solicitous for men who are just. Yes, truly
    the race of the gods is faithful.

Changing in succession,   Str. 4
    they spend one day with their dear father
Zeus, the other deep under the earth   56
    in the hollows of Therapna,
as they fulfill an equal fate, because
Polydeuces chose that life rather than being wholly
divine and living in heaven,
    when Castor was killed in war.
For Idas, somehow angry about cattle,   60
    wounded him with the point of his bronze spear.

ones besides Pellana had athletic games is unknown. Mt. Lycaeon
is in Arcadia, where games for Zeus Lycaeus were held (cf. *Ol.*
9.95).
   [19] A maternal ancestor of Theaeus. For *theoxenia*, entertainment by mortals of the Dioscuri, who supervise games and bestow athletic prowess, see *Ol.* 3.34–41.

PINDAR

ἀπὸ Ταϋγέτου πεδαυγά-
ζων ἴδεν Λυγκεὺς δρυὸς ἐν στελέχει
ἡμένους. κείνου γὰρ ἐπιχθονίων πάν-
των γένετ᾽ ὀξύτατον
ὄμμα. λαιψηροῖς δὲ πόδεσσιν ἄφαρ
ἐξίκεσθαν, καὶ μέγα ἔργον ἐμήσαντ᾽ ὠκέως
65 καὶ πάθον δεινὸν παλάμαις Ἀφαρητί-
δαι Διός· αὐτίκα γάρ
ἦλθε Λήδας παῖς διώκων· τοὶ δ᾽ ἔναν-
τα στάθεν τύμβῳ σχεδὸν πατρωΐῳ·

ἔνθεν ἁρπάξαντες ἄγαλμ᾽ Ἀίδα, ξεστὸν πέτρον,
ἔμβαλον στέρνῳ Πολυδεύκεος· ἀλλ᾽ οὔ νιν φλάσαν
οὐδ᾽ ἀνέχασσαν· ἐφορμαθεὶς δ᾽ ἄρ ἄκοντι θοῷ,
70 ἤλασε Λυγκέος ἐν πλευραῖσι χαλκόν.
Ζεὺς δ᾽ ἐπ᾽ Ἴδᾳ πυρφόρον πλᾶξε ψολόεντα
κεραυνόν·
ἅμα δ᾽ ἐκαίοντ᾽ ἐρῆμοι. χαλεπὰ δ᾽ ἔρις ἀνθρώ-
ποις ὁμιλεῖν κρεσσόνων.

Ε´ ταχέως δ᾽ ἐπ᾽ ἀδελφεοῦ βί-
αν πάλιν χώρησεν ὁ Τυνδαρίδας,
καί νιν οὔπω τεθναότ᾽, ἄσθματι δὲ φρίσ-
σοντα πνοὰς ἔκιχεν.

61 πεδαυγάζων Triclinius: πόδ᾽ αὐγάζων BD¹: πέδ᾽ αὖ γά-
ζων D   62 ἡμένους Boeckh: ἧμενος BD: ἥμενον Aristar-
chus: ἥμένος (= ἡμένους) Didymus
64 ἐμήσαντ᾽ E. Schmid: ἐμνήσατ᾽ B: ἐμνήσαντ᾽ D

120

Watching from Taygetus, Lynceus had seen them[20]   Ant. 4
    sitting in the hollow trunk of an oak tree,
for of all mortals
    he had the sharpest
eyesight. The sons of Aphareus[21] came at once
on swift feet and quickly devised a mighty deed,
and they suffered terribly   65
    at the hands of Zeus, for immediately
the son of Leda[22] came in pursuit, while they took
    a stand against him beside their father's tomb.

From it they seized the grave marker of polished stone   Ep. 4
and threw it against Polydeuces' chest, but they did not
    crush him
or drive him back. He attacked them then with his swift
    javelin
and drove the bronze into Lynceus' side.   70
Zeus hurled against Idas a smoldering thunderbolt of
    fire
and the two men burned all alone. Strife against those
    who are stronger is difficult for men to face.

The son of Tyndareus[23] returned swiftly   Str. 5
    to his mighty brother
and found him not yet dead,
    but gasping hard for breath.

[20] The ancient commentators were divided on whether both brothers were hiding in the tree trunk or only Castor. Boeckh's emendation follows the account in the *Cypria* (*fr.* 11 Allen).

[21] Idas and Lynceus (different from Lynceus, king of Argos, in 12).   [22] Polydeuces.   [23] Polydeuces.

75 θερμὰ δὴ τέγγων δάκρυα στοναχαῖς
ὄρθιον φώνασε· "Πάτερ Κρονίων, τίς δὴ λύσις
ἔσσεται πενθέων; καὶ ἐμοὶ θάνατον σὺν
τῷδ' ἐπίτειλον, ἄναξ.
οἴχεται τιμὰ φίλων τατωμένῳ
φωτί· παῦροι δ' ἐν πόνῳ πιστοὶ βροτῶν

κᾱμάτου μεταλαμβάνειν." ὣς
ἤνεπε· Ζεὺς δ' ἀντίος ἤλυθέ οἱ,
80 καὶ τόδ' ἐξαύδασ' ἔπος· "Ἐσσί μοι υἱός·
τόνδε δ' ἔπειτα πόσις
σπέρμα θνατὸν ματρὶ τεᾷ πελάσαις
στάξεν ἥρως. ἀλλ' ἄγε τῶνδέ τοι ἔμπαν αἵρεσιν
παρδίδωμ'· εἰ μὲν θάνατόν τε φυγὼν καὶ
γῆρας ἀπεχθόμενον
αὐτὸς Οὔλυμπον θέλεις ⟨ναίειν ἐμοὶ⟩
σύν τ' Ἀθαναίᾳ κελαινεγχεῖ τ' Ἄρει,

85 ἔστι σοι τούτων λάχος· εἰ δὲ κασιγνήτου πέρι
μάρνασαι, πάντων δὲ νοεῖς ἀποδάσσασθαι ἴσον,
ἥμισυ μέν κε πνέοις γαίας ὑπένερθεν ἐών,
ἥμισυ δ' οὐρανοῦ ἐν χρυσέοις δόμοισιν."
ὣς ἄρ' αὐδάσαντος οὐ γνώμᾳ διπλόαν θέτο βουλάν,
90 ἀνὰ δ' ἔλυσεν μὲν ὀφθαλμόν, ἔπειτα δὲ φωνὰν
χαλκομίτρα Κάστορος.

75 δὴ E. Schmid: δὲ BD   79 ἀντίος D: ἀντία B
84 ⟨ναίειν ἐμοὶ⟩ suppl. Boeckh: om. BD

Hot indeed were the tears he shed; he groaned   75
and cried aloud, "Father, son of Cronus, what release
will there ever be from sorrows? Grant me death
    along with him here, lord.
Honor disappears when a man loses his friends,
    and few mortals remain faithful in time of toil

to share the labor." Thus he spoke.   Ant. 5
    And Zeus came before him
and proclaimed these words. "You are my son.   80
    But this man was conceived afterwards
by your mother's husband, when that hero came to her
and sowed his mortal seed. But come, I nonetheless
grant you this choice: if you prefer to escape death
    and hateful old age,
and come by yourself to live on Olympus with me and
    with Athena and Ares of the darkened spear,

that destiny is yours. But if you strive on behalf of your   Ep. 5
brother, and intend to share everything equally with   86
    him,
then you may live half the time beneath the earth
and half in the golden homes of heaven."
When he had spoken thus, he[24] set no twofold plan in
    his judgment,
but freed the eye and then the voice   90
    of bronze-armored Castor.

[24] Polydeuces.

NEMEAN 11

The occasion for this poem is the installation of Aristagoras for a year on the governing council of Tenedos. The early editors presumably placed this ode among the epinicia rather than the encomia because of its emphasis on Aristagoras' youthful athletic prowess. Added to the praise of Tenedos and Aristagoras are frequent allusions to the limitations of human life, lost opportunities for success, alternation of achievement and failure, the uncertainty of the future, and the suffering caused by excessive ambition—worthwhile considerations for a future councillor.

Hestia, goddess of the hearth and of town halls, is invoked and requested to welcome Aristagoras into her service (1–3). The council is praised for its rule on Tenedos and its celebration of Zeus, god of hospitality (4–9). After praying that Aristagoras may successfully complete his year's service, the poet praises him for his strength and courage (10–12). Reflections on human achievement, mortality, and the need to celebrate success lead to the announcement that Aristagoras and his family have won sixteen victories at local games in wrestling and the pancratium (13–21).

The poet avers that if Aristagoras' overly cautious parents had not held him back, he would have been victorious in wrestling at Pytho and Olympia (22–29). This prompts the observation that too great or too little confidence can thwart success (29–32). Aristagoras bears the mark of his illustrious ancestry deriving from Sparta and Thebes, but not every generation produces the fruit of achievement (33–43). Men cannot know the future, and we often hope for too much success; moderation is best, for wanting what is impossible results in pain (43–48).

11. ⟨ΑΡΙΣΤΑΓΟΡΑΙ ΤΕΝΕΔΙΩΙ

ΠΡΥΤΑΝΕΙ⟩

Α΄   Παῖ Ῥέας, ἅ τε πρυτανεῖα λέλογχας, Ἑστία,
     Ζηνὸς ὑψίστου κασιγνήτα καὶ ὁμοθρόνου Ἥρας,
     εὖ μὲν Ἀρισταγόραν δέξαι τεὸν ἐς θάλαμον,
     εὖ δ' ἑταίρους ἀγλαῷ σκάπτῳ πέλας,
5   οἵ σε γεραίροντες ὀρθὰν φυλάσσοισιν Τένεδον,

     πολλὰ μὲν λοιβαῖσιν ἀγαζόμενοι πρώταν θεῶν,
     πολλὰ δὲ κνίσᾳ· λύρα δέ σφι βρέμεται καὶ ἀοιδά·
     καὶ ξενίου Διὸς ἀσκεῖται θέμις αἰενάοις
     ἐν τραπέζαις· ἀλλὰ σὺν δόξᾳ τέλος
10   δωδεκάμηνον περᾶσαί νιν ἀτρώτῳ κραδίᾳ.

     ἄνδρα δ' ἐγὼ μακαρίζω μὲν πατέρ' Ἀρκεσίλαν,
     καὶ τὸ θαητὸν δέμας ἀτρεμίαν τε σύγγονον·
     εἰ δέ τις ὄλβον ἔχων μορφᾷ παραμεύσεται ἄλλους,

> inscr. suppl. Boeckh: om. BD
> 10 περᾶσαί νιν Dissen: περᾶσαι σὺν BD
> 11 ἀρκεσίλαν D(schol.)BD: ἀγησίλαν B (cf. fr. 123.15)
> 13 ἄλλους Hartung: ἄλλων BD: ἄλλον Morel

11. FOR ARISTAGORAS
OF TENEDOS

INSTALLATION AS COUNCILOR

Daughter of Rhea, to whom city halls are allotted,   Str. 1
    Hestia,
sister of highest Zeus and of Hera who shares his throne,
welcome Aristagoras into your chamber,
and welcome his companions beside your splendid
    scepter,
who, by honoring you, keep Tenedos upright,   5

often worshiping you first of gods with libations   Ant. 1
and often with savor of sacrifice. The lyre and song
    resound for them,
and the ordinance of Zeus Xenius is venerated
in continuous feasts. May he complete his term
of twelve months in glory and with heart unscathed.   10

As for the man, I count his father Arcesilas blessed,   Ep. 1
and praise him[1] for his admirable build and inborn
    courage.
But if a man possessing riches surpasses others in beauty
    of form,

---

[1] Aristagoras.

127

ἔν τ᾽ ἀέθλοισιν ἀριστεύων ἐπέδειξεν βίαν,
15 θνατὰ μεμνάσθω περιστέλλων μέλη,
καὶ τελευτὰν ἁπάντων γᾶν ἐπιεσσόμενος.

Β΄ ἐν λόγοις δ᾽ ἀστῶν ἀγαθοῖσιν ἐπαινεῖσθαι χρεών,
καὶ μελιγδούποισι δαιδαλθέντα μελίζεν ἀοιδαῖς.
ἐκ δὲ περικτιόνων ἑκκαίδεκ᾽ Ἀρισταγόραν
20 ἀγλααὶ νῖκαι πάτραν τ᾽ εὐώνυμον
ἐστεφάνωσαν πάλᾳ καὶ μεγαυχεῖ παγκρατίῳ.

ἐλπίδες δ᾽ ὀκνηρότεραι γονέων παιδὸς βίαν
ἔσχον ἐν Πυθῶνι πειρᾶσθαι καὶ Ὀλυμπίᾳ ἀέθλων.
ναὶ μὰ γὰρ ὅρκον, ἐμὰν δόξαν παρὰ Κασταλίᾳ
25 καὶ παρ᾽ εὐδένδρῳ μολὼν ὄχθῳ Κρόνου
κάλλιον ἂν δηριώντων ἐνόστησ᾽ ἀντιπάλων,

πενταετηρίδ᾽ ἑορτὰν Ἡρακλέος τέθμιον
κωμάσαις ἀνδησάμενός τε κόμαν ἐν πορφυρέοις
ἔρνεσιν. ἀλλὰ βροτῶν τὸν μὲν κενεόφρονες αὖχαι
30 ἐξ ἀγαθῶν ἔβαλον· τὸν δ᾽ αὖ καταμεμφθέντ᾽ ἄγαν
ἰσχὺν οἰκείων παρέσφαλεν καλῶν
χειρὸς ἕλκων ὀπίσσω θυμὸς ἄτολμος ἐών.

17 ἀγαθοῖσιν ἐπαινεῖσθαι Schroeder: ἀγαθοῖς μὲν αἰνεῖ-
σθαι (μὲν om. B[l]) BDp
18 μελίζεν Pauw: μελιζέμεν codd.
30 ἔβαλον D: ἔλαβον B

128

and in contests displays his strength by winning,
let him remember that mortal are the limbs he clothes   15
and that earth is the last garment of all he will wear.

Yet it is necessary that he be praised in townsmen's   Str. 2
    kindly words,
and that we celebrate and adorn him with honey-
    sounding songs.
Sixteen splendid victories, won from the neighboring
peoples,[2] have crowned Aristagoras and his famous clan   20
in wrestling and in the proud pancratium.

But his parents' overly cautious expectations kept their   Ant. 2
    strong son
from competing in the games at Pytho and Olympia.
For I swear that, in my judgment, had he gone to
    Castalia
and to the well-wooded hill of Cronus, he would have   25
    had
a more noble homecoming than his wrestling opponents,

after celebrating the four-year festival ordained by   Ep. 2
    Heracles
with a victory revel and binding his hair in gleaming
wreaths. But among mortals, empty-minded confidence
casts one man from success, while a timid spirit,   30
holding back by the hand another man too distrustful
of his own strength, deprives him of achievements that
    belong to him.

   [2] I.e. in local games.

PINDAR

Γ´ συμβαλεῖν μὰν εὐμαρὲς ἦν τό τε Πεισάνδρου πάλαι
αἷμ᾽ ἀπὸ Σπάρτας—Ἀμύκλαθεν γὰρ ἔβα σὺν
Ὀρέστᾳ,
35 Αἰολέων στρατιὰν χαλκεντέα δεῦρ᾽ ἀνάγων—
καὶ παρ᾽ Ἰσμηνοῦ ῥοὰν κεκραμένον
ἐκ Μελανίπποιο μάτρως· ἀρχαῖαι δ᾽ ἀρεταί

ἀμφέροντ᾽ ἀλλασσόμεναι γενεαῖς ἀνδρῶν σθένος·
ἐν σχερῷ δ᾽ οὔτ᾽ ὦν μέλαιναι καρπὸν ἔδωκαν
ἄρουραι,
40 δένδρεά τ᾽ οὐκ ἐθέλει πάσαις ἐτέων περόδοις
ἄνθος εὐῶδες φέρειν πλούτῳ ἴσον,
ἀλλ᾽ ἐναμείβοντι. καὶ θνατὸν οὕτως ἔθνος ἄγει

μοῖρα. τὸ δ᾽ ἐκ Διὸς ἀνθρώποις σαφὲς οὐχ ἕπεται
τέκμαρ· ἀλλ᾽ ἔμπαν μεγαλανορίαις ἐμβαίνομεν,
45 ἔργα τε πολλὰ μενοινῶντες· δέδεται γὰρ ἀναιδεῖ
ἐλπίδι γυῖα· προμαθείας δ᾽ ἀπόκεινται ῥοαί.
κερδέων δὲ χρὴ μέτρον θηρευέμεν·
ἀπροσίκτων δ᾽ ἐρώτων ὀξύτεραι μανίαι.

33 μὰν Pauw: λίαν BD
35 χαλκεντέα E. Schmid: χαλκέ τε (= χαλκέων τε) B: χαλ-
κεντέων D
36 ῥοὰν Bergk: ῥοὰν BD
40 περόδοις E. Schmid (cf. Eustathius proem. 3.294.9–10):
περιόδοις BD
42 οὕτως ἔθνος Heyne e paraphr. (γένος): οὕτω σθένος BD

130

It was easy indeed to infer the bloodline of ancient   Str. 3
    Pisander
from Sparta—he came here[3] with Orestes from Amyclae
leading a bronze-clad army of Aeolians—   35
and from the streams of the Ismenus its blending
with that from Melanippus,[4] his mother's ancestor. The
    talents of ancient time

produce their strength in alternating generations of men; Ant. 3
for neither do the dark fields yield continual crops,
nor in all the circling years are trees wont   40
to bear fragrant blossoms of equal worth,
but they vary. In like fashion destiny leads our mortal

race. As for that which comes from Zeus, no clear sign   Ep. 3
attends men, but all the same we embark on ambitious
    projects
and yearn for many accomplishments, for our bodies are   45
    enthralled
to shameless hope, and the streams of foreknowledge lie
    far off.
One must seek due measure of gains;
too painful is the madness of unattainable desires.

[3] To Tenedos.
[4] A Theban champion opposing the Seven (cf. Aesch. *Sept.*
407–414).

ΙΣΘΜΙΟΝΙΚΑΙ

ISTHMIAN ODES

ISTHMIAN 1

The poem opens with a dramatic conceit. Pindar must postpone his composition of a paean (*Pae.* 4) intended for Ceans to perform in honor of Delian Apollo because, it appears, Theban athletes have won six crowns in the Isthmian games and his allegiance to his mother city requires him to celebrate her first. Pindar never mentions the names of the other athletes (although his praise of Castor and Iolaus suggests a variety of events), but concentrates instead on the victory of Herodotus, who drove his own chariot, a noteworthy achievement, since most noblemen hired their charioteers.

The poet assures Thebe, the eponymous nymph of Thebes, that her interests are his foremost concern (1–3). He asks Delos not to resent his postponement of the paean in her honor, for he intends to complete both her poem and this one celebrating the Isthmus, occasioned by the six crowns that Thebans have won there (3–13).

The poet proposes to link Herodotus with the charioteers Castor and Iolaus, who are hymned for their various athletic victories (14–31). After bidding farewell to these heroes, the poet alludes to some misfortune that Asopodorus, the victor's father, had previously suffered, but contrasts it with his present good fortune and comments on the foresight gained through bitter experience (32–40).

The lines that follow express the obligation of poets to praise those who strive hard and at great cost to achieve success (41–46). A priamel listing various occupations and their rewards culminates in the praise earned by athletes and soldiers (47–51).

The poet thanks Poseidon for his help in winning the chariot victory and alludes to other contests won by Herodotus (52–59), but claims that time does not permit mention of all his victories (60–63). The poet hopes that Herodotus will be inspired by this praise to honor Thebes with future victories at Pytho and Olympia (64–67). The poem concludes with a gnomic portrayal of the victor's opposite, a miser who hoards his wealth and gains no post-humous fame (67–68).

1. ‹ΗΡΟΔΟΤΩΙ ΘΗΒΑΙΩΙ

ΑΡΜΑΤΙ›

Α΄ Μᾶτερ ἐμά, τὸ τεόν, χρύσασπι Θήβα,
πρᾶγμα καὶ ἀσχολίας ὑπέρτερον
θήσομαι. μή μοι κρανάα νεμεσάσαι
Δᾶλος, ἐν ᾇ κέχυμαι.
5 τί φίλτερον κεδνῶν τοκέων ἀγαθοῖς;
εἶξον, ὦ Ἀπολλωνιάς· ἀμφοτερᾶν
  τοι χαρίτων σὺν θεοῖς ζεύξω τέλος,

καὶ τὸν ἀκερσεκόμαν Φοῖβον χορεύων
ἐν Κέῳ ἀμφιρύτᾳ σὺν ποντίοις
ἀνδράσιν, καὶ τὰν ἁλιερκέα Ἰσθμοῦ
10 δειράδ'· ἐπεὶ στεφάνους
ἓξ ὤπασεν Κάδμου στρατῷ ἐξ ἀέθλων,
καλλίνικον πατρίδι κῦδος. ἐν ᾇ
  καὶ τὸν ἀδείμαντον Ἀλκμήνα τέκεν

inscr. suppl. E. Schmid: om. BD
6 ἀμφοτερᾶν Boeckh e schol.: ἀμφοτέρων B: ἀμφοτέροις D
11 ἓξ ὤπασεν BD: ἓξ ὤπασαν D¹: ἐξώπασεν Aristarchus

136

1. FOR HERODOTUS
OF THEBES

WINNER, CHARIOT RACE

Mother of mine, Thebe of the golden shield,	Str. 1
I shall put your concern above even my	
pressing obligations. Let not rocky Delos	
be angry with me, on whose behalf I have been toiling.[1]	
What is dearer to good men than their beloved parents?	5
Yield, O island of Apollo, for with divine help	
I shall combine the completion of both poems,	

by celebrating in dance both unshorn Phoebus	Ant. 1
on wave-washed Ceos with its seafaring	
men and the Isthmus' seagirt	
ridge, because it[2] bestowed	10
six crowns on Cadmus' people from its games,	
the glory of victory for their fatherland, in which	
Alcmene too bore her dauntless	

---

[1] In composing a paean (*Pae.* 4) in honor of Delian Apollo.

[2] The Isthmus. Theban athletes seem to have won six victories in the most recent Isthmian games.

παῖδα, θρασεῖαι τόν ποτε Γηρυόνα φρῖξαν κύνες.
ἀλλ᾽ ἐγὼ Ἡροδότῳ τεύ-
    χων τὸ μὲν ἅρματι τεθρίππῳ γέρας,
15 ἀνία τ᾽ ἀλλοτρίαις οὐ χερσὶ νωμάσαντ᾽ ἐθέλω
ἢ Καστορείῳ ἢ Ἰολάοι᾽ ἐναρμόξαι νιν ὕμνῳ.
κεῖνοι γὰρ ἡρώων διφρηλάται Λακεδαίμονι καὶ
    Θήβαις ἐτέκνωθεν κράτιστοι·

Β´ ἔν τ᾽ ἀέθλοισι θίγον πλείστων ἀγώνων,
καὶ τριπόδεσσιν ἐκόσμησαν δόμον
20 καὶ λεβήτεσσιν φιάλαισί τε χρυσοῦ,
γευόμενοι στεφάνων
νικαφόρων· λάμπει δὲ σαφὴς ἀρετά
ἔν τε γυμνοῖσι σταδίοις σφίσιν ἔν
    τ᾽ ἀσπιδοδούποισιν ὁπλίταις δρόμοις,

οἷά τε χερσὶν ἀκοντίζοντες αἰχμαῖς
25 καὶ λιθίνοις ὁπότ᾽ ἐν δίσκοις ἵεν·
οὐ γὰρ ἦν πενταέθλιον, ἀλλ᾽ ἐφ᾽ ἑκάστῳ
ἔργματι κεῖτο τέλος.
τῶν ἀθρόοις ἀνδησάμενοι θαμάκις
ἔρνεσιν χαίτας ῥεέθροισί τε Δίρ-
    κας ἔφανεν καὶ παρ᾽ Εὐρώτᾳ πέλας,

25 ὁπότ᾽ ἐν Hermann: ὁπότε BD: ὁπόταν Trypho ap. Eusta-
thium: ποτ᾽ ἀνὰ Ammonius

138

son, before whom Geryon's fierce dogs once cowered.[3]   Ep. 1
But, for my part, in rendering honor to Herodotus
    for his four-horse chariot, whose reins
he guided with no other hands than his own, I wish   15
to include him in a hymn to Castor or Iolaus,
for they were the mightiest charioteers of the heroes,
    one born in Lacedaemon, the other in Thebes,

and in athletic games they took part in the most contests,   Str. 2
adorning their houses with tripods,
cauldrons, and bowls of gold,   20
whenever they savored the crowns
of victory; and their excellence shines clearly
in the naked foot races and in the races of
    armor with clanging shields;

and how it shone as they hurled javelins from their   Ant. 2
      hands
and when they made casts with discuses of stone   25
(there was no pentathlon, but for each event
a prize was reserved).
They often crowned their hair with thick wreaths from
these events, and appeared beside Dirce's streams
    and close by the Eurotas,

[3] A dog named Orthrus with two (or three) heads guarded
Geryon's cattle on an island near Gadira (Cadiz). Heracles slew
the dog and took the cattle. Only Pindar mentions more than one
dog.

30 Ἰφικλέος μὲν παῖς ὁμόδαμος ἐὼν Σπαρτῶν γένει,
   Τυνδαρίδας δ' ἐν Ἀχαιοῖς
      ὑψίπεδον Θεράπνας οἰκέων ἕδος.
   χαίρετ'· ἐγὼ δὲ Ποσειδάωνι Ἰσθμῷ τε ζαθέᾳ
   Ὀγχηστίαισίν τ' ἀϊόνεσσιν περιστέλλων ἀοιδάν
   γαρύσομαι τοῦδ' ἀνδρὸς ἐν τιμαῖσιν ἀγακλέα τὰν
      Ἀσωποδώρου πατρὸς αἶσαν

Γ΄ Ἐρχομενοῖό τε πατρῴαν ἄρουραν,
36 ἅ νιν ἐρειδόμενον ναυαγίαις
    ἐξ ἀμετρήτας ἁλὸς ἐν κρυοέσσᾳ
    δέξατο συντυχίᾳ·
    νῦν δ' αὖτις ἀρχαίας ἐπέβασε Πότμος
40 συγγενὴς εὐαμερίας· ὁ πονή-
       σαις δὲ νόῳ καὶ προμάθειαν φέρει.

    εἰ δ' ἀρετᾷ κατάκειται πᾶσαν ὀργάν,
    ἀμφότερον δαπάναις τε καὶ πόνοις,
    χρή νιν εὑρόντεσσιν ἀγάνορα κόμπον
    μὴ φθονεραῖσι φέρειν
45 γνώμαις· ἐπεὶ κούφα δόσις ἀνδρὶ σοφῷ
    ἀντὶ μόχθων παντοδαπῶν ἔπος εἰ-
       πόντ' ἀγαθὸν ξυνὸν ὀρθῶσαι καλόν.

---

4 The "Sown Men." After Cadmus slew the dragon that guarded
the fountain of Ares, he sowed the dragon's teeth, from which
armed men grew. The five survivors of these became the ancestors
of the Theban nobility.

140

the one, Iphicles' son belonging to the race of Spartoi,[4]   Ep. 2
the other, Tyndareus' son dwelling among the Achaeans   31
    on his highland home of Therapna.[5]
Farewell. But as I array Poseidon and the sacred
    Isthmus
and Onchestus' shores[6] in my song,
I shall proclaim, while honoring this man, that illustrious
    fortune of his father Asopodorus

and his ancestral soil of Orchomenus,[7]   Str. 3
which welcomed him from the boundless sea,   36
when he was hard pressed by shipwreck
in chilling misfortune.[8]
Now, however, the Destiny of his family has once again
set him aboard the fair weather of old. One   40
    who has toiled also gains foresight for his mind.

If someone is devoted wholeheartedly to excellence   Ant. 3
with both expenses and hard work,
it is necessary to give those who achieve it a lordly vaunt
with no begrudging
thoughts, since it is a light gift for a man who is wise   45
to speak a good word in return for labors of all kinds
    and to raise up a noble tribute shared by all.[9]

[5] These Achaeans were the pre-Dorian population of Laconia in Therapna, on the heights southeast of Sparta.

[6] A Boeotian city northwest of Thebes near Lake Copaïs famous for its sanctuary of Poseidon (cf. *Isth.* 4.19 and *Il.* 2.506).

[7] An ancient city of the Minyae at the northern end of Lake Copaïs (cf. *Ol.* 14).   [8] Probably exile as a result of political unrest; he may also have fought on the side of the Persians at Plataea (Hdt. 9.69).   [9] I.e. by the victor and his polis.

141

PINDAR

μισθὸς γὰρ ἄλλοις ἄλλος ἐπ' ἔργμασιν ἀνθρώποις
    γλυκύς,
μηλοβότᾳ τ' ἀρότᾳ τ' ὀρ-
    νιχολόχῳ τε καὶ ὃν πόντος τράφει·
γαστρὶ δὲ πᾶς τις ἀμύνων λιμὸν αἰανῆ τέταται·
50 ὃς δ' ἀμφ' ἀέθλοις ἢ πολεμίζων ἄρηται κῦδος
    ἁβρόν,
εὐαγορηθεὶς κέρδος ὕψιστον δέκεται, πολια-
    τᾶν καὶ ξένων γλώσσας ἄωτον.

Δ' ἄμμι δ' ἔοικε Κρόνου σεισίχθον' υἱόν
γείτον' ἀμειβομένοις εὐεργέταν
ἁρμάτων ἱπποδρόμιον κελαδῆσαι,
55 καὶ σέθεν, Ἀμφιτρύων,
παῖδας προσειπεῖν τὸν Μινύα τε μυχόν
καὶ τὸ Δάματρος κλυτὸν ἄλσος Ἐλευ-
    σῖνα καὶ Εὔβοιαν ἐν γναμπτοῖς δρόμοις·

Πρωτεσίλα, τὸ τεὸν δ' ἀνδρῶν Ἀχαιῶν
ἐν Φυλάκᾳ τέμενος συμβάλλομαι.
60 πάντα δ' ἐξειπεῖν, ὅσσ' ἀγώνιος Ἑρμᾶς
Ἡροδότῳ ἔπορεν
ἵπποις, ἀφαιρεῖται βραχὺ μέτρον ἔχων

---

[10] Poseidon at nearby Onchestus is credited with helping Herodotus win his Isthmian victory.

142

For a different payment for different tasks is sweet to   Ep. 3
    men,
whether to a shepherd, a plowman, a fowler,
   or to one whom the sea nourishes,
since everyone strives to keep gnawing hunger from his
    belly.
But he who wins luxurious glory in games or as a soldier   50
by being praised gains the highest profit, the finest
   words from tongues of citizens and foreigners.

But it befits us to celebrate Cronus' earthshaking son,   Str. 4
our neighbor[10] and patron of horse racing, as we requite
his assistance to the chariots,
and to invoke your sons,[11] Amphitryon,   55
along with the glen of Minyas,
Demeter's famous sanctuary of Eleusis,
   and Euboea, when telling of circling racecourses.

Protesilas, I include as well your precinct   Ant. 4
at Phylaca belonging to Achaean men.
But recounting all the victories Hermes, patron of   60
    games,
has granted to Herodotus
and his horses, my hymn's brief length forbids.

[11] The Thebans celebrated the Heraclea (honoring Amphitryon's son) and Iolaea (honoring his grandson); Herodotus had won at one or both of these (schol.). The following lines allude to victories won in the Minyeia at Orchomenus, in games dedicated to Demeter at Eleusis, in games on Euboea, and in games honoring Protesilas at Phylaca (in Thessaly).

ὕμνος. ἦ μὰν πολλάκι καὶ τὸ σεσω-
παμένον εὐθυμίαν μείζω φέρει.

εἴη νιν εὐφώνων πτερύγεσσιν ἀερθέντ' ἀγλααῖς
65 Πιερίδων, ἔτι καὶ Πυ-
θῶθεν Ὀλυμπιάδων τ' ἐξαιρέτοις
Ἀλφεοῦ ἔρνεσι φράξαι χεῖρα τιμὰν ἑπταπύλοις
Θήβαισι τεύχοντ'. εἰ δέ τις ἔνδον νέμει πλοῦτον
κρυφαῖον,
ἄλλοισι δ' ἐμπίπτων γελᾷ, ψυχὰν Ἀίδᾳ τελέων
οὐ φράζεται δόξας ἄνευθεν.

And in fact, what is left in silence
   often brings even greater cheer.

May he, lifted on the splendid wings of the melodious   Ep. 4
Pierians, also from Pytho and from the Olympic   65
   games wreathe his hand with choicest garlands
from the Alpheus, thus bringing honor to seven-gated
Thebes. But if a man keeps wealth hidden inside
and attacks others with laughter, he does not consider
   that he is paying up his soul to Hades devoid of fame.

ISTHMIAN 2

Isth. 2 is the last of Pindar's four epinicia honoring the Emmenidae of Acragas. *Pyth.* 6 commemorates Xenocrates' Pythian chariot victory, probably won in 490. *Ol.* 2 and 3 celebrate his brother Theron's Olympic chariot victory in 476. When *Isth.* 2 was composed, perhaps as late as 470, Xenocrates was no longer alive, for Pindar speaks of him in the past tense (36–37). The ode was probably placed in this book because an Isthmian victory is cited first among his past successes. As in the case of *Pyth.* 6, Pindar addresses the ode to Xenocrates' son Thrasybulus, for whom he also wrote an encomium (see *fr.* 124).

The poets of old wrote spontaneous love poetry whenever a beautiful boy took their fancy, but now the Muse sells her poetry and endorses the saying "money makes the man" (1–11). The poet acknowledges Thrasybulus' awareness of this situation and recounts Xenocrates' Isthmian victory (12–17). After briefly mentioning Xenocrates' Pythian victory, the poet recalls the success in the Panathenaea achieved by his charioteer, Nicomachus (18–22), who also won at Olympia for Xenocrates' brother Theron (23–29).

The homes of the Emmenidae are well acquainted with victory celebrations, and the poet finds it easy to bring praise to them (30–34). He hopes in particular to succeed

146

in conveying the kindness of Xenocrates (whose name means "host strength"), who was respectful of his fellow citizens, a breeder of horses, a devoted worshiper of the gods, and a never failing host (35–42).

In the face of men's inclination to envy, the poet exhorts Thrasybulus to keep alive his father's excellence and to make known this poem, which he is sending via Nicasippus (43–48).

2. <ΞΕΝΟΚΡΑΤΕΙ ΑΚΡΑΓΑΝΤΙΝΩΙ

ΑΡΜΑΤΙ>

Α΄   Οἱ μὲν πάλαι, ὦ Θρασύβουλε,
        φῶτες, οἳ χρυσαμπύκων
ἐς δίφρον Μοισᾶν ἔβαι-
        νον κλυτᾷ φόρμιγγι συναντόμενοι,
ῥίμφα παιδείους ἐτόξευον μελιγάρυας ὕμνους,
ὅστις ἐὼν καλὸς εἶχεν Ἀφροδίτας
5   εὐθρόνου μνάστειραν ἁδίσταν ὀπώραν.

ἁ Μοῖσα γὰρ οὐ φιλοκερδής
        πω τότ᾽ ἦν οὐδ᾽ ἐργάτις·
οὐδ᾽ ἐπέρναντο γλυκεῖ-
        αι μελιφθόγγου ποτὶ Τερψιχόρας
ἀργυρωθεῖσαι πρόσωπα μαλθακόφωνοι ἀοιδαί.

inscr. suppl. Triclinius, Heyne: om. BD
6 τότ᾽ D, Clem. Alex.: ποτ᾽ B, schol. Aristoph.
7 μελιφθόγγου Heyne: μελίφθογγοι BD

148

2. FOR XENOCRATES
OF ACRAGAS

WINNER, CHARIOT RACE

The men of long ago,[1] O Thrasybulus,	Str. 1
who used to mount	
the chariot of the golden-wreathed Muses,	
taking with them the glorious lyre,	
freely shot their honey-sounding hymns of love	
at any boy who was beautiful and had the sweetest	
bloom	
of late summer that woos fair-throned Aphrodite.	5

For at that time the Muse was not yet	Ant. 1
greedy for gain nor up for hire,	
nor were sweet, soft-voiced songs	
with their faces silvered over being sold	
from the hand of honey-voiced Terpsichore.[2]	

[1] I.e. poets like Alcaeus, Ibycus, and Anacreon (schol.).
[2] The image is of a prostitute, the madam being the Muse Terpsichore.

149

νῦν δ' ἐφίητι ⟨τὸ⟩ τὠργείου φυλάξαι
10 ῥῆμ' ἀλαθείας ⟨∪–⟩ ἄγχιστα βαῖνον,

"χρήματα χρήματ' ἀνήρ"
   ὃς φᾶ κτεάνων θ' ἅμα λειφθεὶς καὶ φίλων.
ἐσσὶ γὰρ ὦν σοφός· οὐκ ἄγνωτ' ἀείδω
Ἰσθμίαν ἵπποισι νίκαν,
τὰν Ξενοκράτει Ποσειδάων ὀπάσαις,
15 Δωρίων αὐτῷ στεφάνωμα κόμᾳ
πέμπεν ἀναδεῖσθαι σελίνων,

Β′ εὐάρματον ἄνδρα γεραίρων,
   Ἀκραγαντίνων φάος.
ἐν Κρίσᾳ δ' εὐρυσθενὴς
   εἶδ' Ἀπόλλων νιν πόρε τ' ἀγλαΐαν
καὶ τόθι κλειναῖς ⟨τ'⟩ Ἐρεχθειδᾶν χαρίτεσσιν
      ἀραρώς
20 ταῖς λιπαραῖς ἐν Ἀθάναις, οὐκ ἐμέμφθη
ῥυσίδιφρον χεῖρα πλαξίπποιο φωτός,

τὰν Νικόμαχος κατὰ καιρὸν
   νεῖμ' ἁπάσαις ἁνίαις·

9 ⟨τὸ⟩ suppl. Heyne
10 ⟨ἑτᾶς⟩ suppl. Bergk: ⟨ὁδῶν⟩ suppl. Turyn Hermanno
praeeunte
12 ἄγνωτ' DΣ^γρ: ἀγνῶτ' B
19 ⟨τ'⟩ suppl. Bergk
22 νεῖμ' ἁπάσαις Hermann: νωμᾷ πάσαις BD

150

But now she bids us heed the Argive's adage,[3]
which comes . . . closest to the truth: 10

"Money, money makes the man,"   Ep. 1
    said he who lost his possessions and friends as well.
But enough, for you are wise. Not unknown is
the Isthmian chariot victory that I sing,
which Poseidon granted to Xenocrates,
and sent a crown of Dorian parsley   15
for him to bind upon his hair,

thus honoring the man of fine chariots,   Str. 2
    a light to the people of Acragas.
In Crisa mighty Apollo
    beheld him and gave him splendor
there too; and when he gained the glorious favor of
        Erechtheus' descendants
in shining Athens,[4] he had no cause to blame   20
the chariot-preserving hand, which the horse-striking
        man

Nicomachus applied fittingly   Ant. 2
    to all the reins

[3] The scholion attributes it to Aristodemus the Spartan and
quotes Alcaeus (fr. 360): χρήματ' ἄνηρ, πένιχρος δ' οὐδ' εἷς
πέλετ' ἔσλος οὐδὲ τίμιος, "money is the man, and no poor man is
noble or honorable."

[4] At the Panathenaic festival. Erechtheus was a mythical king
of Athens.

PINDAR

ὅν τε καὶ κάρυκες ὡ-
    ρᾶν ἀνέγνον, σπονδοφόροι Κρονίδα
Ζηνὸς Ἀλεῖοι, παθόντες πού τι φιλόξενον ἔργον·
25 ἀδυπνόῳ τέ νιν ἀσπάζοντο φωνᾷ
χρυσέας ἐν γούνασιν πίτνοντα Νίκας

γαῖαν ἀνὰ σφετέραν,
    τὰν δὴ καλέοισιν Ὀλυμπίου Διός
ἄλσος· ἵν' ἀθανάτοις Αἰνησιδάμου
παῖδες ἐν τιμαῖς ἔμιχθεν.
30 καὶ γὰρ οὐκ ἀγνῶτες ὑμῖν ἐντὶ δόμοι
οὔτε κώμων, ὦ Θρασύβουλ', ἐρατῶν,
οὔτε μελικόμπων ἀοιδᾶν.

Γ´ οὐ γὰρ πάγος οὐδὲ προσάντης
    ἁ κέλευθος γίνεται,
εἴ τις εὐδόξων ἐς ἀν-
    δρῶν ἄγοι τιμὰς Ἑλικωνιάδων.
35 μακρὰ δισκήσαις ἀκοντίσσαιμι τοσοῦθ', ὅσον
    ὀργάν
Ξεινοκράτης ὑπὲρ ἀνθρώπων γλυκεῖαν
ἔσχεν. αἰδοῖος μὲν ἦν ἀστοῖς ὁμιλεῖν,

ἱπποτροφίας τε νομίζων
    ἐν Πανελλάνων νόμῳ·

---

5 The Olympic heralds proclaimed a sacred truce in Zeus'
name throughout Greece during the season of the games and also
announced the victors.

152

and whom the heralds of the seasons[5] also recognized,
    the Elean truce-bearers of Cronus' son Zeus,
undoubtedly having experienced some act of hospitality,
and they welcomed him with a sweetly breathing voice,   25
when he fell on the knees of golden Victory

in their land,   Ep. 2
    the one men call Olympian Zeus'
sanctuary. There the sons of Aenesidamus[6]
were joined to immortal honors.
And so, your family's houses are not unfamiliar   30
with delightful victory revels, O Thrasybulus,
nor with songs of honey-sweet acclaim.

For there is no hill,   Str. 3
    nor is the road steep,
when one brings the honors of the Heliconian maidens[7]
    to the homes of famous men.
May I make a long throw with the discus and cast the   35
    javelin as far as
Xenocrates surpassed all men with his sweet disposition.
He was respectful in the company of his townsmen,

he practiced horse-breeding   Ant. 3
    in the Panhellenic tradition,

[6] Aenesidamus was the father of Xenocrates and Theron. Evidently Nicomachus drove the chariot when Theron won his Olympic victory in 476.

[7] The Muses, born in Pieria, dwelt on Mt. Helicon in Boeotia (cf. Hes. *Th.* 1–8).

PINDAR

καὶ θεῶν δαῖτας προσέ-
    πτυκτο πάσας· οὐδέ ποτε ξενίαν
40 οὖρος ἐμπνεύσαις ὑπέστειλ᾽ ἱστίον ἀμφὶ τράπεζαν·
ἀλλ᾽ ἐπέρα ποτὶ μὲν Φᾶσιν θερείαις,
ἐν δὲ χειμῶνι πλέων Νείλου πρὸς ἀκτάν.

μή νυν, ὅτι φθονεραὶ
    θνατῶν φρένας ἀμφικρέμανται ἐλπίδες,
μήτ᾽ ἀρετάν ποτε σιγάτω πατρῴαν,
45 μηδὲ τούσδ᾽ ὕμνους· ἐπεί τοι
οὐκ ἐλινύσοντας αὐτοὺς ἐργασάμαν.
ταῦτα, Νικάσιππ᾽, ἀπόνειμον, ὅταν
ξεῖνον ἐμὸν ἠθαῖον ἔλθῃς.

39 δαῖτας Morel e schol.: διαίτας BD

154

and welcomed all the feasts
   of the gods. And never did an oncoming wind
cause him to furl the sails at his hospitable table,   40
but he would travel to Phasis in summer seasons,
while in winter he would sail to the shore of the Nile.[8]

Therefore, since envious hopes   Ep. 3
   hang about the minds of mortals,
let the son never keep silent his father's excellence
nor these hymns, for I truly   45
did not fashion them to remain stationary.[9]
Impart these words to him, Nicasippus,[10]
when you visit my honorable host.

[8] I.e. no circumstances curbed his generosity. A summer wind
favored traveling to the Phasis River (in Colchis), a winter wind
south to the Nile.

[9] I.e. like statues (cf. *Nem.* 5.1–2).

[10] Otherwise unknown, his name means "horse victor."

ISTHMIAN 3

This and the following ode for Melissus of Thebes are often treated as one poem by editors because they are metrically identical. They are separated, however, in one of the two important MSS (B) and the scholia treat them as two poems. In addition, they celebrate two different occasions: *Isth.* 3 makes a passing reference to an Isthmian victory, but emphasizes a Nemean chariot victory; *Isth.* 4 celebrates a victory in the pancratium at the Isthmus, with no mention of a chariot victory. A plausible assumption is that after *Isth.* 4 was composed, Melissus won the chariot race at Nemea, and instead of writing its companion poem in a different meter, as is the case with other pairs of odes (e.g., *Ol.* 4 and 5, *Ol.* 10 and 11, and *Pyth.* 4 and 5), Pindar composed a triad in the identical meter, which adumbrates several themes treated more extensively in *Isth.* 4.

The ode opens with generalized observations on the need to praise any citizen who is successful or prosperous and is not excessive in his behavior (1–3). Zeus is responsible for great achievements, and a proper reverence makes prosperity more enduring (4–6). A poet is obligated to praise a successful man (7–8).

Melissus is celebrating two victories, one at the Isthmus, the other at Nemea in the chariot race (9–13). He has inherited his ability from famous ancestors on both

156

sides of his family, the Cleonymidae and the Labdacidae, who were devoted to chariot racing (13–17b). The poem closes with a gnomic statement contrasting the vicissitudes of an individual's lifetime with the abiding favor enjoyed by sons of gods (18–18b).

3. ⟨ΜΕΛΙΣΣΩΙ ΘΗΒΑΙΩΙ

ΙΠΠΟΙΣ⟩

Εἴ τις ἀνδρῶν εὐτυχήσαις
   ἢ σὺν εὐδόξοις ἀέθλοις
ἢ σθένει πλούτου κατέχει φρασὶν αἰανῆ κόρον,
ἄξιος εὐλογίαις ἀστῶν μεμίχθαι.
Ζεῦ, μεγάλαι δ' ἀρεταὶ θνατοῖς ἕπονται
5 ἐκ σέθεν· ζώει δὲ μάσσων
   ὄλβος ὀπιζομένων, πλαγίαις δὲ φρένεσσιν
οὐχ ὁμῶς πάντα χρόνον θάλλων ὁμιλεῖ.

εὐκλέων δ' ἔργων ἄποινα
   χρὴ μὲν ὑμνῆσαι τὸν ἐσλόν,
χρὴ δὲ κωμάζοντ' ἀγαναῖς χαρίτεσσιν βαστάσαι.
ἔστι δὲ καὶ διδύμων ἀέθλων Μελίσσῳ
10 μοῖρα πρὸς εὐφροσύναν τρέψαι γλυκεῖαν
ἦτορ, ἐν βάσσαισιν Ἰσθμοῦ
   δεξαμένῳ στεφάνους, τὰ δὲ κοίλᾳ λέοντος
ἐν βαθυστέρνου νάπᾳ κάρυξε Θήβαν

inscr. suppl. Callierges: om. BD

158

3. FOR MELISSUS OF THEBES

WINNER, CHARIOT RACE

If a man is successful,   Str.
    either in glorious games
or with mighty wealth, and keeps down nagging excess
        in his mind,
he deserves to be included in his townsmen's praises.
Zeus, great achievements come to mortals
from you, and men's happiness has a longer life   5
    when they are reverent, but does not flourish
as well for all time when it dwells with shifty minds.

In recompense for glorious deeds   Ant.
    one must hymn the good man
and must exalt him, as he revels, with gentle poems of
        praise.
Melissus has the good fortune of twin prizes
to turn his heart to sweet   10
festivity, for he won crowns in the Isthmian
    glens, and then in the hollow valley
of the deep-chested lion he had Thebe proclaimed[1]

[1] By the herald who announced his victory at Nemea; Thebe is
the eponymous nymph of Thebes.

159

ἱπποδρομίᾳ κρατέων· ἀνδρῶν δ' ἀρετάν
σύμφυτον οὐ κατελέγχει.
15 ἴστε μὰν Κλεωνύμου
δόξαν παλαιὰν ἅρμασιν·
καὶ ματρόθε Λαβδακίδαισιν σύννομοι
17b πλούτου διέστειχον τετραοριᾶν πόνοις.
αἰὼν δὲ κυλινδομέναις ἀμέραις ἄλλ' ἄλλοτ' ἐξ
18b ἄλλαξεν. ἄτρωτοί γε μὰν παῖδες θεῶν.

by winning in the chariot race. He brings no disgrace   Ep.
upon the prowess inherited from his kinsmen.
Surely you[2] know the ancient fame   15
of Cleonymus with chariots,
and on his mother's side as relatives of the Labdacidae
they devoted their wealth to the toils of four-horse   17b
    chariots.
As the days roll by, one's life changes now this way
now that, but the sons of the gods remain unwounded.[3]   18b

   [2] In the plural, thus addressed to the audience.
   [3] For the contrast between the vicissitudes that beset individuals and the abiding good fortune of the gods or a family, see *Ol.* 2.35–47, *Pyth.* 5.54–55, *Pyth.* 7.19–21, *Nem.* 6.1–7, and *Isth.* 4.4–21.

ISTHMIAN 4

This poem continues to treat themes touched upon in *Isth.* 3. Of particular note are the successes and misfortunes of the victor's clan, which was famous for its prowess in the past, but recently had lost four men in war (perhaps in the battle of Plataea in 479). The victory of Melissus in the pancratium at the Isthmus has awakened memory of his clan's earlier victories, but has also called to mind their failure to win Panhellenic crowns. Pindar rarely provides details about an athlete's appearance, but here he stresses the fact that Melissus was a pancratiast of small stature who used his courage and skill to overcome bigger opponents.

Melissus' Isthmian victory and the achievements of his clan, the Cleonymidae, furnish many avenues for praise (1–5). Although individuals are subject to vicissitudes, the Cleonymidae have always been famous for their hospitality, lack of arrogance, and unsurpassed achievements, particularly in horse breeding and warfare (5–15). Four of them, however, were killed in battle on a single day (16–17b). Now the spring has come again with the celebration of a victory at the Isthmus, which has reawakened the clan's former fame in chariot racing at Athens and Sicyon (18–27). They also competed in the crown games, but were unsuccessful (28–33). The gnomic observation that a weaker man can overcome a stronger one by skill leads to the example of Ajax, whose valor went unrewarded by the Greeks at Troy (34–36b). Homer, however, immortalized his excellence in verse (37–42).

The poet hopes to accomplish for Melissus what Homer did for Ajax (43–45), and praises him for his courage and skill, especially the latter, because he was small (45–51). His slight stature calls forth the example of the Theban hero Heracles, who skillfully defeated the much stronger Antaeus (52–55).

After briefly sketching the career of Heracles and his apotheosis on Olympus (55–60), the poet describes the evening sacrifices performed at Thebes honoring him and his sons (61–66), and mentions the following day's athletic games, at which Melissus was twice victorious as an adult and once as a boy (67–71b). The poem concludes with brief praise of his trainer Orseas (71b–72b).

4. ⟨ΜΕΛΙΣΣΩΙ ΘΗΒΑΙΩΙ

ΠΑΓΚΡΑΤΙΩΙ⟩

Α΄ Ἔστι μοι θεῶν ἕκατι
  μυρία παντᾷ κέλευθος,
ὦ Μέλισσ᾽, εὐμαχανίαν γὰρ ἔφανας Ἰσθμίοις,
ὑμετέρας ἀρετὰς ὕμνῳ διώκειν·
αἷσι Κλεωνυμίδαι θάλλοντες αἰεί
5 σὺν θεῷ θνατὸν διέρχον-
  ται βιότου τέλος. ἄλλοτε δ᾽ ἀλλοῖος οὖρος
πάντας ἀνθρώπους ἐπαΐσσων ἐλαύνει.

τοὶ μὲν ὦν Θήβαισι τιμά-
  εντες ἀρχᾶθεν λέγονται
πρόξενοί τ᾽ ἀμφικτιόνων κελαδεννᾶς τ᾽ ὀρφανοί
ὕβριος· ὅσσα δ᾽ ἐπ᾽ ἀνθρώπους ἄηται
10 μαρτύρια φθιμένων ζωῶν τε φωτῶν
  ἀπλέτου δόξας, ἐπέψαυ-
  σαν κατὰ πὰν τέλος· ἀνορέαις δ᾽ ἐσχάταισιν
οἴκοθεν στάλαισιν ἅπτονθ᾽ Ἡρακλείαις·

inscr. suppl. Boeckh: om. BD
5 βιότου Donaldson: βίου BD

164

4. FOR MELISSUS OF THEBES

WINNER, PANCRATIUM

I have, through the gods' favor,	Str. 1
countless roads in every direction,	
O Melissus—since at the Isthmian games you revealed	
an abundant resource—	
to pursue in song your family's achievements,	
in which the Cleonymidae ever flourish	
with a god's help, as they travel to the mortal end	5
of life. At different times different winds	
rush upon all humans and drive them on.	

But from the beginning they are said	Ant. 1
to have been honored in Thebes	
as hosts of neighboring peoples and free of loud-voiced	
arrogance; and as for all the testimonials wafted among	
mankind	
of endless fame won by men living or dead,	10
they have attained them in all fullness,	
and by their unexcelled manly deeds	
have grasped from their home[1] the pillars of Heracles;	

[1] For the expression, see *Ol.* 3.43–44.

PINDAR

καὶ μηκέτι μακροτέραν σπεύδειν ἀρετάν.
ἱπποτρόφοι τ᾽ ἐγένοντο,

15   χαλκέῳ τ᾽ Ἄρει ἅδον.
ἀλλ᾽ ἀμέρᾳ γὰρ ἐν μιᾷ
τραχεῖα νιφὰς πολέμοιο τεσσάρων

17b ἀνδρῶν ἐρήμωσεν μάκαιραν ἑστίαν·
νῦν δ᾽ αὖ μετὰ χειμέριον ποικίλα μηνῶν ζόφον

18b χθὼν ὥτε φοινικέοισιν ἄνθησεν ῥόδοις

B΄   δαιμόνων βουλαῖς. ὁ κινη-
     τὴρ δὲ γᾶς Ὀγχηστὸν οἰκέων

20   καὶ γέφυραν ποντιάδα πρὸ Κορίνθου τειχέων,
τόνδε πορὼν γενεᾷ θαυμαστὸν ὕμνον
ἐκ λεχέων ἀνάγει φάμαν παλαιάν
εὐκλέων ἔργων· ἐν ὕπνῳ
    γὰρ πέσεν· ἀλλ᾽ ἀνεγειρομένα χρῶτα λάμπει,
Ἀοσφόρος θαητὸς ὣς ἄστροις ἐν ἄλλοις·

25   ἅ τε κἂν γουνοῖς Ἀθανᾶν
     ἅρμα καρύξαισα νικᾶν
ἔν τ᾽ Ἀδραστείοις ἀέθλοις Σικυῶνος ὤπασεν
τοιάδε τῶν τότ᾽ ἐόντων φύλλ᾽ ἀοιδᾶν.
οὐδὲ παναγυρίων ξυνᾶν ἀπεῖχον
καμπύλον δίφρον, Πανελλά-
    νεσσι δ᾽ ἐριζόμενοι δαπάνᾳ χαῖρον ἵππων·

30   τῶν ἀπειράτων γὰρ ἄγνωτοι σιωπαί.

18 ποικίλα Hartung: ποικίλων BD

166

let no one strive for yet more distant achievement.   Ep. 1
They were breeders of horses
and found favor with bronze Ares.   15
However, in a single day
a cruel blizzard of war stripped
their blessed hearth of four men.   17b
But now again, after a winter's gloom lasting months,
it is as if the dappled earth had blossomed with red roses   18b

by the gods' designs. The shaker of the earth   Str. 2
    dwelling at Onchestus[2]
and at the sea bridge before the walls of Corinth   20
by granting this marvelous hymn to the clan
is rousing from its bed their ancient fame
for glorious deeds, for it had fallen
    asleep; but now it is awake and its body shines
like the Morning Star, splendid to behold among the
        other stars.

That fame heralded their chariot's victory   Ant. 2
    both on the heights of Athens
and in the games of Adrastus at Sicyon, and granted   26
such leaves of song as these from men who lived then.
Nor did they hold back their curved chariot
from national festivals, but competing with all Hellenes
    they rejoiced to spend wealth on horses,
since to those who do not take part belongs oblivious   30
        silence.

[2] For Poseidon's sanctuary at Onchestus, see *Isth.* 1.33.

PINDAR

ἔστιν δ᾽ ἀφάνεια τύχας καὶ μαρναμένων,
πρὶν τέλος ἄκρον ἱκέσθαι·
τῶν τε γὰρ καὶ τῶν διδοῖ·
καὶ κρέσσον᾽ ἀνδρῶν χειρόνων
35   ἔσφαλε τέχνα καταμάρψαισ᾽· ἴστε μάν
35b   Αἴαντος ἀλκὰν φοίνιον, τὰν ὀψίᾳ
      ἐν νυκτὶ ταμὼν περὶ ᾧ φασγάνῳ μομφὰν ἔχει
36b   παίδεσσιν Ἑλλάνων ὅσοι Τροίανδ᾽ ἔβαν.

Γ᾽   ἀλλ᾽ Ὅμηρός τοι τετίμα-
          κεν δι᾽ ἀνθρώπων, ὃς αὐτοῦ
      πᾶσαν ὀρθώσαις ἀρετὰν κατὰ ῥάβδον ἔφρασεν
      θεσπεσίων ἐπέων λοιποῖς ἀθύρειν.
40   τοῦτο γὰρ ἀθάνατον φωνᾶεν ἕρπει,
      εἴ τις εὖ εἴπῃ τι· καὶ πάγ-
          καρπον ἐπὶ χθόνα καὶ διὰ πόντον βέβακεν
      ἐργμάτων ἀκτὶς καλῶν ἄσβεστος αἰεί.

      προφρόνων Μοισᾶν τύχοιμεν,
          κεῖνον ἅψαι πυρσὸν ὕμνων
      καὶ Μελίσσῳ, παγκρατίου στεφάνωμ᾽ ἐπάξιον,
45   ἔρνεϊ Τελεσιάδα. τόλμᾳ γὰρ εἰκώς
      θυμὸν ἐριβρεμετᾶν θηρῶν λεόντων

33 διδοῖ Triclinius: διδοῖ τέλος BD
46 θηρῶν Heyne: θηρᾶν BD

168

But even when men strive, fortune remains hidden	Ep. 2
before they reach the final goal,	
for she gives some of this and some of that,	
and the skill of inferior men can overtake	
and bring down a stronger man. Surely you know of	35
Ajax's bloodstained valor, which he pierced late at night	35b
on his own sword, and thereby casts blame	
upon[3] all the sons of the Hellenes who went to Troy.	36b

But Homer, to be sure, has made him honored	Str. 3
among mankind, who set straight	
his entire achievement and declared it with his staff[4]	
of divine verses for future men to enjoy.	
For that thing goes forth with immortal voice	40
if someone says it well, and over the all-fruitful	
earth and through the sea has gone	
the radiance of noble deeds forever undimmed.	

May I find the favor of the Muses	Ant. 3
to light such a beacon-fire of hymns	
for Melissus too, Telesiadas' offspring, a crown worthy	
of the pancratium. For he resembles the boldness	45
of loudly roaring wild lions in his heart	

[3] Or *incurs the blame of.*

[4] The staff was the emblem of the rhapsodic poets, the sons of Homer (cf. *Nem.* 2.1–3), who performed epic poetry.

ἐν πόνῳ, μῆτιν δ᾽ ἀλώπηξ,
αἰετοῦ ἅ τ᾽ ἀναπιτναμένα ῥόμβον ἴσχει·
χρὴ δὲ πᾶν ἔρδοντ᾽ ἀμαυρῶσαι τὸν ἐχθρόν.

     οὐ γὰρ φύσιν Ὠαριωνείαν ἔλαχεν·
50 ἀλλ᾽ ὀνοτὸς μὲν ἰδέσθαι,
συμπεσεῖν δ᾽ ἀκμᾷ βαρύς.
καί τοί ποτ᾽ Ἀνταίου δόμους
Θηβᾶν ἄπο Καδμεῖᾶν μορφὰν βραχύς,
53b ψυχὰν δ᾽ ἄκαμπτος, προσπαλαίσων ἦλθ᾽ ἀνήρ
τὰν πυροφόρον Λιβύαν, κρανίοις ὄφρα ξένων
54b ναὸν Ποσειδάωνος ἐρέφοντα σχέθοι,

Δ´ υἱὸς Ἀλκμήνας· ὃς Οὔλυμ-
πόνδ᾽ ἔβα, γαίας τε πάσας
56 καὶ βαθύκρημνον πολιᾶς ἁλὸς ἐξευρὼν θέναρ,
ναυτιλίαισί τε πορθμὸν ἡμερώσαις.
νῦν δὲ παρ᾽ Αἰγιόχῳ κάλλιστον ὄλβον
ἀμφέπων ναίει, τετίμα-
ταί τε πρὸς ἀθανάτων φίλος, Ἥβαν τ᾽ ὀπυίει,
60 χρυσέων οἴκων ἄναξ καὶ γαμβρὸς Ἥρας.

   51 ἀκμᾷ Pauw: αἰχμᾷ BD
   56 βαθύκρημνον Heyne: βαθυκρήμνου BD
   58 Αἰγιόχῳ Triclinius: Αἰγιόχῳ Διὶ BD

---

  5 Perhaps an allusion to a maneuver in the pancratium, which allowed ground wrestling. The fox that plays dead by lying on its

during the struggle, but in skill he is a fox,
    which rolls on its back to check the eagle's swoop.[5]
One must do everything to diminish one's opponent.

For he was not granted the build of an Orion;   Ep. 3
but although he was paltry to look at,   50
to fall in with he was heavy in his strength.
Yes, long ago a man came to Antaeus' home
in wheat-bearing Libya from Cadmean Thebes,
short of stature, but of unbending spirit,   53b
to wrestle with him and stop him from roofing
Poseidon's temple with the skulls of strangers.[6]   54b

He was Alcmene's son, who went to Olympus,   Str. 4
    after exploring all the lands
and the cliff-walled hollow of the gray sea,   56
and making safe the route for shipping.[7]
But now he lives with the Aegis-Bearer,[8] enjoying
the noblest happiness: he is honored as a friend
    by the immortals, he is married to Hebe,
he is lord of a golden home and son-in-law to Hera.   60

back to catch birds is well known in medieval fables; see K. Varty,
Reynard the Fox (Leicester 1967), illus. 147–153 (I owe this ob-
servation to J. Rusten).

[6] Whenever Antaeus, a son of Poseidon and Gaea (Earth), was
thrown, he would rise stronger because of contact with his mother.
Heracles overcame him by holding him in the air. Pindar is con-
flating him with Busiris, the Egyptian son of Poseidon who sacri-
ficed all visiting strangers.

[7] By ridding it of pirates and monsters (schol.).

[8] Zeus.

τῷ μὲν Ἀλεκτρᾶν ὕπερθεν
    δαῖτα πορσύνοντες ἀστοί
καὶ νεόδματα στεφανώματα βωμῶν αὔξομεν
ἔμπυρα χαλκοαρᾶν ὀκτὼ θανόντων,
τοὺς Μεγάρα τέκε οἱ Κρεοντὶς υἱούς·
65 τοῖσιν ἐν δυθμαῖσιν αὐγᾶν
    φλὸξ ἀνατελλομένα συνεχὲς παννυχίζει,
αἰθέρα κνισάεντι λακτίζοισα καπνῷ,

καὶ δεύτερον ἆμαρ ἐτείων τέρμ᾽ ἀέθλων
γίνεται, ἰσχύος ἔργον.
ἔνθα λευκωθεὶς κάρα
70 μύρτοις ὅδ᾽ ἀνὴρ διπλόαν
νίκαν ἀνεφάνατο παίδων ⟨τε⟩ τρίταν
71b πρόσθεν, κυβερνατῆρος οἰακοστρόφου
γνώμᾳ πεπιθὼν πολυβούλῳ· σὺν Ὀρσέᾳ δέ νιν
72b κωμάξομαι τερπνὰν ἐπιστάζων χάριν.

71 ⟨τε⟩ suppl. Hermann
72b κωμάξομαι D: κωμάζομαι B | ἐπιστάζων Triclinius e
schol.: ἀποστάζων B: ἐπιστοχάζων D

In his honor, above the Electran Gates[9]   Ant. 4
    we citizens prepare a feast
and a newly built circle of altars[10] and multiply
burnt offerings for the eight bronze-clad who died,
the sons that Megara, Creon's daughter, bore to him.
For them at sunset the flame rises   65
    and burns all night long,
kicking heaven with its savor of smoke.

And on the second day is the conclusion   Ep. 4
of the annual games, the labor of strength.[11]
There did this man, his head made white
with myrtle,[12] bring to light a double   70
victory, and a third previously among boys,
when he heeded his guiding helmsman's   71b
judgment rich in counsel.[13] I shall sing of him with
      Orseas
in my revel song as I shed upon them delightful grace.   72b

[9] One of the main gates of Thebes.
[10] Presumably one for each of Heracles' sons.
[11] Either a general description of the athletic events (Bury) or
a specific reference to the pancratium (Sandys).
[12] Victors in the Iolaea were crowned with myrtle (schol.).
[13] His trainer Orseas.

ISTHMIAN 5

This is the last of the three poems Pindar composed for the sons of Lampon. Phylacidas, younger brother of Pytheas (celebrated in *Nem.* 5), had won an Isthmian victory as a boy (celebrated in *Isth.* 6). As usual in odes to Aeginetan victors, Pindar includes praise of the sons of Aeacus. Here he concentrates on the martial exploits of Achilles, which provide a transition to his praise of the Aeginetan sailors for their bravery during the battle of Salamis. The poem was therefore composed sometime after 480. Theia, addressed in the poem's opening, is a little known goddess mentioned as the mother of the Sun, Moon, and Dawn in Hesiod's *Theogony* 371–374. Here she seems to represent the principle of light and sight. The designation "of many names" indicates the multitude of ways in which her powers are manifested.

A hymn to Theia associates her power with the luster of gold and with the spectacle of competing ships and chariots (1–6). A series of gnomic observations on the glory won by victorious athletes with the help of the gods leads to the conclusion that mortals cannot aim for more than a portion of success and fame (7–16).

After briefly mentioning the victories of Phylacidas and Pytheas, the poet announces his desire to sing of the Aeacidae (17–22). A gnomic reflection on the need for praising successful toil is supported by the example of brave warriors whose deeds have become the subjects of poetry (22–29). A priamel lists heroes celebrated in various cities and culminates in the Aeacidae, who twice sacked Troy (30–38). After invoking the Muse, the poet lists four heroes from the Trojan War and asks who defeated them, but instead of providing the name of Achilles gives that of his ancestral homeland, Aegina (38–45).

Of all that the poet could say in praise of Aegina, he singles out her sailors' valor in the bloody battle of Salamis (46–50), but quickly stops himself from exulting and turns to the city's achievements in athletics (51–54). The victor's family serves as an example to aspiring athletes of the hard work required for success (54–58). The poet reiterates his praise for Phylacidas and for his brother Pytheas, who appears to have coached him (59–63).

5. ‹ΦΥΛΑΚΙΔΑΙ ΑΙΓΙΝΗΤΗΙ

ΠΑΓΚΡΑΤΙΩΙ›

Α΄ Μᾶτερ Ἀελίου πολυώνυμε Θεία,
    σέο ἕκατι καὶ μεγασθενῆ νόμισαν
    χρυσὸν ἄνθρωποι περιώσιον ἄλλων·
    καὶ γὰρ ἐριζόμεναι
5 νᾶες ἐν πόντῳ καὶ ‹ὑφ᾽› ἅρμασιν ἵπποι
    διὰ τεάν, ὤνασσα, τιμὰν ὠκυδινά-
      τοις ἐν ἁμίλλαισι θαυμασταὶ πέλονται·

    ἔν τ᾽ ἀγωνίοις ἀέθλοισι ποθεινόν
    κλέος ἔπραξεν, ὅντιν᾽ ἀθρόοι στέφανοι
    χερσὶ νικάσαντ᾽ ἀνέδησαν ἔθειραν
10 ἢ ταχυτᾶτι ποδῶν.
    κρίνεται δ᾽ ἀλκὰ διὰ δαίμονας ἀνδρῶν.
    δύο δέ τοι ζωᾶς ἄωτον μοῦνα ποιμαί-
      νοντι τὸν ἄλπνιστον εὐανθεῖ σὺν ὄλβῳ,

inscr. suppl. Triclinius: om. BD
2 σέο Bergk: σέο γ᾽ BD

176

5. FOR PHYLACIDAS
OF AEGINA

WINNER, PANCRATIUM

Mother of the Sun, Theia of many names,   Str. 1
because of you men value gold as mighty
above all other things;
then too, when ships contend
on the sea or horses yoked to chariots,   5
it is through your honor, O queen, that they become
    wondrous to behold in swiftly turning encounters;

and in athletic competitions a man gains   Ant. 1
the glory he desires, when thick crowns
wreathe his hair after winning victory with his hands
or the swiftness of his feet.   10
But men's valor is determined by the gods.
There are truly two things alone that foster the finest
    sweetness of life in blossoming prosperity:

---

5 ⟨ὑφ'⟩ suppl. Bergk e schol.: καὶ ἐν ἅρμασιν B: καὶ
ἅρμασιν D   12 ἄλπνιστον Σ^γρ: ἀνέλπιστον BD: ἄλπι-
στον Callierges, Wackernagel

εἴ τις εὖ πάσχων λόγον ἐσλὸν ἀκούῃ.
μὴ μάτευε Ζεὺς γενέσθαι· πάντ' ἔχεις,
15 εἴ σε τούτων μοῖρ' ἐφίκοιτο καλῶν.
θνατὰ θνατοῖσι πρέπει.
τὶν δ' ἐν Ἰσθμῷ διπλόα θάλλοισ' ἀρετά,
Φυλακίδα, κεῖται, Νεμέᾳ δὲ καὶ ἀμφοῖν
Πυθέᾳ τε, παγκρατίου. τὸ δ' ἐμόν
20 οὐκ ἄτερ Αἰακιδᾶν κέαρ ὕμνων γεύεται·
σὺν Χάρισιν δ' ἔμολον Λάμπωνος υἱοῖς

Β΄ τάνδ' ἐς εὔνομον πόλιν. εἰ δὲ τέτραπται
θεοδότων ἔργων κέλευθον ἂν καθαράν,
μὴ φθόνει κόμπον τὸν ἐοικότ' ἀοιδᾷ
25 κιρνάμεν ἀντὶ πόνων.
καὶ γὰρ ἡρώων ἀγαθοὶ πολεμισταί
λόγον ἐκέρδαναν· κλέονται δ' ἔν τε φόρμιγ-
γεσσιν ἐν αὐλῶν τε παμφώνοις ὁμοκλαῖς

μυρίον χρόνον· μελέταν δὲ σοφισταῖς
Διὸς ἕκατι πρόσβαλον σεβιζόμενοι·
30 ἐν μὲν Αἰτωλῶν θυσίαισι φαενναῖς
Οἰνεΐδαι κρατεροί,
ἐν δὲ Θήβαις ἱπποσόας Ἰόλαος
γέρας ἔχει, Περσεὺς δ' ἐν Ἄργει, Κάστορος δ' αἰχ-
μᾷ Πολυδεύκεός τ' ἐπ' Εὐρώτα ῥεέθροις.

18 Φυλακίδα, κεῖται BD: Φυλακίδ', ἄγκειται Maas e schol.

178

if a man succeeds and hears his praises sung.   Ep. 1
Do not seek to become Zeus; you have all there is,
if a share of those blessings should come to you.   15
Mortal things befit mortals.
For you, Phylacidas, a flourishing double achievement
is stored up at the Isthmus, and at Nemea for both you
and Pytheas in the pancratium. But my heart
tastes no hymns without including the Aeacidae,   20
for I have come with the Graces at the bidding of
        Lampon's sons[1]

to this law-abiding city.[2] If someone has entered   Str. 2
into the clear road of divinely granted deeds,
do not grudge to blend into your song a fitting vaunt
in return for toils,   25
for among the heroes brave warriors also
gained praise and are celebrated on lyres
        and in the full range of pipes' harmonies

for time beyond measure, and, thanks to Zeus, reverence   Ant. 2
for them has provided a theme for wise poets.
In the splendid sacrifices of the Aetolians   30
the mighty sons of Oeneus[3] have their honor,
while in Thebes it is horse-driving Iolaus;[4]
it is Perseus in Argos, and the spearmen Castor and
        Polydeuces by the streams of the Eurotas;

[1] Phylacidas and Pytheas.
[2] Aegina.   [3] Meleager and Tydeus.
[4] Iphicles' son and Heracles' nephew.

ἀλλ᾽ ἐν Οἰνώνᾳ μεγαλήτορες ὀργαί
35 Αἰακοῦ παίδων τε· τοὶ καὶ σὺν μάχαις
δὶς πόλιν Τρώων πράθον, ἑσπόμενοι
Ἡρακλῆι πρότερον,
καὶ σὺν Ἀτρείδαις. ἔλα νῦν μοι πεδόθεν·
λέγε, τίνες Κύκνον, τίνες Ἕκτορα πέφνον,
40 καὶ στράταρχον Αἰθιόπων ἄφοβον
Μέμνονα χαλκοάραν· τίς ἄρ᾽ ἐσλὸν Τήλεφον
τρῶσεν ἑῷ δορὶ Καΐκου παρ᾽ ὄχθαις;

Γ´ τοῖσιν Αἴγιναν προφέρει στόμα πάτραν,
διαπρεπέα νᾶσον· τετείχισται δὲ πάλαι
45 πύργος ὑψηλαῖς ἀρεταῖς ἀναβαίνειν.
πολλὰ μὲν ἀρτιεπής
γλῶσσά μοι τοξεύματ᾽ ἔχει περὶ κείνων
κελαδέσαι· καὶ νῦν ἐν Ἄρει μαρτυρήσαι
κεν πόλις Αἴαντος ὀρθωθεῖσα ναύταις

ἐν πολυφθόρῳ Σαλαμὶς Διὸς ὄμβρῳ
50 ἀναρίθμων ἀνδρῶν χαλαζάεντι φόνῳ.
ἀλλ᾽ ὅμως καύχαμα κατάβρεχε σιγᾷ·
Ζεὺς τά τε καὶ τὰ νέμει,
Ζεὺς ὁ πάντων κύριος. ἐν δ᾽ ἐρατεινῷ

36 πράθον ἑσπόμενοι B: πάθον ἑπόμενοι D
48 κελαδέσαι Bruno Keil: κελαδῆσαι BD
52 τά τε καὶ Boeckh: τάδε καὶ BD

---

5 The ancient name for Aegina.
6 The command is addressed to the Muse in her chariot,

but in Oenona[5] it is the great-hearted spirits   Ep. 2
of Aeacus and his sons, who twice in battles   35
destroyed the Trojans' city, first
as followers of Heracles,
then with the Atreidae. Drive me now up from the
      plain;[6]
tell which men slew Cycnus, which ones slew Hector
and the fearless general of the Ethiopians,   40
Memnon of the bronze armor? Who then wounded
      noble Telephus
with his spear by the banks of the Caïcus?[7]

One's mouth proclaims Aegina as their homeland,   Str. 3
that illustrious island. From of old has she been built
as a bastion for men to scale with lofty achievements.   45
My fluent tongue
has many arrows to ring out in praise
of them, and recently in war Salamis, the city of Ajax,
      could attest that it was preserved by her sailors

during Zeus' devastating rain,   Ant. 3
that hailstorm of gore for countless men.[8]   50
But nevertheless, drench your boast in silence;
Zeus dispenses a variety of things,
Zeus the lord of all. And in poetry's delightful

calling for a more elevated treatment in the manner of epic. A
scholion, however, interprets πεδόθεν to mean "from the begin-
ning."

  [7] A river in Mysia. Although the first three questions are posed
in the plural, Achilles is the answer to all four.

  [8] For the acclaim won by the Aeginetans in the battle of
Salamis, see Hdt. 8.93.

PINDAR

μέλιτι καὶ τοιαίδε τιμαὶ καλλίνικον
    χάρμ᾽ ἀγαπάζοντι. μαρνάσθω τις ἔρδων

55 ἀμφ᾽ ἀέθλοισιν γενεὰν Κλεονίκου
    ἐκμαθών· οὔτοι τετύφλωται μακρός
    μόχθος ἀνδρῶν οὐδ᾽ ὁπόσαι δαπάναι
    ἐλπίδων ἔκνισ᾽ ὄπιν.
    αἰνέω καὶ Πυθέαν ἐν γυιοδάμαις
60 Φυλακίδᾳ πλαγᾶν δρόμον εὐθυπορῆσαι,
    χερσὶ δεξιόν, νόῳ ἀντίπαλον.
    λάμβανέ οἱ στέφανον, φέρε δ᾽ εὔμαλλον μίτραν,
    καὶ πτερόεντα νέον σύμπεμψον ὕμνον.

    54 μαρνάσθω Triclinius: μαρνάσθω δέ BD
    58 ἐλπίδων ἔκνισ᾽ ὄπιν Ceporinus: ἐλπίδων ἔκνιξ᾽ ὄπιν B:
    ἐλπίδων ἔκνιζ᾽ ὄπιν D: ἐλπίδων ἔκνιξ᾽ ὀπί Aristarchus: ἐλπίδ᾽
    ἔκνιξαν ὄπιν Wilamowitz

182

honey such honors as these[9] also welcome
    joyous song of victory. Let a man strive to perform

in the games after thoroughly learning about the family   Ep. 3
of Cleonicus,[10] for the long hard work of their men   56
is certainly not hidden, nor have all their costs
vexed the zeal of their hopes.
I praise Pytheas too among those who subdue bodies[11]
for guiding straight the course of Phylacidas' blows,   60
being quick with his hands and a good match with his
    mind.
Take up a crown for him, bring a fillet of fine wool,
and send along this winged new hymn.

[9] I.e. victories in athletics.

[10] Father of Lampon and grandfather of Phylacidas (schol.).

[11] I.e. pancratiasts. Pytheas had apparently coached his younger brother.

ISTHMIAN 6

This is chronologically the second of the three odes written for the sons of Lampon. It is preceded by *Nem.* 5 for Phylacidas' older brother Pytheas and followed by *Isth.* 5 for Phylacidas' subsequent Isthmian victory. A prominent theme of the ode is the greatness of sons. The opening simile highlights the successes of Lampon's sons, the central narrative concentrates on Heracles' prayer that Telamon may father a great son, and in the poem's conclusion Lampon is praised for the care he lavishes on his sons. A parallel motif is that of a drink offering, which also appears in the opening, in the narrative, and at the end of the poem.

This ode is likened to the second of three libations at a symposium: the first was occasioned by Pytheas' Nemean victory, the present one celebrates Phylacidas' Isthmian victory, and the poet prays that a third may be called for by an Olympic victory (1–9). If a man's hard work and expenditure lead to success and subsequent fame, then he has reached the limits of mortal success (10–13). Lampon hopes to accomplish this before he dies and the poet asks the Fates to fulfill that wish for his friend (14–18).

When the victor is from Aegina, the poet is obligated to praise the Aeacidae, whose numerous deeds are famous throughout the world, whether those of Peleus, Ajax, or

184

Telamon (19–27), the last-mentioned of whom was Heracles' ally in the taking of Troy and in the destruction of the Meropes and of Alcyoneus (27–35). Upon coming to Telamon's house to summon him to Troy, Heracles poured a libation and prayed that Telamon's wife Eriboea would bear him a brave son (35–49). Zeus answered by sending an eagle (*aietos*) and Heracles urged Telamon to name his son Ajax accordingly (49–56).

Citing insufficient time to recount all their deeds, the poet breaks off his treatment of the Aeacidae and turns to the two brothers and their uncle Euthymenes, whom he intends to praise in the briefest terms (56–59). After summarily listing their combined victories, which have brought glory in song to the clan of the Psalychiadae, their grandfather Themistius, and their city, he turns to their father Lampon, praising the diligent training he has given his sons and his civic-mindedness, hospitality, good sense, and knowledge of athletics (60–73). The poem ends with Pindar's offering to them a drink of the Muses' water from the fountain of Dirce at Thebes (74–75).

6. ⟨ΦΥΛΑΚΙΔΑΙ ΑΙΓΙΝΗΤΗΙ

ΠΑΙΔΙ ΠΑΓΚΡΑΤΙΩΙ⟩

Α΄ Θάλλοντος ἀνδρῶν ὡς ὅτε συμποσίου
δεύτερον κρατῆρα Μοισαίων μελέων
κίρναμεν Λάμπωνος εὐαέθλου γενεᾶς ὕπερ, ἐν
 Νεμέᾳ μὲν πρῶτον, ὦ Ζεῦ,
τὶν ἄωτον δεξάμενοι στεφάνων,
5 νῦν αὖτε Ἰσθμοῦ δεσπότᾳ
Νηρεΐδεσσί τε πεντήκοντα παίδων ὁπλοτάτου
Φυλακίδα νικῶντος. εἴη δὲ τρίτον
σωτῆρι πορσαίνοντας Ὀ-
 λυμπίῳ Αἴγιναν κάτα
σπένδειν μελιφθόγγοις ἀοιδαῖς.

10 εἰ γάρ τις ἀνθρώπων δαπάνᾳ τε χαρείς
καὶ πόνῳ πράσσει θεοδμάτους ἀρετάς

inscr. suppl. Schroeder: om. BD
5 αὖτε Hermann cum cod. D schol. *Isth.* 5 inscr.: αὖτ᾽ ἐν BD

186

6. FOR PHYLACIDAS
OF AEGINA

WINNER, BOYS' PANCRATIUM

As when a drinking party of men is thriving,   Str. 1
so we are mixing a second bowl of the Muses' songs
in honor of Lampon's prize-winning offspring,
    for first at Nemea, O Zeus,
by your favor they[1] received the choicest of crowns,[2]
and now again, since by the grace of the Isthmus' lord   5
and the fifty Nereids the youngest of the sons,
Phylacidas, is victorious. May there be a third bowl
for us to prepare
    for the Olympian Savior and pour upon Aegina
a libation of honey-voiced songs.[3]

For if a man, delighting in expenditure and hard work,   Ant. 1
accomplishes divinely fashioned deeds of excellence,   11

---

[1] Or *we*.

[2] I.e. for Pytheas' Nemean victory.

[3] The first libation at a symposium is to Olympian Zeus, the
second to the heroes, and the third to Zeus Savior (schol.). *Nem.* 5
was the first libation (to Zeus, patron of the Nemean games), this
ode is the second (celebrating Telamon and Heracles), the third,
to the Olympian Savior, will celebrate an Olympic victory.

σύν τέ οἱ δαίμων φυτεύει δόξαν ἐπήρατον, ἐ-
σχατιαῖς ἤδη πρὸς ὄλβου
βάλλετ᾽ ἄγκυραν θεότιμος ἐών.
τοίαισιν ὀργαῖς εὔχεται
15 ἀντιάσαις Ἀίδαν γῆράς τε δέξασθαι πολιόν
ὁ Κλεονίκου παῖς· ἐγὼ δ᾽ ὑψίθρονον
Κλωθὼ κασιγνήτας τε προσ-
εννέπω ἑσπέσθαι κλυταῖς
ἀνδρὸς φίλου Μοίρας ἐφετμαῖς.

ὔμμε τ᾽, ὦ χρυσάρματοι Αἰακίδαι,
20 τέθμιόν μοι φαμὶ σαφέστατον ἔμμεν
τάνδ᾽ ἐπιστείχοντα νᾶσον ῥαινέμεν εὐλογίαις.
μυρίαι δ᾽ ἔργων καλῶν τέ-
τμανθ᾽ ἑκατόμπεδοι ἐν σχερῷ κέλευθοι
καὶ πέραν Νείλοιο παγᾶν καὶ δι᾽ Ὑπερβορέους·
οὐδ᾽ ἔστιν οὕτω βάρβαρος
οὔτε παλίγγλωσσος πόλις
25 ἅτις οὐ Πηλέος ἀίει κλέος ἥ-
ρωος, εὐδαίμονος γαμβροῦ θεῶν,

Β´ οὐδ᾽ ἅτις Αἴαντος Τελαμωνιάδα
καὶ πατρός· τὸν χαλκοχάρμαν ἐς πόλεμον
ἆγε σὺν Τιρυνθίοισιν πρόφρονα σύμμαχον ἐς
Τροΐαν, ἥρωσι μόχθον,

17 ἑσπέσθαι Pauw: σπέσθαι BD
25 ἀίει Hermann e schol. (κατακούει): ἀΐει BD

and in addition fortune plants lovely fame for him,
    at the limits of happiness he has already
cast his anchor as one honored by the gods.
The son of Cleonicus[4] prays
that with feelings such as these he may meet Hades   15
and welcome gray old age, and I myself call upon
Clotho enthroned on high and her sister Fates[5]
    to follow the noble
commands of the man who is my friend.

And as for you, O Aeacidae with your golden chariots,   Ep. 1
I declare that I have the clearest mandate,   20
when coming to this island, to shower you with praises.
Countless roads, one after another, one hundred feet
    wide, have been cut for their noble deeds
beyond the springs of the Nile and through the
        Hyperboreans,[6]
and there is no city so alien
    or of such backward speech
that it does not hear tell of the fame of the hero Peleus,   25
    the blessed son-in-law of the gods,

or of Telamonian Ajax   Str. 2
or of his father, whom Alcmene's son led
as an eager ally into bronze-loving war, when he went
    with his men from Tiryns[7] in ships to Troy,

---

[4] Lampon.   [5] Atropos and Lachesis.   [6] As far south
as the sources of the Nile and as far north as the land of the Hyper-
boreans (those beyond the North Wind); for a similar inclusive
doublet, see *Isth.* 2.41–42.   [7] Heracles performed most of
his labors for Eurystheus, king of Tiryns.

Λαομεδοντιᾶν ὑπὲρ ἀμπλακιᾶν
30 ἐν ναυσὶν Ἀλκμήνας τέκος.
εἷλε δὲ Περγαμίαν, πέφνεν δὲ σὺν κείνῳ Μερόπων
ἔθνεα καὶ τὸν βουβόταν οὔρεϊ ἴσον
Φλέγραισιν εὑρὼν Ἀλκυο-
νῆ, σφετέρας δ᾽ οὐ φείσατο
χερσὶν βαρυφθόγγοιο νευρᾶς

35 Ἡρακλέης. ἀλλ᾽ Αἰακίδαν καλέων
ἐς πλόον <– –> κύρησεν δαινυμένων.
τὸν μὲν ἐν ῥινῷ λέοντος στάντα κελήσατο νε-
κταρέαις σπονδαῖσιν ἄρξαι
καρτεραίχμαν Ἀμφιτρυωνιάδαν,
ἄνδωκε δ᾽ αὐτῷ φέρτατος
40 οἰνοδόκον φιάλαν χρυσῷ πεφρικυῖαν Τελαμών.
ὁ δ᾽ ἀνατείναις οὐρανῷ χεῖρας ἀμάχους
αὔδασε τοιοῦτον ἔπος·
"Εἴ ποτ᾽ ἐμὰν, ὦ Ζεῦ πάτερ,
θυμῷ θέλων ἀρᾶν ἄκουσας,

νῦν σε, νῦν εὐχαῖς ὑπὸ θεσπεσίαις
45 λίσσομαι παῖδα θρασὺν ἐξ Ἐριβοίας

36 ⟨γάμον⟩ vel ⟨γάμους⟩ suppl. Von der Mühll: ⟨κεῖνον⟩
suppl. Schroder: alii alia   42 τοιοῦτον Heyne: τοιοῦτόν τι
BD   44 θεσπεσίαις Ceporinus: θεσπεσίαν BD

[8] When Heracles saved Laomedon's daughter Hesione, who
was about to be sacrificed to a sea monster sent by Poseidon,

190

that labor for the heroes,
on account of Laomedon's crimes.[8]   30
He took Pergamum, and with that man[9] slew the tribes
of the Meropes[10] and that cowherd great as a mountain,
Alcyoneus,[11] when he encountered him
    at Phlegrae, and did not hold back
his hands from his deep-toned bowstring,

Heracles, that is. But when he came to summon Aeacus'   Ant. 2
    son[12]
to the voyage . . . he found them dining.   36
As Amphitryon's son, a mighty spearman, stood there
    in his lion's skin, matchless Telamon bade him
pour out the first libations of nectar
and handed up to him
the wine-receiving bowl bristling with gold.   40
And he, stretching his invincible hands upwards to
        heaven,
spoke out such words as these:
    "If ever, O father Zeus,
you heard my prayers with a willing heart,

now, now with holy prayers   Ep. 2
I entreat you to bring to term from Eriboea for this man   45

Laomedon refused to give him the horses he had promised.
    [9] Telamon.   [10] Inhabitants of Cos (cf. *Il.* 14.255 and
15.28).   [11] A giant who stole the cattle of Helius and was as-
sociated with the Giants against whom Heracles fought alongside
the Olympians at Phlegrae (cf. Apollod. 1.6.1 and *Nem.* 1.67–68).
The same three exploits are named at *Nem.* 4.25–30.
    [12] Telamon.

ἀνδρὶ τῷδε ξεῖνον ἀμὸν μοιρίδιον τελέσαι·
τὸν μὲν ἄρρηκτον φυάν, ὥσ-
περ τόδε δέρμα με νῦν περιπλανᾶται
θηρός, ὃν πάμπρωτον ἀέθλων κτεῖνά ποτ' ἐν Νεμέᾳ·
θυμὸς δ' ἐπέσθω." ταῦτ' ἄρα
οἱ φαμένῳ πέμψεν θεός

50   ἀρχὸν οἰωνῶν μέγαν αἰετόν· ἁ-
δεῖα δ' ἔνδον νιν ἔκνιξεν χάρις,

Γ´   εἶπέν τε φωνήσαις ἅτε μάντις ἀνήρ·
"Ἔσσεταί τοι παῖς, ὃν αἰτεῖς, ὦ Τελαμών·
καί νιν ὄρνιχος φανέντος κέκλευ ἐπώνυμον εὐ-
ρυβίαν Αἴαντα, λαῶν
ἐν πόνοις ἔκπαγλον Ἐνυαλίου."

55   ὣς ἦρα εἰπὼν αὐτίκα
ἕζετ'. ἐμοὶ δὲ μακρὸν πάσας <ἀν>αγήσασθ' ἀρετάς·
Φυλακίδᾳ γὰρ ἦλθον, ὦ Μοῖσα, ταμίας
Πυθέᾳ τε κώμων Εὐθυμέ-
νει τε· τὸν Ἀργείων τρόπον
εἰρήσεταί που κἀν βραχίστοις·

60   ἄραντο γὰρ νίκας ἀπὸ παγκρατίου
τρεῖς ἀπ' Ἰσθμοῦ, τὰς δ' ἀπ' εὐφύλλου Νεμέας,

46 τῷδε Triclinius: τοῖδε B^{ec}: τόνδε D | ξεῖνον B: κεῖνον D
47 με νῦν Stephanus: μίμνοι BD
53 κέκλευ Melanchthon: κέκλετ' BD
56 ἀναγήσασθ' Mingarelli: ἀγήσασθ' BD
59 που κἀν Heyne: που κὲν B: πα κ' ἐν D

192

a bold son to be my destined guest-friend,
one with a body as impenetrable as this hide
   now wrapped around me from the
beast I once slew in Nemea as the very first of my labors,
and may he have a heart to match." Then, after
   he had said this, the god sent him
the king of birds, a great eagle.   50
   Sweet joy thrilled him within,

and he spoke out like a seer and said,   Str. 3
"You shall have the son you request, O Telamon;
and call him, as namesake of the bird that appeared,
   mighty Ajax, awesome among the host
in the toils of Enyalius."[13]
After speaking thus, he immediately   55
sat down. But it would take me too long to recount all
   their deeds,
since I have come, O Muse, as steward
of the revel songs for Phylacidas, Pytheas,
   and Euthymenes.[14] In the Argive manner
it will be stated, I think, in the briefest terms:[15]

these splendid boys and their uncle took away three   Ant. 3
victories in the pancratium from the Isthmus and others   61

[13] An epithet of Ares.

[14] Their maternal uncle (schol.).

[15] The Argives, like the Spartans, had a reputation for brevity
in speech (cf. Aesch. *Supp.* 200–201).

193

ἀγλαοὶ παῖδές τε καὶ μάτρως. ἀνὰ δ' ἄγαγον ἐς
    φάος οἵαν μοῖραν ὕμνων·
τὰν Ψαλυχιαδᾶν δὲ πάτραν Χαρίτων
ἄρδοντι καλλίστᾳ δρόσῳ,
65 τόν τε Θεμιστίου ὀρθώσαντες οἶκον τάνδε πόλιν
θεοφιλῆ ναίοισι. Λάμπων δὲ μελέταν
ἔργοις ὀπάζων Ἡσιό-
    δου μάλα τιμᾷ τοῦτ' ἔπος,
υἱοῖσί τε φράζων παραινεῖ,

ξυνὸν ἄστει κόσμον ἑῷ προσάγων
70 καὶ ξένων εὐεργεσίαις ἀγαπᾶται,
μέτρα μὲν γνώμᾳ διώκων, μέτρα δὲ καὶ κατέχων·
γλῶσσα δ' οὐκ ἔξω φρενῶν· φαί-
    ης κέ νιν ἄνδρ' ἐν ἀεθληταῖσιν ἔμμεν
Ναξίαν πέτραις ἐν ἄλλαις χαλκοδάμαντ' ἀκόναν.
πίσω σφε Δίρκας ἁγνὸν ὕ-
    δωρ, τὸ βαθύζωνοι κόραι
75 χρυσοπέπλου Μναμοσύνας ἀνέτει-
    λαν παρ' εὐτειχέσιν Κάδμου πύλαις.

72 ἄνδρ' ἐν ἀεθληταῖσιν E. Schmid: ἄνδρ' ἐν ἀθληταῖσιν
BD: ἀνδράσιν ἀεθληταῖσιν Heyne

194

from leafy Nemea.[16] And what a portion
  of hymns have they brought to light!
They refresh the clan of the Psalychiadae
with the finest dew of the Graces;
having exalted the house of Themistius,[17] they dwell   65
in this city beloved by the gods. In devoting industry
to his deeds, Lampon holds in particular
  honor that saying of Hesiod,[18]
which he quotes and recommends to his sons,

as he brings to his own city an adornment all share   Ep. 3
and is beloved for his acts of kindness to foreigners,   70
pursuing due measure in judgment and holding fast to it;
his tongue does not stray from his thoughts; you would
  say that among athletes the man is a bronze-taming
whetstone from Naxos compared to other stones.[19]
I shall offer them a drink of Dirce's[20] sacred water,
  which the deep-bosomed daughters
of golden-robed Mnemosyne made to surge   75
  by the well-walled gates of Cadmus.

[16] Or *three victories, one from the Isthmus and the others from leafy Nemea.*

[17] Phylacidas' maternal grandfather (schol.).

[18] Hes. *Op.* 412: μελέτη δέ τοι ἔργον ὀφέλλει, "industry advances work."

[19] For the excellent qualities of Naxian whetstones, see Pliny *NH* 36.54, 164 and 37.109.

[20] A spring near Thebes, the city of Cadmus.

ISTHMIAN 7

The occasion of the ode, Strepsiades' victory at the Isthmus, is given but passing mention; instead, the poet concentrates on the victor's uncle, also named Strepsiades, who died in battle defending his homeland of Thebes. Because Pindar provides no specific information about the battle, there is little agreement on the poem's date.

In a lengthy priamel, the poet asks Thebe, the eponymous nymph of the city, which former distinction has pleased her most, and provides as possible answers numerous gods, heroes, and military successes associated with Thebes (1–15). After meditating on the role of song in preserving the memory of bygone deeds, he issues an exhortation to celebrate Strepsiades' recent Isthmian victory in the pancratium (16–22).

The poet declares that the victor has shared his crown with his uncle of the same name who was killed in battle (23–25). After extolling the glory that accrues to one who dies defending his homeland, the poet addresses the uncle and compares him to the heroic warriors Meleager, Hector, and Amphiaraus for fighting and dying in the forefront of the army (26–36).

The poet expresses his personal grief at the elder Strepsiades' death, but finds consolation in the recent victory and prays that the present happiness may continue

(37–39). Speaking in the first person, the poet recommends enjoying each day as it comes, while avoiding overreaching ambitions such as those that caused Bellerophon's demise (40–48). The poem ends with a prayer that Strepsiades may go on to win a Pythian victory (49–51).

7. ⟨ΣΤΡΕΨΙΑΔΗΙ ΘΗΒΑΙΩΙ

ΠΑΓΚΡΑΤΙΩΙ⟩

Α΄ Τίνι τῶν πάρος, ὦ μάκαιρα Θήβα,
καλῶν ἐπιχωρίων μάλιστα θυμὸν τεόν
εὔφρανας; ἦρα χαλκοκρότου πάρεδρον
Δαμάτερος ἁνίκ᾽ εὐρυχαίταν
5 ἄντειλας Διόνυσον, ἢ χρυσῷ μεσονύκτιον
νείφοντα δεξαμένα τὸν φέρτατον θεῶν,

ὁπότ᾽ Ἀμφιτρύωνος ἐν θυρέτροις
σταθεὶς ἄλοχον μετῆλθεν Ἡρακλείοις γοναῖς;
ἢ ἀμφὶ πυκναῖς Τειρεσίαο βουλαῖς;
ἢ ἀμφ᾽ Ἰόλαον ἱππόμητιν;
10 ἢ Σπαρτῶν ἀκαμαντολογχᾶν; ἢ ὅτε καρτερᾶς
Ἄδραστον ἐξ ἀλαλᾶς ἄμπεμψας ὀρφανόν

inscr. suppl. edd.: om. BD
8–9 ἢ E. Schmid: ἢ ὅτ᾽ BD

---

[1] Dionysus is often associated with Demeter, but it was Cybele who was normally worshiped to the clanging of cymbals.

7. FOR STREPSIADES
OF THEBES

WINNER, PANCRATIUM

In which of your land's former glories,	Str. 1
O blessed Thebe, did your heart	
take most delight? Was it when you raised up	
flowing-haired Dionysus as companion to Demeter	
of the ringing bronze?[1] or when, in a midnight	5
snowstorm	
of gold, you received the greatest of the gods,[2]	

when he stood in Amphitryon's doorway	Ant. 1
and sought his wife to beget Heracles?	
or because of Teiresias' profound counsels?	
or because of the skillful horseman, Iolaus?	
or for the Spartoi of the unwearied spears?[3] or when you	10
sent back Adrastus from the fierce battle deprived	

[2] Zeus. Pindar has transferred the shower of gold from the legend of Danaë to that of Alcmene (schol.). Pindar's Zeus also "snows" gold at *Ol.* 7.34.

[3] For the Spartoi ("Sown Men"), see *Pyth.* 9.82 and *Isth.* 1.30.

PINDAR

μυρίων ἑτάρων ἐς Ἄργος ἵππιον;
ἢ Δωρίδ' ἀποικίαν οὕνεκεν ὀρθῷ
ἔστασας ἐπὶ σφυρῷ
Λακεδαιμονίων, ἕλον δ' Ἀμύκλας
15 Αἰγεῖδαι σέθεν ἔκγονοι, μαντεύμασι Πυθίοις;
ἀλλὰ παλαιὰ γάρ
εὕδει χάρις, ἀμνάμονες δὲ βροτοί,

Β΄ ὅ τι μὴ σοφίας ἄωτον ἄκρον
κλυταῖς ἐπέων ῥοαῖσιν ἐξίκηται ζυγέν·
20 κώμαζ' ἔπειτεν ἁδυμελεῖ σὺν ὕμνῳ
καὶ Στρεψιάδᾳ· φέρει γὰρ Ἰσθμοῖ
νίκαν παγκρατίου, σθένει τ' ἔκπαγλος ἰδεῖν τε μορ-
φάεις, ἄγει τ' ἀρετὰν οὐκ αἴσχιον φυᾶς.

φλέγεται δὲ ἰοπλόκοισι Μοίσαις,
μάτρωί θ' ὁμωνύμῳ δέδωκε κοινὸν θάλος,
25 χάλκασπις ᾧ πότμον μὲν Ἄρης ἔμειξεν·
τιμὰ δ' ἀγαθοῖσιν ἀντίκειται.
ἴστω γὰρ σαφὲς ὅστις ἐν ταύτᾳ νεφέλᾳ χάλα-
ζαν αἵματος πρὸ φίλας πάτρας ἀμύνεται,

22 αἴσχιον B: αἴσχθιον D: αἰσχίω Triclinius
27 πρό E. Schmid: πρὸς BD

4 The Dorian conquest of Lacedaemon was accomplished

200

of countless companions to Argos, land of horses?   Ep. 1
or because you established
on firm footing the Dorian colony
of the Lacedaemonians, and your offspring, the
    Aegeidae,
took Amyclae in accordance with the Pythian oracles?[4]   15
But the ancient
splendor sleeps; and mortals forget

what does not attain poetic wisdom's choice pinnacle,   Str. 2
yoked to glorious streams of verses.
Therefore celebrate in a sweetly sung hymn   20
Strepsiades too, for he is winner of victory at the
    Isthmus
in the pancratium; he is awesome in strength and
    handsome to behold,
   and his success is no worse than his looks.

He is being set ablaze by the violet-haired Muses   Ant. 2
and has given a share of his crown to his namesake
    uncle,
whom Ares of the bronze shield brought to his fated   25
    end;
but honor is laid up as a recompense for brave men.
For let him know well, whoever in that cloud of war
   defends his dear country from the hailstorm of blood

with the taking of Amyclae, a few miles south of Sparta (cf. *Pyth.*
1.65–66). Schol. 18c reports Aristotle as saying (in his lost treatise
on the Spartan constitution) that when the Spartans were told
by an oracle to make allies of the Aegeidae in their war against
Amyclae, they went to Thebes and obtained their alliance.

λοιγὸν ἄντα φέρων ἐναντίῳ στρατῷ,
ἀστῶν γενεᾷ μέγιστον κλέος αὔξων
30 ζώων τ' ἀπὸ καὶ θανών.
τὺ δέ, Διοδότοιο παῖ, μαχατάν
αἰνέων Μελέαγρον, αἰνέων δὲ καὶ Ἕκτορα
Ἀμφιάραόν τε,
εὐανθέ' ἀπέπνευσας ἁλικίαν

Γ' προμάχων ἀν' ὅμιλον, ἔνθ' ἄριστοι
36 ἔσχον πολέμοιο νεῖκος ἐσχάταις ἐλπίσιν.
ἔτλαν δὲ πένθος οὐ φατόν· ἀλλὰ νῦν μοι
Γαιάοχος εὐδίαν ὄπασσεν
ἐκ χειμῶνος. ἀείσομαι χαίταν στεφάνοισιν ἁρ-
μόζων· ὁ δ' ἀθανάτων μὴ θρασσέτω φθόνος.

40 ὅ τι τερπνὸν ἐφάμερον διώκων
ἕκαλος ἔπειμι γῆρας ἔς τε τὸν μόρσιμον
αἰῶνα. θνᾴσκομεν γὰρ ὁμῶς ἅπαντες·
δαίμων δ' ἄισος· τὰ μακρὰ δ' εἴ τις
παπταίνει, βραχὺς ἐξικέσθαι χαλκόπεδον θεῶν
ἕδραν· ὅ τοι πτερόεις ἔρριψε Πάγασος

45 δεσπόταν ἐθέλοντ' ἐς οὐρανοῦ σταθμούς
ἐλθεῖν μεθ' ὁμάγυριν Βελλεροφόνταν

28 ἄντα φέρων Thiersch: ἀμύνων BD: ἀμφιβαλὼν A. W.
Mair
36 ἐσχάταις ἐλπίσιν Callierges: ἐσχάταις ἐπ' ἐλπίς . . B
(ἐλπίσιν B¹): ἐσχάτοισιν ἐπ' ἐλπίδιν D
43 ἄισος Benedictus cum paraphr.: ἄιστος BD

by turning the onslaught against the opposing army,   Ep. 2
that he fosters the greatest glory for his townsmen's race,
both while he lives and after he is dead.   30
And you, son of Diodotus, as you emulated the warrior
Meleager and emulated Hector
and Amphiaraus,
you breathed out your youth in full blossom

in the host of fighters at the forefront, where the bravest   Str. 3
bore war's strife with their ultimate hopes.   36
I suffered grief beyond telling, but now
the Earthholder[5] has granted me fair weather
after the storm. I shall fit wreaths to my hair and sing—
     may the envy of the immortals cause no disruption.

By pursuing the pleasure that comes day by day,   Ant. 3
I shall calmly approach old age and my fated   41
lifetime. For we all alike die,
but our fortune is unequal. If a man peers at distant
things, he is too little to reach the gods' bronze-paved
     dwelling. Indeed, winged Pegasus threw

his master, when Bellerophon desired to enter   Ep. 3
the habitations of heaven and the company   46

[5] Poseidon, tutelary god of the Isthmian games.

PINDAR

Ζηνός. τὸ δὲ πὰρ δίκαν
γλυκὺ πικρότατα μένει τελευτά.
ἄμμι δ', ὦ χρυσέᾳ κόμᾳ θάλλων, πόρε, Λοξία,
50 τεαῖσιν ἀμίλλαισιν
εὐανθέα καὶ Πυθόι στέφανον.

of Zeus. A most bitter end awaits
that sweetness which is unjust.
But grant us, O Loxias[6] luxuriating in your golden hair,
a crown in full blossom   50
in your contests at Pytho as well.

[6] A title of Apollo.

ISTHMIAN 8

The dominant theme of the ode is "deliverance." The prominent treatment of the war ending in the expulsion of the Persians in 479 provides a somber backdrop for the joyful celebration portrayed in the opening five lines and makes it likely that Cleandrus won his Isthmian victory in the following year. Since Thebes had joined with the Persians at the battle of Plataea, whereas Aegina had remained loyal to the Greek cause, lines 16–18 may be seen as justifying a Theban's praise of Aegina by appeal to their past kinship. Many have seen in the myth's broad outlines (a threat to divine order averted by the gods at the cost of death in battle) parallels with events on the historical level (the Persian invasion and the death of Nicocles, the victor's cousin). Because Cleandrus appears to be young, many editors assume that his victory is in the boys' (or youths') division, but that remains uncertain.

One of the young celebrants is told to go to Cleandrus' home and there begin the revel in honor of his victories at the Isthmus and Nemea (1–5). Although grieved, the poet accepts the invitation to compose this song, since it is time to cease from sorrow now that the gods have removed the Persian threat from Hellas (5–12). Although life is full of uncertainty, one must live in the present with confident hopes, especially when one has freedom (12–15a).

A Theban poet is obligated to praise Aegina, for their namesake nymphs were born as twin daughters of Asopus (16–21).

Praise of the Aeacidae for their bravery and good judgment prompts the observation that even the gods recognized their virtue when Zeus and Poseidon were quarreling over marriage to Thetis (21–29). Themis prophesied in the divine council that Thetis was destined to bear a son greater than his father, and urged the gods to marry her to the virtuous Peleus and let her bear his son (30–45). The gods assented, and the youthful exploits of her son Achilles became the subject of poetry (45–48). After providing a catalog of Achilles' victims at Troy, the poet reports that the Muses sang the dirge at his funeral, since the gods deemed him worthy of such tribute (49–60).

Applying the same principle, the poet honors in song the deceased Nicocles, who is his day had been a victorious boxer at the Isthmus (61–65). Cleandrus has lived up to his cousin's achievement and has won previous victories at Megara and Epidaurus (65a–68). He deserves praise for his youthful accomplishments (69–70).

8. ⟨ΚΛΕΑΝΔΡΩΙ ΑΙΓΙΝΗΤΗΙ

ΠΑΓΚΡΑΤΙΩΙ⟩

Α΄ Κλεάνδρῳ τις ἁλικίᾳ
    τε λύτρον εὔδοξον, ὦ νέοι, καμάτων
  πατρὸς ἀγλαὸν Τελεσάρχου παρὰ πρόθυρον
  ἰὼν ἀνεγειρέτω
  κῶμον, Ἰσθμιάδος τε νί-
  κας ἄποινα, καὶ Νεμέᾳ
  5 ἀέθλων ὅτι κράτος ἐξ-
    εὗρε· τῷ καὶ ἐγώ, καίπερ ἀχνύμενος
  5a θυμόν, αἰτέομαι χρυσέαν καλέσαι
    Μοῖσαν. ἐκ μεγάλων δὲ πενθέων λυθέντες
  6a μήτ᾽ ἐν ὀρφανίᾳ πέσωμεν στεφάνων,
    μήτε κάδεα θερά-
    πευε· παυσάμενοι δ᾽ ἀπράκτων κακῶν
  γλυκύ τι δαμωσόμεθα καὶ μετὰ πόνον·
  ἐπειδὴ τὸν ὑπὲρ κεφαλᾶς

inscr. suppl. Heyne: om. BD

8. FOR CLEANDRUS
OF AEGINA

WINNER, PANCRATIUM

In honor of youthful Cleandrus, let one of you go,   Str. 1
    O young men, to the splendid portal
of his father Telesarchus
to awaken the revel, as a glorious requital
for his efforts and a reward
    both for his Isthmian victory and because at Nemea
he gained triumph in the contests.   5
    And so I too, although grieved
at heart, am asked to invoke the golden   5a
Muse. And, having been released from great sorrows,
let us not fall into a dearth of crowns,   6a
nor should you[1] nurse
    your troubles. Let us cease from incurable[2] ills
and sing for the citizens a sweet song even after toil,
since a god has turned away

[1] The poet is addressing himself.
[2] Or *unavailing*.

PINDAR

10 λίθον γε Ταντάλου παρά
    τις ἔτρεψεν ἄμμι θεός,

Β΄ ἀτόλματον Ἑλλάδι μό-
    χθον. ἀλλ᾽ ἐμοὶ δεῖμα μὲν παροιχόμενον
    καρτερὰν ἔπαυσε μέριμναν· τὸ δὲ πρὸ ποδός
    ἄρειον ἀεὶ βλέπειν
    χρῆμα πάν· δόλιος γὰρ αἰ-
      ὼν ἐπ᾽ ἀνδράσι κρέμαται,
15 ἑλίσσων βίου πόρον· ἱ-
      ατὰ δ᾽ ἐστὶ βροτοῖς σύν γ᾽ ἐλευθερίᾳ
15a καὶ τά. χρὴ δ᾽ ἀγαθὰν ἐλπίδ᾽ ἀνδρὶ μέλειν.
    χρὴ δ᾽ ἐν ἑπταπύλοισι Θήβαις τραφέντα
16a Αἰγίνᾳ Χαρίτων ἄωτον προνέμειν,
    πατρὸς οὕνεκα δίδυ-
      μαι γένοντο θύγατρες Ἀσωπίδων
    ὁπλόταται, Ζηνί τε ἅδον βασιλέι.
    ὁ τὰν μὲν παρὰ καλλιρόῳ
20 Δίρκᾳ φιλαρμάτου πόλι-
      ος ᾤκισσεν ἀγεμόνα·

Γ΄ σὲ δ᾽ ἐς νᾶσον Οἰνοπίαν
    ἐνεγκὼν κοιμᾶτο, δῖον ἔνθα τέκες

10 λίθον γε Ταντάλου Bergk: τε Ταντάλου λίθον B^ac D:
γε Ταντάλου λίθον B^pc(schol.)BD: τὸν Ταντάλου λίθον
Heimsoeth   11 παροιχόμενον Benedictus: παροιχομένων
BDΠ²⁴   13 βλέπειν Π²⁴: om. BD
    17 Ἀσωπίδων Heyne: Ἀσωπίδων θ᾽ D

210

from over our heads   10
    the very rock of Tantalus,[3]

that unbearable labor for Hellas.   Str. 2
    But for me the passing of fear has halted
my strong anxiety;[4] and it is always best to look
at each thing
right at our feet, for over men hangs
    a treacherous time
as it unrolls the course of life, but even this   15
    can be healed for mortals so long as they have
freedom. A man must cherish good hope.   15a
And one raised in seven-gated Thebes
must offer the choicest gift of the Graces to Aegina,   16a
because these[5] were twins, the youngest daughters
    of their father Asopus,
and they found favor with king Zeus,
who established one beside the beautiful stream
of Dirce to dwell as mistress   20
    of a chariot-loving city;

but you he brought to the island of Oenopia[6]   Str. 3
    and slept with you, and there you bore divine

[3] Tantalus was punished by living in fear of a boulder suspended above his head (cf. *Ol.* 1.57–58), here a metaphor for the Persian invasion of 480.   [4] παροιχομένων, found in the MSS and P. Oxy. 2439, gives a strained reading: "the fear of evils (now) gone halted my strong endeavor (i.e. as a poet)."

[5] The eponymous nymphs Thebe and Aegina. Asopus is a Boeotian river.   [6] Like Oenona, an ancient name for Aegina reflecting its viticulture.

Αἰακὸν βαρυσφαράγῳ πατρὶ κεδνότατον
ἐπιχθονίων· ὃ καί
δαιμόνεσσι δίκας ἐπεί-
ραινε· τοῦ μὲν ἀντίθεοι
25 ἀρίστευον υἱέες υἱ-
έων τ᾽ ἀρηίφιλοι παῖδες ἀνορέᾳ
25a χάλκεον στονόεντ᾽ ἀμφέπειν ὅμαδον,
σώφρονές τ᾽ ἐγένοντο πινυτοί τε θυμόν.
26a ταῦτα καὶ μακάρων ἐμέμναντ᾽ ἀγοραί,
Ζεὺς ὅτ᾽ ἀμφὶ Θέτιος
ἀγλαός τ᾽ ἔρισαν Ποσειδὰν γάμῳ,
ἄλοχον εὐειδέα θέλων ἑκάτερος
ἐὰν ἔμμεν· ἔρως γὰρ ἔχεν.
30 ἀλλ᾽ οὔ σφιν ἄμβροτοι τέλε-
σαν εὐνὰν θεῶν πραπίδες,

Δ΄ ἐπεὶ θεσφάτων ⟨ἐπ⟩άκου-
σαν· εἶπε δ᾽ εὔβουλος ἐν μέσοισι Θέμις,
εἵνεκεν πεπρωμένον ἦν, φέρτερον πατέρος
ἄνακτα γόνον τεκεῖν
ποντίαν θεόν, ὃς κεραυ-
νοῦ τε κρέσσον ἄλλο βέλος
35 διώξει χερὶ τριόδον-
τός τ᾽ ἀμαιμακέτου, Ζηνὶ μισγομέναν

27 ἔρισαν Benedictus: ἔρισας D
29 ἔχεν E. Schmid cum paraphr. (κατεῖχεν): ἔσχεν D
31 ἐπάκουσάν Triclinius: ἤκουσαν D
32 εἵνεκεν D: οὔνεκεν Donaldson

Aeacus, dearest of mortals to his loud-thundering
father, a man who
settled disputes even for the gods.[7]
   His god-like sons
and their war-loving sons[8]   25
   were the foremost in courage
to tend the groaning din of bronze war,   25a
and they were wise and prudent at heart.
Even the assembly of the blessed gods remembered this,   26a
when Zeus and splendid Poseidon
   quarreled over marriage to Thetis,
each wishing her to be his own beautiful
wife, because love held them in its grip.
But the gods' immortal minds   30
   did not accomplish that wedlock for them,

when they heard what was ordained.   Str. 4
   For wise-counseling Themis said in their midst
that it was fated for the goddess of the sea
to bear a royal son mightier
than his father, who would wield
   another kind of weapon
stronger than the thunderbolt   35
   or the tireless trident, if she was joined

[7] Although Aeacus settled disputes for men (Paus. 1.39.6) and became a judge in the underworld, no arbitration for gods is otherwise known.   [8] His sons were Peleus and Telamon; his grandsons, Achilles and Ajax.

32–33 πατέρος ἄνακτα γόνον Ahlwardt: γόνον ἄνακτα πατρὸς D   35 Ζηνὶ Triclinius: διὶ D

35a ἢ Διὸς παρ' ἀδελφεοῖσιν. "ἀλλὰ τὰ μέν
παύσατε· βροτέων δὲ λεχέων τυχοῖσα
36a υἱὸν εἰσιδέτω θανόντ' ἐν πολέμῳ,
χεῖρας Ἄρεΐ <τ'> ἐν-
αλίγκιον στεροπαῖσί τ' ἀκμὰν ποδῶν.
τὸ μὲν ἐμόν, Πηλέι γέρας θεόμορον
ὀπάσσαι γάμου Αἰακίδᾳ,
40 ὅν τ' εὐσεβέστατον φάτις
Ἰαολκοῦ τράφειν πεδίον·

Ε´ ἰόντων δ' ἐς ἄφθιτον ἄν-
τρον εὐθὺς Χείρωνος αὐτίκ' ἀγγελίαι·
μηδὲ Νηρέος θυγάτηρ νεικέων πέταλα
δὶς ἐγγυαλιζέτω
ἄμμιν· ἐν διχομηνίδες-
σιν δὲ ἑσπέραις ἐρατόν
45 λύοι κεν χαλινὸν ὑφ' ἥ-
ρωι παρθενίας." ὣς φάτο Κρονίδαις
45a ἐννέποισα θεά· τοὶ δ' ἐπὶ γλεφάροις
νεῦσαν ἀθανάτοισιν· ἐπέων δὲ καρπός
46a οὐ κατέφθινε. φαντὶ γὰρ ξύν' ἀλέγειν
καὶ γάμον Θέτιος ἄ-
νακτα, καὶ νεαρὰν ἔδειξαν σοφῶν

37 <τ'> suppl. Boeckh
38–39 Πηλέι γέρας θεόμορον ὀπάσσαι γάμου Αἰακίδᾳ
Hermann: Πηλεῖ θεάμοιρον ὀπάσαι γάμου Αἰακίδᾳ γέρας D
40 φάτις Bothe: φασὶν D

214

to Zeus or to Zeus' brothers. "Come, stop this.   35a
Let her win a mortal's bed
and see her son die in war,   36a
a match for Ares with his hands,
    and like lightning in the power of his feet.
My advice is to grant the divine gift
of this marriage to Aeacus' son Peleus,
who is said to be the most pious man   40
    the plain of Iolcus has reared.

Let the announcement go without delay   Str. 5
    straight to the immortal cave of Chiron,[9]
and do not allow Nereus' daughter
to place in our hands the leaves of strife
a second time. But during the evenings
    of a full moon,[10] let her loosen
the lovely bridle of her virginity   45
    in submission to that hero." Thus spoke the goddess
as she addressed Cronus' sons, and they nodded assent   45a
with their immortal brows. The fruit of her words
did not wither away, for they say that the lord[11]   46a
joined the others in favoring that marriage of Thetis,
    and the mouths of wise poets have revealed

[9] Chiron married Peleus and Thetis (cf. *Nem.* 3.56–57).

[10] A favored time for celebrating great events, whether a noble marriage (cf. Eur. *IA* 717) or games (cf. *Ol.* 3.19–20 and *Ol.* 10.73–75).

[11] Zeus.

στόματ᾽ ἀπείροισιν ἀρετὰν Ἀχιλέος·
ὃ καὶ Μύσιον ἀμπελόεν
50 αἵμαξε Τηλέφου μέλα-
νι ῥαίνων φόνῳ πεδίον

Ϝ´ γεφύρωσέ τ᾽ Ἀτρεΐδαι-
σι νόστον, Ἑλέναν τ᾽ ἐλύσατο, Τροΐας
ἶνας ἐκταμὼν δορί, ταί νιν ῥύοντό ποτε
μάχας ἐναριμβρότου
ἔργον ἐν πεδίῳ κορύσ-
σοντα, Μέμνονός τε βίαν
55 ὑπέρθυμον Ἕκτορά τ᾽ ἄλ-
λους τ᾽ ἀριστέας· οἷς δῶμα Φερσεφόνας
55a μανύων Ἀχιλεύς, οὖρος Αἰακιδᾶν,
Αἴγιναν σφετέραν τε ῥίζαν πρόφαινεν.
56a τὸν μὲν οὐδὲ θανόντ᾽ ἀοιδαί γ᾽ ἔλιπον,
ἀλλά οἱ παρά τε πυ-
ρὰν τάφον θ᾽ Ἑλικώνιαι παρθένοι
στάν, ἐπὶ θρῆνόν τε πολύφαμον ἔχεαν.
ἔδοξ᾽ ἦρα καὶ ἀθανάτοις,
60 ἐσλόν γε φῶτα καὶ φθίμε-
νον ὕμνοις θεᾶν διδόμεν.

56a οὐδὲ Boeckh: οὔτε D | γ᾽ ἔλιπον Hermann: ἔλιπον D:
ἐπέλιπον Snell
60 ἐσλόν γε Callierges: ἐς λόγον γε D

216

Achilles' youthful excellence to those unaware of it.[12]
He also bloodied the vine-clad
plain of Mysia   50
    with the dark drops of Telephus' gore,

he bridged a return home   Str. 6
    for the Atreidae and rescued Helen,
after cutting out Troy's sinews[13] with his spear; they
had previously checked him
from marshaling the work
    of man-slaying battle in the plain: proud
and mighty Memnon, Hector, and other champions,   55
    to whom Achilles, guardian of the Aeacidae,
showed the house of Persephone,   55a
and made famous Aegina and his own descent.
Not even when he died did songs abandon him,   56a
but the Heliconian maidens stood beside
    his pyre and his tomb
and poured over him their dirge of many voices.[14]
Indeed, the immortals too thought it best
to entrust a brave man like that, even though dead,   60
    to the hymns of the goddesses.

[12] For his youthful exploits, see *Nem.* 3.43–52.
[13] I.e. defenders who sustained Troy, listed below.
[14] For the dirge of the Muses (Heliconian maidens) over
Achilles, see *Od.* 24.60–61, where ἀμειβόμεναι ὀπὶ καλῇ corre-
sponds to πολύφαμον.

217

PINDAR

Ζ΄ τὸ καὶ νῦν φέρει λόγον, ἔσ-
συταί τε Μοισαῖον ἅρμα Νικοκλέος
μνᾶμα πυγμάχου κελαδῆσαι. γεραίρετέ νιν,
ὃς Ἴσθμιον ἂν νάπος
Δωρίων ἔλαχεν σελί-
νων· ἐπεὶ περικτίονας
65 ἐνίκασε δή ποτε καὶ
κεῖνος ἄνδρας ἀφύκτῳ χερὶ κλονέων.
65a τὸν μὲν οὐ κατελέγχει κριτοῦ γενεά
πατραδελφεοῦ· ἁλίκων τῷ τις ἁβρόν
66a ἀμφὶ παγκρατίου Κλεάνδρῳ πλεκέτω
μυρσίνας στέφανον, ἐ-
πεί νιν Ἀλκαθόου τ' ἀγὼν σὺν τύχᾳ
ἐν Ἐπιδαύρῳ τε νεότας δέκετο πρίν·
τὸν αἰνεῖν ἀγαθῷ παρέχει·
70 ἥβαν γὰρ οὐκ ἄπειρον ὑ-
πὸ χειᾷ καλῶν δάμασεν.

63 ἂν νάπος Hermann: ἀνάπος D
65 ἀφύκτῳ Triclinius: ἀφύκτε D: ἀφύκτᾳ Maas
69 παρέχει Triclinius: παρέχειν D
70 χειᾷ Triclinius: χόα πω D: κόλπῳ Theiler: κόλπου D. C.
Young

218

That principle holds true now as well,   Str. 7
    and the Muses' chariot is speeding forward
to sing a memorial to the boxer Nicocles.[15] Praise him,[16]
who won the Dorian parsley
in the Isthmian glen,
    since that man too in his day
conquered the men who lived around him,   65
    by driving them back with his inescapable hand.
Upon him the offspring[17] of his father's noble brother   65a
casts no shame. Therefore, let one of his comrades,
in honor of the pancratium, weave for Cleandrus   66a
a luxurious crown of myrtle,
    since the contest of Alcathoös[18] and the youth
in Epidaurus welcomed him before with good fortune.
A good man has the means to praise him,
for he has not suppressed in a hole   70
    a youth without experience of noble deeds.

[15] Cleandrus' cousin (cf. 65a).

[16] The plural imperative is addressed to the celebrants (and perhaps also the Muses).

[17] Cleandrus.

[18] The games in honor of Alcathoös, son of Pelops, were held at Megara. A crown of myrtle was evidently the prize there or at the Asclepieia in Epidaurus.

ISTHMIAN 9

These eight dactylo-epitritic verses from the opening of an epinician for an Aeginetan are preserved in the Laurentian MS (D) after *Isth.* 8. They contain topics often found in Pindar's other odes to Aeginetans.

9. ‹. . . ΑΙΓΙΝΗΤΗΙ›

Κλεινὸς Αἰακοῦ λόγος, κλεινὰ δὲ καὶ ναυ-
  σικλυτὸς Αἴγινα· σὺν θεῶν δέ νιν αἴσᾳ
Ὕλλου τε καὶ Αἰγιμιοῦ
Δωριεὺς ἐλθὼν στρατός
ἐκτίσσατο· τῶν μὲν ὑπὸ στάθμᾳ νέμονται
5 οὐ θέμιν οὐδὲ δίκαν
ξείνων ὑπερβαίνοντες· οἷοι δ᾽ ἀρετάν
δελφῖνες ἐν πόντῳ, ταμίαι τε σοφοί
Μοισᾶν ἀγωνίων τ᾽ ἀέθλων.

4 ἐκτίσσατο· τῶν Hermann: ἐκτήσατο· τὰ D

9. FOR AN UNKNOWN

VICTOR FROM AEGINA

Famous is the story of Aeacus, and famous too is Aegina,   Str.
    renowned for her navy. By the destiny of the gods
the Dorian army of Hyllus
and of Aegimius came and
founded her.[1] Her citizens live in obedience to their
    rule,
transgressing neither divine law nor justice   5
due to strangers. As for their excellence,
they are like dolphins in the sea, and wise stewards
of the Muses and of athletic contests.

[1] For the Dorian conquest of southern Greece, see *Pyth.*
1.61–65.

SELECTED FRAGMENTS

INTRODUCTION

Apart from eight lines of a ninth *Isthmian* ode preserved in codex D, fragments of Pindar's poems have come to us from two sources: brief quotations by ancient authors or copies found on papyrus, particularly on those from Oxyrhynchus.

Since the monumental edition of Boeckh (1821), the fragments of the thirteen books of Pindar's non-epinician poems have been arranged according to the list of works given in the Ambrosian life (1.3.6–9 Drachmann): hymns, paeans, dithyrambs (2 books), prosodia (2), partheneia (2), poems separate from the partheneia, hyporchemata (2), encomia, and threnoi.[1]

In making selections for this edition I have included fragments generally believed to be from Pindar that (1) offer sufficient continuous text to make sense; (2) treat a god or other important subject; (3) are part of a longer poem; or (4) have a well-attested Nachleben. I have supplied very selective critical notes; for a full account readers are re-

---

[1] The list provided by P. Oxy. 2438.36–39 (first published in 1961 and emended by I. Gallo) gives a different order and omits one book of hyporchemata: dithyrambs (2), prosodia (2), paeans, partheneia (3), encomia (in which are also skolia), hymns, hyporchemata, and threnoi.

ferred to the edition of H. Maehler (1989), upon which the present work is principally based, and A. Turyn (1952).

In the case of quotations by ancient authors, I have supplied enough context to make clear the point of the citation or to add further information. Although the steady accumulation of new fragments and new classifications of already existing ones have made renumbering desirable, I have followed that of Maehler's edition.

The symbol ⊗ indicates the beginning or end of a fragmentary poem. For papyri appearing in *The Oxyrhynchus Papyri*, I provide the volume and year. On the Greek side Pindaric scholia are cited according to Heyne's numeration (used by Drachmann), on the English side according to Maehler's.

ΕΠΙΝΙΚΟΙ ΙΣΘΜΙΟΝΙΚΑΙΣ

2,3   ΚΑΣΜΥΛΩΙ ΡΟΔΙΩΙ ΠΥΚΤΩΙ

2 Schol. Lucian. *dial. mort.* 10 p. 255.23 Rabe τοῦτον
γοῦν τὸν Τροφώνιον καὶ τὸν ἄλλον (ἀδελφὸν coni.
Rabe) μέμνηται Πίνδαρος ἐν τῇ ᾠδῇ τῶν Ἰσθμιονικῶν
τῇ εἰς Κασμύλον (Rohde: κασμηλον cod.) Ῥόδιον
πύκτην· ἱστορεῖ δὲ οὕτως (Rohde: οὗτος cod.)·

ὁ δ' ἐθέλων τε καὶ δυνάμενος ἁβρὰ πάσχειν
τὰν Ἀγαμήδεϊ Τροφωνίῳ θ' Ἑκαταβόλου
συμβουλίαν λαβών . . .

2 Τρεφωνίῳ Schroeder

3 Plut. *consol. Apoll.* 14.109A καὶ περὶ Ἀγαμήδους δὲ
καὶ Τροφωνίου φησὶ Πίνδαρος τὸν νεὼν τὸν ἐν Δελ-
φοῖς οἰκοδομήσαντας αἰτεῖν παρὰ τοῦ Ἀπόλλωνος
μισθόν, τὸν δ' αὐτοῖς ἐπαγγείλασθαι εἰς ἑβδόμην
ἡμέραν ἀποδώσειν, ἐν τοσούτῳ δ' εὐωχεῖσθαι παρα-
κελεύσασθαι· τοὺς δὲ ποιήσαντας τὸ προσταχθὲν τῇ
ἑβδόμῃ νυκτὶ κατακοιμηθέντας τελευτῆσαι.

ODES FOR ISTHMIAN
VICTORS

2,3   FOR CASMYLUS OF RHODES, BOXER

2 Scholion on Lucian, *Dialogues of the Dead*. "Pindar mentions this Trophonius and the other (*or* his brother) in the Isthmian ode to Casmylus the Rhodian boxer.[1] He tells the following":

> He who is willing and able to live luxuriously,
> by taking the advice of the Far-Shooter[2]
> given to Agamedes and Trophonius[3]

[1] Son of Euagoras, contemporary of Diagoras of Rhodes (cf. *Ol.* 7); see also A.P. 16.23 (attributed to Simonides).
[2] Apollo.
[3] Builders of Apollo's temple at Delphi.

3 Plutarch, *Letter of Consolation to Apollonius*. "And of Agamedes and Trophonius Pindar says that after building the temple in Delphi they asked for their wages from Apollo, who promised to pay them on the seventh day and encouraged them to feast in the meantime. They did what they were ordered, and on the seventh night, after going to sleep, they died."

5 Apollon. *synt.* 2.114 p. 213.14 Uhlig (idem *de pron.* p. 48.20 Schneider) ἀλλὰ καὶ τὸ ἐν Ἰσθμιονίκαις Πινδάρου ἐτάραξεν τοὺς ὑπομνηματισαμένους·

Αἰολίδαν δὲ Σίσυφον κέλοντο
ᾧ παιδὶ τηλέφαντον ὄρσαι
γέρας φθιμένῳ Μελικέρτᾳ

schol. Pind. *Isth.* argum. a (3.192.13 Drachmann) χορεύουσαι τοίνυν ποτὲ αἱ Νηρεΐδες ἐπεφάνησαν τῷ Σισύφῳ καὶ ἐκέλευσαν εἰς τιμὴν τοῦ Μελικέρτου ἄγειν τὰ Ἴσθμια.

5 Apollonius Dyscolus, *On Syntax*. "But this too in Pindar's *Isthmians* confounded the commentators":

> They ordered Sisyphus, son of Aeolus,
> to raise up a far-shining honor[4]
> for his dead son, Melicertes.

[4] I.e. to institute the Isthmian games. Melicertes is elsewhere the son of Athamas and Ino (cf. Apollodorus 1.9.1).

Scholion, *Introduction to the Isthmian Odes*. "And so, a chorus of Nereids once appeared to Sisyphus and ordered him to conduct the Isthmian games in honor of Melicertes."

ΥΜΝΟΙ

29–35   Hymn. 1

<ΘΗΒΑΙΟΙΣ ΕΙΣ ΔΙΑ?>

29 Ps.-Lucian. *encom. Demosth.* 19 (3.371 Jacobitz) ὥσπερ οὖν ὁ Πίνδαρος ἐπὶ πολλὰ τῷ νῷ τραπόμενος οὕτως πως ἠπόρηκεν·

A΄ 	Ἰσμηνὸν ἢ χρυσαλάκατον Μελίαν
	ἢ Κάδμον ἢ Σπαρτῶν ἱερὸν γένος ἀνδρῶν
	ἢ τὰν κυανάμπυκα Θήβαν
		ἢ τὸ πάντολμον σθένος Ἡρακλέος
5 	ἢ τὰν Διωνύσου πολυγαθέα τιμὰν
	ἢ γάμον λευκωλένου Ἁρμονίας
	ὑμνήσομεν;

HYMNS

29–35   Hymn 1

FOR THE THEBANS IN HONOR OF ZEUS(?)

This hymn, which opened Pindar's book of hymns, consists
of portions pieced together from many sources. Its sub-
jects included an opening catalog of famous Thebans, the
marriage of Cadmus and Harmonia, and the unions of
Zeus that produced the Horae, Artemis and Apollo, and
Athena. For an overview, see B. Snell, "Pindar's Hymn to
Zeus," in *The Discovery of the Mind*, tr. T. G. Rosenmeyer
(Harvard 1953).

29 Ps.-Lucian, *In Praise of Demosthenes.* "After Pindar
turned his mind to many topics, he expressed his perplex-
ity thus":

> Shall it be Ismenus, or Melia of the golden spindle,
> or Cadmus, or the holy race of the Spartoi,
> or Thebe of the dark-blue fillet,
>   or the all-daring strength of Heracles,
> or the wondrous honor of Dionysus,   5
>   or the marriage of white-armed Harmonia
>   that we shall hymn?

PINDAR

schol. p. 225.27 Rabe ἀρχαὶ ταῦτα τῶν Πινδάρου τοῦ
μελοποιοῦ ὕμνων. schol. Pind. *Nem.* 10.1a ὁ δὲ Πίν-
δαρος ὅτε βούλοιτο ἐπαινεῖν τὰς πατρίδας τῶν νενικη-
κότων, ἀθροίζειν εἴωθε τὰ πεπραγμένα ταῖς πόλεσι
περιφανῆ, καθὼς ἐν τῇ ᾠδῇ, ἧς ἡ ἀρχή· Ἰσμηνὸν—
Μελίαν. Plut. *de glor. Ath.* 4.347F ἡ δὲ Κόριννα τὸν
Πίνδαρον, ὄντα νέον ἔτι καὶ τῇ λογιότητι σοβαρῶς
χρώμενον, ἐνουθέτησεν ὡς ἄμουσον ὄντα καὶ μὴ ποι-
οῦντα μύθους, ὃ τῆς ποιητικῆς ἔργον εἶναι συμβέβη-
κε, γλώττας δὲ καὶ καταχρήσεις καὶ μεταφράσεις καὶ
μέλη καὶ ῥυθμοὺς ἡδύσματα τοῖς πράγμασιν ὑπο-
τιθέντα. σφόδρ᾽ οὖν ὁ Πίνδαρος ἐπιστήσας τοῖς λε-
γομένοις ἐποίησεν ἐκεῖνο τὸ μέλος (vv. 1, 2, 4 et 5).
δειξαμένου δὲ τῇ Κορίννῃ γελάσασα ἐκείνη τῇ χειρὶ
δεῖν ἔφη σπείρειν, ἀλλὰ μὴ ὅλῳ τῷ θυλάκῳ.

32 Aristid. *or.* 3.620 (1.498 Lenz-Behr) κἂν τοῖς ὕμνοις
διεξιὼν περὶ τῶν ἐν ἅπαντι τῷ χρόνῳ συμβαινόντων
παθημάτων τοῖς ἀνθρώποις καὶ τῆς μεταβολῆς τὸν
Κάδμον φησὶν ἀκοῦσαι τοῦ Ἀπόλλωνος μουσικὰν
ὀρθὰν ἐπιδεικνυμένου. Plut. *de Pyth. orac.* 6.397A ὁ δὲ
Πίνδαρος "ἀκοῦσαι," φησί, "τοῦ θεοῦ τὸν Κάδμον
ἐπιδεικνυμένου μουσικὰν ὀρθάν," οὐχ ἡδεῖαν οὐδὲ
τρυφερὰν οὐδ᾽ ἐπικεκλασμένην τοῖς μέλεσιν.

μουσικὰν ὀρθὰν ἐπιδεικνυμένου

Scholion on Ps.-Lucian *ad loc.* "These are the first lines of the hymns of Pindar the lyric poet." Scholion on *Nem.* 10.1. "When Pindar wished to praise the victors' homelands, he was in the habit of cataloguing the conspicuous accomplishments of the cities, as in the ode which begins with 'Shall it be Ismenus, or Melia.'" Plutarch, *Were the Athenians More Famous in War or in Wisdom?* "Corinna warned Pindar, who was still young and prided himself on his eloquence, that he was unpoetic for not telling myths, which are the proper business of poetry, but that he supported his works with unusual words, strange usages, paraphrases, songs, and rhythms, which are just embellishments of the subject matter. So Pindar, taking her words to heart, composed that famous poem, 'Shall it be Ismenus . . . ?' When he showed it to her, she laughed and said that one should sow with the hand, not with the whole sack."

32 Aristides, *Oration* 3 (*In Defense of the Four*). "And even in the hymns, when (Pindar) narrates the sufferings and change of fortune that befall men throughout the whole of time, he says that Cadmus heard Apollo performing correct music." Plutarch, *The Oracles at Delphi.* "Pindar says, 'Cadmus heard the god performing correct music,' not sweet nor voluptuous nor with its melodies suddenly changing."

performing correct music

PINDAR

30 Clem. Alex. *strom.* 5.14.137.1 Πίνδαρος δὲ ἄντικρυς
καὶ σωτῆρα Δία συνοικοῦντα Θέμιδι εἰσάγει, βασιλέα
σωτῆρα δίκαιον ἑρμηνεύων ὧδέ πως·

πρῶτον μὲν εὔβουλον Θέμιν οὐρανίαν
χρυσέαισιν ἵπποις Ὠκεανοῦ παρὰ παγὰν
Μοῖραι ποτὶ κλίμακα σεμνὰν
    ἆγον Οὐλύμπου λιπαρὰν καθ᾽ ὁδὸν
5   σωτῆρος ἀρχαίαν ἄλοχον Διὸς ἔμμεν·
ἁ δὲ τὰς χρυσάμπυκας ἀγλαοκάρ-
πους τίκτεν ἀλαθέας Ὥρας.

7 ἀλαθέας Ὥρας Boeckh ex Hesychio (α 2733): ἀγαθὰ
σωτῆρας Clemens

33 Plut. *quaest. Plat.* 8.4.3.1007Β ἔνιοι τῶν Στωικῶν . . .
τὴν δ᾽ οὐσίαν αὐτοῦ (sc. τοῦ χρόνου) καὶ τὴν δύναμιν
οὐ συνορῶντες, ἣν ὅ γε Πίνδαρος ἔοικεν οὐ φαύλως
ὑπονοῶν εἰπεῖν·

ἄνα⟨κτα⟩ τὸν πάντων ὑπερ-
βάλλοντα Χρόνον μακάρων

1 ἄνα⟨κτα⟩ suppl. Heyne

33b Clem. Alex. *strom.* 1.21.107.2 (2.69 Stählin) Πίνδα-
ρος γράφει·

ἐν χρόνῳ δ᾽ ἔγεντ᾽ Ἀπόλλων

236

30 Clement of Alexandria, *Miscellanies*. "Pindar right away introduces Zeus Savior's marriage to Themis, calling him a just, savior king in these words":

> First did the Fates bring wise-counseling, heavenly
>   Themis
> on golden horses from the springs of Oceanus
> along a shining road
>   to the hallowed stair of Olympus
> to be the primordial wife of Zeus Savior;   5
>   and she bore the golden-filleted
>   bearers of splendid fruit, the ever-true Horae.[5]

[5] According to Hes. *Th.* 901–904 Themis bore both the Horae and the Fates to Zeus

33 Plutarch, *Platonic Questions*. "Some Stoics . . . not realizing its (time's) essence and power, which Pindar seems to have surmised astutely when he said":

> Time, the lord surpassing
>   all the blessed gods

33b Clement of Alexandria, *Miscellanies*. "Pindar writes":

> in the course of time Apollo was born

PINDAR

33c Theophr. *phys. opin. fr.* 12 (*Doxogr.* p. 487 Diels) ap. Ps.-Philon. περὶ ἀφθαρσίας κόσμου 23 (6.109 Cohn-Wendland) Πίνδαρος ἐπὶ τῆς Δήλου φησί·

χαῖρ᾽, ὦ θεοδμάτα, λιπαροπλοκάμου
παίδεσσι Λατοῦς ἱμεροέστατον ἔρνος,
πόντου θύγατερ, χθονὸς εὐρεί-
ας ἀκίνητον τέρας, ἄν τε βροτοί
5   Δᾶλον κικλήσκοισιν, μάκαρες δ᾽ ἐν Ὀλύμπῳ
τηλέφαντον κυανέας χθονὸς ἄστρον.

2 παίδεσσι Boeckh: παῖδ᾽ οἱ M: παῖδες οἱ UHP
6 τηλέφαντον Bergk: τηλέφατον codd.

33d PSI 14.1391, vv. 7–11. Strabo 10.5.2 φησὶν ὁ Πίνδαρος·

ἦν γὰρ τὸ πάροιθε φορητὰ
κυμάτεσσιν παντοδαπῶν ἀνέμων
ῥιπαῖσιν· ἀλλ᾽ ἁ Κοιογενὴς ὁπότ᾽ ὠδί-
νεσσι θυίοισ᾽ ἀγχιτόκοις ἐπέβα
5   νιν, δὴ τότε τέσσαρες ὀρθαί
πρέμνων ἀπώρουσαν χθονίων,
ἂν δ᾽ ἐπικράνοις σχέθον
πέτραν ἀδαμαντοπέδιλοι
κίονες, ἔνθα τεκοῖ-
10   σ᾽ εὐδαίμον᾽ ἐπόψατο γένναν.
.]. . ισ[

238

33c Theophrastus, *Doctrines of the Natural Philosophers.* "Pindar says of Delos":

> Hail, O heaven-built island, offshoot most desirable
> to the children[6] of shining-haired Leto,
> daughter of the sea,[7] immobile marvel
>   of the broad earth, whom mortals
> call Delos, but the blessed gods on Olympus   5
>   call the far-shining star[8] of the dark-blue earth.

[6] Apollo and Artemis, who were born on Delos.
[7] Delos was born from the sea, like Rhodes (cf. *Ol.* 7).
[8] Asteria ("star") was an old name for Delos (cf. *Pae.* 5.42).

33d Strabo 10.5.2. "Pindar says (of Delos)":

> For previously it was carried
>   on the waves by the blasts of winds
> of all sorts. But when Coeus' daughter,[9]
>   frantic with the pains of approaching birth,
>   set foot on it, then did four upright columns   5
> with bases of adamant rise
> from their foundations in the earth
> and on their capitals support
> the rock. There, after giving birth,
>   she beheld her blessed offspring.   10

[9] Leto.

---

2 ⟨τ'⟩ ἀνέμων suppl. Schneider
3 κοιογενὴς V: καιογενὴς rell.
4–5 ἐπέβα νιν V: ἐπιβαίνειν rell.

34 Heph. p. 51.16 Consbruch ἀντεστραμμένον δέ ἐστι τούτῳ (sc. τῷ Πλατωνικῷ) τὸ Πινδαρικὸν καλούμενον·

ὃς καὶ τυπεὶς ἁγνῷ πελέκει τέκετο ξαν-
    θὰν Ἀθάναν

35 Heph. p. 51.7 Consbruch

κείνων λυθέντες σαῖς ὑπὸ χερσίν, ἄναξ

31 Aristid. *or.* 2.420 (1.277 Lenz-Behr) Πίνδαρος . . . ἐν Διὸς γάμῳ καὶ τοὺς θεοὺς αὐτούς φησιν ἐρομένου τοῦ Διός, εἴ του δέοιντο, αἰτῆσαι ποιήσασθαί τινας αὐτῷ θεούς, οἵτινες τὰ μεγάλα ταῦτα ἔργα καὶ πᾶσάν γε δὴ τὴν ἐκείνου κατασκευὴν κατακοσμήσουσι λόγοις καὶ μουσικῇ.

35a Aristid. *or.* 43.30 (2.347 Keil) αὐτὸς (sc. Ζεὺς) ἂν μόνος εἰπὼν ἃ χρὴ περὶ αὑτοῦ, θεὸς ἅτε

πλέον τι λαχών·

τοῦτο γὰρ οὖν Πινδάρῳ κάλλιον ἢ ἄλλ᾽ ὁτιοῦν ὁτῳοῦν εἴρηται περὶ Διός.

35b Plut. *consol. Apoll.* 28.116D ὁ δὲ Πίνδαρός (φη-
    σιν)·

σοφοὶ δὲ καὶ τὸ μηδὲν ἄγαν ἔπος αἴνη-
    σαν περισσῶς

240

34 Hephaestion, *Handbook on Meters*. "The converse of that (i.e. the Platonic *metron*) is this one called the 'Pindaric'":

who,[10] struck with a sacred ax, gave birth
    to fair-haired Athena

[10] Zeus.

35 The Same.

having been released from them[11] by your hands, lord

[11] The Titans' bonds (cf. *Pyth.* 4.291).

31 Aristides, *Oration* 2 (*In Defense of Oratory*). "Pindar . . . says in the marriage of Zeus, that when he asked the gods themselves if they needed anything, they requested that he create for himself some gods,[12] who would adorn with words and music those great works and all those arrangements of his."

[12] I.e. the Muses.

35a Aristides, *Oration* 43 (*To Zeus*). "Zeus . . . alone could speak correctly about himself—as a god

allotted a larger share,

for this expression by Pindar surpasses anything else said by anyone about Zeus."

35b Plutarch, *Letter of Consolation to Apollonius*. "Pindar says":

the wise have also given surpassing praise
    to the saying, "nothing too much"

35c Heliod. ap. Priscian. *Gr. Lat.* 3.428.17 Keil idem (sc. Heliodorus) ostendit Pindarum etiam trisyllabos in fine versus posuisse,

νόμων ἀκούοντες θεόδματον κέλαδον

36 ΕΙΣ ΑΜΜΩΝΑ

Schol. Pind. *Pyth.* 9.90bc τὴν Λιβύην Διὸς κῆπον λέγει (*Pyth.* 9.53) . . . διὰ τὸ τὸν Ἄμμωνα Δία νομίζεσθαι·

⊗   Ἄμμων Ὀλύμπου δέσποτα

37 ΕΙΣ ΠΕΡΣΕΦΟΝΗΝ

vit. Pind. Ambr. (1.2.9 Drachmann) ἡ Δημήτηρ ὄναρ ἐπιστᾶσα αὐτῷ ἐμέμψατο ὅτι μόνην τῶν θεῶν οὐχ ὕμνησεν· ὁ δ᾽ εἰς αὐτὴν ἐποίησε ποίημα οὗ ἡ ἀρχή·

⊗   Πότνια θεσμοφόρε χρυσάνιον

38 Aristid. *or.* 3.466 (1.451 Lenz-Behr) πάνυ γὰρ μετ᾽ ἀληθείας (Πίνδαρος) ὕμνησεν·

ἐν ἔργμασιν δὲ νικᾷ τύχα,
οὐ σθένος

242

35c Priscian, *Grammar.* "The same Heliodorus[13] shows that Pindar put even three syllables (viz. tribrachs) at the end of a verse":

hearing the divinely fashioned sound of melodies

[13] Metrician, 1st cent. A.D. This quotation is an iambic trimeter that concludes with ◡◡◡ instead of the usual ◡–.

36 IN HONOR OF AMMON

Scholion on *Pyth.* 9.53. "He calls Libya the garden of Zeus . . . because Ammon is considered to be Zeus":

Ammon, master of Olympus

37 IN HONOR OF PERSEPHONE

The Ambrosian Life of Pindar. "Demeter appeared to him in a dream and criticized him because she was the only goddess he had not hymned. He composed a poem for her which begins":

O law-bringing mistress of the golden reins[14]

[14] According to Pausanias, the epithet χρυσάνιον applies to Hades: hence Boeckh conjectured χρυσανίου ⟨Ἄιδου δάμαρ⟩ "wife of Hades of the golden reins." The Ambrosian life and Eustathius ascribe the ode to Demeter; Pausanias to Persephone.

38 Aristides, *Oration* 3 (*In Defense of the Four*). "In complete truth Pindar sang":

in deeds fortune prevails,
not strength

42 Stob. *flor.* 4.45.1 (5.993 Wachsmuth-Hense) Πινδά-
ρου ὕμνων·

   . . . ἀλλοτρίοισιν μὴ προφαίνειν, τίς φέρεται
μόχθος ἄμμιν· τοῦτό γέ τοι ἐρέω·
καλῶν μὲν ὦν μοῖράν τε τερπνῶν
ἐς μέσον χρὴ παντὶ λαῷ
5 δεικνύναι· εἰ δέ τις ἀνθρώ-
    ποισι θεόσδοτος ἀτλάτα κακότας
προστύχῃ, ταύταν σκότει κρύπτειν ἔοικεν.

6 ἀτλάτα κακότας Boeckh: ἀτληκηκότας Vind.

43 Athen. 12.7.513C τοιοῦτός ἐστιν καὶ (Ἀμφιάραος)
ὁ παραινῶν Ἀμφιλόχῳ τῷ παιδί·

   "ὦ τέκνον, ποντίου θηρὸς πετραίου
χρωτὶ μάλιστα νόον
προσφέρων πάσαις πολίεσσιν ὁμίλει·
τῷ παρεόντι δ᾽ ἐπαινήσαις ἑκών
5 ἄλλοτ᾽ ἀλλοῖα φρόνει."

51a–d   ΕΙΣ ΑΠΟΛΛΩΝΑ ΠΤΩΙΟΝ

51a Strabo 9.2.33 (ex Apollodoro) οἱ δὲ ποιηταὶ
κοσμοῦσιν ἄλση καλοῦντες τὰ ἱερὰ πάντα, κἂν ᾖ
ψιλά· τοιοῦτόν ἐστι καὶ τὸ τοῦ Πινδάρου περὶ τοῦ
Ἀπόλλωνος λεγόμενον·

42 Stobaeus, *Anthology* (*One Must Display Successes, Hide Failures, and Make Good Use of What is at Hand*). "From Pindar's hymns":

> . . . do not display to strangers what toil
> we are bearing; this at least I shall tell you:
> one must show one's portion
> of noble and pleasant things openly
> to all the people; but if any heaven-sent,   5
>   unbearable trouble befalls men,
> it is fitting to hide it in darkness.

43 Athenaeus, *Scholars at Dinner.* "Similar is the man (sc. Amphiaraus) who advises his son Amphilochus":

> "O son, make your mind most like
> the skin of the rocky sea creature[15]
> in all the cities you visit;
> readily praise the person who is present,
> but think differently at other times."   5

[15] The octopus (cf. Theognis 215).

51a–d   IN HONOR OF APOLLO PTOIUS

This poem in honor of Apollo, father of Tenerus and Ismenus by Melia, relates the founding of his oracle and temple at the foot of Mt. Ptoïon in Boeotia.

51a Strabo, *Geography* (quoting Apollodorus). "But the poets are using embellishment when they call all sacred places groves (ἄλση), even if they are bare of trees. An example is what Pindar says about Apollo":

προ[.]ινηθεὶς ἐπῆεν
γᾶν τε ⟨πᾶσαν⟩ καὶ θάλασσαν
καὶ σκοπιαῖσιν [ἄκρ]αις ὀρέων ὕπερ ἔστα
καὶ μυχοὺς διζάσατο βαλλόμενος κρηπῖδας ἀλσέων.

1 προ[......]ις V: [....]ινηθεὶς Α
2 τε ⟨πᾶσαν⟩ καὶ Turyn: τε καὶ codd.: τε καὶ ⟨πᾶσαν⟩
Meineke
3 [ἄκρ]αις suppl. Meineke: [...]αις A: om. V
4 διζάσατο Meineke, Wilamowitz: δινάσατο V: δεινάσατο
A

51b Strabo 9.2.33 τὸ δὲ Τηνερικὸν πεδίον ἀπὸ Τηνέ-
ρου προσηγόρευται· μυθεύεται δ᾽ Ἀπόλλωνος υἱὸς ἐκ
Μελίας, προφήτης τοῦ μαντείου κατὰ τὸ Πτῷον ὄρος,
ὅ φησιν εἶναι τρικόρυφον ὁ αὐτὸς ποιητής·

κ</αί ποτε τὸν τρικάρανον
Πτωΐου κευθμῶνα κατέσχεθε κοῦ[ρος]

2 κοῦ[ρος] Snell: κού[ρα] Reitzenstein

51c Schol. Paus. 9.23.6 Πίνδαρος δὲ ἐν ὕμνοις Ἀπόλ-
λωνος καὶ τῆς Ἀθάμαντος θυγατρὸς Ζευξίππης (sc.
υἱὸν εἶναί φησι τὸν Πτῷον).

51d Strabo 9.2.34 ὁ αὐτὸς ποιητὴς (sc. Πίνδαρος) . . .
καὶ τὸν Τήνερον καλεῖ

⟨–∪∪?⟩ ναοπόλον μάντιν δαπέδοισιν ὁμοκλέα

246

. . . he traversed
all the land and sea
and stood over the lofty look-outs of mountains
and explored the depths, as he laid the foundations of
    groves.

51b Strabo, *Geography*. "The Teneric plain is named
for Tenerus. In myth he was the son of Apollo by Melia,
prophet of the oracle on Mt. Ptoïon, which the same poet
(sc. Pindar) says is three-peaked":

. . . and one day the son[16]
inhabited the three-peaked cavern of Ptoïon.

[16] Ptoïos, son of Apollo and Zeuxippe, for whom the mountain
in northern Boeotia was named. Others read daughter (i.e.
Zeuxippe, daughter of Athamas, king of Orchomenus); cf.
Herodian, *On Orthography* (in R. Reitzenstein, *Geschichte der
griechischen Etymologika*, p. 305): "Mt. Ptoïon, with a long 'i' in
Pindar: 'and one day the daughter inhabited the three-peaked
cavern of Ptoïon.'"

51c Scholion on Pausanias, *Description of Greece*. "In his
hymns Pindar says that Ptoïus was the son of Apollo and of
Zeuxippe, Athamas' daughter."

51d Strabo, *Geography of Greece*. "And the same poet
calls Tenerus"

the temple-tending seer with the same name as the
    plains

ΠΑΙΑΝΕΣ

The paean, whose name derives from *iē Paian*, a cry addressed to Apollo (cf. *h. Hom.* 3.517), was sung on numerous occasions, primarily to Apollo in his role as healer or protector (*Il.* 1.473), but also as a song of hope before battle (*Pae.* 2), of joy after victory (*Il.* 22.391), or during a banquet or symposium (Alcman, *fr.* 98).

Choruses danced Pindar's paeans, as is made clear by *Isth.* 1.7–9, where Pindar speaks of dancing to Phoebus on Ceos with seafaring men (undoubtedly a reference to *Pae.* 4). Accompaniment was with lyre, pipes, or both; the extant paeans exhibit a considerable variety of metrical (mainly Aeolic) and stanzaic forms. The titles given by the Hellenistic editors normally indicate the performers (or

Pae. 1

52a P. Oxy. 841 (5, 1908) [ΘΗΒΑΙΟΙΣ]

πρὶν ὀδυνηρὰ γήραος σ[. . . . . μ]ολεῖν,
πρίν τις εὐθυμίᾳ σκιαζέτω
νόημ' ἄκοτον ἐπὶ μέτρα, ἰδών

1 σ[χεδὸν μ] Grenfell-Hunt

PAEANS

commissioners) in the dative and the place of performance by εἰς ("to") plus accusative.

The Hellenistic editors collected Pindar's paeans into one book. The principal source is P. Oxy. 841, published in 1908 by Grenfell and Hunt, which gives fragments from ten paeans. Many additional fragments were published in 1961 by E. Lobel in volume 26 of *The Oxyrhynchus Papyri*, some of which Snell-Maehler have classed as paeans but are probably not.

For detailed studies of Pindar's paeans, see I. Rutherford, *Pindar's* Paeans: *A Reading of the Fragments with a Survey of the Genre* (Oxford 2001) and S. L. Radt, *Pindars zweiter und sechster Paian* (Amsterdam 1958). In general, see L. Käppel, *Paian: Studien zur Geschichte einer Gattung* (Berlin 1992).

Paean 1

52a   FOR THE THEBANS

Oxyrhynchus papyrus (2nd cent. A.D.)

> Before the pains of old age . . . arrive,[1]
> let a man shelter in cheerfulness
> a mind without rancor in moderation, having seen

---

[1] Or *before reaching the pains.*

δύναμιν οἰκόθετον.

5 ἰ]ὴ ἰή, νῦν ὁ παντελὴς Ἐνιαυτός
   ῝Ωρα[ί] τε Θεμίγονοι
   πλάξ]ιππον ἄστυ Θήβας ἐπῆλθον
   Ἀπόλ]λωνι δαῖτα φιλησιστέφανον ἄγοντες·
   Παιὰ]ν δὲ λαῶν γενεὰν δαρὸν ἐρέπτοι
10 σαό]φρονος ἄνθεσιν εὐνομίας. ⊗

7 πλάξ]ιππον Housman
9 Παιὰ]ν D'Alessio
10 σαό]φρονος D'Alessio: σώ]φρονος Grenfell-Hunt

Pae. 2

52b P. Oxy. 841 (5, 1908) [ΑΒΔΗΡΙΤΑΙΣ]

Α′ Ναΐδ]ος Θρονίας ῎Αβδηρε χαλκοθώραξ
    Ποσ]ειδᾶνός τε παῖ,
    σέθ]εν Ἰάονι τόνδε λαῷ
    παι]ᾶνα [δι]ώξω
5   Δηρηνὸν Ἀπόλλωνα πάρ τ' Ἀφρο[δίταν ∪–
    (desunt vv. 6–22)
    [13 ll.] . κα[. .]

1 suppl. Bury
2–5 suppl. Grenfell-Hunt

---

4 A local cult name of Apollo.

the resource stored in his house.
Iē Iē,[2] now have the all-concluding Year   5
and the Horae, daughters of Themis,
come to the horse-driving city of Thebe,
bringing to Apollo the crown-loving feast.
Long may Paean wreathe the people's offspring
with the flowers of wise order.[3]   10

---

[2] An exclamation, frequent in paeans, usually addressed to Apollo as Paean ("Healer"), but also to Hera in *Pae*. 21. For a discussion of the cry's origin, see Athen. 15.701B–F.

[3] For Eunomia (Order), one of the Horae, see *Ol*. 9.16, *Ol*. 13.6, and Bacch. 13.186–189.

Paean 2

52b Same papyrus   FOR THE ABDERITES

Abdera was settled by Teos in the sixth century and fought against the local Thracians to maintain itself. As a result of the Ionian revolt in 499 Darius destroyed Teos, but Abderites resettled the mother city (cf. 28–30). The poet recalls the colony's previous success against Paeonians (61–63), a setback (63–64), and a victory in a battle at Mt. Melamphyllon, which was apparently predicted by Hecate (68–79). The poet prays for a final, decisive campaign against the Thracians (104–106).

Abderus of the bronze breastplate, son of the Naiad   Str. 1
Thronia and Poseidon,
beginning with you I shall set in motion
    this paean for the Ionian people
to Apollo Derenus[4] and Aphrodite . . .   5
        (lines 6–22 are missing)

.   .   .   .   .   .   Ep. 1

. .]ạ τινα [τάνδε] ναίω
25 Θ[ρ]αϊκίαν γ[αῖ]αν ἀμπελό[εσ]σάν τε καί
εὔκαρπον· μή μοι μέγας ἕρπων
κάμοι ἐξοπίσω χρόνος ἔμπεδος.
νεόπολίς εἰμι· ματρὸς
δὲ ματέρ᾽ ἐμᾶς ἔτεκον ἔμπαν
30 πολεμίῳ πυρὶ πλαγεῖ-
σαν. εἰ δέ τις ἀρκέων φίλοις
ἐχθροῖσι τραχὺς ὑπαντιάζει,
μόχθος ἡσυχίαν φέρει
καιρῷ καταβαίνων.
35 ἰὴ ἰὲ Παιάν, ἰὴ ἰέ· Παιὰν
δὲ μήποτε λείποι.

Βʹ —∪–∪∪–] ἀλκαὶ δὲ τεῖχος ἀνδρῶν
ὕψιστον ἵστατ]αι
∪∪∪–∪]ρα· μάρναμαι μὰν
40 ∪̠–∪∪δάοις·
——∪ Ποσ]ειδάṇιọ[ν γ]ένος [——∪—
τῶν γὰρ ἀṇτομένων
∪∪∪–∪] φέρεσθαι
——∪∪]ως ἑκὰς
45 –∪–πο]τικύρσῃ
——∪∪κα]ὶ μανίει
∪∪–∪——]

—∪–∪∪–∪̠–∪λ]αὸν ἀστῶν

I dwell in this
Thracian land of plentiful vines   25
and bountiful fruits. May mighty time hereafter
not tire of its steadfast march for me.
I am of a young city, but all the same
    I gave birth to my mother's mother,
after she was stricken by enemy fire.   30
    If, to aid friends,
one sternly opposes enemies,
the effort brings peace
    when it proceeds in due measure.
Iē ie, Paean, iē ie. May Paean   35
    never leave us.

    . . . men's valor stands   Str.2
as the loftiest wall
            I am truly fighting
            against enemies.   40
    the offspring of Poseidon
for of those engaging
            to be carried
            far from
            he encounters   45
            and is angry

   . . . . . .

    the host of citizens   Ant. 2

---

25 suppl. Grenfell-Hunt
29 ἔτεκον pap.: ἔπιδον Grenfell-Hunt
38 suppl. Grenfell-Hunt, Bury e schol.
45 suppl. Grenfell-Hunt   46 suppl. Snell

PINDAR

×-×-∪-]

50 ∪∪∪-∪∪]οι· τὸ δ' εὐβου-
λίᾳ τε καὶ α[ἰδ]οῖ
ἐγκείμενο[ν] αἰεὶ θάλλει μαλακαῖς ε[ὐ]δίαι[ς·]
καὶ τὸ μὲν διδότω
θεός· [ὁ δ]' ἐχθρὰ νοήσαις
55 ἤδη φθόνος οἴχεται
τῶν πάλαι προθανόντων·
χρὴ δ' ἄνδρα τοκεῦσι⟨ν⟩ φέρειν
βαθύδοξον αἶσαν.

τοὶ σὺν πολέμῳ κτησάμ[ενοι
60 χθόνα πολύδωρον, ὄλ[βον
ἐγκατέθηκαν πέραν Ἀ[θόῳ] Παιόνων
αἰχματᾶν [λαοὺς ἐλάσαντε]ς
ζαθέας τροφοῦ· ἀλλὰ [βαρεῖα μέν
ἐπέπεσε μοῖρα· τλάντ[ω]ν
65 δ' ἔπειτα θεοὶ συνετέλεσσα[ν.
ὁ δὲ καλόν τι πονή[σ]αις
εὐαγορίαισι φλέγει·
κείνοις δ' ὑπέρτατον ἦλθε φέγγος
ἄντα δ[υ]σμενέων Μελαμ-
70 φύλλου προπάροιθεν.

51–52, 54 suppl. Grenfell-Hunt
59–62 suppl. von Arnim
63 suppl. Jurenka, von Arnim

254

. . . . . .

That which relies   50
   upon good counsel and respect[5]
always flourishes in gentle tranquillity,
and may the god grant it.
   But hate-mongering envy
has now disappeared   55
   for those who died long ago:
a man must give his forefathers
   their due portion of ample glory.

By dint of war they won   Ep. 2
   this bountiful land and established   60
their prosperity after chasing
the tribes of Paeonian warriors beyond
Athos,[6] their divine nurse. But a grievous
misfortune befell them; yet they persevered
   and afterwards the gods joined to fulfill it.   65
A man who performs a noble labor
   is lit up by praises.
Upon them came the most exalted light[7]
against their enemies
   before Melamphyllon.[8]   70

[5] In peacetime *aidōs* consists of reverence for the laws and re-
spect for fellow citizens; in war it connotes bravery.

[6] The geography is imprecise. The Paeonians were located to
the northwest of Abdera near the Strymon River; Mt. Athos is
southwest.

[7] Of victory.

[8] A mountain in Thrace (cf. Pliny NH 4.11.50).

255

ἰὴ ἰὲ Παιάν, ἰὴ ἰέ· Παιὰν
δὲ μήποτε λείποι.

Γ′ "ἀ]λλά μιν ποταμῷ σχεδὸν μολόντα φύρσει
βαιοῖς σὺν ἔντεσιν
75   ποτὶ πολὺν στρατόν·" ἐν δὲ μηνὸς
πρῶτον τύχεν ἆμαρ·
ἄγγελλε δὲ φοινικόπεζα λόγον παρθένος
εὐμενὴς Ἑκάτα
τὸν ἐθέλοντα γενέσθαι.
80   ν]ῦν δ᾽ αὖ γ[λ]υκυμάχανο̣ν̣
(desunt vv. 81–94)

95   [‒‒∪∪‒‒∪∪‒]
. .∪. .]ε καλέοντι μολπαί
Δᾶλο]ν ἀν᾽ εὔοδμον ἀμφί τε Παρ[νασ]σίαις
πέτραις ὑψηλαῖς θαμὰ Δ[ελφ]ῶν
λιπαρ]άμπυ[κε]ς ἱστάμεναι χορὸν
100   ταχύ]ποδα π̣[αρ]θ̣ένοι χαλ-
κέᾳ] κ̣ελαδ[έον]τι γλυκὺν αὐδᾷ
τρόπ]ον· ἐμο̣[ὶ δ᾽ ἐπ]έ̣ξ̣[ω]ν̣ ἐσ̣[.]
. . . ε]ὐκλέα [.‒. .‒.]ν̣ χά[ρ]ιν,

80 ν]ῦν suppl. von Arnim
97 suppl. Housman
99 suppl. Snell
100–101 suppl. Grenfell-Hunt
102 suppl. Snell

PAEAN 2

Iē ie, Paean, iē ie. May Paean
    never leave us.

"But when the enemy has come near the river,   Str. 3
he will confound him with a few arms
against a large army."[9] That day fell   75
    on the first of the month,
and Hecate, the maiden with ruddy feet,
was graciously announcing her prophecy
    eager for fulfillment.
But now the sweetly accomplishing . . .   80
        (lines 81–94 are missing)

.   .   .   .   .   .   Ep. 3
    songs are calling   96
throughout fragrant Delos, and among the lofty rocks
of Parnassus often do the maidens of Delphi
with shining headbands join
in swift-footed dance and sing   100
    a sweet strain with ringing
voice. But for me . . .
    famous . . . grace of words,

[9] This is presumably a prophecy spoken by Hecate before the
victory. It is not clear why she is said to have ruddy feet (77).
Demeter has the same epithet at *Ol.* 6.94.

Ἄβδ]ηρε, καὶ στ[ρατὸν] ἱπποχάρμαν

105 σᾷ] βίᾳ πολέ[μ]ῳ τελευ-
ταί]ῳ προβι[β]άζοις.
ἰὴ ἰὲ Παιάν, ἰὴ ἰέ· Παιὰν
δὲ μήποτε λείποι. ⊗

104–106 suppl. Grenfell-Hunt, Bury

Pae. 4

52d P. Oxy. 841 (5, 1908) [ΚΕΙΟΙΣ]

A΄ ‿‿–‿‿–‿‿] Ἄρτεμιν·

  ––‿––‿‿]υσομαι

  ––‿––‿‿]ος αὐδάν·

  ‿‿‿––‿‿γυν]αικῶν ἑδνώσεται

5 ‿–‿–×–]ῳδ᾽ ἐπέων δυνατώτερον·

  –––‿‿]α κατὰ πᾶσαν ὁδόν

  ‿‿–‿– ἡ]συχίαν Κέῳ

   –‿‿–‿‿–]

   –‿‿––‿‿–]

10 ‿‿–‿‿–‿‿]άλλεται

inscr. ΕΙΣ ΔΗΛΟΝ Grenfell-Hunt: ΕΙΣ ΚΑΡΘΑΙΑΝ Hope, Rutherford
4 ἑδνώσατο schol.

---

10 The scholion reads the aorist (ἑδνώσατο) and says it means "to be hymned."

Abderus, and in your might may you lead forth
our army that delights in horses   105
     for a final war.
Iē ie, Paean, iē ie. May Paean
     never leave us.

Paean 4

52d Same papyrus   FOR THE CEANS

Pindar undoubtedly refers to this poem at *Isth.* 1.7–9,
where he says that he will dance to Phoebus on Ceos with
seafaring men. The theme of the poem ("be it ever so hum-
ble, there's no place like home"), which has antecedents in
Telemachus' praise of Ithaca (*Od.* 4.605–606) and in the
portrayal of rocky Delos herself in *h. Hom. Apol.* 51–60,
is exemplified in the paean by Melampus of Pylos and
Euxantius of Ceos, who refused to leave their homes for
more prestigious situations.

                    Artemis   Str. 1
                    I shall
                    voice
     of women, he will receive (song) as a wedding-gift[10]
                    of verses, more powerful;   5
               on every road
          peace for Ceos.

          .   .   .   .   .   .
          .   .   .   .   .   .
            10

PINDAR

‿‿–‿‿–]ν χρόνον ὀρνύει
––‿–] Δᾶλον ἀγακλέα
––‿––] Χάρισι· Κάρθαι-
    α μὲν ‿–– ἐλα]χύνωτον στέρνον χθονός
15 ‿–‿–×–   ]νιν Βαβυλῶνος ἀμείψομαι
––––‿‿–   ]έχεται̣ πεδίων
‿‿–‿––‿‿   ]οι· θεῶν
  –‿‿–‿‿–   ]
  –‿‿––‿‿   ]ρη·
20 ‿‿–‿‿–‿‿   ]ν ἰχθύσιν.

ἤτοι καὶ ἐγὼ σ[κόπ]ελον ναίων δια-
    γινώσκομαι μὲν ἀρεταῖς ἀέθλων
Ἑλλανίσιν, γινώσκ[ο]μα̣[ι] δὲ καὶ
    μοῖσαν παρέχων ἅλις·
25 [ε]ἰ καί τι Διω[νύσ]ου ἄρο[υρ]α φέρει
βιόδωρον ἀμαχανίας ἄκος,
ἄνιππός εἰμι καὶ βουνομίας ἀδαέστερος·
ἀλλ᾿ ὅ γε Μέλαμπος οὐκ ἤθελεν
λιπὼν πατρίδα μο[να]ρχε[ῖν] Ἄργει
30 θέμενος οἰ[ω]νοπόλον γέρας.
ἰὴ ἰή, ὦ ἰὲ Πα[ιάν.]

14 suppl. Grenfell-Hunt
25 suppl. Grenfell-Hunt, Nairn

---

[11] One of five cities on Ceos (schol.). Strabo 10.5.6 names four.
[12] The scholion seems to point out that there are no plains on the islands.   [13] The island's pride in athletic victories is evi-

260

time, it arouses   Ant. 1
very famous Delos
with the Graces. Carthaea[11]
    a narrow ridge of land
I will (not) trade it for Babylon   15
    of plains[12]
        of the gods.

.   .   .   .   .   .
    .   .   .   .   .   .

            fish.   20

Truly, I too, who dwell on a rock,   Ep. 1
    am renowned for achievements among Hellenes
in games,[13] and also known
    for providing poetry in abundance.[14]
And although the land produces a share of Dionysus'   25
life-giving remedy for helplessness,[15]
I am without horses and know little of cattle-pasturing.
But Melampus,[16] at least, was not willing
to leave his homeland[17] to be sole ruler in Argos
and give up his office of divination.   30
Iē iē, O ie Paean.

dent in the inscription found at Ioulis that lists Cean victors (IG
XII 5.608).   [14] The reference can be to the amount of poetry
their victories have occasioned or to the Cean poets Simonides
and Bacchylides (whose first two odes celebrate Cean victors).
    [15] Wine.   [16] A seer from Pylos, Jason's cousin (cf. *Pyth.*
4.126). Very different accounts of Melampus' actions are given in
Herodotus (9.34), Apollodorus (1.9.12.8), and Pausanias (2.18.4).
    [17] Or *having left his homeland, Melampus was not willing*. In
all other accounts Melampus did in fact leave Pylos.

PINDAR

B′ τὸ δὲ οἴκοθεν ἄστυ κα̣[ὶ −∪−
    καὶ συγγένει᾽ ἀνδρὶ φ[∪−∪−
    στέρξαι· ματ[αί]ων δὲ [∪∪−−
35 ἑκὰς ἐόντων· λόγο[ν ἄν]α̣κ̣τος Εὐξαν[τίου
    ἐπαίνεσα̣ [Κρητ]ῶν μαιομένων ὃς ἀνα[ίνετο
    αὐταρχεῖν, πολίων δ᾽ ἑκατὸν πεδέχει[ν
    μέρος ἕβδομον Πασιφά[α]α̣ς ⟨σὺν⟩ υἱ-
    οῖ]σι· τέρας δ᾽ ἑὸν εἶ-
40 πέν σφι· "τρέω τοι πόλεμον
    Διὸς Ἐννοσίδαν τε βαρ[ύ]κτυπον.

    χθόνα τοί ποτε καὶ στρατὸν ἀθρόον
    πέμψαν κεραυνῷ τριόδοντί τε
    ἐς τὸν βαθὺν Τάρταρον ἐμὰν μα-
45 τέρα λιπόντες καὶ ὅλον οἶκον εὐερκέα·
    ἔπειτα πλούτου πειρῶν μακάρων τ᾽ ἐπιχώριον
    τεθμὸν π[ά]μπαν ἐρῆμον ἀπωσάμενος
    μέγαν ἄλλοθι κλᾶρον ἔχω; λίαν
    μοι [δέο]ς ἔμπεδον εἴ-
50 η κεν. ἔα, φρήν, κυπάρισ-
    σον, ἔα δὲ νομὸν Περιδάιον.

34 δ᾽ [ἔπλετ᾽ ἔρως τῶν suppl. Housman
36 suppl. Housman, Grenfell-Hunt
38 ⟨σὺν⟩ add. Housman
49 suppl. Housman

18 Housman's supplement gives the sense of the gnome: "But to foolish men belongs a love of things far away" (cf. *Pyth.* 3.20–23).

262

PAEAN 4

| One's home town and . . . | Str. 2 |
| and kinsfolk for a man . . . | |

to be content. But to foolish men . . .
    of things far away.[18] I approve the words of lord   35
        Euxantius,[19]
who refused to rule over the Cretans, although they
    were eager,
and to share a seventh part of one hundred
cities with the sons of Pasiphaë.[20]
    But he told them his own omen:
    "Truly I fear war   40
    with Zeus and I fear loud-rumbling Earthshaker.[21]

With their thunderbolt and trident they once   Ant. 2
sent the land and all the people
into deep Tartarus, sparing my mother
    and the entire well-fenced house.   45
Then, am I to pursue wealth and reject as totally void
this land's ordinance from the blessed gods,
in order to have a great inheritance elsewhere? Too
      great
    would be my constant
    fear. Give up, my mind, the cypress tree,[22]   50
    give up the pasture land around Ida.[23]

[19] Son of Minos and Dexithea, king of Ceos (cf. Bacch. 1.118–128 and 2.8).

[20] Wife of Minos, mother of the Minotaur. For "Crete of the hundred cities," see *Il.* 2.649.   [21] Poseidon.

[22] There are many cypresses in Crete (schol.). Plut. *de exil.* 9.602F gives a garbled version of lines 50–53.

[23] The main mountain on Crete.

ἐμοὶ δ᾽ ὀλίγον δέδοται θά[μνου ‿‿,
    οὐ πενθέων δ᾽ ἔλαχον, ⟨οὐ⟩ στασίων
    (desunt vv. 54–57)

58   ‿–‿–‿––‿‿–‿‿–‿–] πέρι
    (desunt vv. 59–61)

62   ἰὴ ἰή, ὦ ἰὲ Παιάν. ⊗

52 suppl. Snell
53 ⟨οὐ⟩ add. Blass

Pae. 5

52e P. Oxy. 841 (5, 1908)

[ΑΘΗΝΑΙΟΙΣ? ΕΙΣ ΔΗΛΟΝ]
    (restant frustula vv. 16–21, desunt cetera)

35   [–‿‿–‿‿ Εὔ-]
    βοιαν ἕλον καὶ ἔνασσαν·

Η´   ἰήιε Δάλι᾽ Ἄπολλον·
    καὶ σποράδας φερεμήλους
    ἔκτισαν νάσους ἐρικυδέα τ᾽ ἔσχον

40   Δᾶλον, ἐπεί σφιν Ἀπόλλων
    δῶκεν ὁ χρυσοκόμας
        Ἀστερίας δέμας οἰκεῖν·

Θ´   ἰήιε Δάλι᾽ Ἄπολλον·
    Λατόος ἔνθα με παῖδες
45   εὐμενεῖ δέξασθε νόῳ θεράποντα
    ὑμέτερον κελαδεννᾷ

264

PAEAN 4

To me has been given a small (portion?) of bush(?) . . .   Ep. 2
    but I have been allotted no sorrows, no civil strife.
        (lines 54–57 are missing)
                 around   58
        (lines 59–61 are missing)
Iē iē, O ie Paean.

Paean 5

52e   FOR THE ATHENIANS(?) TO DELOS

Same papyrus
        (lines 1–34 are missing or fragmentary)
              They[24]   35
    took Euboea and settled there;

Iēie Delian Apollo—   Str. 8
and they colonized the scattered, sheep-bearing
islands, and they took widely famed
Delos, when golden-haired Apollo   40
gave them the body
    of Asteria[25] to dwell on.

Iēie Delian Apollo—   Str. 9
There may you children[26] of Leto
with a glad mind welcome me as your attendant   45
with the ringing, .

---

[24] Ionians from Athens (schol.).   [25] Leto's sister, pursued by Zeus, who turned into the island Ortygia, later called Delos (cf. *Pae.* 7b.43–52).   [26] Apollo and Artemis.

σὺν μελιγάρυϊ παι-
  ᾶνος ἀγακλέος ὀμφᾷ. ⊗

Pae. 6

52f   [ΔΕΛΦΟΙΣ ΕΙΣ ΠΥΘΩ]

P. Oxy. 841 (5, 1908); PSI 2.147, vv. 6, 61–70, 104–111,
125–183; P. Oxy. 1792 (26, 1961), vv. 128–131, 134–136.

Α΄   Πρὸς Ὀλυμπίου Διός σε, χρυσέα
             κλυτόμαντι Πυθοῖ,
          λίσσομαι Χαρίτεσ-
             σίν τε καὶ σὺν Ἀφροδίτᾳ
5   ἐν ζαθέῳ με δέξαι χρόνῳ
          ἀοίδιμον Πιερίδων προφάταν·
          ὕδατι γὰρ ἐπὶ χαλκοπύλῳ
          ψόφον ἀιὼν Κασταλίας
          ὀρφανὸν ἀνδρῶν χορεύσιος ἦλθον

6 ἀοιδίμων Πˢ

---

27 Or *famous*.
28 The Cephisus river flowed into the Castalian spring through
the mouths of bronze lions (schol.).

honey-voiced sound
    of a far-famed paean.

Paean 6

52f   FOR THE DELPHIANS TO PYTHO

The poem was performed at Delphi for a festival called the
theoxenia, at which gods were entertained (61). The main
narrative (79–120) concerns Apollo's efforts to delay Troy's
fall and his vengeance for Priam's death on Neoptolemus,
who was cut down during a quarrel in Apollo's own pre-
cinct. The last triad of the extant text consists of praise of
Aegina and the Aeacidae (123–183). Scholion 150a on
Nem. 7 reads: "Aristodemus [says] that because he was
blamed by the Aeginetans for having seemed in his paeans
to say that Neoptolemus had gone to Delphi to rob the
temple, now, as if to defend him, says that he did not die
robbing the temple, but was killed upholding his honor
over sacrificial meats." From this notice and other com-
ments in the scholia many scholars have argued that *Nem.*
7 was written to correct a slight to the Aeginetans in *Pae.* 6,
but no convincing case has been made for any slight in *Pae.*
6 and the relationship of the two poems remains unclear.

In the name of Olympian Zeus, I beseech you,   Str. 1
    golden Pytho famous for seers,
with the Graces
    and Aphrodite
welcome me in this holy time,   5
the tuneful[27] prophet of the Pierians.
For having heard, by the water from the bronze gates,[28]
    the murmur of Castalia
devoid of men's dancing, I have come

267

PINDAR

10   ἔταις ἀμαχανίαν ἀ[λ]έξων
        τεοῖσιν ἐμαῖς τε τιμ[α]ῖς·
      ἤτορι δὲ φίλῳ παῖς ἅτε ματέρι κεδνᾷ
        πειθόμενος κατέβαν στεφάνων
        καὶ θαλιᾶν τροφὸν ἄλσος Ἀ-
15   πόλλωνος, τόθι Λατοΐδαν
        θαμινὰ Δελφῶν κόραι
      χθονὸς ὀμφαλὸν παρὰ σκιάεντα μελπ[ό]μεναι
        ποδὶ κροτέο[ντι γᾶν θο]ῷ
        (desunt vv. 19–49)
50   καὶ πόθεν ἀθαν[άτων ἔρις ἄ]ρξατο·
        ταῦτα θεοῖσι [μ]έν
      πιθεῖν σοφοὺ[ς] δυνατόν,
      βροτοῖσιν δ᾽ ἀμάχανο[ν εὑ]ρέμεν·
        ἀλλὰ παρθένοι γάρ, ἴσατ[ε], Μο[ῖ]σαι,
55   πάντα, κε[λαι]νεφεῖ σὺν
        πατρὶ Μναμοσ[ύν]ᾳ τε
        τοῦτον ἔσχετ[ε τεθ]μόν,
      κλῦτε νῦν· ἔρα[ται] δέ μο[ι]
      γλῶσσα μέλιτος ἄωτον γλυκὺν [∪∪−−
60   ἀγῶνα Λοξίᾳ καταβάντ᾽ εὐρὺν
        ἐν θεῶν ξενίᾳ.

50 suppl. Diehl
54 ἴσατ[ε] Ferrari: ἰσ[σ]ατ[ε] pap.: ἴσθ᾽ ὅτ[ι] Jurenka
60 Λοξίᾳ Grenfell-Hunt

268

to ward off helplessness from your kinsmen   10
    and from my own honors;[29]
for in heeding my own heart, as a child
    obeys his dear mother, I have come
    to Apollo's precinct, nurse of crowns
    and feasts, where the maidens of Delphi   15
    often sing to Leto's son
at the shady navel of the earth
and beat the ground with a rapid foot . . .
            (lines 19–49 are missing)
and as to whence the immortals' strife began,   50
    it is possible for the gods
to entrust that to wise men,
but mortals have no way to find it.
    But, virgin Muses, because you know
all things—along with your father   55
    of the dark clouds and Mnemosyne[30]
    you have that privilege—
hear me now. My tongue longs (to sing?)
the sweet essence of honey . . .
    having come to the broad gathering for Loxias[31]   60
    in the guest-feast of the gods.

[29] Or *privileges*. The poet will gain honors (or exercise his privileges) by bringing his song to the chorus of Delphians.

[30] For the Muses as daughters of Zeus and Mnemosyne (Memory), see *Isth.* 6.75.

[31] Apollo's title as oracle-giver.

B΄   θύεται γὰρ ἀγλααῖς ὑπὲρ Πανελ-
      λάδος, ἄν τε Δελφῶν
      ἔθ[ν]ος εὔξατο λι-
65   μοῦ θ[∪–∪–∪– –
      ἐκδι[∪–∪– –∪–
      φιλει[∪– –∪∪–∪ᗊ–
      Κρόν[ιε ∪∪∪–∪∪–
      πρύτα[νι ∪– –∪∪–
70   τοὶ πα[∪– –∪–∪∪ᗊ–
      χρησ[τ]η[ρι –∪∪–∪– –
      Πυ]θωνόθ[εν –∪– –
      καί ποτε [∪∪– –∪∪–∪∪– –
      Πανθοο[–∪∪–∪∪–
75   δ᾽ ἐς Τροΐα[ν ∪∪–∪∪
      ἤνεγκε[ν ∪∪– θρασυμή-
      δεα πάις [–∪–
      ∪∪–∪–] ὃν ἐμβα[λ – –∪–∪∪–
      Πάριος ἑ[καβόλος βροτη-
80   σίῳ δέμαϊ θεός,
      Ἰλίου δὲ θῆκεν ἄφαρ
      ὀψιτέραν ἅλωσιν,

      κυανοπλόκοιο παῖδα ποντίας
        Θέτιος βιατάν,

74 παν θοὸ[ν Snell   76 suppl. Housman
79 suppl. Grenfell-Hunt
81 Ἰλίου Πs: Ἰλίῳ pap.

For sacrifice is made on behalf of splendid Pan-Hellas,[32]   Str. 2
    which the race of the Delphians
prayed (to be relieved?) of famine . . .

      65

    .   .   .   .   .   .

    .   .   .   .   .   .

son of Cronus
    ruler
they who   70
oracle(s)
    from Pytho
and once
    Panthoös[33]
    and to Troy . . .   75
    he brought . . . bold-counseling(?)
    son . . .
        whom shot . . .
the far-shooting god[34]
    in the human form of Paris,   80
and he at once delayed
the capture of Ilion,

by binding in savage slaughter   Ant. 2
    the powerful son[35]

[32] A designation of all of Greece, reflecting the Panhellenic status of Delphi, which helped stop a drought in the time of Aeacus (cf. Paus. 2.29.7–8).

[33] A priest of Apollo at Troy (cf. *Il.* 3.146 and Verg. *Aen.* 2.319). Snell read παν θοὸ[ν ("... swift") as a reference to Achilles.

[34] I.e. Apollo.   [35] Achilles, shot by Paris. Hyginus 107 also says that he was killed by Apollo disguised as Paris.

271

85   πιστὸν ἕρκος Ἀχαι-
      ῶν, θρασεῖ φόνῳ πεδάσαις·
    ὅσσα τ᾽ ἔριξε λευκωλένῳ
    ἄκναμπτον Ἥρᾳ μένος ἀν[τ]ερείδων
    ὅσα τε Πολιάδι. πρὸ πόνων

90   δέ κε μεγάλων Δαρδανίαν
    ἔπραθεν, εἰ μὴ φύλασσεν Ἀπό[λ]λ[ω]ν·
    νέφεσσι δ᾽ ἐν χρυσέοις Ὀλύμποι-
      ο καὶ κορυφα[ῖσι]ν ἵζων
    μόρσιμ᾽ ἀνα[λ]ύεν Ζεὺς ὁ θεῶν σκοπὸς οὐ τόλ-

95   μα· περὶ δ᾽ ὑψικόμῳ [Ἑ]λένᾳ
    χρῆν ἄρα Πέργαμον εὐρὺ[ν] ἀ-
      ιστῶσαι σέλας αἰθομένου
    πυρός· ἐπεὶ δ᾽ ἄλκιμον
    νέκυν [ἐ]ν τά[φῳ] πολυστόνῳ θέντο Πηλείδαν,

100   ἁλὸς ἐπὶ κῦμα βάντες [ἦ]λ-
      θον ἄγγελο[ι] ὀπίσω
    Σκυρόθεν Ν[ε]οπτόλεμο[ν
    εὐρυβίαν ἄγοντες,

    ὃς διέπερσεν Ἰλίου πόλ[ιν·

105   ἀλλ᾽ οὔτε ματέρ᾽ ἔπειτα κεδνάν
    εἶδεν οὔτε πατρῴαις ἐν ἀρού[ραις
    ἵππους Μυρμιδόνων,
    χαλκοκορυ[στ]ὰν [ὅ]μιλον ἐγε[ίρ]ων.
 .   σχεδὸν δ[ὲ Το]μάρου Μολοσσίδα γαῖαν

91 ἔπραθον Bury   96–97 suppl. Schroeder

of the dark-haired sea-goddess Thetis,   85
    the trusty bastion of the Achaeans.
What great strife he waged with white-armed Hera
as he pitted his unyielding strength against her,
and what strife against Polias![36] Before great toils
    he would have sacked Dardania,   90
had Apollo not been on guard.
But Zeus, the watcher of the gods, sitting on the peaks
    among the golden clouds of Olympus,
did not dare to undo the things that were fated.
    And on account of high-haired Helen,   95
    it was necessary after all for the gleam
    of blazing fire to destroy spacious Pergamum.
    And after they had placed the valiant corpse
of Peleus' son in his much-bewailed tomb,
messengers crossed the wave of the sea   100
    and came back
from Scyros
bringing mighty Neoptolemus,

who sacked the city of Ilion.   Ep. 2
But afterwards he saw neither his dear mother   105
nor the horses of the Myrmidons
in his father's fields,
as he marshaled the bronze-helmeted host.
Near Tomarus[37] he came to the land of Molossia

[36] Athena Polias, guardian of the city. Apollo is the subject of this sentence, Achilles of the next.

[37] A mountain near Dodona in Epirus.

PINDAR

110   ἐξίκετ᾽ οὐδ᾽ [ἀ]νέμους ἔ[λ]α[θ]εν
    οὐδὲ τὸν [ε]ὐρυφαρέτραν Ἑκαβόλον·
    ὤ[μο]σε [γὰρ θ]εός,
    γέ[ρον]θ᾽ ὅ[τι] Πρίαμον
    π[ρ]ὸς ἑρκεῖον ἤναρε βωμὸν ἐ[π-
115   εν]θορόντα, μή νιν εὔφρον᾽ ἐς οἶ[κ]ον
    μήτ᾽ ἐπὶ γῆρας ἱξέ-
    μεν βίου· ἀμφιπόλοις δὲ
    μ]υριᾶν περὶ τιμᾶν
    δηρι]αζόμενον κτάνεν
120   ⟨ἐν⟩ τεμέ]νεϊ φίλῳ γᾶς παρ᾽ ὀμφαλὸν εὐρύν.
    ⟨ἰὴ⟩ ἰῆτε νῦν, μέτρα παιηό-
    ν]ων ἰῆτε, νέοι.

Γ´   ὀνομακλύτα γ᾽ ἔνεσσι Δωριεῖ
    μ[ε]δέοισα [πό]ντῳ
125   νᾶσος, [ὦ] Διὸς Ἑλ-
    λανίου φαεννὸν ἄστρον.
    οὔνεκεν οὔ σε παιηόνων
    ἄδορπον εὐνάξομεν, ἀλλ᾽ ἀοιδᾶν
    ῥόθια δεκομένα κατερεῖς
130   πόθεν ἔλαβες ναυπρύτανιν

110 suppl. Grenfell-Hunt
112 γὰρ suppl. Housman
113 suppl. Snell
118 μυρίαν vel μυριᾶν schol. *Nem.* 7.94a: ζ(ητεῖται) Πυθιᾶν
schol. pap.: κυριᾶν Housman: μοιριᾶν Boeckh
119 suppl. Grenfell-Hunt

274

and did not escape the winds   110
nor the broad-quivered Far-Shooter,
    for the god had sworn,
that because he had killed aged Priam,
who leapt up towards the courtyard altar,[38]
    he would not come to his welcoming home   115
nor to an old age
    in life. He slew him as he
    was quarreling with attendants
over countless[39] honors
in his own sanctuary at the broad navel of the earth.   120
    Iē sing[40] now, young men,
    sing the measures of paeans.

Island[41] whose name is famous indeed,   Str. 3
    you live and rule in the Dorian sea,
O shining star   125
    of Zeus Hellanius.[42]
Therefore we shall not put you to bed
without a banquet of paeans; rather,
as you receive waves of songs you will recount
    where you got your ship-ruling   130

[38] The altar of Zeus Herceius, located in the court (cf. *Od.* 22.334–335).

[39] Or (reading κυριᾶν) *appointed*. As in v. 11 τιμαί could mean "privileges."

[40] Iēte ("sing," "sing iē"?) appears only here; its meaning and that of the "measures of paeans" are unclear.

[41] Aegina.

[42] One of Zeus' titles (cf. *Nem.* 5.10).

δαίμονα καὶ τὰν θεμίξενον ἀρετ[άν.
ὁ πάντα τοι τά τε καὶ τὰ τεύχων
σὸν ἐγγυάλιξεν ὄλβον
εὐρύο[πα] Κρόνου παῖς, ὑδάτ‹εσσ›ι δ' ἐπ' Ἀσ[ω-
135   ποῦ π[οτ' ἀ]πὸ προθύρων βαθύκολ-
πον ἀνερέψατο παρθένον
Αἴγιναν· τότε χρύσεαι ἀ-
έρος ἔκρυψαν κόμ[α]ι
ἐπιχώριον κατάσκιον νῶτον ὑμέτερον,
140   ἵνα λεχέων ἐπ' ἀμβρότων
(restant frustula vv. 141–175)
176   . . .]ύπων[. . .]ειν ἀπείρονας ἀρετάς
Αἰακ]ιδᾶν· φ[ιλεῖ]τε
. . .]ι πόλιν πατρίαν, φί-
λων] δ' εὔφ[ρον]α λαόν
180   . .] γονευ[ ]στεφάνοισι παν
εὐ]θαλέος ὑγιε[ίας] σκιάζετε· Μοισᾶν
δ'] ἐπαβολέοντ[ι] πολλάκι, Παιάν, δέ-
ξ'] ἐννόμων θ[αλί]αν. ⊗

177 Αἰακ] suppl. Turyn
177–183 suppl. Snell

fortune and that virtue of just regard for strangers.
Truly, the far-seeing son of Cronus
   who accomplishes all things, both this and that,
has bestowed prosperity on you, and by the waters
   of the Asopus[43] he once carried off   135
     from her portal the deep-bosomed virgin,
     Aegina. Then the golden tresses
     of the air hid
the shadowy ridge of your native land,[44]
so that in an immortal bed . . .   140
    (lines 141–175 are missing or fragmentary)
                  boundless achievements   176
of the Aeacidae. Love[45]
   . . . the homeland city,
   the kindly people of friends
. . . shade over with garlands   180
of flourishing health. Of the Muses
   from one often having a share(?), Paean, receive
   the feast(?) of lawful men.[46]

[43] A river near Thebes; Thebe and Aegina were daughters of
Asopus (cf. *Isth.* 8.17–18).

[44] The nymph and the island are fused in the imagery.

[45] The plural imperatives "love" and "shade over" are presum-
ably addressed to all the gods present at the *theoxenia*.

[46] I have printed Snell's conjectures in the final fragmentary
lines, although the meaning is often unclear.

Pae. 7

52g ΘΗΒΑΙΟΙΣ Ε̣[ΙΣ
ΠΡΟΣ . . . [

P. Oxy. 841 (5, 1908); PSI 2.147, vv. 1–13.

A´ Μαντευμάτ̣[ω]ν τε θεσπεσίων δοτῆρα
καὶ τελεσσιε[πῆ]
θεοῦ ἄδυτον [. . . . .]ον ἀγλαάν τ᾽ ἐς αὐλάν
Ὠκεανοῖο̣ [   ]ν Μελίας
5 Ἀπόλλωνί γ᾽ [   ] .´ [
ὀρ‹ε›ιδρόμον τ̣[ε
σὺν ἀπιομ[ήδ]ει φιλα̣[
    γα να‹ί›ειν το[. . ?]νδέλ . [
χέων ῥαθά[μιγ]γα πλ̣[
10 Χαρίτεσσί μοι ἄγχι θ[
γλυκὺν κατ᾽ αὐλὸν αἰθερ[
ἰόντι τηλαυγέ᾽ ἀγ κορυφὰν [
ἥρωα Τήνερον λέγομεν [
. . . .]α ταύρων ε̣ι[
15 . . . .]ν προβωμ[
. . . .]οιτ . τ . μο[. . . .]παρα[
. . . . κελ]ά̣δησαν αὐδάν·
. . . . . .]αντεσι χρηστήριον

2 [πῆ] suppl. Wilamowitz: [πὲς] suppl. Galiano
6 ‹ε› add. Schroeder
7–8 suppl. Snell
9 suppl. Vitelli

Paean 7

52g   FOR THE THEBANS TO . . .
                       FOR . . .

Same papyri

(I come to?) the giver of divine oracles	Str. 1
and to the word-fulfilling	
sanctuary of the god[47] . . . and to the splendid hall	
of Oceanus' daughter . . . Melia	
for Apollo at least	5
and running on the mountains	
with kindly	
to dwell	
pouring a drop	
with the Graces for me near	10
on the sweet pipe, sky	
going on the far-shining peak	
we speak of the hero Tenerus	
of bulls	
before the altar	15

  . . . . . .

     they sang a song
      oracle

[47] Apollo. Tenerus, his son by Melia, was the prophet both of Apollo Ptoïus in the plain that bears his name and of Apollo Ismenius in Thebes (cf. *Pyth.* 11.4–6 and *Pae.* 9.41–46).

Pae. 7b

52h Π[ ] . . [. .]ΑΙΣ ΕΙΣ ΔΗΛΟ[Ν

P. Oxy. 2240 (26, 1961), init. vv. 1–10; P. Oxy. 2442 (26, 1961), fin. vv. 1–19, init. vv. 47–57; P. Oxy. 841 (5, 1908), vv. 6–52.

⊗ Ἀπολλο[ν --∪∪–   ]
      σὲ καὶ . [∪∪–.   ]
   μα̣τ̣ερ[   ]
   παιαν[   ] . [.]ι̣[ ]
5   στεφ[   ]εὐανθέος
    ἔρνεσ[   ]α̣ . .
    μή μο[ι   ]υ̣ς̣
    ἀρχομ[   ] . ραν
    ἥρωϊ[   ]χων
10 κελαδήσαθ᾽ ὕμνους,
    Ὁμήρου [δὲ μὴ τρι]πτὸν κατ᾽ ἀμαξιτόν
    ἰόντες, ἀ[λλ᾽ ἀλ]λοτρίαις ἀν᾽ ἵπποις,
    ἐπεὶ αυ[˙ π]τανὸν ἅρμα
    Μοισα[   ]μεν.
15 ἐ]πεύχο[μαι] δ᾽ Οὐρανοῦ τ᾽ εὐπέπλῳ θυγατρὶ
    Μναμ[ο]σύ[ν]ᾳ κόραισί τ᾽ εὐ-
       μαχανίαν διδόμεν.
    τ]υφλα̣[ὶ γὰ]ρ ἀνδρῶν φρένες,
    ὅ]στις ἄνευθ᾽ Ἑλικωνιάδων
20 βαθεῖαν ε . . [. .] . ων ἐρευνᾷ σοφίας ὁδόν.

Paean 7b

52h   FOR THE . . . TO DELOS

Same papyri (plus another, early 2nd cent. A.D.)

Apollo	Str.
you and	
mother	
paean	
crown . . . flowering	5
garlands	
do not for me	
begin	
for the hero	
sing hymns	10
and not going on the trodden highway of Homer,	
but on another's horses,	
since . . . winged chariot	
Muse(s) . . . I (ride?).	
And I pray to	15
Uranus' well-robed daughter,	
Mnemosyne, and to her children[48]	
to provide facility,	
for blind are the minds of men,	
if anyone without the Heliconians	
seeks the deep path of wisdom.	20

[48] The Muses, called the Heliconians in 19.

---

11 suppl. Snell, Lobel
12 suppl. Snell
15–19 suppl. Grenfell-Hunt

ἐμοὶ δὲ τοῦτο[ν δ]ι̣έδω-
κ . ν] ἀθάνατ̣[ο]ν πόνον
(restant frustula vv. 23–40)

[. . . . . .]α[
.]υνας· τί πείσομα[ι
ἦ Διὸς οὐκ ἐθέλο[ισα
Κοίου θυγάτηρ π[
45   ἄπιστά μ[ο]ι δέδο[ι]κα κ̣αμ̣[
    δέ μιν ἐν πέλ[α]γ[ο]ς
ῥιφθεῖσαν εὐαγέα πέτραν φανῆναι·
καλέοντί μιν Ὀρτυγίαν ναῦται πάλαι.
πεφόρητο δ᾽ ἐπ᾽ Αἰγαῖον θαμά,
50   τᾶς ὁ κράτιστος
    ἐράσσατο μιχθείς
τοξοφόρον τελέσαι γόνον
    (desunt vv. 53–57 ⊗)

46 suppl. Wilamowitz
50 τᾶς = τέως V. Schmidt: ἇς = ἕως Grenfell-Hunt

Pae. 8

52i   ΔΕΛ]ΦΟΙΣ [ΕΙΣ ΠΤΘΩ

P. Oxy. 841 (5, 1908), vv. 1–3, 66–70, 72–75, 79–99; P. Oxy.
1791 (15, 1922), vv. 63–81; P. Oxy. 2442 (26, 1961), vv. 67–

inscr. suppl. Maehler

But to me (they) have handed over	Ant.
this immortal task	

(lines 23–40 are missing or fragmentary)

. . . . . .	Ep.

   " . . . What shall I suffer?"
So spoke the daughter[49]
of Coeus, unwilling[50] . . . of Zeus

Things unbelievable to me I fear . . .   45
   but (they say that) having been thrown
into the sea, she appeared as a conspicuous rock.
Sailors have called her Ortygia[51] since olden times.
And she was often borne over the Aegean,

until the most powerful one   50
desired to lie with her[52]
and produce bow-bearing offspring . . .

[49] Asteria; she and Leto were daughters of the Titan Coeus (cf. Hes. *Th.* 409 and *Pae.* 12.13).

[50] Presumably unwilling to marry Zeus (cf. Callimachus, *h. Del.* 36–40).

[51] For Ortygia as another name for Delos, see Ap. Rhod. 1.537 and Verg. *Aen.* 3.124.

[52] Leto. According to *fr.* 33d, Delos became stationary when Leto arrived there to give birth to Apollo and Artemis.

Paean 8

52i   FOR THE DELPHIANS TO PYTHO

Various papyri

This fragment tells of the second and third temples of Apollo built at Delphi. According to Pausanias (10.5.9) the first temple was constructed of laurel branches brought from Tempe. The second temple, built by bees of beeswax

99. cf. Paus. 10.5.12 τὰ μέντοι ἄλλα με οὐκ ἔπειθεν ὁ
λόγος ἢ Ἡφαίστου τὸν ναὸν τέχνην εἶναι ἢ τὰ ἐς τὰς
ᾠδοὺς τὰς χρυσᾶς, ἃς δὴ Πίνδαρος ἦσεν ἐπ᾽ ἐκείνῳ τῷ
ναῷ· χρύσειαι—ἄειδον κηληδόνες.

Κλυτοὶ μάντι[ες] Ἀπόλλωνος,
ἐγὼ μὲν ὑπὲρ χθονός
ὑ]πέρ τ᾽ ὠκεανοῦ
Θέμιδός τ᾽ ἐπι[
    (desunt vv. 5–50, restant frustula vv. 51–61)
62   Ἰυγ[γ
    ναόν· τὸν μὲν Ὑπερβορ[έοις
    ἄνεμος ζαμενὴς ἔμ‹ε›ιξ[
65   ὦ Μοῖσαι· το‹ῦ› δὲ παντέχ[νοις
    Ἀφαίστου παλάμαις καὶ Ἀθά[νας

3–4 suppl. Grenfell-Hunt
63 suppl. Hunt
64 ‹ε› add. Snell
65–66, 68 suppl. Hunt

and feathers, was sent by Apollo to the Hyperboreans. Pausanias disputes Pindar's account about the third temple, supposedly made of bronze (10.5.12): "I remain unpersuaded by other aspects of the story, how the temple was the work of Hephaestus and the parts relating to the golden singers, which Pindar included in his song on this temple ('above the pediment sang golden Charmers')." Pausanias goes on to say that there were varying accounts of the temple's disappearance: "Some say that it plunged into a chasm, others that it was melted by fire." The fourth temple was built by Trophonius and Agamedes (cf. *fr.* 2).

Famous seers of Apollo,
I (have come?) over the land,
over the ocean,
and to (the shrine?) of Themis[53] . . .
> (lines 5–61 are missing or fragmentary)

Charmers[54]   Ep.
temple. The one[55] a furious wind   63
brought to the Hyperboreans . . .
O Muses. But of the other,[56] what arrangement   65
was shown by the all-fashioning skills

[53] The name Themis appears in a scholion and if it belongs here, it might refer to Delphi's earlier connection with Ge-Themis (cf. *Pyth.* 11.9 and Paus. 10.5.6).

[54] Golden birds (wrynecks) that graced the third temple at Delphi. Cf. Philostr. Apol. T. 6.11: ἑνὸς δὲ αὐτῶν καὶ χρυσᾶς ἴυγγας ἀνάψαι λέγεται Σειρήνων τινὰ ἐπεχούσας πειθώ ("And from one of them [sc. Apollo's temples] it is said that golden wrynecks were attached that possessed, as it were, the attraction of sirens.").   [55] The second temple.   [56] The third temple.

τίς ὁ ῥυθμὸς ἐφαίνετο;
χάλκεοι μὲν τοῖχοι χάλκ[εαί
   θ᾽ ὑπὸ κίονες ἔστασαν,
70 χρύσεαι δ᾽ ἐξ ὑπὲρ αἰετοῦ
ἄειδον Κηληδόνες.
ἀλλά μιν Κρόνου παῖ[δες
κεραυνῷ χθόν᾽ ἀνοιξάμ[ε]νο[ι
ἔκρυψαν τὸ [π]άντων ἔργων ἱερώτ[ατον

75 γλυκείας ὀπὸς ἀγασ[θ]έντες,
ὅτι ξένοι ἔφ[θ]<ι>νον
   ἄτερθεν τεκέων
ἀλόχων τε μελ[ί]φρονι αὐδ[ᾷ   θυ-
μὸν ἀνακρίμναντες· επε[
80 λυσίμβροτον παρθενίᾳ κε[
ἀκηράτων δαίδαλμα [
   ἐνέθηκε δὲ Παλλὰς ἀμ[
φωνᾷ τά τ᾽ ἐόντα τε κα[ὶ
πρόσθεν γεγενημένα
85 . . . . . .]ται Μναμοσύνα[
   ]παντα σφιν ἔφρα[σ . ν
   (restant frustula vv. 87–99)

72 suppl. Lobel
74 suppl. Hunt
76, 78, 83, 86 suppl. Lobel

of Hephaestus and Athena?
The walls were of bronze and bronze
    columns stood in support,
and above the pediment   70
sang six golden Charmers.
But the children of Cronus split open
the earth with a thunderbolt
and buried that most holy of all works,

in astonishment at the sweet voice   Str.
because strangers were perishing   76
away from their children
and wives as they suspended their hearts
    on the honey-minded song[57] . . .
the man-releasing contrivance(?)   80
of undamaged . . . to the virgin[58] . . .
and Pallas put (enchantment?)
into their voice and Mnemosyne[59]
    declared to them
all the things that are   85
and happened before . . .
        (lines 87–99 are fragmentary)

[57] Cf. Athen. 7.290E: τί διαφέρειν οὗτος ὑμῖν δοκεῖ τῶν παρὰ Πινδάρῳ Κηληδόνων, αἳ κατὰ τὸν αὐτὸν τρόπον ταῖς Σειρῆσι τοὺς ἀκρωμένους ἐποίουν ἐπιλανθανομένους τῶν τροφῶν διὰ τὴν ἡδονὴν ἀφαναίνεσθαι; ("How do you think that man differs from the Charmers in Pindar, which, just like the Sirens, made their listeners forget those who reared them and wither away in pleasure?").

[58] Probably the Delphic priestess.

[59] Or *the daughters of Mnemosyne* (i.e. the Muses).

PINDAR

Pae. 8a

52i(A) P. Oxy. 841 (5, 1908)

(restant frustula vv. 1–9)

10   σπεύδοντ᾽, ἔκλαγξέ ⟨θ᾽⟩ ἱερ[
      δαιμόνιον κέαρ ὀλοαῖ-
        σι στοναχαῖς ἄφαρ,
      καὶ τοιᾷδε κορυφᾷ σά-
        μαινεν λόγων· ὦ παναπ.[εὐ-
15   ρ[ύ]οπα Κρονίων τελεῖς σ[
      π[ε]πρωμέναν πᾶθαν α[
        νικα Δαρδανίδαις Ἑκάβ[
     . .] ποτ᾽ εἶδεν ὑπὸ σπλάγχ[νοις
      φέροισα τόνδ᾽ ἀνέρ᾽· ἔδοξ[ε γάρ
20   τεκεῖν πυρφόρον ἐρι[
      Ἑκατόγχειρα, σκληρᾷ [
      Ἴλιον πᾶσάν νιν ἐπὶ π[έδον
      κατερείψαι· ἔειπε δὲ μ[
     . . .] . ᾽[.]ᾳ τέρας ὑπνα[λέον
25   . . . . .]λε προμάθεια
      (restant frustula vv. multorum)

10 ⟨θ᾽⟩ add. Grenfell-Hunt
15 τελεῖς Π^{ac} ([ἐπι]τελέσεις schol.): τέλει Π^{pc}
18 suppl. Grenfell-Hunt
19 suppl. Snell
20 Ἐρι[νὺν suppl. Grenfell-Hunt
22, 24 suppl. Grenfell-Hunt

Paean 8a

52i(A) Oxyrhynchus papyrus (early 2nd cent. A.D.)

(lines 1–9 are missing or fragmentary)
(him[60]) hastening, and her[61] divinely inspired heart   10
immediately cried out
    with dreadful groanings
and she indicated with
    purport of words such as this: "O all . . .
    far-seeing son of Cronus, you will fulfill[62]   15
the fated suffering
    when Hecabe (told) the Dardanidae,[63]
(the vision) she once saw, when she
was carrying this man[64] in her womb: she thought
that she gave birth to a fire-bearing . . .   20
Hundred-hander,[65] who with harsh (force?)
dashed all Ilion
onto the plain. And she said
            the dream-omen
            foresight.   25

[60] Probably Paris.
[61] Probably Cassandra.
[62] The scholion apparently read τελεῖς "you will fulfill."
[63] The Trojans; Dardanus was the legendary founder of Troy.
[64] Paris (Alexander).
[65] Apollodorus 3.12.5 reports that Hecabe dreamed she gave birth to a firebrand that burned the city. See Frazer *ad loc.* Hundred-handed elsewhere applies to the Giant Briareus, who fought on Zeus' side against the Titans (cf. *Il.* 1.401–406). Grenfell-Hunt's conjecture of Ἐρι[νὺν envisions a hundred-handed Fury.

Pae. 9

52k   [ΘΗΒΑΙΟΙΣ ΕΙΣ ΙΣΜΗΝΙΟΝ]

P. Oxy. 841 (5, 1908), vv. 9–18, 34–49. Dion. Hal. *Demosth.*
7 (1.142 Usener-Radermacher) ταῦτα . . . εἰ λάβοι
μέλη καὶ ῥυθμοὺς ὥσπερ οἱ διθύραμβοι καὶ τὰ
ὑπορχήματα, τοῖς Πινδάρου ποιήμασιν ἐοικέναι δό-
ξειεν ἂν τοῖς εἰς τὸν ἥλιον εἰρημένοις, ὥς γ᾽ ἐμοὶ
φαίνεται· ἀκτὶς—τέρας· πολέμου δὶς ἅμα—μεταπεί-
σομαι.

Αʹ   Ἀκτὶς ἀελίου, τί πολύσκοπ᾽ ἐμήσαο,
        ὦ μᾶτερ ὀμμάτων, ἄστρον ὑπέρτατον
        ἐν ἀμέρᾳ κλεπτόμενον; ⟨τί δ᾽⟩ ἔθηκας ἀμάχανον
        ἰσχύν ⟨τ᾽⟩ ἀνδράσι καὶ σοφίας ὁδόν,
5   ἐπίσκοτον ἀτραπὸν ἐσσυμένα;
        ἐλαύνεις τι νεώτερον ἢ πάρος;
        ἀλλά σε πρὸς Διός, ἱπποσόα θοάς,
        ἱκετεύω, ἀπήμονα
        εἰς ὄλβον τινὰ τράποιο Θήβαις,
10   ὦ πότνια, πάγκοινον τέρας

        ⌣]ρα[–⌣⌣–⌣⌣–⌣⌣–⌣–]
        [––⌣–⌣––⌣⌣–⌣–]
        ⌣]ῶνος [––], πολέμοιο δὲ σᾶμα φέρεις τινός,

1 ἐμήσαο Bergk: μησθ codd.: μήσεαι Blass
3 ⟨τί δ᾽⟩ add. Diehl   4 ⟨τ᾽⟩ add. Blass
7 ἱπποσόα θοάς Bergk, Blass: ἱπποσθαθοὰς codd.

Paean 9

52k FOR THE THEBANS TO THE ISMENION

Oxyrhynchus papyrus (early 2nd cent. A.D.)

Dionysius of Halicarnassus, *On the Style of Demosthenes.*
"I believe that this passage (viz. from Plato) . . . if it had
songs and rhythms like dithyrambs and hyporchemata,
would resemble the poem Pindar addressed to the sun."
Scholars have speculated that the total eclipse of 463 B.C.
is the most likely one to be referred to in the poem.

Beam of the sun, what have you contrived, far-seeing one,	Str. 1
O mother of eyesight, supreme star,	
by being hidden in daytime? Why have you confounded	
men's strength and wisdom's way	
by hastening on a darkened path?	5
Are you bringing some unprecedented disaster?	
But, swift driver of horses, in the name of Zeus	
I beseech you,	
turn this universal omen, O lady,	
into some harmless blessing for Thebes.	10

. . . . . .	Ant. 1
. . . . . .	
are you bringing the portent of some war,	

---

13 πολέμοιο δὲ σᾶμα Scaliger, Grenfell-Hunt: πολέμου δὶς
ἅμα codd.

ἢ καρποῦ φθίσιν, ἢ νιφετοῦ σθένος
15 ὑπέρφατον, ἢ στάσιν οὐλομέναν
ἢ πόντου κενεώσιας ἂμ πέδον,
ἢ παγετὸν χθονός, ἢ νότιον θέρος
ὕδατι ζακότῳ ῥέον,
ἢ γαῖαν κατακλύσαισα θήσεις
20 ἀνδρῶν νέον ἐξ ἀρχᾶς γένος;

ὀλοφύ⟨ρομαι οὐ⟩δέν, ὅ τι πάντων μέτα πείσομαι
(desunt vv. 22–32)

B´ . . . . . .
ἐκράνθην ὑπὸ δαιμονίῳ τινί
35 λέχει πέλας ἀμβροσίῳ Μελίας
ἀγαυὸν καλάμῳ συνάγεν θρόον
μήδεσί τε φρενὸς ὑμ[ε]τέραν χάριν.
λιτανεύω, Ἑκαβόλε,
Μοισαίαις ἀν[α]τιθεὶς τέχνα[ι]σι
40 χρηστήριον . [.]πωλοῦτ̣[. .(.)]ι

ἐν ᾧ Τήνερον εὐρυβίαν θεμίτ[ων ∪–
ἐξαίρετον προφάταν ἔτεκ[εν λέχει
κόρα μιγεῖσ᾽ Ὠκεανοῦ Μελία σέο, Πύθι[ε.

16 κενεώσιας Schroeder: κενέωσιν codd. | ἂμ Hermann:
ἀλλὰ codd.
18 ῥέον Schroeder: ἱερόν codd.
19 θήσεις Barnes: θήσει pap.
42 suppl. Grenfell-Hunt

292

or the failure of crops, or a mighty snowstorm
beyond telling, or murderous civil war,   15
or the sea emptying over the plain,
or freezing of the earth, or a wet summer
flowing with raging rain,
or will you flood the land and make
a new race of men from the beginning?   20

I bewail nothing that I shall suffer along with   Ep. 1
      everyone
          (lines 22–32 are missing)

   .   .   .   .   . .   Str. 2
I have been ordained by some divine . . .
to compose, beside the immortal couch of Melia,   35
a noble song with the pipe
and by the skills of my mind in your honor.
I entreat you, Far-Shooting god,
as I dedicate to the Muses' arts
your oracle[66] . . .   40

in which Melia, daughter of Oceanus,   Ant. 2
having shared your bed, Pythian god,
bore mighty Tenerus, chosen prophet of oracles.

[66] At the Ismenion in Thebes (schol.).

τῷ] Κάδμου στρατὸν καὶ Ζεάθου πό[λιν,
45   ἀκερσεκόμα πάτερ, ἀνορέας
ἐπέτρεψας ἕκατι σαόφρονος.
καὶ γὰρ ὁ πόντιος Ὀρσ[ιτ]ρίαινά νιν
περίαλλα βροτῶν τίεν,
Εὐρίπου τε συνέτεινε χῶρον
     (desunt reliqua)

44 καί pap.: ἂν Wilamowitz

Pae. 12

52m   [ΝΑΞΙΟΙΣ ΕΙΣ ΔΗΛΟΝ?]

P. Oxy. 1792 (15, 1922)

              [ ]με[. . . . . .]ωνιο[
. . .] . οισιν ἐννέ[α Μοί]σαις
.]αλαδαρτεμι . [. .] . ωϊονασ[
. .]χος ἀμφέπο[ισ᾿ ἄν]θεα τοια[ύτας
5   .]ὑμνήσιος δρέπῃ· θαμὰ δ᾿ ἔρ[χεται
Να]ξόθεν λιπαροτρόφων θυσί[ᾳ
μή]λων Χαρίτεσσι μίγδαν
Κύ]νθιον παρὰ κρημνόν, ἔνθα [
κελαινεφέ᾿ ἀργιβρένταν λέγο[ντι
10 Ζῆνα καθεζόμενον
κορυφαῖσιν ὕπερθε φυλάξαι π[ρ]ονοί[ᾳ,

2 suppl. Lobel   4 suppl. Lobel, Grenfell-Hunt, Snell
5–6 suppl. Grenfell-Hunt, Lobel
7–8 suppl. Grenfell-Hunt   9 suppl. Schroeder
11 suppl. Lobel

PAEAN 9

To him, unshorn father, you entrusted
the people of Cadmus and Zethus' city[67]   45
because of his wise courage.
For the sea god Wielder of the Trident[68]
honored him above all mortals,
and he sped (his chariot) to the region of Euripus[69]

    . . .

[67] Thebes, whose walls were built by Amphion and Zethus (cf. *Od.* 11.262–264).

[68] Poseidon.

[69] The channel between Euboea and Attica.

Paean 12

52m   FOR THE NAXIANS TO DELOS(?)

Oxyrhynchus papyrus (early 2nd cent. A.D.)

     .   .   .   .   .   .

       with the nine Muses
    Artemis(?)
(you)[70] in attendance cull the flowers of such
hymnic song. Often there comes . . .   5
from Naxos for the sacrifice
of richly-fed sheep, together with the Graces,
to the slope of Cynthus,[71] where
they say dark-clouded, thunder-flashing
Zeus, sitting   10
above the heights, kept watch with forethought,

[70] The missing female subject of this sentence is perhaps Asteria, Leto's sister.

[71] The highest hill on Delos.

ἁνίκ᾽ ἀγανόφρων
Κοίου θυγάτηρ λύετο τερπνᾶς
ὠδῖνος· ἔλαμψαν δ᾽ ἀελίου δέμας ὅπω[ς
15 ἀγλαὸν ἐς φάος ἰόντες δίδυμοι
παῖδες, πολὺν ῥόθ[ο]ν ἴεσαν ἀπὸ στομ[άτων
᾽Ε]λείθυιά τε καὶ Λά[χ]εσις· τε̣λέ[.]αι δ᾽ ολ[
κα]τελάμβανον . [. . .]
. .]εφθέγξαντο δ᾽ ἐγχώριαι
20 ἀγ]λαὸς ἆς ἀν᾽ ἕρκε̣[.] . . . [
(restant frustula)

14 suppl. Maas

Pae. 14

52o P. Oxy. 2441 (26, 1961)

(restant frustula vv. 8–30)
31 εὐδοξίας δ᾽ ἐπίχειρα δε[
θε· λίγεια μὲν Μοῖσ᾽ ἀφα . [
μων τελευταῖς ὀαρίζε[ι
λόγον τερπνῶν ἐπέων [
35 μνάσει δὲ καί τινα ναίο[ν-
θ᾽ ἑκὰς ἡρωΐδος
θεαρίας· βασανι-
σθέντι δὲ χρυσῷ τέλος . [
γνώμας δὲ ταχείας συν[
40 σοφίᾳ γὰρ ἀείρεται πλει[⊗

33, 35 suppl. Lobel

when the gentle-minded
daughter[72] of Coeus was being released from her
    sweet
birth-pains. The twin children shone like the sun
when they came into the splendid light,   15
and Eleithyia and Lachesis[73] sent forth
much shouting from their mouths . . .
were taking
and the local (women) proclaimed . . .
the splendid . . .   20

[72] Leto.
[73] One of the Fates.

Paean 14

52o Oxyrhynchus papyrus (Early 2nd cent. A.D.)

    (lines 8–30 are missing or fragmentary)
and the wages of fame   31
    the high-voiced Muse
    in the rites speaks softly
an utterance of sweet verses . . .
and she will make even a person dwelling   35
    far away be mindful of the heroic
spectacle.[74] For, when it has been tested,
    gold . . . the end . . .
and swift thoughts
for . . . is lifted up with wisdom . . .   40

[74] Or *sacred mission*. Plutarch (*qu. Gr.* 293C) mentions a Delphic festival called the Heroïs, which is perhaps being referred to here.

Pae. 15

52p   Α[Ι]ΓΙΝΗΤΑΙΣ ΕΙ[Σ] ΑΙΑΚΟΝ

P. Oxy. 2441 (26, 1961)

Α´ Τῷδ᾽ ἐν ἄματι τερπνῷ
    ἵπποι μὲν ἀθάναται
    Ποσειδᾶνος ἄγοντ᾽ Αἰακ[,
    Νηρεὺς δ᾽ ὁ γέρων ἔπετα[ι·
5   πατὴρ δὲ Κρονίων μολ[
    πρὸς ὄμμα βαλὼν χερὶ [
    τράπεζαν θεῶν ἐπ᾽ ἀμβ[ρο
    ἵνα οἱ κέχυται πιεῖν νε[κταρ

    ἔρχεται δ᾽ ἐνιαυτῷ
10 ὑπερτάταν [.υ.]ονα . . .

4, 7–8 suppl. Lobel

Pae. 16

52q P. Oxy. 2440 (26, 1961). Plut. *de def. orac.* 7.413C
κατεκρίθη δὲ θνατοῖς ἀγανώτατος ἔμμεν ὥς φησιν ὁ
Πίνδαρος.

    . . . .]ονδ᾽ ἐφ[
    . . . .]ν ἄναξ Ἄπολλον
    . . . .]α μὲν γὰρ εὔχομαι
    . . . . .]θέλοντι δόμεν

PAEAN 15

Paean 15

52p   FOR THE AEGINETANS TO AEACUS

Same papyrus

On this pleasant day — Str.
the immortal horses
of Poseidon are carrying (to Aeacus?) . . .
and the old man Nereus[75] follows;
and father Zeus, son of Cronus . . . — 5
having cast his eye . . . with his hand . . .
to the (immortal?) table of the gods,
where nectar is poured for him to drink.

And there comes in a year — Ant.
the highest . . . — 10

[75] The Old Man of the Sea, father of Aeacus' wife, Psamatheia.

Paean 16

52q Oxyrhynchus papyrus (late 2nd cent. A.D.)

Plutarch, *On the Obsolescence of Oracles.* "He (sc. Apollo) was judged to be most gentle to mortals, as Pindar says."

. . . . . .

lord Apollo,
for I pray
with willing (mind?) to give

5   . . . .]ι δύναμις ἀρκεῖ·
κατεκρίθης δὲ θνα-
τοῖς ἀγανώτατος ἔμμεν
. . . .]μα[.]νατ[. . .] . οιναρ

Pae. 18

52s   Α]ΡΓΕΙΟΙΣ . . [. .]Σ ΗΛΕΚΤΡΥΩ[Ν . . .

P. Oxy. 2442 (26, 1961)

Αʹ   Ἐν Τυν]δαριδᾶν ἱερῷ
τεμέ]νει πεφυτευμένον ἄ[λσος
ἀνδ]ρὶ σοφῷ παρέχει μέλος [
. . . .] . ν᾽ ἀμφὶ πόλιν φλεγε[
5   . . . .]ν ὕμνων σέλας ἐξ ἀκαμαν[το . . .
. . . . .]ι[.]ʹ. μενος οὔ κεν ἐς ἀπλακ[
. . . . . . .π]ερὶ [Δ]αρδανίᾳ
            ] . ι οἷά ποτε Θήβᾳ
            ]τε καὶ ἁν[ί]κα ναύλοχοι
10   ]ήλασαν [ἐ]ννύχιον κρυφα[
           ]λεκ . [. . . . . .] . . [.]

1 suppl. Snell, Lobel   2–3, 7, 9–10 suppl. Lobel

Pae. 20

52u P. Oxy. 2442 (26, 1961)

(restant frustula vv. 1–6)
7   . . μεν . [. . . . .] . [.] δ[ι]ὰ θυρᾶν ἐπειδ[
ὄφιες θεόπομπ[οι   ]

7–19 suppl. Lobel

                    power suffices;   5
          and you were judged to be
             most gentle to mortals.

                    Paean 18

52s   FOR THE ARGIVES . . . ELECTRYON[76]

Oxyrhynchus papyrus (3rd cent. A.D.)

    The grove planted in the sacred precinct   Str.
    of the Tyndaridae
    provides song to the man who is wise
             about the city blazes(?)
    the gleam of hymns from unwearying (tongue?)   5
             (I would not fall?) into error
       around Dardania[77]
             such as once at Thebes
             and when the pirates
             drove secretly at night . . .   10

[76] Father of Alcmene, inadvertently killed by Amphitryon,
who fled to Thebes. Lines 9–10 may refer to the raid of the
Teleboae and Taphians against Electryon and his sons (cf. Ap.
Rhod. 1.747–750).
[77] Troy.

                    Paean 20

52u   Same papyrus. This fragment recounts the infant
Heracles' battle with the snakes sent by Hera, a theme also
treated at *Nem.* 1.35–50.

             (lines 1–6 are fragmentary)
                    through the doors   7
       the heaven-sent snakes

. . . ζ . . ἐπὶ βρέφος οὐρανίου Διός

10   . . . . .] . [.]νθ', ὁ δ' ἀντίον ἀνὰ κάρα τ' ἄειρ[ε
        . . . . .] χειρὶ μελέων ἄπο ποικίλον
σπά]ργανον ἔρριψεν ἑάν τ' ἔφανεν φυάν
        . . . ὀμμ]άτων ἄπο σέλας ἐδίνασεν.
        . . . .] ἄπεπλος ἐκ λεχέων νεοτόκων

15   ]οθ[.]νόρουσε περὶ φόβῳ.
                ] . οἶκον Ἀμφιτρύωνος
        δεί]ματι σχόμεναι φύγον
                ] . α πᾶσαι
        ἀ]μφίπολ[οι Κεφ[αλ]λαν[
        (restant frustula vv. 20–23)

Pae. 21

52v P. Oxy. 2442

        . . . .

        ἰὴ ἰὲ βασίλειαν Ὀλυ[μ]πίω[ν
        νύμφαν ἀριστόπο[σ]ιν

54 Strabo 9.3.6 (τὸν τόπον) ἐκάλεσαν τῆς γῆς ὀμφα-
λόν, προσπλάσαντες καὶ μῦθον ὅν φησι Πίνδαρος, ὅτι
συμπέσοιεν ἐνταῦθα οἱ αἰετοὶ οἱ ἀφεθέντες ὑπὸ τοῦ
Διός, ὁ μὲν ἀπὸ τῆς δύσεως, ὁ δ' ἀπὸ τῆς ἀνατολῆς.
Paus. 10.16.3 τὸν δὲ ὑπὸ Δελφῶν καλούμενον ὀμφαλὸν
λίθου πεποιημένον λευκοῦ, τοῦτο εἶναι τὸ ἐν μέσῳ γῆς
πάσης αὐτοί τε λέγουσιν οἱ Δελφοί, καὶ ἐν ᾠδῇ τινι
Πίνδαρος ὁμολογοῦντά σφισιν ἐποίησεν.

. . . toward the child of heavenly Zeus
    but he was lifting up his head to face them   10
. . . with his hand he threw from his limbs the elaborate
swaddling cloth and revealed his natural force
    from his eyes he whirled a flash.
. . . without a robe from her bed fresh with birthing
    she leapt up in fear.   15
        the house of Amphitryon . . .
        gripped by panic,
            all the
    Cephallenian[78] maidservants fled.

[78] Cephallene was called Dulichium before the time of Amphitryon (schol.). Amphitryon had taken Cephallene when he attacked the Teleboae.

Paean 21

52v Same papyrus. Twenty-four fragmentary verses in another column of the same papyrus with a refrain addressed to Hera were included among the paeans by Snell-Maehler. I give only the refrain.

iē, ie Queen of the Olympians,
wife of the best husband.

54 Strabo, *Geography of Greece.* "They called the place the navel of the earth, having made up a story, which Pindar tells, that the eagles set free by Zeus, one from the west, the other from the east, met there." Pausanias, *Description of Greece.* "What is called the 'navel' by the Delphians is made of white stone, and they themselves claim that it is in the center of the whole earth, and what Pindar says in one of his odes agrees with them."

PINDAR

61 Stob. *ecl.* 2.1.8 (2.4 Wachsmuth-Henze) Πίνδαρος
παιάνων·

τί ἔλπεαι σοφίαν ἔμμεν, ἃν ὀλίγον τοι
ἀνὴρ ὑπὲρ ἀνδρὸς ἴσχει;
οὐ γὰρ ἔσθ᾽ ὅπως τὰ θεῶν
βουλεύματ᾽ ἐρευνάσει βροτέᾳ φρενί·
5   θνατᾶς δ᾽ ἀπὸ ματρὸς ἔφυ.

4 ἐρευνάσει Boeckh: ἐρευνᾶσαι codd.

70, 249b (70) schol. Pind. *Pyth.* 12.44a ἐν γὰρ τῷ Κη-
φισσῷ οἱ αὐλητικοὶ κάλαμοι φύονται· εἴρηται δὲ καὶ
ἐν παίσι περὶ αὐλητικῆς. (249b) Ammon. schol. Hom.
Φ 195 [P. Oxy. 221 (2, 1899)] τοῦτο δὲ ἐμφαί[νει]ν καὶ
Πίνδαρον λέγοντα τὸν αὐλητικὸν κ[ά]λαμον Ἀχε-
λωΐου κ[ράν]αν ⟨τρέφειν, ἤτοι⟩ (suppl. Wilamowitz et
Schroeder) τ[ο]ῦ ὕδατος·

πρόσθα μὲν ἲς Ἀχελωΐου τὸν ἀοιδότατον
Εὐρωπία κράνα Μέλ[α]ν[ό]ς τε ῥοαί
τρέφον κάλαμον

2 suppl. et ποταμοῦ post τε del. Wilamowitz

304

61 Stobaeus, *Selections* (*On Those Investigating Divine Matters*). "From Pindar's paeans":

> What do you imagine wisdom to be, which
> one man possesses in slightly greater degree than
>   another?
> For it is impossible that he will search out the gods'
> plans with a mortal mind,
> since he was born from a mortal mother.   5

70, 249b (70) Scholion on *Pyth.* 12.25. "Because reeds for pipes grow in the Cephissus; there is also mention of pipe-playing in the paeans." (249b) Scholia of Ammonius on *Iliad* 21 (preserved on a papyrus of the late 1st–early 2nd cent. A.D.). "Pindar shows this when he says that the spring of Acheloös (or of its water) nourishes the pipe-reed":

> Formerly, the power of the Acheloös,[79]
> Europa's spring, and the streams of the Melas
> nourished the most melodious reed.

[79] The Acheloös and Melas are rivers near Orchomenus in Boeotia, famous for reeds used for making pipes (cf. *Pyth.* 12.25–27). The spring of Europa (if the text is correct) is not otherwise known.

ΔΙΘΥΡΑΜΒΟΙ

The dithyramb, whose origins are obscure, is first mentioned in connection with drunken revelry in celebration of Dionysus in the mid-seventh century B.C. by Archilochus (*fr.* 120 West). Around 600 B.C. Arion is credited with introducing formal improvements and a circular chorus at Corinth (where at *Ol.* 13.18–19 Pindar says the dithyramb was invented), while around 500 B.C. Lasus of Hermione (Pindar's teacher according to the *Vita Thomana*) improved the music and dance and helped institute dithyrambic contests in Athens, in which, accord-

Dith. 1

70a P. Oxy. 1604 (13, 1919)

```
                ]αποδανα[
              ]ν λεγόντων [
            ]ιον ἄνακτα [
          ]λειβόμενον δ . [
5       ]υσε πατέρα Γοργόν[ων
        Κυ]κλώπων· πτόλις α . [
```

---

¹ Phorcus, father of the Gorgons (cf. 17) and grandfather of Polyphemus the Cyclops (cf. *Od.* 1.71–72).

DITHYRAMBS

ing to P. Oxy. 2438, Pindar was victorious in 497/6. Simonides is credited with 56 victories in dithyrambic contests, but not a single verse of his dithyrambs survives. The substantial portions of five dithyrambs and part of a sixth by Bacchylides (15–20) show that the mythical narratives need not be concerned with Dionysus. The Alexandrian editors collected Pindar's dithyrambs into two rolls. For a detailed study, see M. J. H. Van Der Weiden, *The Dithyrambs of Pindar: Introduction, Text and Commentary* (Amsterdam 1991).

Dith. 1

70a Oxyrhynchus papyrus (late 2nd cent. A.D.). The myth in this very fragmentary piece evidently concerns Perseus, his escape from the sea (16) and his exploits with the Gorgons (17). Because Argos is mentioned in line 7, some editors have conjectured that the poem was composed for the Argives.

. . . .

> of them saying
>   lord
> poured out
>   father[1] of the Gorgons   5
> of the Cyclopes. The city

]ν ἐν Ἄργει μεγάλῳ . . [
]ποι ζυγέντες ἐρατᾷ δόμον
]ντ' Ἄβαντος,
10   τοὺς   ]λεεν.
εὐ]δαιμόνων βρομιάδι θοίνᾳ πρέπει
]κορυφάν
]θέμεν· εὐάμπυκες
ἀέ]ξετ' ἔτι, Μοῖσαι, θάλος ἀοιδᾶν
15   ]γὰρ εὔχομαι. λέγοντι δὲ βροτοί
]α φυγόντα νιν καὶ μέλαν ἕρκος ἅλμας
κορᾶν] Φόρκοιο, σύγγονον πατέρων,
(restant frustula vv. 18–38)

10 τοὺς e schol.   17 κορᾶν e schol.

Dith. 2

70b   ]ΗΡΑΚΛΗΣ Η ΚΕΡΒΕΡΟΣ
ΘΗΒΑΙΟΙΣ

P. Oxy. 1604 (13, 1919). Strabo 10.3.13 Πίνδαρος ἐν τῷ διθυράμβῳ οὗ ἡ ἀρχή· πρὶν—διθυράμβων, μνησθεὶς τῶν περὶ τὸν Διόνυσον ὕμνων τῶν τε παλαιῶν καὶ τῶν ὕστερον, μεταβὰς ἀπὸ τούτων φησί· σοὶ μὲν κατάρχειν, μᾶτερ μεγάλα, πάρα ῥόμβοι κυμβάλων· ἐν δὲ καχλάδων κρόταλ', αἰθομένα τε δᾴς ὑπὸ ξανθαῖσι πεύκαις. Dion. Hal. de comp. verb. 14 ἄχαρι δὲ καὶ ἀηδὲς τὸ σ καὶ πλεονάσαν σφόδρα λυπεῖ· θηριώδους γὰρ καὶ ἀλόγου μᾶλλον ἢ λογικῆς ἐφάπτεσθαι δοκεῖ φωνῆς ὁ συριγμός· τῶν γοῦν παλαιῶν τινες σπανίως

in great Argos
yoked . . . lovely . . . house
of Abas[2]

them   10
of fortunate ones . . . for the dionysiac[3] feast it is fitting
the peak
to put(?). You Muses with beautiful headbands,
continue to foster the garland of songs
for I pray. Mortals tell that   15
he having fled the black enclosure of the sea
of the daughters(?) of Phorcus,[4] relative of the fathers

[2] King of Argos (cf. *Pyth.* 8.55).
[3] The adjective βρομιάδι ("dionysiac") is derived from Βρό-
μιος ("Loud-Roarer"), one of Dionysus' cult names (cf. *Dith.* 2.6).
[4] The Gorgons (cf. *Pyth.* 12.13).

Dith. 2

70b   HERACLES OR CERBERUS
FOR THE THEBANS

Same papyrus. Strabo, *Geography of Greece.* "In the
dithyramb which begins 'In the past,' Pindar, after men-
tioning both earlier and later hymns on the subject of
Dionysus, moves on from them and says: 'Great Mother,
the whirlings of tambourines are at hand to lead off, and
there too castanets clang and the blazing torch beneath
the yellow pine trees.'" Dionysius of Halicarnassus, *On
Literary Composition.* "The sigma is neither charming nor
pleasant and is very offensive when overused, for a hiss is
considered to pertain more to the sound of a wild and irra-
tional animal than to that of a rational being. And so a num-
ber of the ancient poets used it sparingly and guardedly,

309

ἐχρῶντο αὐτῷ καὶ πεφυλαγμένως, εἰσὶ δ᾽ οἳ καὶ
ἀσίγμους ὅλας ᾠδὰς ἐποίουν· δηλοῖ δὲ τοῦτο καὶ
Πίνδαρος ἐν οἷς φησι· πρὶν μὲν—ἀνθρώποις. Athen.
10.455BC Πίνδαρος δὲ πρὸς τὴν ἀσιγμοποιηθεῖσαν
ᾠδήν, ὡς ὁ αὐτός φησι Κλέαρχος, οἱονεὶ γρίφου τινὸς
ἐν μελοποιίᾳ προβληθέντος, ὡς πολλῶν τούτῳ
προσκρουόντων διὰ τὸ ἀδύνατον εἶναι ἀποσχέσθαι
τοῦ σίγμα καὶ διὰ τὸ μὴ δοκιμάζειν, ἐποίησε· πρὶν
μὲν—ἀνθρώποις. ταῦτα σημειώσαιτ᾽ ἄν τις πρὸς τοὺς
νοθεύοντας Λάσου τοῦ Ἑρμιονέως τὴν ἄσιγμον ᾠδήν,
ἥτις ἐπιγράφεται Κένταυροι. καὶ ὁ εἰς τὴν Δήμητρα δὲ
τὴν ἐν Ἑρμιόνῃ ποιηθεὶς τῷ Λάσῳ ὕμνος ἄσιγμός
ἐστιν.

A′ Πρὶν μὲν ἕρπε σχοινοτένειά τ᾽ ἀοιδὰ
   διθυράμβων
 καὶ τὸ σὰν κίβδηλον ἀνθρώποισιν ἀπὸ στομάτων,
 διαπέπ[τ]α[νται . . . .] . . . . [
5 κλοισι νέαι [. . . . ε]ἰδότες
 οἶαν Βρομίου [τελε]τάν
 καὶ παρὰ σκᾶ[πτ]ον Διὸς Οὐρανίδαι
 ἐν μεγάροις ἵσταντι. σεμνᾷ μὲν κατάρχει
 Ματέρι πὰρ μεγάλᾳ ῥόμβοι τυπάνων,

inscr. Κ]ΑΤΑ[ΒΑΣΙΣ] ΗΡΑΚΛΕΟΥ[Σ] Snell
9 τυπάνων Bury: τυμπάνων pap.: κυμβάλων Strabo

310

and some even composed entire odes without sigmas.
Pindar illustrates this when he says: 'In the past . . . .'"
Athenaeus, *Scholars at Dinner*. "Regarding the poem com-
posed without the letter sigma, the same Clearchus said
that Pindar wrote the following, a kind of riddle put in lyric
poetry, since many had criticized him for not avoiding the
use of the letter sigma and they disapproved of it: 'In the
past . . . .' One should take note of this in response to those
who reject the asigmatic ode of Lasus of Hermione enti-
tled *Centaurs*. Also, the hymn to Demeter of Hermione
written by Lasus contains no sigma."

In the past the song of dithyrambs came forth   Str. 1
      stretched like a measuring line[5]
and the *san*[6] came falsely from the mouths of men,
but new . . . have been thrown open . . .
                        knowing   5
what kind of festival of Bromius[7]
the Uranidae hold also beside the scepter of Zeus
in their halls. In the presence of the venerable
Great Mother[8] the whirlings of tambourines lead off,

[5] Or *long-drawn-out*. The meaning is unclear. Later authors
use the term of poems to mean prolix (Philostr. *Her.* 19.17) or of
cola to mean lengthy (Hermog. *Inv.* 1.5, 4.4).

[6] The Dorians called the letter sigma *san* (Hdt. 1.139). It is not
clear whether Pindar is referring to Lasus of Hermione as one
who avoided sigmas (as not being genuine) and is contrasting his
own dithyramb (which contains them), or if he simply disapproves
of the asigmatic dithyramb.

[7] Bromius, a cult name of Dionysus, means "Loud-Roarer."

[8] Cybele, the Phrygian goddess (also known as Rhea, wife of
Cronus). For her association with Dionysus, cf. Eur. *Ba.* 78–82.

10   ἐν δὲ κέχλαδ[εν] κρόταλ᾽ αἰθομένα τε
        δαῖς ὑπὸ ξανθαῖσι πεύκαις·
    ἐν δὲ Ναΐδων ἐρίγδουποι στοναχαί
    μανίαι τ᾽ ἀλαλαί τ᾽ ὀρίνεται ῥιψαύχενι
    σὺν κλόνῳ.
15   ἐν δ᾽ ὁ παγκρατὴς κεραυνὸς ἀμπνέων
    πῦρ κεκίνη[ται τό τ᾽] Ἐννυαλίου
    ἔγχος, ἀλκάεσσά [τ]ε Παλλάδο[ς] αἰγίς
    μυρίων φθογγάζεται κλαγγαῖς δρακόντων.

    ῥίμφα δ᾽ εἶσιν Ἄρτεμις οἰοπολὰς ζεύ-
20   ξαισ᾽ ἐν ὀργαῖς
    Βακχίαις φῦλον λεόντων α[∪∪–∪∪–
    ὁ δὲ κηλεῖται χορευοίσαισι κα[ὶ θη-
    ρῶν ἀγέλαις. ἐμὲ δ᾽ ἐξαίρετο[ν
    κάρυκα σοφῶν ἐπέων
25   Μοῖσ᾽ ἀνέστασ᾽ Ἑλλάδι κα[λ]λ[ιχόρῳ
    εὐχόμενον βρισαρμάτοις ο[–∪ Θήβαις,
    ἔνθα ποθ᾽ Ἁρμονίαν [φ]άμα γα[μετάν
    Κάδμον ὑψη[λαῖ]ς πραπίδεσ[σι λαχεῖν κεδ-
    νάν· Δ[ιὸ]ς δ᾽ ἄκ[ουσεν ὀ]μφάν,
30   καὶ τέκ᾽ εὔδοξο[ν παρ᾽] ἀνθρώπο[ις γενεάν.
    Διόνυσ[.] ´ θ. [. . . . . . .] ´ τ[.]χ[
    ματέ[ρ
    πει . [

10 κέχλαδ[εν] Schroeder: κέχλαδ[ον] Grenfell-Hunt: κε-
χλάδων Strabo

there too the castanets ring, and the blazing torch   10
    beneath the yellow pine trees;
there too the loud-sounding groans of the Naiads
and the ecstatic cries are aroused
in the agitation of tossing necks.
There too the all-powerful, fire-breathing thunderbolt   15
is shaken, as is Enyalius'[9]
spear, and the intrepid aegis of Pallas
rings out with the hisses of countless snakes.

And lightly comes solitary Artemis,   Ant. 1
    having yoked the race of lions   20
in bacchic frenzy . . .
and he[10] is charmed by the dancing herds
    even of wild beasts. And the Muse has appointed me
as her chosen herald of wise verses
for Hellas of wide dancing spaces,   25
boasting for Thebes, powerful in chariots,
where, the story goes, Cadmus once won
Harmonia as his cherished bride with his lofty mind.
    She heeded the voice of Zeus
and gave birth to a child[11] famous among men.   30
Dionysus
mother . . .

[9] A title of Ares.   [10] Dionysus.   [11] Semele.

---

13 ῥιψαύχενι Plut. 417C et 706E: ἐριαύχενι Plut. 623B:
ὑψαύχενι pap.   21 ἀ[γρότερον Βρομίῳ Bury, Schroeder
22–23 suppl. Housman   25 suppl. Bury
26 suppl. Grenfell-Hunt   27 suppl. Housman
28, 30 suppl. Bury

81 Aristid. *or.* 2.229 (1.209 Lenz-Behr) τεκμαίρομαι
ἔργοισιν Ἡρακλέος αὐτοῖς τούτοις, ὅτι καὶ ἑτέρωθι
μεμνημένος περὶ αὐτῶν ἐν διθυράμβῳ τινί·

–∪––– σὲ δ᾽ ἐγὼ παρά μιν

αἰνέω μέν, Γηρυόνα, τὸ δὲ μὴ Δί

φίλτερον σιγῶμι πάμπαν· –∪––

οὐ γὰρ εἰκός, φησίν, ἁρπαζομένων τῶν ὄντων καθῆ-
σθαι παρ᾽ ἑστίᾳ καὶ κακὸν εἶναι.

Dith. 3

70c P. Oxy. 1604 (13, 1919)

]ναλ[

]

]ιτο μὲν στάσις·

]πόδα

5   ]κατε[. . . . .]ον κυανοχίτων

]τεὰν τε[λετ]ὰν μελίζοι

]πλόκον σ[τεφά]νων κισσίνων

]κρόταφον [ ]

]εων ἐλθὲ φίλαν δὴ πόλεα

10   ]ιόν τε σκόπελον γείτονα πρύτανιν[

]αμα καὶ στρατιά

6–7, 19 suppl. Grenfell-Hunt

DITHYRAMB 2

81 Aristides, *Oration* 2 (*In Defense of Oratory*). "I adduce the very deeds of Heracles, because elsewhere in mentioning them in a dithyramb, he says

> . . . in comparison to him[12]
> I praise you, Geryon, but about that which is
> less pleasing to Zeus I would keep completely silent;

for it is not proper, when your possessions are being stolen, to sit by your hearth and play the coward."

[12] Heracles, who stole Geryon's cattle (cf. *fr.* 169.6–8). This fragment is joined to *Dith.* 2 because of its meter.

Dith. 3

70c Same papyrus

> .   .   .   .   .   .
> .   .   .   .   .   .
>   civil strife
>   foot
>   with a dark-blue tunic   5
> may (someone) sing of your festival[13]
> a wreath of ivy crowns
> temple[14] . . .
>   come[15] to the city that is dear indeed
>   and the neighboring rock that is lord   10
>   and the host

[13] Of Dionysus.
[14] Of the head, presumably where the crowns are placed.
[15] Singular imperative, presumably addressed to Dionysus. Bury conjectures that the city is Corinth, the neighboring rock (10) is the Acrocorinth, and the neck (14) is the Isthmus.

PINDAR

```
      ]τ᾽ ἀκναμπτεὶ κρέμασον
      ]ς τε χάρμας
      ]π̣[. . . .]ν̣τος αὐχὴν ῥύοιτο πα[
15         ]ων πέλοι
           ]λ̣αν πόνο̣ι̣ χορῶν [
           ]ε̣ες τ᾽ ἀοιδαί,
           ]οιο φῦλον ω[
19       ]ε̣ πετάλοις ἠρ[ινοῖς
```

(restant frustula vv. 22–26, desunt cetera)

Dith. 4

70d P. Oxy. 2445 (26, 1961)

(restant frustula vv. 1–13)

```
      ]φύτευε{ν} ματρί
15    ] . αν λέχεά τ᾽ ἀνα[γ]καῖα δολ[
      ]α̣ν·
      Κρ]ο̣νίων νεῦσεν ἀνάγκᾳ[
         ]δολιχὰ δ᾽ ὁδ[ὸ]ς̣ ἀθανάτω[ν
```

(restant frustula vv. 19–34)

```
35  . . . μ]έμηλεν πατρὸς νόῳ,
```

15–43 suppl. Lobel

---

18 Or *was planting*. The mother is Danaë; the subject could be Polydectes or Perseus.
19 Cf. τό τ᾽ ἀναγκαῖον λέχος of Danaë's enslavement at *Pyth.* 12.15.
20 Presumably the way to the Gorgons.
21 Zeus, Perseus' father.

316

inflexibly hang up[16]
and spear-heads[17]
      may the neck rescue
      may it be   15
      labors of choruses
      and songs
      tribe
      leaves of spring

[16] An imperative, perhaps addressed to Dionysus.

[17] The scholion glosses χάρμας as τὰς ἐπιδορατίδας ("spear-heads"). The schol. at *Ol.* 9.86 reports that Ibycus (*fr.* 340 PMGF) and Stesichorus (*fr.* 267 PMGF) also used the word in that sense.

Dith. 4

70d Oxyrhynchus papyrus (late 2nd cent. A.D.)

This dithyramb contains an account of Perseus familiar from *Pyth.* 10.44–48 and *Pyth.* 12.6–17. Polydectes, the ruler of Seriphus, held Danaë, Perseus' mother, in bondage as his concubine. With the help of Athena (and here Hermes as well) Perseus cut off Medusa's head, returned to Seriphus, and turned the inhabitants to stone. Numerous small fragments of papyrus forming parts of this dithyramb are not reproduced here.

      (lines 1–13 are fragmentary)
was planning[18] for the mother
    and the bed of compulsion[19]   15

. . . . . .

the Son of Cronus nodded his consent by necessity
           long is the road of the immortals[20]
      (lines 19–34 are fragmentary)
it concerned the father's[21] mind   35

.....]σσέ νιν ὑπάτοισιν βουλεύμασι‹ν›·
Ὀλυμ]πόθεν δέ οἱ χρυσόρραπιν ὦρσεν Ἑρμᾶν . [
καὶ π]ολίοχον Γλαυ-
    κώπιδ]ᾳ· τὸ μὲν ἔλευσεν· ἴδον τ᾽ ἄποπτα
40   .....] · ἦ γὰρ [α]ὐτῶν μετάστασιν ἄκραν[
. . θη]κε· πέτραι δ᾽ [ἔφ]ᾳ[ν]θεν ἀντ[ὶ] φωτῶν
.....]ν τ᾽ ἔρωτος ἀντ᾽ ἀμοιβὰν ἐδάσσατο[
στρα]τάρχῳ·
    (restant frustula vv. 44–47 et aliorum multorum)

41 [ἔφ]ᾳ[ν]θεν Snell: [ἐπ]ᾶ[χ]θεν Lobel

75   ΑΘΗΝΑΙΟΙΣ

Dion. Hal. *de comp. verb.* 22 ποιητῶν μὲν οὖν Πίνδαρος
ἀρκέσει παραληφθείς, συγγραφέων δὲ Θουκυδίδης·
κράτιστοι γὰρ οὗτοι ποιηταὶ τῆς αὐστηρᾶς ἁρμονίας.
ἀρχέτω δὲ Πίνδαρος, καὶ τούτου διθύραμβός τις οὗ
ἔστιν ἀρχή·

⊗   Δεῦτ᾽ ἐν χορόν, Ὀλύμπιοι,
    ἐπί τε κλυτὰν πέμπετε χάριν, θεοί,
    πολύβατον οἵ τ᾽ ἄστεος ὀμφαλὸν θυόεντ᾽
    ἐν ταῖς ἱεραῖς Ἀθάναις
5   οἰχνεῖτε πανδαίδαλόν τ᾽ εὐκλέ᾽ ἀγοράν·
    ἰοδέτων λάχετε στεφάνων τᾶν τ᾽ ἐαρι-
        δρόπων ἀοιδᾶν,

6 τᾶν τ᾽ ἐαριδρόπων Usener: ἄντε ἀριδρόπων F: τ᾽ ἀντ᾽
ἐαριδρέπων P: τάν τε ἀριδρέπτων E

318

him with the highest plans
From Olympus he sent to him Hermes of the golden
        wand
and the city-protecting Gray-Eyed Goddess.[22]
    He brought it,[23] and they saw things not to be seen
        Truly he(?) made their transformation   40
            extreme(?);
    and they became stones instead of humans,
    and he gave requital for his lovemaking
to the commander.[24]

            (lines 44–47 are fragmentary)

[22] For Athena's assistance to Perseus, see *Pyth.* 10.45 and
Pyth. 12.18–19.
[23] Probably Medusa's head.
[24] Polydectes.

75   FOR THE ATHENIANS

Dionysius of Halicarnassus, *On Literary Composition.*
"From the poets it will suffice to cite Pindar and from
prose authors Thucydides, because they are the best writ-
ers in the austere style. Let Pindar lead off. A dithyramb of
his begins thus":

Come to the chorus, Olympians,
and send over it glorious grace, you gods
who are coming to the city's crowded, incense-rich
        navel[25]
in holy Athens
and to the glorious, richly adorned agora.   5
Receive wreaths of plaited violets and the songs
        plucked in springtime,

[25] Perhaps the altar of the twelve gods in the agora.

PINDAR

Διόθεν τέ με σὺν ἀγλαΐᾳ
ἴδετε πορευθέντ' ἀοιδᾶν δεύτερον
ἐπὶ τὸν κισσοδαῆ θεόν,
10   τὸν Βρόμιον, τὸν Ἐριβόαν τε βροτοὶ καλέομεν,
γόνον ὑπάτων μὲν πατέρων μελπόμεν‹οι›
γυναικῶν τε Καδμεϊᾶν {Σεμέλην}.
ἐναργέα τ' ἔμ' ὥτε μάντιν οὐ λανθάνει,
φοινικοεάνων ὁπότ' οἰχθέντος Ὡρᾶν θαλάμου
15   εὔοδμον ἐπάγοισιν ἔαρ φυτὰ νεκτάρεα.
τότε βάλλεται, τότ' ἐπ' ἀμβρόταν χθόν' ἐραταί
ἴων φόβαι, ῥόδα τε κόμαισι μείγνυται,
ἀχεῖ τ' ὀμφαὶ μελέων σὺν αὐλοῖς,
οἰχνεῖ τε Σεμέλαν ἑλικάμπυκα χοροί.

11 μελπόμενοι Hermann: μέλπε P: μέλπομεν FMVE
12 Σεμέλην FMVE: ἔμολον P: secl. Boeckh
13 ἐναργέα τ' ἔμ' ὥτε μάντιν van Groningen: ἐναργέα
νεμέω μάντιν P: ἐν ἄλγεα τεμέωι τε μάντιν F: ἐν ἀργέα νεμέα
μάντιν MV   14 φοινικοεάνων Koch: φοινικοεάων F: φοί-
νικος ἑανῶν PMVE
15 ἐπάγοισιν F: ἐπαΐωσιν PMVE
18 ἀχεῖ τ' F: ἀχεῖται Apollon.: οἰχνεῖ τ' PMVE

76, 77   ΑΘΗΝΑΙΟΙΣ
76 Aristoph. Eq. 1329 Ὦ ταὶ λιπαραὶ καὶ ἰοστέφανοι
καὶ ἀριζήλωτοι Ἀθῆναι. schol. Aristoph. Ach. 637 παρὰ
τὰ ἐκ τῶν Πινδάρου διθυράμβων· αἱ λιπαραὶ καὶ
ἰοστέφανοι Ἀθῆναι. schol. Aristoph. Nub. 299 Πίνδα-
ρος· Ὦ ταὶ λιπαραὶ καὶ ἀοίδιμοι, Ἑλλάδος ἔρεισμα,

and look upon me with favor as I proceed from Zeus
with splendor of songs secondly[26]
to that ivy-knowing god,
whom we mortals call Bromius and Eriboas[27]   10
as we sing of the offspring of the highest of fathers
and of Cadmean women.[28]
Like a seer, I do not fail to notice the clear signs,
when, as the chamber of the purple-robed Horae[29] is
    opened,
the nectar-bearing flowers bring in the sweet-   15
    smelling spring.
Then, then, upon the immortal earth are cast
the lovely tresses of violets, and roses are fitted to hair
and voices of songs echo to the accompaniment of
    pipes
and choruses come to Semele of the circling
    headband.

[26] The meaning of "from Zeus" and "secondly" is not clear.
Perhaps the poet begins his song with Zeus before turning to
Dionysus.
[27] "Loud-Roarer" and "Loud-Shouter" are cult names of
Dionysus.
[28] I.e. of Zeus and Semele.
[29] The goddesses of the seasons.

76, 77   FOR THE ATHENIANS

76 Aristophanes, *Knights* 1329. "O shining and violet-
crowned and widely admired Athens." scholion on Aris-
tophanes, *Acharnians* 637. "A parody of the passage from
Pindar's dithyrambs, 'shining and violet-crowned Ath-

κλειναὶ Ἀθᾶναι. schol. Aristid. *or.* 1.401 (3.341 Dindorf)
τὸ δὲ ἔρεισμα πολλοὶ μὲν καὶ ἄλλοι καὶ Πίνδαρος δέ
φησιν· ἔρεισμ᾽ Ἀθήνας δαιμόνιον πτολίεθρον.

⊗   Ὦ ταὶ λιπαραὶ καὶ ἰοστέφανοι καὶ ἀοίδιμοι,
    Ἑλλάδος ἔρει-
        σμα, κλειναὶ Ἀθᾶναι, δαιμόνιον πτολίεθρον.

77 Plut. *de glor. Ath.* 7.350A ὥς φησιν αὐτὸς (sc. Πίν-
δαρος) ἐπ᾽ Ἀρτεμισίῳ·

   ὅθι παῖδες Ἀθαναίων ἐβάλοντο φαεννάν
   κρηπῖδ᾽ ἐλευθερίας

78 Plut. *de glor. Ath.* 7.349C κλῦθι ἄννα (lacuna) γω
Πολέμου—ἄνδρες τὸν ἱρόθυτον θάνατον, ὡς ὁ Θηβαῖ-
ος Ἐπαμεινώνδας εἶπεν, ὑπὲρ πατρίδος καὶ τάφων καὶ
ἱερῶν ἐπιδιδόντες ἑαυτοὺς τοῖς καλλίστοις καὶ λαμ-
προτάτοις ἀγῶσιν.

⊗   Κλῦθ᾽ Ἀλαλά, Πολέμου θύγατερ,
    ἐγχέων προοίμιον, ᾷ θύεται
    ἄνδρες ὑπὲρ πόλιος τὸν ἱρόθυτον θάνατον

   1 Κλῦθ᾽ Ἀλαλά Plut. 483D   3 ὑπὲρ πόλιος Bergk e
Plut. 349C (ὑπὲρ πατρίδος) et Herodian. (ὑπὲρ πόλεων)

cf. schol. Aesch. *Pers.* 49 (ἐν διθυράμβῳ). schol. anon. P.
Ryl. 535 [Πιν]δαρικόν (δαγ-: Roberts) ἐστι τὸ σχῆμα,
[οἷον τὸ] θύεται ἄνδρες.

322

ens.'" scholion on Aristides, *Oration* 1 (*Panathenaic Oration*). "Pindar, along with many others, says: 'Athens, bulwark, divine citadel.'"

O shining and violet-crowned and celebrated in song,
bulwark of Hellas,
famous Athens, divine citadel.

77 Plutarch, *On the Fame of the Athenians*. "As Pindar himself says concerning Artemisium[30]"

where the sons of the Athenians laid the bright
foundation of freedom.

[30] The encounter off the northern tip of Euboea between the Athenian and Persian fleets in late summer 480 (cf. Hdt. 8.1–18 and Simonid. *frr.* 532 and 533) was a prelude to the victory at Salamis.

78 The same. "As the Theban Epaminondas said when they were devoting themselves to the noblest and most distinguished of struggles for their homeland, tombs, and temples,"

Hear me, Battle Cry, daughter of War,
prelude to spears, to whom men offer[31]
a holy sacrifice of death on behalf of their city.

[31] A scholion on Aesch. *Pers.* 49 reports that this comes from a dithyramb. Scholion on a Rylands papyrus. "It is the 'Pindaric figure' (*schema Pindaricum*) as in θύεται ἄνδρες ('men offers')."

81 Vid. *Dith.* 2.

83 Schol. Pind. *Ol.* 6.152 διὰ τὴν ἀγροικίαν καὶ τὴν
ἀναγωγίαν τὸ παλαιὸν οἱ Βοιωτοὶ ὕες ἐκαλοῦντο·
καθάπερ καὶ αὐτὸς ἐν τοῖς διθυράμβοις· ἦν ὅτε σύας
τὸ Βοιώτιον ἔθνος ἔλεγον.

ἦν ὅτε σύας Βοιώτιον ἔθνος ἔνεπον

τὸ post σύας schol. Pind.: om. Strabo, Galen. | ἔνεπον Strabo,
Galen.: ἔλεγον schol. Pind.

81 See *Dith.* 2.

83 Scholion on *Ol.* 6.90. "Because of their rusticity and vulgarity, Boeotians were long ago called pigs, just as Pindar himself said in his dithyrambs":

> there was a time when they called the Boeotian
> people pigs

ΠΡΟΣΟΔΙΑ

89a   ΕΙΣ ΑΡΤΕΜΙΝ?

Schol. Aristoph. *Eq.* 1264 τοῦτο ἀρχὴ προσοδίου Πινδά-
ρου· ἔχει δὲ οὕτως·

⊗   Τί κάλλιον ἀρχομένοισ(ιν ?) ἢ καταπαυομένοισιν
    ἢ βαθύζωνόν τε Λατώ
    καὶ θοᾶν ἵππων ἐλάτειραν ἀεῖσαι;

92 Strabo 13.4.6 Πίνδαρος δὲ συνοικειοῖ τοῖς ἐν τῇ
Κιλικίᾳ τὰ ἐν Πιθηκούσσαις . . . καὶ τὰ ἐν Σικελίᾳ· καὶ
γὰρ τῇ Αἴτνῃ φησὶν ὑποκεῖσθαι τὸν Τυφῶνα τόν ποτε
(sequitur *Pyth.* 1.17–19), καὶ πάλιν·

    κείνῳ μὲν Αἴτνα δεσμὸς ὑπερφίαλος
    ἀμφίκειται

---

[2] Boeckh included *frr.* 92 and 93 among the prosodia because
Porphyrion, *de Abst.* 3.16 reports that Pindar treated Typhos' pur-
suit of the gods in them.

PROSODIA
(PROCESSIONAL ODES)

Too little remains from the two books of Pindar's prosodia or from Bacchylides' one book (*frr.* 11–13) to generalize about the form and content of these odes, which were accompanied by the pipe and, as the name implies, probably involved processions to temples and holy places.

89a   TO ARTEMIS(?)

Scholion on Aristophanes, *Knights* 1264. "This is the beginning of a Pindaric processional ode, which reads as follows":

> What is more noble when beginning or ending
> than to sing of deep-bosomed Leto
> and the driver[1] of swift horses?

[1] Artemis.

92 Strabo, *Geography of Greece*. "Pindar associates the territory of Pithecussae and of Sicily with that of Cilicia, for he says that Typhos lies beneath Aetna (he quotes *Pyth.* 1.17–19), and further":[2]

> around him Aetna, an enormous confinement,
> lies.

PINDAR

93 Idem καὶ πάλιν·

ἀλλ' οἷος ἄπλατον κεράιζε θεῶν
Τυφῶνα πεντηκοντοκέφαλον ἀνάγκᾳ Ζεὺς πατήρ
ἐν Ἀρίμοις ποτέ.

2 ἑκατοντακάρανον Hermann

93 The same. "And further":

but father Zeus alone of the gods was slaying
unapproachable, fifty-headed[3] Typhos by force
once among the Arimoi.[4]

[3] Elsewhere in Pindar Typhos has one hundred heads.
[4] Cf. *Il.* 2.783 and Hes. *Th.* 304. It is uncertain whether this is a
people or place—or where either is located.

ΠΑΡΘΕΝΕΙΑ

Partheneia were sung by girls to the accompaniment of the pipe and included dancing. The earliest extant example is that of Alcman, *fr.* 1. In discussing the austere style of Pindar, Dionysius of Halicarnassus (*de Dem.* 39) observes that his partheneia require a different style, "although even in these appears a similar sort of nobility and seriousness." According to Proclus (Phot. *Bibl.* 321a34 and b23) one species of partheneion was the daphnephoricon, an ode sung at a festival celebrated by a procession

Parth. 1

94a P. Oxy. 659 (4, 1904) ⟨ΘΗΒΑΙΟΙΣ?⟩

ρη[. .].χο[   ]ερσ[
αιτι[. .]σαλ[. . . . .] . [. . . .]
δεῖ δεσμὸς [. . .]οσ[. . . .]θειαισερ[ ]
. ω . ενα κ[αρ]δίᾳ
5   μάντις ὡς τελέσσω

ἱεραπόλος· τιμαὶ
δὲ βροτοῖσι κεκριμέναι·

4 suppl. Snell

330

PARTHENEIA (MAIDEN-ODES)

bearing branches of bay to the temple of Apollo at Thebes. Pausanias 9.10.4 says of it: "The following custom is, as far as I know, still observed in Thebes. They choose a boy from a noble family who is both handsome and strong as priest for a year to Apollo Ismenius. His title is *daphnephorus*, because the boys wear wreaths of laurel leaves." Pindar composed three books of partheneia, one of which was entitled (according to some sources) "poems separate from the partheneia."

Parth. 1

94a   FOR THE THEBANS(?)

Oxyrhynchus papyrus (1st cent. B.C.). Although this fragment is on the same papyrus as *Parth.* 2 and also celebrates the family of Aeoladas, it is probably not to be classified as a partheneion since the speaker is male (cf. φιλέων, 11).

bond must . . .
    heart
    that I may fulfill as a   5

prophet-priest. Various honors   Str.
    have been allotted to mortals,

παντὶ δ᾽ ἐπὶ φθόνος ἀνδρὶ κεῖται
ἀρετᾶς, ὁ δὲ μηδὲν ἔχων ὑπὸ σι-
10   γᾷ μελαίνᾳ κάρα κέκρυπται.

φιλέων δ᾽ ἂν εὐχοίμαν
      Κρονίδαις ἐπ᾽ Αἰολάδᾳ
καὶ γένει εὐτυχίαν τετάσθαι
ὁμαλὸν χρόνον· ἀθάναται δὲ βροτοῖς
15   ἀμέραι, σῶμα δ᾽ ἐστὶ θνατόν.

ἀλλ᾽ ᾧτινι μὴ λιπότε-
      κνος σφαλῇ πάμπαν οἶκος βιαί-
      ᾳ δαμεὶς ἀνάγκᾳ,
ζώει κάματον προφυγὼν ἀνια-
20   ρόν· τὸ χ[ὰ]ρ πρὶν γενέ-
      [σθαι ∪–∪––]

20–21 suppl. Grenfell-Hunt

Parth. 2

94b P. Oxy. 659 (4, 1904)
‹ΑΓΑΣΙΚΛΕΙ ΘΗΒΑΙΩΙ ΔΑΦΝΗΦΟΡΙΚΟΝ
(ΕΙΣ ΙΣΜΗΝΙΟΝ?)›

Α΄   ‿ū–∪∪] χρυσοπ[επλ ū–∪–
      . . .]δωμ[. . .] . λέσηστ[. . . .]με . [–∪–
ἧκε]ι γὰρ ὁ [Λοξ]ίας

3–4 suppl. Schroeder, Grenfell-Hunt

but upon every man lies envy
for his achievement, while he who has nothing
    hides his head under black silence.   10

In friendship would I pray   Ant.
    to the children of Cronus to extend success
upon Aeoladas and his race
for unbroken time. Humans have immortal
    days, but their body is mortal.   15

But he, whose house does not fail   Ep.
    of children and is not completely
    overwhelmed by the force of necessity,
lives free from painful
    toil, for before   20
    having been born . . .

Parth. 2

94b   DAPHNEPHORICON FOR
            AGASICLES OF THEBES
            (TO THE ISMENION?)

Same papyrus. This daphnephoricon honors Aeoladas,
whose son Pagondas later commanded the Thebans at the
battle of Delium in 424 (cf. Thuc. 4.91–93), and whose
grandson, Agasicles, was the *daphnephorus*. In this poem
the speaker is female. See Appendix for a genealogy of the
family.

           golden(robed)   Str. 1

   . . . . . .

For Loxias has come

π]ρ[ό]φρω[ν] ἀθανάταν χάριν
5   Θήβαις ἐπιμείξων.

ἀλλὰ ζωσαμένα τε πέπλον ὠκέως
       χερσίν τ᾽ ἐν μαλακαῖσιν ὄρπακ᾽ ἀγλαόν
δάφνας ὀχέοισα πάν-
       δοξον Αἰολάδα σταθμόν
10   υἱοῦ τε Παγώνδα

ὑμνήσω στεφάνοισι θάλ-
       λοισα παρθένιον κάρα,
σειρῆνα δὲ κόμπον
       αὐλίσκων ὑπὸ λωτίνων
15   μιμήσομ᾽ ἀοιδαῖς

Β΄   κεῖνον, ὃς Ζεφύρου τε σιγάζει πνοὰς
       αἰψηράς, ὁπόταν τε χειμῶνος σθένει
φρίσσων Βορέας ἐπι-
       σπέρχησ᾽ ὠκύαλον †τε πόντου†
20   ῥ]ιπὰν †ἐτάραξε καὶ†
       (desunt vv. aut 8 aut 23)
       . . . .]φεν[. . . .].[
30   . . . . .]ασ⟦ικ⟧μ[ι]ζωννα[

Γ΄   πολ]λὰ μὲν [τ]ὰ πάροιθ[∪–×–∪–
       δαιδάλλοισ᾽ ἔπεσιν, τὰ δ᾽ α[×–∪–
Ζεὺς οἶδ᾽, ἐμὲ δὲ πρέπει

gladly to shed immortal glory
on Thebes.   5

But quickly tying up my robe   Ant. 1
    and carrying in my gentle hands a splendid branch
of laurel, I shall hymn
    the all-glorious house of Aeoladas
and of his son Pagondas,   10

my maidenly head flourishing   Ep. 1
    with garlands,
    and I shall imitate in my songs,
to the accompaniment of lotus pipes,
    that siren's loud song   15

which silences the swift blasts   Str. 2
    of Zephyr, and whenever with the strength of
        winter
chilling Boreas rages
    swiftly over the sea . . .
stirs up the blast . . .   20
    (8 or 23 verses are missing, two are fragmentary)

many are the former things . . .   Str. 3
    as I adorn them in verses, while the others . . .   32
Zeus knows, but it is proper for me

31, 37 suppl. Grenfell-Hunt

παρθενήια μὲν φρονεῖν
35 γλώσσᾳ τε λέγεσθαι·

ἀνδρὸς δ᾽ οὔτε γυναικός, ὧν θάλεσσιν ἔγ-
κειμαι, χρή μ[ε] λαθεῖν ἀοιδὰν πρόσφορον.
πιστὰ δ᾽ Ἀγασικλέει
μάρτυς ἤλυθον ἐς χορόν
40 ἐσλοῖς τε γονεῦσιν

ἀμφὶ προξενίαισι· τί-
μαθεν γὰρ τὰ πάλαι τὰ νῦν
τ᾽ ἀμφικτιόνεσσιν
ἵππων τ᾽ ὠκυπόδων πο[λυ-
45 γνώτοις ἐπὶ νίκαις,

Δ´ αἷς ἐν ἀιόνεσσιν Ὀγχη[στοῦ κλυ]τᾶς,
ταῖς δὲ ναὸν Ἰτωνίας ἀ[μφ᾽ εὐκλέ]α
χαίταν στεφάνοις ἐκό-
σμηθεν ἔν τε Πίσᾳ περιπ[
(desunt vv. aut 8 aut 23)
ρίζα τέ [∪ – –
σε]μνὸν αν[∪∪ – ∪] Θ[ή-
60 βαις] ἑπταπύλοισ⟨ιν⟩.

41–42 τίμαθεν γὰρ Wilamowitz: τιμαθεντας pap.
44, 46 suppl. Grenfell-Hunt
47 suppl. Schroeder   59–60, 62 suppl. Grenfell-Hunt

    to think maidenly thoughts
and to say them with my tongue.   35

Neither for a man nor woman, to whose offspring   Ant. 3
    I am devoted, must I forget a fitting song.
As a faithful witness for Agasicles
    I have come to the dance
and for his noble parents   40

because of their hospitality, for both of old   Ep. 3
    and still today they have been honored
    by their neighbors
for their celebrated victories
    with swift-footed horses,   45

for which on the shores of famous Onchestus[1]   Str. 4
    and also by the glorious temple of Itonia[2]
they adorned their hair with garlands
    and at Pisa[3] . . .
            (8 or 23 verses are missing)
(and the root?)
holy . . . to Thebes
    of the seven gates.   60

[1] A Boeotian city northwest of Thebes (cf. *Isth*. 1.33).
[2] Athena Itonia, whose temple was near Coronea, where the Pan-Boeotian games were held.
[3] Site of the Olympic games.

PINDAR

E´ ἐνῆκεν καὶ ἔπειτ[. . . . .]λος
τῶνδ᾽ ἀνδρῶν ἕνε[κε]ν μερίμνας σώφρονος
ἐχθρὰν ἔριν οὐ παλίγ-
γλωσσον, ἀλλὰ δίκας [ὁ]δούς
65 π[ισ]τὰς ἐφίλη[σε]ν.

Δαμαίνας πα[. .]ρ . . [. . .]ῳ νῦν μοι ποδὶ
στείχων ἀγέο· [τ]ὶν γὰρ ε[ὔ]φρων ἕψεται
πρῶτα θυγάτηρ [ὁ]δοῦ
δάφνας εὐπετάλου σχεδ[ό]ν
70 βαίνοισα πεδίλοις,

Ἀνδαισιστρότα ἂν ἐπά-
σκησε μήδεσ[ι.] . [.]τ[.] . . [ ]
ἁ δ᾽ ἔρ[γμ]ασι [--
μυρίων ε[. . . . .]αις
75 ζευξα[∪∪--

F´ μὴ νῦν νέκτα[ρ . . . .]νας ἐμᾶς
διψῶντ᾽ α[. . . . .] παρ᾽ ἁλμυρόν
οἴχεσθον· ἐ[--∪--
(desunt vv. 10, restant frustula vv. 89–107)

64 suppl. Puech
65 ἐφίλη[σε]ν Grenfell-Hunt: ἐφίλη[σα]ν Puech
67–69 suppl. Grenfell-Hunt
73 suppl. Schroeder

338

And then (bitter anger?) provoked	Str. 5
on account of these men's wise ambition	
a hateful and unrelenting strife,	
but he[4] cherished the faithful	
ways of justice.	65

. . . [5] of Damaena, stepping forth now	Ant. 5
with a . . . foot, lead the way for me, since the first	
to follow you on the way will be your kindly daughter,	
who beside the branch of leafy bay	
walks on sandals.	

whom Andaesistrota has trained	Ep. 5
in skills . . .	
and she, with works	
of innumerable	
having yoked	75

Do not, you two, thirsting for nectar . . . of mine,	Str. 6
go to the	
salty . . . [6]	

[4] Or (reading ἐφίλη[σα]ν) they.
[5] It is not clear whether her father or son should be understood here.
[6] After a lacuna of 10 or 25 lines, only scraps of some nineteen lines remain.

94c ΔΑΙΦΑΝΤΩΙ ΘΗΒΑΙΩΙ
ΔΑΦΝΗΦΟΡΙΚΟΝ ⟨ΕΙΣ ΙΣΜΗΝΙΟΝ?⟩

vit. Pind. Ambr. (1.3.3 Drachmann) γήμας δὲ Μεγά-
κλειαν τὴν Λυσιθέου καὶ Καλλίνης ἔσχεν υἱὸν Δα-
ΐφαντον, ᾧ καὶ δαφνηφορικὸν ᾆσμα ἔγραψεν, καὶ
θυγατέρας δύο, Πρωτομάχην καὶ Εὔμητιν. *vit. Pind.* P.
Oxy. 2438.24 ff. πα]ρθενείοις·[Πρ]ωτομάχης κ[αὶ Εὐ-
μήτιδος θ]υγατέρων δ . [ ] . ων ἀδελφὸν . [ ]ν
θυγατέρας δ᾽ ε[ἶχε Πρ]ω[το]μάχην κ[αὶ Εὔμητι]ν ὧν
μνημονε[ύει καὶ ἐν τ]ῇ ᾠδῇ ἧς ἡ ἀρ[χή· ὁ Μοι-
σα]γέτας με καλεῖ χ[ορεῦσαι .]πολλων[(suppl. Lobel,
Gallo; dubium utrum ad duo carmina an ad unum haec
spectent).

⊗   Ὁ Μοισαγέτας με καλεῖ χορεῦσαι

Heph. 14.2 p. 44 Consbruch τὸ καλούμενον Πινδαρικὸν
ἑνδεκασύλλαβον . . . οἷον·

ἄγοις, ὦ κλυτά, θεράποντα, Λατοῖ

94c   DAPHNEPHORICON FOR
DAÏPHANTUS OF THEBES
(TO THE ISMENION?)

The Ambrosian Life of Pindar. "Having married Mega-
cleia, whose parents were Lysitheus and Calline, he had a
son, Daïphantus, for whom he wrote a daphnephoricon,
and two daughters, Protomache and Eumetis." *Oxyrhyn-
chus Life of* Pindar. " . . . in the maiden-odes; Protomache
and Eumetis, his daughters . . . brother . . . and he had
daughters named Protomache and Eumetis, whom he
mentions in the ode which begins":

The leader[7] of the Muses summons me to dance,

[7] Apollo.

Hephaestion, *Handbook on Meters.* "The so-called Pinda-
ric hendecasyllabic, such as (the line cited above) and":

may you lead your attendant, O glorious Leto[8]

[8] For the poet as the attendant of Leto's children, see *Pae.*
5.44–48.

ΚΕΧΩΡΙΣΜΕΝΑ ΤΩΝ
ΠΑΡΘΕΝΕΙΩΝ

95 *vit. Pind. Ambr.* (1.2.5 Drachmann) ὁ γοῦν Πὰν ὁ
θεὸς ὤφθη μεταξὺ τοῦ Κιθαιρῶνος καὶ τοῦ Ἑλικῶνος
ᾄδων παιᾶνα Πινδάρου· διὸ καὶ ᾆσμα ἐποίησεν εἰς τὸν
θεὸν ἐν ᾧ χάριν ὁμολογεῖ τῆς τιμῆς αὐτῷ, οὗ ἡ ἀρχή·

⊗ Ὦ Πάν, Ἀρκαδίας μεδέων
   καὶ σεμνῶν ἀδύτων φύλαξ,

schol. Pind. *Pyth.* 3.139a πάρεδρος ὁ Πὰν τῇ Ῥέα, ὡς
αὐτὸς ὁ Πίνδαρος ἐν τοῖς κεχωρισμένοις τῶν παρ-
θεν‹εί›ων φησίν· Ὦ Πάν, Ἀρκαδίας μεδέων, ἕως τοῦ

      Ματρὸς μεγάλας ὀπαδέ,
      σεμνᾶν Χαρίτων μέλημα
5   τερπνόν

      1 Πάν schol. Pind.: Πὰν Πὰν vit. Pind. Ambr. et Eustath.
      4 μέλημα BCE: ἄγαλμα DG

342

POEMS SEPARATE FROM
THE PARTHENEIA

The Ambrosian life cites two books of partheneia and
a third called "poems separate from the partheneia." A
scholion on *Pyth.* 3.78 places Pindar's ode to Pan in this
book. For a detailed treatment of these fragments, see L.
Lehnus, *L'Inno a Pan di Pindaro* (Milan 1979).

95 *The Ambrosian Life of Pindar.* "In any case, the god
Pan was seen between Cithaeron and Helicon singing one
of Pindar's paeans. And so he composed an ode for the god
in which he acknowledged gratitude for the honor the god
had given him; it begins":

> O Pan, ruler of Arcadia
> and guardian of the holy shrines,

Scholion on *Pyth.* 3.78. "Pan is a companion of Rhea, as
Pindar himself says in the poems separate from the par-
theneia, from 'O Pan, ruler of Arcadia' to":

> companion of the Great Mother,[1]
> the holy Graces' delightful
> darling   5

---

[1] Rhea (or Cybele).

PINDAR

96 Aristot. *rhet.* 2.24.1401a15 ἢ εἴ τις κύνα ἐγκωμιάζων τὸν ἐν τῷ οὐρανῷ συμπαραλαμβάνοι, ἢ τὸν Πᾶνα, ὅτι Πίνδαρος ἔφησεν·

> ὦ μάκαρ, ὅν τε μεγάλας
> θεοῦ κύνα παντοδαπόν
> καλέοισιν Ὀλύμπιοι

104b   ΔΑΦΝΗΦΟΡΙΚΟΝ ΕΙΣ
      ΓΑΛΑΞΙΟΝ

Plut. *de Pyth. or.* 29.409B οἱ μὲν οὖν περὶ τὸ Γαλάξιον τῆς Βοιωτίας κατοικοῦντες ᾔσθοντο τοῦ θεοῦ (sc. Ἀπόλλωνος) τὴν ἐπιφάνειαν ἀφθονίᾳ καὶ περιουσίᾳ γάλακτος·

> προβάτων γὰρ ἐκ πάντων κελάρυξεν,
> ὡς ἀπὸ κρανᾶν φέρτατον ὕδωρ,
> θηλᾶν γάλα· τοὶ δ' ἐπίμπλαν ἐσσύμενοι πίθους·
> ἀσκὸς δ' οὔτε τις ἀμφορεὺς ἐλίννεν δόμοις,
5   πέλλαι γὰρ ξύλιναι πίθοι ‹τε› πλῆσθεν ἅπαντες

1 προβάτων Leonicus: πρὸ πάντων codd.
    3 θηλᾶν Wilamowitz: θήλεον codd. | ἐπίμπλαν Schroeder:
ἐπίμπλων codd.
    5 ξύλιναι Wilamowitz: ξύλινοι codd. | ‹τε› suppl. Ed.
Schwartz

96 Aristotle, *Rhetoric*. "Or, if in praising a dog, one would include the one in the sky (sc. Sirius) or Pan, because Pindar said":

> O blessed one, whom the Olympians
> call the multiform dog
> of the great goddess

104b DAPHNEPHORICON TO
THE GALAXION

Plutarch, *The Oracles at Delphi No Longer Given in Verse*. "Those who lived around the Galaxion[2] in Boeotia became aware of the god's presence by the unstinting profusion of milk."

> For, like the finest water from springs,
> milk gushed forth from the teats
> of all the flocks; the people rushed to fill the jars,
> and not a single wineskin or amphora remained in
>   their homes,
> for all the wooden buckets and jars were filled.   5

[2] A temple to Apollo Galaxius on a small river of the same name.

ΥΠΟΡΧΗΜΑΤΑ

In hyporchemata there was a close connection between song and dance (cf. *fr.* 107ab). Athenaeus (14.631c) says: "The hyporchematic [dance] is one in which the chorus sings as it dances . . . In Pindar this is danced by Spartan men, and the hyporchematic dance is for men as well as

105ab   ΙΕΡΩΝΙ ΣΤΡΑΚΟΣΙΩΙ

Schol. *Nem.* 7.1a καταφέρεται εἰς τοῦτο ὁ Πίνδαρος ὅταν ὑπῇ τις ὁμωνυμία, οἷον (sequitur *fr.* 120) καὶ

(a) ⊗   Σύνες ὅ τοι λέγω,
ζαθέων ἱερῶν ἐπώνυμε
πάτερ, κτίστορ Αἴτνας·

cf. schol. Pind. *Pyth.* 2.127 τὸν ἐπίνικον (*Pyth.* 2) ἐπὶ μισθῷ συντάξας ὁ Πίνδαρος ἐκ περιττοῦ συνέπεμψεν αὐτῷ προῖκα ὑπόρχημα, οὗ ἡ ἀρχή· σύνες—ἐπώνυμε.

HYPORCHEMATA
(DANCE–ODES)

women." Judging from the extant fragments, the topics included encomia (*fr.* 105ab), praises of the gods' powers (*fr.* 108ab), political advice (*fr.* 110), and stories of Heracles (*fr.* 111). Pindar composed two books of hyporchemata.

105ab   FOR HIERON OF SYRACUSE

Scholion on *Nem.* 7.1. "Pindar is drawn to this (viz. word-play) whenever there is some similar name, as (*fr.* 120) and":

> Understand what I tell you,
> you whose name means holy temples,[1]
> father, founder of Aetna.

[1] A play on Ἱέρων (Hieron) and ἱερῶν (temples).

Cf. Scholion on *Pyth.* 2.69. "After composing the epinician (*Pyth.* 2) on hire, Pindar sent Hieron an extra hyporchema gratis, which began: 'Understand what I tell you.'"

PINDAR

Schol. Aristoph. *Av.* 941 ff. καὶ ταῦτα παρὰ τὰ ἐκ
Πινδάρου· ἔχει δὲ οὕτως·

(b)   νομάδεσσι γὰρ ἐν Σκύθαις ἀλᾶται στρατῶν,
5   ὃς ἀμαξοφόρητον οἶκον οὐ πέπαται,
    ἀκλεὴς ⟨δ'⟩ ἔβα.

6 ⟨δ'⟩ suppl. Boeckh

106 Athen. epit. 1.28A (Eustath. *Od.* 1822.5 et 1569.44)
Πίνδαρος δ' ἐν τῇ εἰς Ἱέρωνα Πυθικῇ ᾠδῇ·

⊗   Ἀπὸ Ταϋγέτοιο μὲν Λάκαιναν
    ἐπὶ θηρσὶ κύνα τρέχειν
    πυκινώτατον ἑρπετόν·
    Σκύριαι δ' ἐς ἄμελξιν γλάγεος αἶγες ἐξοχώταται·
5   ὅπλα δ' ἀπ' Ἄργεος, ἅρμα Θη-
    βαῖον, ἀλλ' ἀπὸ τᾶς ἀγλαοκάρπου
6   Σικελίας ὄχημα δαιδάλεον ματεύειν.

2 τρέχειν Athen.: τρέφειν Eustath.
4 γλάγεος Schneidewin: γάλακτος Athen.: γλάγους
Eustath.
5 ἀλλ' ἀπὸ τῆς schol. Aristoph.: ἀπὸ τῆς Athen.: ἀλλ' ἀπ'
Schroeder

107ab Plut. *quaest. symp.* 9.15.748B δηλοῖ δ' ὁ μάλι-
στα κατωρθωκέναι δόξας ἐν ὑπορχήμασι καὶ γεγο-
νέναι πιθανώτατος ἑαυτοῦ τὸ δεῖσθαι τὴν ἑτέραν τῆς
ἑτέρας (sc. τὴν ποίησιν τῆς ὀρχήσεως)· τὸ γὰρ

348

Scholion on Aristophanes, *Birds* 941–943. "These, too, parody verses from Pindar, which read as follows":

for among the nomadic Scythians the man is   (b)
        excluded from the folk
who does not possess a house borne on a wagon,   5
and he goes without glory.[2]

[2] The scholion on Aristophanes, *Birds* 942 explains that when the Scythians packed up to move, anyone without a wagon was dishonored by them.

106 Athenaeus, *Scholars at Dinner.* "And Pindar in the Pythian[3] ode to Hieron":

From Taygetus [comes] the Laconian dog,
the smartest creature at chasing down
wild prey;
the goats from Scyros are best for milking;
arms from Argos, the chariot from Thebes;   5
    but from Sicily of the splendid fruit
seek an intricately wrought mule car.

[3] Clearly a mistake.

107ab Plutarch, *Table-Talk.* "The writer who is considered to have been the most successful in hyporchemata and the most persuasive clearly shows that the one art (i.e. poetry) needs the other (i.e. dance). Take the passage":

349

PINDAR

(a)   Πελασγὸν ἵππον ἢ κύνα
       Ἀμυκλᾶίαν ἀγωνίῳ
       ἐλελιζόμενος ποδὶ μιμέο καμπύλον μέλος διώκων,
       οἷ ἀνὰ Δώτιον ἀνθεμόεν πεδί-
          ον πέταται θάνατον κεροέσσᾳ
5   εὑρέμεν ματεῖσ' ἐλάφῳ·
       τὰν δ' ἐπ' αὐχένι στρέφοι-
       σαν {ἕτερον} κάρα πάντ' ἐπ' οἶμον . . .

1 Πελασγὸν Meineke: ἀπέλαστον Plut.
4 οἷ Reinach: οἷος Plut. | κεροέσσᾳ Wyttenbach: κεράσασα Plut.
5 ματεῖσ' Schroeder: μανύων Plut.
6 ἕτερον secl. Schroeder | πάντ' ἐπ' οἶμον Schneidewin: πάντα ἕτοιμον Plut.

Idem 748C αὐτὸς γοῦν ἑαυτὸν οὐκ αἰσχύνεται περὶ τὴν ὄρχησιν οὐχ ἧττον ἢ τὴν ποίησιν ἐγκωμιάζων, ὅταν λέγῃ . . . ἐλαφρὸν—τρόπον. Athen. 5.10.181B Κρητικὰ καλοῦσι τὰ ὑπορχήματα· Κρῆτα—Μολοσσόν.

(b)   ἐλαφρὸν ὄρχημ' οἶδα ποδῶν μειγνύμεν·
       Κρῆτα μὲν καλέοντι τρόπον, τὸ δ' ὄργανον
       Μολοσσόν.

108ab Epist. Socr. 1.7 (p. 610 Hercher = 11.6 Köhl) ἀπειθεῖν δὲ αὐτῷ ὀκνῶ καὶ τὸν Πίνδαρον ἡγούμενος εἰς τοῦτο εἶναι σοφόν, ὅς φησιν·

Imitate the Pelasgian[4] horse or dog   (a)
from Amyclae[5] as you shake with your foot
in the contest and drive forward the curved song,[6]
even as it[7] flies over the flowery
    Dotian plain,[8] seeking to find death
for the horned deer;   5
and as she turns her head on her neck
    (the dog pursues?) her along every path.

4 In Thessaly, famous for horses.
5 A city south of Sparta in an area famous for hunting dogs (cf.
fr. 106.1–3).
6 The adjective καμπύλος ("curved") is used of a chariot else-
where in Pindar; its application to the song is not clear.
7 The dog.
8 In Thessaly.

(b) The same. "In any case, he is not ashamed to praise
himself as much for his dancing as for his poetry, when he
says" (vv. 1–2). Athenaeus, *Scholars at Dinner.* "They call
hyporchemata Cretan" (v. 2).

I know how to join in the light dancing of feet;   (b)
they call the style[9] Cretan, but the instrument[10]
    Molossian.

9 Either of the music or of the dance.
10 Perhaps a pipe. Molossia is in Epirus.

108ab (a) [Socrates'] *Letters.* "I hesitate to disbelieve
him (sc. a god), in that I consider Pindar to be wise in this
matter, when he says:

PINDAR

(a)   θεοῦ δὲ δείξαντος ἀρχάν
ἕκαστον ἐν πρᾶγος, εὐθεῖα δή
κέλευθος ἀρετὰν ἑλεῖν,
τελευταί τε καλλίονες.

σχεδὸν γὰρ οὕτω που αὐτῷ ἔχει τὸ ὑπόρχημα.

Clem. Alex. *strom.* 5.14.101 (2.393 Stählin) ὁ μελοποιὸς δέ·

(b)   θεῷ δὲ δυνατὸν μελαίνας
ἐκ νυκτὸς ἀμίαντον ὄρσαι φάος,
κελαινεφέι δὲ σκότει
καλύψαι σέλας καθαρόν

5   ἀμέρας

1–2 ἐκ μελαίνας Clemens: transp. Blass
4–5 καθαρὸν ἀμέρας σέλας Clemens: transp. Blass

110, 109   ΘΗΒΑΙΟΙΣ

110 Stob. *ecl.* 4.9.3 (4.321 Wachsmuth-Henze) Πίνδαρος ὑπορχημάτων·

γλυκὺ δὲ πόλεμος ἀπείροισιν, ἐμπείρων δέ τις
ταρβεῖ προσιόντα νιν καρδίᾳ περισσῶς

1 γλυκὺ δὲ πόλεμος ἀπείροισιν Stobaeus, schol. Thuc. 2.8.1 [P. Oxy. 853 (6, 1908)]: γλυκὺς ἀπείρῳ πόλεμος schol. Hom., Eustath., schol. Thuc. 1.80.1 | ἐμπείρων Stobaeus: πεπειραμένων Eustath.

352

When a god has shown the beginning (a)
for each endeavor, straight indeed
is the path to achieve excellence
and more noble the results.

For the hyporchema says this more or less."

(b) Clement of Alexandria, *Miscellanies*. "The lyric poet
(says)":

A god can make unsullied light (b)
spring from dark night
and in black-clouded darkness
hide the pure gleam
of day. 5

110, 109   FOR THE THEBANS

110 Stobaeus, *Anthology (On War)*. "Pindar, in his hyp-
orchemata":

Sweet is war to those without experience, but anyone
    who has experienced it
dreads its approach exceedingly in his heart.

PINDAR

109 Stob. *ecl.* 4.16.6 (4.395 Wachsmuth-Henze) Πινδά-
ρου ὑπορχημάτων·

τὸ κοινόν τις ἀστῶν ἐν εὐδίᾳ
τιθεὶς ἐρευνασάτω μεγαλάνορος Ἡσυχίας
  τὸ φαιδρὸν φάος,
στάσιν ἀπὸ πραπίδος ἐπίκοτον ἀνελών,
πενίας δότειραν, ἐχθρὰν κουροτρόφον

3 ἀνελών Grotius: ἀνέμων Stobaeus

cf. Polyb. 4.31.6 οὐδὲ γὰρ Θηβαίους ἐπαινοῦμεν κατὰ
τὰ Μηδικά, διότι τῶν ὑπὲρ τῆς Ἑλλάδος ἀποστάντες
κινδύνων τὰ Περσῶν εἵλοντο διὰ τὸν φόβον, οὐδὲ
Πίνδαρον τὸν συναποφηνάμενον αὐτοῖς ἄγειν τὴν
ἡσυχίαν διὰ τῶνδε τῶν ποιημάτων· τὸ κοινόν—φάος.

111 Erotian. *gloss. Hippocr.* p. 20.20 Nachmanson, s.v.
αἰών· ὁ νωτιαῖος μυελός . . . καὶ Πίνδαρος ἐν ὑπορ-
χήμασι λέγων· ἐνέπισε—ἐρραίσθη. P. Oxy. 2446 (26,
1961), vv. 2–9.

. . . .
ἐνέπισε κεκραμέν᾿ ἐν αἵματι, πολλὰ
  δ᾿ ἕλκε᾿ ἔμβαλλε   ] . νωμῶν τραχὺ
  ῥόπαλον,
τέλος δ᾿ ἀείραις πρὸς στιβαρὰς ἐπάραξε

3 ἕλκε᾿ Heringa: ἕλκεα πλευρὰς codd. | ἔμβαλε νωμῶν
Vulcanius: ἔμβαλλεν ὦμον codd.
4 ἐπάραξε H: ἀπάραξε AL: ἄραξε Zuntz

354

109 Stobaeus, *Anthology (On Peace)*. "Pindar, in his hyp-orchemata."

Let any townsman who would put the public good
in fair weather seek out proud Peace's[11]
    shining light,
having plucked from his mind wrathful discord,
giver of poverty, hateful nurse of children.

[11] I.e. peaceful concord within the state.

Polybius, *History*. "We do not praise the Thebans during the Persian War for deserting Hellas in its crisis and siding with the Persians out of fear, nor do we praise Pindar for encouraging them to remain inactive with these verses" (1–2).

111 Oxyrhynchus papyrus (2nd/3rd cent. A.D.). Erotian, *Glossary to Hippocrates*, s.v. αἰών. "spinal marrow . . . and Pindar says in his hyporchemata":

   .   .   .   .   .   .

he made him drink[12] . . . mixed in blood,
    and was inflicting many wounds . . . wielding his
        rough club,
but finally he lifted him up and crushed him against
        his own

[12] Probably a description of Heracles' fight with Antaeus, whom he defeated by lifting off the ground and crushing (cf. *Isth.* 4.52–55).

5   πλευράς,   αἰὼν δὲ δι' ὀστέων ἐρραίσθη

             ]·' αιμαπολ[

           ]δ' ἐγκεφαλ . [

           ]δε θυγατερ . [

           ]ντις ἰδὼν δ[

ribs, and his marrow was shattered throughout his   5
    bones

                    blood
                    brain(s)
                     daughter
                       having seen

ΕΓΚΩΜΙΑ

Encomia (literally poems of praise performed ἐν κώμῳ "in the revel") appear to be intended primarily for performance after a banquet (cf. *fr.* 124ab). They are sometimes difficult to distinguish from scolia (e.g., *frr.* 122, 125, and 128). The extant examples reveal a more personal treat-

118, 119   ΘΗΡΩΝΙ ΑΚΡΑΓΑΝΤΙΝΩΙ

118 Schol. A Pind. *Ol.* 2.39a εὖ δὲ τὸ τῶν Κάδμου θυγατέρων μεμνῆσθαι, ἵνα οἰκείῳ παραδείγματι χρήσηται· τὸ γὰρ τοῦ Θήρωνος γένος ἐνθένδε κατάγεσθαί φησιν ὁ Πίνδαρος ἐν ἐγκωμίῳ οὗ ἀρχή·

⊗   Βούλομαι παίδεσσιν Ἑλλάνων

119 Schol. B Pind. *Ol.* 2.15d ἔνιοι δέ φασιν ὅτι οἱ τοῦ Θήρωνος πρόγονοι οὐδόλως εἰς τὴν Γέλαν κατῆραν, ἀλλ᾽ εὐθὺς εἰς τὴν Ἀκράγαντα ἀπὸ Ῥόδου· ὡς καὶ ὁ Πίνδαρος λέγει·

ἂν δὲ Ῥόδον κατῴκισθεν . . .
ἔνθεν δ᾽ ἀφορμαθέντες ὑψηλὰν πόλιν ἀμφινέμονται,
πλεῖστα μὲν δῶρ᾽ ἀθανάτοις ἀνέχοντες,
ἕσπετο δ᾽ αἰενάου πλούτου νέφος.

358

ENCOMIA (EULOGIES)

ment of their subjects than those in the epinicia, often in terms of erotic desire, and even with humor, as in *fr.* 122 for Xenophon of Corinth. For a detailed commentary, see B. A. van Groningen, *Pindare au Banquet* (Leiden 1960).

118, 119   FOR THERON OF ACRAGAS

118 Scholion on *Ol.* 2.22. "He does well to mention Cadmus' daughters, so as to employ an example of a relative, for Pindar says that Theron's family derives from them in an encomium which begins":

I wish, for the sons of the Hellenes

119 Scholion on *Ol.* 2.8. "Some say that Theron's ancestors did not come to Gela at all, but directly to Acragas from Rhodes, as Pindar says":

and they settled in Rhodes . . .
Having set out from there, they inhabit a lofty city,[1]
and as they offer the most gifts to the immortals,
a cloud of ever-flowing wealth has followed them.

[1] Acragas.

PINDAR

120, 121   ΑΛΕΞΑΝΔΡΩΙ ΑΜΥΝΤΑ

120 Schol. Pind. *Nem.* 7.1a καταφέρεται εἰς τοῦτο ὁ
Πίνδαρος ὅταν ὑπῇ τις ὁμωνυμία, οἷον·

⊗   Ὀλβίων ὁμώνυμε Δαρδανιδᾶν,
παῖ θρασύμηδες Ἀμύντα

121 Dion. Hal. *Demosth.* 26 (1.185 Usener-Radermacher)
Πίνδαρος τοῦτο πεποίηκεν εἰς Ἀλέξανδρον τὸν Μακε-
δόνα, περὶ τὰ μέλη καὶ τοὺς ῥυθμοὺς μᾶλλον ἢ περὶ
τὴν λέξιν ἐσπουδακώς.

. . . πρέπει δ᾽ ἐσλοῖσιν ὑμνεῖσθαι . . .
. . . καλλίσταις ἀοιδαῖς.
τοῦτο γὰρ ἀθανάτοις τιμαῖς ποτιψαύει μόνον,
θνᾴσκει δὲ σιγαθὲν καλὸν ἔργον ⟨∪–⟩

1 δ᾽ ἐσλοῖσιν Sylburg: δὲ ὅλοισιν codd.
3 ῥηθέν post μόνον del. Bothe
4 δὲ σιγαθὲν Barnes: δ᾽ ἐπιταθὲν codd.

122   ΞΕΝΟΦΩΝΤΙ ΚΟΡΙΝΘΙΩΙ

Athen. 13.33.573E (=Chamaeleon, *fr.* 31 Wehrli) καὶ οἱ
ἰδιῶται δὲ κατεύχονται τῇ θεῷ τελεσθέντων περὶ ὧν ἂν
ποιῶνται τὴν δέησιν ἀπάξειν αὐτῇ καὶ τὰς ἑταίρας.
ὑπάρχοντος οὖν τοῦ τοιούτου νομίμου περὶ τὴν θεὸν
Ξενοφῶν ὁ Κορίνθιος ἐξιὼν εἰς Ὀλυμπίαν ἐπὶ τὸν
ἀγῶνα καὶ αὐτὸς ἀπάξειν ἑταίρας εὔξατο τῇ θεῷ

360

120, 121   FOR ALEXANDER, SON OF
                      AMYNTAS

120 Scholion on *Nem.* 7.1. "Pindar is drawn to this (viz. wordplay) whenever there is some similar name, as":

Namesake[2] of the blessed Trojans,
bold-counseling son of Amyntas

  [2] I.e. Alexander (=Paris). Alexander I ("the Philhellene") was king of Macedonia c. 495–450 B.C.

121 Dionysius of Halicarnassus, *On the Style of Demosthenes*. "Pindar composed this for Alexander the Macedonian, with more concern for the sound and rhythm than for the sense."

. . . it is proper for good men to be hymned
. . . with the most noble songs,
for that alone touches upon immortal honors,
but a noble deed dies when left in silence . . .

122   FOR XENOPHON OF CORINTH

Athenaeus, *Scholars at Dinner*. "And private citizens (viz. in Corinth) promise the goddess (Aphrodite) that if their prayers are answered they will even dedicate prostitutes to her. Since such a custom existed concerning the goddess, Xenophon of Corinth, when setting out for the Olympic games, promised the goddess that if he won he would dedicate prostitutes to her. Pindar first wrote an encomium to

PINDAR

νικήσας. Πίνδαρός τε τὸ μὲν πρῶτον ἔγραψεν εἰς
αὐτὸν ἐγκώμιον . . . (Ol. 13), ὕστερον δὲ καὶ σκόλιον τὸ
παρὰ τὴν θυσίαν ᾀσθέν, ἐν ᾧ τὴν ἀρχὴν εὐθέως
πεποίηται πρὸς τὰς ἑταίρας, αἳ παραγενομένου τοῦ
Ξενοφῶντος καὶ θύοντος τῇ Ἀφροδίτῃ συνέθυσαν·
διόπερ ἔφη· ὦ Κύπρου—ἰανθείς· ἤρξατο δ' οὕτως τοῦ
μέλους· πολύξεναι—καλόν. ἀρξάμενος δ' οὕτως ἑξῆς
φησιν· ἀλλὰ θαυμάζω—γυναιξίν. δῆλον γὰρ ὅτι πρὸς
τὰς ἑταίρας διαλεγόμενος ἠγωνία ποῖόν τι φανήσεται
τοῖς Κορινθίοις τὸ πρᾶγμα. πιστεύων δέ, ὡς ἔοικεν,
αὐτὸς αὑτῷ πεποίηκεν εὐθέως· ἐδιδάξαμεν—βασάνῳ.

Αʹ   Πολύξεναι νεάνιδες, ἀμφίπολοι
      Πειθοῦς ἐν ἀφνειῷ Κορίνθῳ,
      αἵ τε τᾶς χλωρᾶς λιβάνου ξανθὰ δάκρη
      θυμιᾶτε, πολλάκι ματέρ' ἐρώτων
         οὐρανίαν πτάμεναι
5   νοήματι πρὸς Ἀφροδίταν,

Βʹ   ὑμῖν ἄνευθ' ἐπαγορίας ἔπορεν,
      ὦ παῖδες, ἐρατειναῖς ⟨ἐν⟩ εὐναῖς
      μαλθακᾶς ὥρας ἀπὸ καρπὸν δρέπεσθαι.
      σὺν δ' ἀνάγκᾳ πᾶν καλόν . . .
      (desunt vv. 10–12)

362

him (*Ol.* 13), but later wrote a scolion as well, sung at the sacrifice, the opening of which he composed as an address to the prostitutes, who joined the celebration when Xenophon was present and performing the sacrifice. That is why he said (vv. 18–20), but he began the song in this way (vv. 1–9), and continued (vv. 13–15). It is clear that in addressing the prostitutes the poet was anxious about how the subject would appear to the Corinthians, but trusting, it appears, in his own integrity, he immediately added (v. 16)."

Young women who welcome many guests, attendants   Str. 1
of Persuasion[3] in rich Corinth,
you who burn the yellow tears of fresh
incense, often soaring in your thoughts
   to the heavenly
mother of loves, Aphrodite,   5

you, O children, she has permitted to cull   Str. 2
without blame in delightful acts of love
the fruit of soft youth.
Under compulsion all is fair . . .

  .   .   .   .   .   .

[3] Peitho is often associated with erotic attraction and desire (cf. *Pyth.* 9.39a and *fr.* 123.14).

---

3 αἴ τε τᾶς χλωρᾶς Tittmann: διαιτε τασχειρας A
4 θυμιᾶτε Tittmann e Zonara: τε ἡμῖν A
5 νοήματι πρὸς Wilamowitz: νοήματι ποττὰν A: νόημα πρὸς τὰν Boeckh   6 ἄνευθ᾽ ἐπαγορίας Meineke: ἄνωθεν ἀπαγορίας A   7 ⟨ἐν⟩ suppl. Boeckh

(Γ´) ἀλλὰ θαυμάζω, τί με λέξοντι Ἰσθμοῦ
δεσπόται τοιάνδε μελίφρονος ἀρχὰν
εὑρόμενον σκολίου

15 ξυνάορον ξυναῖς γυναιξίν.

Δ´ διδάξαμεν χρυσὸν καθαρᾷ βασάνῳ
. . . .
ὦ Κύπρου δέσποινα, τεὸν δεῦτ᾽ ἐς ἄλσος
φορβάδων κορᾶν ἀγέλαν ἑκατόγγυι-
ον Ξενοφῶν τελέαις
20 ἐπάγαγ᾽ εὐχωλαῖς ἰανθείς.

13 Ἰσθμοῦ Casaubonus: ὁμοῦ A

123   ΘΕΟΞΕΝΩΙ ΤΕΝΕΔΙΩΙ

Athen. 13.601D μνησθεὶς δὲ καὶ τοῦ Τενεδίου Θεοξένου
ὁ Πίνδαρος, ὃς ἦν αὐτοῦ ἐρώμενος, τί φησιν;

⊗   Χρῆν μὲν κατὰ καιρὸν ἐρώ-
των δρέπεσθαι, θυμέ, σὺν ἁλικίᾳ·
τὰς δὲ Θεοξένου ἀκτῖνας πρὸς ὄσσων
μαρμαρυζοίσας δρακείς
ὃς μὴ πόθῳ κυμαίνεται, ἐξ ἀδάμαντος
5   ἢ σιδάρου κεχάλκευται μέλαιναν καρδίαν

2 πρὸς ὄσσων Kaibel: προσώπου Athen. 601D: ὄσσων
Athen. 564E

364

. . . . . .   Str. 3
. . . . . .

But I wonder what the lords of the Isthmus
will say of my devising such a beginning as this
    for a honey-minded scolion[4]

to accompany women shared in common.   15

We test gold on a pure touchstone   Str. 4

. . . . . .
O mistress[5] of Cyprus, here into your precinct
Xenophon has brought a hundred-bodied
    herd of girls to graze,
in gladness at the fulfillment of his prayers.   20

[4] An after-dinner song evidently placed in the book of encomia
by the early editors. For the relationship of scolia to encomia, see
A. E. Harvey, "The Classification of Greek Lyric Poetry," *Classical
Quarterly* 5 (1955) 161–175.

[5] Aphrodite.

123   FOR THEOXENUS OF TENEDOS

The same. "And what does Pindar say when he mentions
Theoxenus of Tenedos, who was his beloved?"

One should cull love, my heart,   Str.
    as appropriate during youth,
but whoever has seen those rays
flashing from Theoxenus' eyes
and is not flooded with desire
has a black heart forged from adamant or steel   5

PINDAR

ψυχρᾷ φλογί, πρὸς δ' Ἀφροδί-
    τας ἀτιμασθεὶς ἑλικογλεφάρου
ἢ περὶ χρήμασι μοχθίζει βιαίως
ἢ γυναικείῳ θράσει
ψυχρὰν φορεῖται πᾶσαν ὁδὸν θεραπεύων.
10   ἀλλ' ἐγὼ τᾶς ἕκατι κηρὸς ὣς δαχθεὶς ἕλᾳ

ἱρᾶν μελισσᾶν τάκομαι, εὖτ' ἂν ἴδω
παίδων νεόγυιον ἐς ἥβαν·
ἐν δ' ἄρα καὶ Τενέδῳ
Πειθώ τ' ἔναιεν καὶ Χάρις
15   υἱὸν Ἀγησίλα.

9 ψυχρὰν A: ψυχὰν Schneider
10 τᾶς ἕκατι Wilamowitz: δεκατιτας A: τᾶσδ' ἕκατι Her-
mann· θεᾶς ἕκατι Schneidewin
10–11 ἕλᾳ ἱρᾶν Bergk: ἐλεηρὰν A

124ab ΘΡΑΣΥΒΟΤΛΩΙ ΑΚΡΑΓΑΝΤΙΝΩΙ

(a) Athen. 11.480C καὶ τῶν μὲν Ἀττικῶν ⟨κυλίκων⟩
μνημονεύει Πίνδαρος ἐν τοῖσδε· ὦ Θρασύβουλ'—κέν-
τρον. (b) idem 11.782D αὔξει γὰρ καὶ τρέφει μεγαλύνει
τε τὴν ψυχὴν ἡ ἐν τοῖς πότοις διατριβή, ἀναζωπυ-
ροῦσα καὶ ἀνεγείρουσα μετὰ φρονήσεως τὸν ἑκάστου
νοῦν, ὥς φησιν ὁ Πίνδαρος· ἁνίκ'—πλουτέοντες, εἶτ'
ἐπάγει· ἀέξονται—δαμέντες.

366

with a cold flame, and is dishonored   Ant.
   by bright-eyed Aphrodite,
or toils compulsively for money,
or with womanly courage
is carried in service to an utterly cold path.[6]
But I, because of her,[7] melt like the wax   10

of holy bees bitten by the sun's heat, whenever I look   Ep.
upon the new-limbed youth of boys.
So, after all, in Tenedos
Persuasion and Grace dwell
in the son of Hagesilas.   15

[6] The text is uncertain, but seems to describe one who is devoted exclusively to heterosexual love.

[7] Aphrodite.

124ab FOR THRASYBULUS OF ACRAGAS

Pindar addressed two epinicia (*Pyth.* 6 and *Isth.* 2) to Thrasybulus of Acragas, son of Xenocrates and nephew of Theron (celebrated in *Ol.* 2 and 3).

(a) The same. "And Pindar mentions Attic cups in the following verses (vv. 1–4)." (b) The same. "For time spent in drinking expands, nourishes, and enlarges the soul, by rekindling and awakening each person's mind with thoughts, as Pindar says (vv. 5–8). He then continues (v. 11)."

PINDAR

Α΄   ᾿Ω Θρασύβουλ᾿, ἐρατᾶν ὄχημ᾿ ἀοιδᾶν
      τοῦτό ⟨τοι⟩ πέμπω μεταδόρπιον. ἐν ξυνῷ κεν εἴη
      συμπόταισίν τε γλυκερὸν καὶ Διωνύσοιο καρπῷ

Β΄   καὶ κυλίκεσσιν Ἀθαναίαισι κέντρον·
5   ἁνίκ᾿ ἀνθρώπων καματώδεες οἴχονται μέριμναι
      στηθέων ἔξω· πελάγει δ᾿ ἐν πολυχρύσοιο
            πλούτου

Γ΄   πάντες ἴσᾳ νέομεν ψευδῆ πρὸς ἀκτάν·
      ὃς μὲν ἀχρήμων, ἀφνεὸς τότε, τοὶ δ᾿ αὖ
            πλουτέοντες
            . . . . . .

Δ΄   . . . . . .
11   ⟨–⟩ ἀέξονται φρένας ἀμπελίνοις τόξοις δαμέντες

2 ⟨τοι⟩ suppl. Boeckh
7 ἴσᾳ Hermann: ἴσα CE

124c Athen. 14.641B Ἀριστοτέλης δ᾿ ἐν τῷ περὶ μέθης
(fr. 104 Rose) τὰ τραγήματά φησι λέγεσθαι ὑπὸ τῶν
ἀρχαίων τρωγάλια· ὡσεὶ γὰρ ἐπιδορπισμὸν εἶναι·
Πίνδαρος δέ ἐστιν ὁ εἰπών·

      δείπνου δὲ λήγοντος γλυκὺ τρωγάλιον
      καίπερ πεδ᾿ ἄφθονον βοράν

368

O Thrasybulus, I am sending you this chariot of   Str. 1
    lovely songs
for after dinner. Amid the company may it be a sweet
    goad
for your drinking companions, for the fruit of
    Dionysus,

and for the Athenian drinking cups,   Str. 2
when men's wearisome cares vanish   5
from their breasts, and on a sea of golden wealth

we all alike sail to an illusory shore;   Str. 3
then the pauper is rich, while the wealthy

  .   .   .   .   .   .

  .   .   .   .   .   .   Str. 4
. . . increase in their minds, overcome by the arrows   11
    of the vine.

124c The same. "Aristotle says in his treatise *On Inebria-
tion* that τραγήματα ("desserts") were called τρωγάλια
by the ancients, for they are, as it were, an after-dinner
meal. Pindar is the one who said":

when the dinner ceases, dessert is pleasant
even after a bountiful meal

PINDAR

124d, 125, 126 ΙΕΡΩΝΙ ΣΤΡΑΚΟΣΙΩΙ

124d Philod. *de mus.* 4.12 p. 76 Kemke

βαρβι[τί]ξαι θυμὸν ἀμβλὺν ὄντα καὶ φωνὰν ἐν
    οἴνῳ

καὶ [γ]λυκὺ τρωγάλιον αὐτὴν ⟨τὴν μουσικὴν⟩ εἶναι
λεγόντων παρὰ τὰ δεῖπνα.

125 Athen. 14.635B Ἀριστόξενος (*fr.* 99 Wehrli) δὲ τὴν
μάγαδιν καὶ τὴν πηκτίδα χωρὶς πλήκτρου διὰ ψαλμοῦ
παρέχεσθαι τὴν χρείαν· διόπερ καὶ Πίνδαρον εἰρηκέ-
ναι ἐν τῷ πρὸς Ἱέρωνα σκολίῳ τὴν μάγαδιν ὀνομά-
σαντα ψαλμὸν ἀντίφθογγον. idem 635D ἀρχαῖόν
ἐστιν ὄργανον ἡ μάγαδις, σαφῶς Πινδάρου λέγοντος
τὸν Τέρπανδρον ἀντίφθογγον εὑρεῖν τῇ παρὰ Λυδοῖς
πηκτίδι τὸν βάρβιτον·

> τόν ῥα Τέρπανδρός ποθ' ὁ Λέσβιος εὗρεν
> πρῶτος, ἐν δείπνοισι Λυδῶν
> ψαλμὸν ἀντίφθογγον ὑψηλᾶς ἀκούων πακτίδος

2 Λυδῶν Schneider: λύδιον A

126 Athen. 12.512D (= Heracl. Pont. *fr.* 55 Wehrli) Πίν-
δαρος παραινῶν Ἱέρωνι τῷ Συρακοσίων ἄρχοντι·

> μηδ' ἀμαύρου τέρψιν ἐν βίῳ· πολύ τοι
> φέριστον ἀνδρὶ τερπνὸς αἰών.

370

124d, 125, 126   FOR HIERON OF SYRACUSE

124d Philodemus, *On Music*:

> to arouse with the *barbitos* a mind that is dull and a
>   voice in its cups

"and it (sc. music) is a sweet dessert when they recite it
at the dinner."[8]

[8] The text of this papyrus from Herculaneum is very corrupt
and the meaning uncertain.

125 Athenaeus, *Scholars at Dinner*: "Aristoxenus says
that the *magadis* and the *pēktis* can be played without a
plectrum by plucking; and for that very reason, he says, in
the scolion to Hieron Pindar named the *magadis* and said
'voice-answering plucking.'" The same. "The *magadis* is an
ancient instrument, and Pindar clearly says that Terpander
invented the *barbitos* 'answering the voice' of the *pēktis*
used by the Lydians":

> which [*barbitos*] once Terpander[9] of Lesbos was first
>   to invent, as he heard, during banquets of the Lydians,
> the voice-answering plucking of the high-pitched
>   *pēktis*.[10]

[9] Terpander composed in Sparta in the mid-seventh cent. B.C.
[10] The *barbitos* and the *pēktis* were varieties of lyre; the
barbitos (*lyra maior*) was an octave lower than the *pēktis*.

126 The same. "In his advice to Hieron, the ruler of the
Syracusans, Pindar says":

> and do not diminish enjoyment in life, since by far
>   the best thing for a man is an enjoyable lifetime.

PINDAR

127 Athen. 13.601C (e Chamaeleonte) καὶ Πίνδαρος δ᾽ οὐ μετρίως ὢν ἐρωτικός φησιν·

Εἴη καὶ ἐρᾶν καὶ ἔρωτι
χαρίζεσθαι κατὰ καιρόν·
μὴ πρεσβυτέραν ἀριθμοῦ
δίωκε, θυμέ, πρᾶξιν.

128 Athen. 10.427D (=Theophr. *fr.* 118 Wimmer) ἀλλ᾽ ἦν ἀπ᾽ ἀρχῆς τὸ μὲν σπένδειν ἀποδεδομένον τοῖς θεοῖς, ὁ δὲ κότταβος τοῖς ἐρωμένοις . . . διὸ καὶ τὰ σκολιὰ καλούμενα μέλη τῶν ἀρχαίων ποιητῶν πλήρη ἐστί· λέγω δ᾽ οἷον καὶ Πίνδαρος πεποίηται·

χάριτάς τ᾽ Ἀφροδισίων ἐρώτων,
ὄφρα σὺν Χειμάρῳ μεθύων Ἀγαθωνίδᾳ
βάλω κότταβον

2 Χειμάρῳ anonymus: χειμαμάρῳ A | Ἀγαθωνίδᾳ Wilamowitz: ἀγάθωνι δὲ A

372

127 The same. "And Pindar, who was no moderate lover, says":

May it be mine both to make love
and to gratify another's love when appropriate:
do not, my heart, pursue
a deed more advanced than the number of your years.

128 The same. "But from the beginning the libation was reserved for the gods, while the cottabus was for the beloved . . . and therefore the songs of the ancient poets called scolia are full of (the cottabus); I mean the kind Pindar composed":

the charms of Aphrodite's love-making,
so that, while getting drunk with Chimarus,
I may toss the cottabus[11] for Agathonidas.

[11] A game in which the drinker tried to toss the last drops from his cylix into a metal basin, naming his beloved as he did so.

ΘΡΗΝΟΙ

The threnos is a choral poem of lament accompanied by
the pipe. A number of passages quoted by ancient authors
describing the soul's status after death fall in this category.
In 1961 E. Lobel published numerous scraps from a late
2nd cent. papyrus (P. Oxy. 2447), two of which overlap

Thren. 3

128c Schol. Eur. *Rhes.* 895 cod. A Ἰαλέμῳ αὐ̣θ. [. .
ἔ]λεγον προωνομάσθαι ἐπὶ τιμῇ Ἰαλέμου τοῦ Ἀπόλ-
λωνος καὶ Καλλιόπης, ὥς φησι Πίνδαρος·

Ἔντι μὲν χρυσαλακάτου τεκέων Λατοῦς ἀοιδαί
ὥ[ρ]ιαι παιάνιδες· ἐντὶ [δὲ] καί

2 ὥ[ρ]ιαι suppl. Hermann | [δὲ] suppl. Wilamowitz

374

THRENOI (DIRGES)

fragments (128c and 129) already assigned to the threnoi. The exiguous remains of *Thren.* 1, 2, 4, and 5 have been omitted here. For a detailed commentary, see M. Cannatà Fera, *Pindarus: Thenorum Fragmenta* (Rome 1990).

Thren. 3

Although P. Oxy. 2447, fr. 4(b) only preserves the initial letters of vv. 1–5, it indicates that we have the beginning of a threnos. Unfortunately, the text, deriving from a scholion in one ms. of Euripides, is very corrupt. The opening is in the form of a priamel, culminating in the dirges sung for Calliope's sons, Linus, Hymenaeus, Ialemus, and evidently for Orpheus as well.

128c Scholion on Euripides, *Rhesus* 895. ". . . the lament was named before in honor of Ialemus, the son of Apollo and Calliope, as Pindar says (vv. 1–11)."

> There are paean-songs in due season belonging to the children[1]
>   of Leto with the golden distaff; there are also songs . . .

---

[1] Apollo and Artemis.

θάλλοντος ἐκ κισσοῦ στέφανον Διο[νύ]σου

ο[βρομι< >? παιόμεναι· †τὸ δὲ κοιμίσαν†

5   τρεῖς υἷας ἐκ Καλλιόπας, ὥς οἱ σταθῇ μνάμα<τ᾽>

ἀποφθιμένων·

ἁ μὲν εὐχαίταν Λίνον αἴλινον ὕμνει,

ἁ δ᾽ Ὑμέναιον, <ὃν> ἐν γάμοισι χροϊζόμενον

νυκτὶ σύμπρωτον λάβεν ἔσχατος ὕμνων·

ἁ δὲ < > Ἰάλεμον ὠμοβόλῳ

10   νούσῳ πεδαθέντα σθένος·

υἱὸν Οἰάγρου <δὲ>

Ὀρφέα χρυσάορα . . .

3 θάλλοντος Wilamowitz: θάλλοντες A | στέφανον A: στε-
φάνων Wilamowitz | ἐκ post στέφανον del. Wilamowitz

4 ὄ[ρθιαι Maehler: ο[ὕρεσιν Lehnus | βρομί<ο>παιόμεναι
Cannatà Fera: βρομί<ου> π<έρι μ>αιόμεναι Handley | τὸ δὲ A:
ταὶ δὲ Schneidewin

5 υἷας ἐκ legit Maehler | σταθῇ μνάμα<τ᾽> Maehler: σταθ
μνάμα A

6 εὐχαίταν Maehler: εὐχέταν A

7 <ὃν> suppl. Hermann | ἐν γάμοισι Welcker: ἐργάμοισι A

8 νυκτὶ legit Maehler | ἔσχατος ὕμνων Maehler: ἐσχατ
ὕμν(ον) A: ἐσχάτοις ὕμνοις Hermann et Schneidewin

9 ὠμοβόλῳ Hermann: ὁμοβόλῳ A

10 ὅτι post νούσῳ del. Hermann | πεδαθέντα Schneidewin:
παῖδα θέντοι A

11 <δὲ> suppl. Wilamowitz

12 huc add. Bergk e schol. A Hom. O 256 (4.67.16 Erbse) καὶ
Πίνδαρος χρυσάορα Ὀρφέα φησί.

Dionysus' crown of flourishing ivy
. . . Bromius . . . stricken . . . but (other songs) put to
    sleep
three sons of Calliope, so that memorials of the dead   5
    might be set up for her.
The one[2] sang *ailinon*[3] for long-haired Linus;
another sang of Hymenaeus, whom the last of hymns[4]
    took
when at night his skin was first touched in marriage;
and another sang of Ialemus, whose strength
was fettered by a flesh-rending disease;   10
and the son of Oeagrus[5] . . .

Orpheus of the golden lyre . . .

[2] Presumably "song" is the subject.

[3] A ritual cry of lament (cf. Aesch. *Ag.* 121), with perhaps wordplay (alas, Linus).

[4] I.e. a dirge, when he died on his wedding night.

[5] A scholion on *Pyth.* 4.176 (where Orpheus is Apollo's son) says that Pindar (among others) called Orpheus the son of Oeagrus. For Orpheus as son of Calliope, cf. Tim. *Pers.* 221–223.

PINDAR

Thren. 6

128f P. Oxy. 2447 (26, 1961), vv. 3–8. schol. Ap. Rhod. 1.57a ὁ δὲ Ἀπολλώνιος παρὰ Πινδάρου εἴληφε λέγοντος· ὁ δὲ—γᾶν.

(restant frustula vv. 1–2)

       ]αρ[ ]τευοντι[
           ]κλειτα . [
5   ]και Καστ[
           ]αιαιαν[
ὁ δὲ χλωραῖς
οἴχεται Καινεὺς σχίσαις ὀρθῷ ποδί
γᾶν.

cf. Plut. *de absurd. Stoic. opin.* 1.1057D ὁ Πινδάρου Καινεὺς εὔθυναν ὑπεῖχεν, ἀπιθάνως ἄρρηκτος σιδήρῳ καὶ ἀπαθὴς τὸ σῶμα πλασσόμενος, εἶτα καταδὺς ἄτρωτος ὑπὸ γῆν σχίσας ὀρθῷ ποδὶ γᾶν.

129, 131a, 130   Thren. 7

129 P. Oxy. 2447 (26, 1961), vv. 7–15. Plut. *consol. ad Apoll.* 35.120C λέγεται δ᾽ ὑπὸ μὲν τοῦ μελικοῦ Πινδάρου ταυτὶ περὶ τῶν εὐσεβῶν ἐν Ἅιδου· τοῖσι—βωμοῖς.

τοῖσι λάμπει μὲν μένος ἀελίου
τὰν ἐνθάδε νύκτα κάτω,

378

Thren. 6

128f The same papyrus gives scraps of vv. 3–8. A scholion on Apollonius Rhodius, *Argonautica*. "Apollonius took it from Pindar, who said" (vv. 7–9):

> (lines 1–2 are fragmentary)
> > excel(?)
> > famous(?)
> > and Castor(?)   5

> .   .   .   .   .   .
>   But Caeneus,[6] (struck with) green (fir trees)
> disappears after splitting the earth with his upright
> foot.

[6] A Thessalian hero and ally of the Lapithae against the Centaurs. He was invulnerable, but the Centaurs succeeded in subduing him by bashing him upright into the ground with fir trees. Cf. Ap. Rhod. 1.63–64: "But unbroken and unbending, he sank beneath the earth, hammered by the downward force of mighty pine trees."

Cf. Plutarch, *The Stoics Talk More Paradoxically Than the Poets*. "Pindar's Caeneus used to be criticized for being an implausible creation—invulnerable to iron, feeling nothing in his body, and finally having sunk unwounded under the ground, 'after splitting the earth with his upright foot.'"

129, 131a, 130   Thren. 7

129 Same papyrus (vv. 7–15). Plutarch, *Letter of Consolation to Apollonius*. "The following is said by the lyric poet Pindar about the pious in Hades":

> For them shines the might of the sun
> below during nighttime up here,

PINDAR

φοινικορόδοις ⟨δ᾽⟩ ἐνὶ λειμώνεσσι προάστιον αὐτῶν
καὶ λιβάνων σκιαρᾶν ⟨   ⟩
5 καὶ χρυσοκάρποισιν βέβριθε ⟨δενδρέοις⟩
καὶ τοὶ μὲν ἵπποις γυμνασίοισι ⟨τε – –⟩
      τοὶ δὲ πεσσοῖς
τοὶ δὲ φορμίγγεσσι τέρπονται, παρὰ δέ σφισιν
      εὐανθὴς ἅπας τέθαλεν ὄλβος·
ὀδμὰ δ᾽ ἐρατὸν κατὰ χῶρον κίδναται
†αἰεὶ . . θύματα μειγνύντων πυρὶ τηλεφανεῖ
10 ⟨παντοῖα θεῶν ἐπὶ βωμοῖς⟩
                ]εοι μοῖρ᾽ ἔνθα . [
                ]δώροις βουθυ[
                ]φαν ἄλοχόν [
                ]αν·
15   ]πρὸς [Ὄ]λυμπον [

3 ⟨δ᾽⟩ suppl. Boeckh
4 λιβάνων σκιαρᾶν ⟨ ⟩ Snell: λιβάνῳ σκιαρὰν (-ρὸν B)
Plut.
5 ⟨δενδρέοις⟩ suppl. Wilamowitz
6 ⟨τε⟩ suppl. Boeckh

131a Plut. *consol. ad Apoll.* 35.120D καὶ μικρὸν προ-
ελθὼν ἐν ἄλλῳ θρήνῳ περὶ ψυχῆς λέγων φησίν·

ὄλβιοι δ᾽ ἅπαντες αἴσᾳ λυσιπόνων τελετᾶν

ὄλβιοι . . . λυσιπόνων τελετᾶν Wilamowitz: ὀλβίᾳ . . .
λυσίπονον τελετάν codd.

380

and in meadows of red roses their country abode
is laden with . . . shady frankincense trees
and trees with golden fruit,   5
and some take delight in horses and exercises,
    others in draughts,
and others in lyres; and among them
    complete happiness blooms and flourishes.
A fragrance spreads throughout the lovely land,
as they continually mingle offerings of all kinds
(with far-shining fire on the gods' altars).[7]   10
        portion from there
        gifts, oxen-sacrifice(s)
        wife

  .   .   .   .   .   .

        to Olympus   15

[7] The papyrus omits v. 10 in the passage from Plutarch.

131a Plutarch, ibid. "And, a bit further on in another
threnos, when speaking about the soul, he says":

  happy are all those with the good fortune of toil-
      relieving rites

130 Plut. *de lat. vid.* 7.1130C ἡ δὲ τρίτη τῶν ἀνοσίως βεβιωκότων καὶ παρανόμως ὁδός ἐστιν, εἰς ἔρεβός τι καὶ βάραθρον ὠθοῦσα τὰς ψυχάς,

> ἔνθεν τὸν ἄπειρον ἐρεύγονται σκότον
> βληχροὶ δνοφερᾶς νυκτὸς ποταμοὶ

131b Plut. *consol. ad Apoll.* 35.120C

> σῶμα μὲν πάντων ἕπεται θανάτῳ περισθενεῖ,
> ζωὸν δ᾽ ἔτι λείπεται αἰῶνος εἴδω-
>   λον· τὸ γάρ ἐστι μόνον
> ἐκ θεῶν· εὕδει δὲ πρασσόντων μελέων, ἀτὰρ εὑ-
>   δόντεσσιν ἐν πολλοῖς ὀνείροις
> δείκνυσι τερπνῶν ἐφέρποισαν χαλεπῶν τε κρίσιν.

133 Plat. *Men.* 81B λέγει δὲ καὶ Πίνδαρος καὶ ἄλλοι . . . τὴν ψυχὴν τοῦ ἀνθρώπου εἶναι ἀθάνατον . . . δεῖν δὴ διὰ ταῦτα ὡς ὁσιώτατα διαβιῶναι τὸν βίον·

> οἷσι δὲ Φερσεφόνα ποινὰν παλαιοῦ πένθεος
> δέξεται, ἐς τὸν ὕπερθεν ἅλιον κείνων ἐνάτῳ ἔτεϊ
> ἀνδιδοῖ ψυχὰς πάλιν, ἐκ τᾶν βασιλῆες ἀγαυοί
> καὶ σθένει κραιπνοὶ σοφίᾳ τε μέγιστοι
> 5 ἄνδρες αὔξοντ᾽· ἐς δὲ τὸν λοιπὸν χρόνον ἥροες ἁ-
>   γνοὶ πρὸς ἀνθρώπων καλέονται.

---

10 For a discussion of the "ancient grief" as Persephone's for the killing of her son Dionysus by the Titans, see R. S. Bluck, *Plato's Meno* (Cambridge 1964) 278.

130 Plutarch, *Is "Live Unknown" a Wise Precept?* "The third way[8] is for those who have lived unholy and criminal lives; it plunges their souls into a pit of darkness":

> from there sluggish rivers of gloomy night
> belch forth an endless darkness

[8] For a discussion of the three ways, see M. M. Willcock, *Pindar Victory Odes* (Cambridge 1995) 171–172.

131b Plutarch, *Letter of Consolation to Apollonius*:

> The body of all men is subject to overpowering death,
> but a living image[9] of life still remains,
>   for it alone is
> from the gods. It slumbers while the limbs are active,
>   but to men as they sleep, in many dreams
> it reveals an approaching decision of things pleasant
>   or distressful.

[9] I.e. the soul.

133 Plato, *Meno*. "Among others Pindar says . . . that the soul of man is immortal . . . that therefore it is indeed necessary to live one's entire life as piously as possible":

> But for those from whom Persephone accepts requital
> for the ancient grief,[10] in the ninth year she returns
> their souls to the upper sunlight; from them arise
> proud kings and men who are swift in strength
> and greatest in wisdom, and for the rest of time   5
>   they are called sacred heroes by men.

134 Stob. *ecl.* 4.39.6 (5.903 Wachsmuth-Hense) Πινδά-
ρου θρήνων·

εὐδαιμόνων δραπέτας οὐκ ἔστιν ὄλβος

135 Schol. Pind. *Ol.* 1.127a καὶ ἐν θρήνοις τὸν αὐτὸν
ἀριθμὸν τίθησι τῶν ὑπὸ τοῦ Οἰνομάου ἀναιρεθέντων
μνηστήρων·

πέφνε δὲ τρεῖς καὶ δέκ᾽ ἄνδρας·
τετράτῳ δ᾽ αὐτὸς πεδάθη

136a Aristid. *or.* 31.12 (2.215 Keil) ἐπέρχεταί μοι τὸ τοῦ
Πινδάρου προσθεῖναι,

ἄστρα τε καὶ ποταμοὶ καὶ κύματα πόντου

τὴν ἀωρίαν τὴν σὴν ἀνακαλεῖ.

137   ΙΠΠΟΚΡΑΤΕΙ? ΑΘΗΝΑΙΩΙ

Clem. Alex. *strom.* 3.3.17 (2.203 Stählin) Πίνδαρος περὶ
τῶν ἐν Ἐλευσῖνι μυστηρίων λέγων ἐπιφέρει·

ὄλβιος ὅστις ἰδὼν κεῖν᾽ εἶσ᾽ ὑπὸ χθόν·
οἶδε μὲν βίου τελευτάν,
οἶδεν δὲ διόσδοτον ἀρχάν

1 κεῖν᾽ εἶσ᾽ Teuffel: ἐκεῖνα κοινὰ εἰσ᾽ Clemens

134 Stobaeus, *Anthology (On Happiness)*. "From Pindar's threnoi":

the happiness of blessed men is no fugitive

135 Scholion on *Ol.* 1.79. "In the threnoi as well he gives the same number of suitors slain by Oenomaus":

he killed thirteen men;
he himself was checked by the fourteenth

136a Aristides, *Oration* 31 *(Funeral Oration for Eteoneus)*. "It occurs to me to add the line of Pindar,

the stars and rivers and waves of the sea,

invoke again and again your untimely death."

137   FOR HIPPOCRATES OF ATHENS(?) [11]

Clement of Alexandria, *Miscellanies*. "In speaking of the Eleusinian mysteries, Pindar adds":

Blessed is he who sees them[12] and goes beneath the
        earth;
    he knows the end of life
and knows its Zeus-given beginning.

[11] The inscription is derived from a scholion on *Pyth.* 7.18 ff., which says that Pindar wrote a threnos for Hippocrates, a relative of the victor Megacles.
[12] The mysteries.

INCERTORUM LIBRORUM
FRAGMENTA

140a P. Oxy. 408 (3, 1903)

(restant frustula vv. 1–24, desunt vv. 25–47)

φ[ι]λ[.]ν μι[– –

τοὶ πρόıδ[ο]ν αἶσαν α̣[
50   ζοι τότ᾽ ἀμφε . ουτα̣τ . [
'Ηρακλέης· ἁλίαι[. .] . . [
ναὶ μολόντας [.]υ̣[. .]π̣[.] . [.] . σο̣ε̣ν
θο . . οι φύγον ον[. . . . .] . [.] . . .
πάντων γὰρ ὑπ[έ]ρβιος ανα . σε̣φα[
55   ψυχὰν κενεῶ[ν] εμε[.] . ἔ̣ρ̣υ̣κ̣ε̣ν . . [
λαῶν ξενοδα[ΐ]κτα βασιλῆ[-]
      ος ἀτασθαλίᾳ κοτέω[ν] θαμά,
ἀρχαγέτᾳ τε [Δ]άλου
πίθετο παῦσε̣έ̣ν̣ [τ᾽] ἔργ᾽ ἀναιδῆ . . . .
60   γάρ σε λ[ι]γυσφα̣ρ̣ά̣γ̣ω̣ν κ̣λ̣υ̣τᾶ̣ν̣ ἀυ-
τά, 'Εκαβόλε̣, φορμίγγων.

49 suppl. Snell   54–58 suppl. Grenfell-Hunt
59 ἔργ᾽ ἀναιδῆ legit Snell

FRAGMENTS FROM
UNIDENTIFIABLE BOOKS

140a Papyrus (early 2nd cent. A.D.)

The subject of the fragment is Heracles' vengeance on Laomedon for refusing to pay him his promised reward after he rescued Laomedon's daughter Hesione from a sea monster. Heracles' campaign against Troy is also mentioned at *Nem.* 3.36–37 and *Isth.* 6.27–31.

> (lines 1–24 and 48 are fragmentary, 25–47 are missing)
> they foresaw their fate . . .   [Ant.]
>   then . . .   50
> Heracles; of the sea . . .
> (them) coming on ship
>   they fled . . .
> for of all . . . the powerful man . . .
> he restrained the soul of vain men . . .   55
> often angry at the wickedness of the people's
>   guest-murdering king,[1]
> and he obeyed the colony-founder of Delos[2]
> and stopped the shameless deeds . . .
>   for the sound of the glorious shrill-voiced   60
>   lyres (celebrates?) you, Far-Shooter.

[1] Laomedon (cf. 68).

[2] For Apollo as colony-founder, see *Pyth.* 5.60.

387

PINDAR

μνάσθηθ' ὅτι τοι ζαθέας
Πάρου ἐν γυάλοις ἔσσατο ἄ[ν]ακτι
βωμὸν πατρί τε Κρονίῳ τιμάεν-
65 τι πέραν ἰσθμὸν διαβαίς,
ὅτε Λαομέδον-
τι πεπρωμένοι᾿ ἤρχετο
μόροιο κάρυξ.

ἦν γάρ τι παλαίφατον [. .] . . . ον
70 ἷκε συγγόνους
τρεῖς π[. .] . εω[.]ν κεφαλὰν . . ρ . . ται[
ἐπιδ[. . . . .]αιμα[. .] . [. . . .] . [
(restant frustula vv. 73–80 ⊗)

140b P. Oxy. 408 (3, 1903); schol. Pind. *Ol*. 10.17i, vv. 4–
5; Plut. *qu. conv.* 7.5.2.704F, vv. 15–17

A´⊗ Ἴων[
ἀοιδ[ὰν κ]αὶ ἁρμονίαν
αὐλ[οῖς ἐ]πεφράσ[ατο
τῶ[ν γε Λο]κρῶν τις, οἵ τ᾿ ἀργίλοφον
5 πὰρ Ζεφυρίου κολώναν
ν[. . . ὑπὲ]ρ Αὐσονία[ς ἁλός

3 suppl. Schroeder
4 γε suppl. Garrod
6 ἁλός suppl. Wilamowitz

388

Remember that he[3] set up an altar to you
in the valleys of holy Paros, lord,
and to his honored father, son of Cronus,
    after crossing over the isthmus,[4]   65
when as herald
    he began the doom
fated for Laomedon.

For there was an ancient pronouncement . . .   [Ep.]
he came to   70
three kinsmen . . . head . . .

   3 Heracles; Apollodorus 2.5.9 mentions Heracles' sojourn in
Paros during his quest for Hippolyte's belt, after which he went to
Troy.
   4 The Hellespont, or perhaps the Isthmus of Corinth.

140b Same papyrus; scholion on *Ol.* 10.13 (vv. 4–5); Plu-
tarch, *Table-Talk* (vv. 15–17). The relationship of this frag-
ment to the preceding one is not clear.

(Ionian?)   Str. 1
one[5] of the Locrians, who (dwell?) by the
white-topped hill of Zephyrion[6]
above the Ausonian sea,[7]
devised the song and musical mode   5
for pipes

   5 Probably a reference to Xenocritus (or Xenocrates), who in-
vented the Locrian musical mode (cf. Athen. 14.625E and schol.
Ol. 10.17k and 18b).
   6 The headland of Epizephyrian Locri.
   7 The Adriatic.

PINDAR

λι[. . . . . .]ις ἀνθ . [
οἷον [ὄ]χημα λιγ[υ
κες λό[γ]ον παιηο[ν
10 Ἀπόλλωνί τε καὶ [
ἄρμενον. ἐγὼ μ[
παῦρα μελ[ι]ζομεν[
[γλώ]σσαργον ἀμφέπω[ν ἐρε-
θίζομαι πρὸς αυ . [
15 ἁλίου δελφῖνος ὑπόκρισιν,
τὸν μὲν ἀκύμονος ἐν πόντου πελάγει
αὐλῶν ἐκίνησ' ἐρατὸν μέλος.

8–9 [εὐπλε]κὲς suppl. Fileni
9 λό[γ]ον Maehler: Λο[κρ]ὸν Ferrari
12 μελ[ι]ζομέν[ου τέχναν Grenfell-Hunt
13 suppl. Grenfell-Hunt

140c Plut. *de def. orac.* 30.426C οἱ Τυνδαρίδαι τοῖς
χειμαζομένοις βοηθοῦσιν

ἐπερχόμενόν τε μαλάσσοντες βίαιον
πόντον ὠκείας τ' ἀνέμων . . . ῥιπάς

140d Clem. Alex. *strom.* 5.14.129 (2.413 Stählin) Πίνδα-
ρός τε ὁ μελοποιὸς οἷον ἐκβακχεύεται, ἄντικρυς εἰπών·

τί θεός; τὸ πάν.

ὅτι post τὸ del. Schroeder

390

. . . . . .
such a chariot . . . (high-pitched?)
   word . . . paean(s) . . .
fitting for Apollo and   10
      I . . .
singing a few songs,
cherishing the garrulous . . .
   am incited to . . .
in the manner of a dolphin of the sea,   15
which the lovely melody of pipes
excited in the expanse of the waveless deep.

140c Plutarch, *On the Obsolescence of Oracles*. "The
Tyndaridae come to the aid of men being tossed in a
storm":

   calming the violent advance
   of the sea and the swift blasts of the winds

140d Clement of Alexandria, *Miscellanies*. "And how the
lyric poet Pindar swells with enthusiasm when he says out-
right":

   What is god? Everything.

PINDAR

141 Didym. Caec. *de trin.* 3.1 p. 320 ed. Bon. καὶ οἱ ἔξω
φασίν·

θεὸς ὁ πάντα τεύχων βροτοῖς
καὶ χάριν ἀοιδᾷ φυτεύει

143 Plut. *de superst.* 6.167F κοινὸν ἀνθρώπων τὸ μὴ
πάντα διευτυχεῖν (ὁ Πίνδαρος θεούς φησι)·

κεῖνοι γάρ τ' ἄνοσοι καὶ ἀγήραοι
πόνων τ' ἄπειροι, βαρυβόαν
πορθμὸν πεφευγότες Ἀχέροντος

146 Schol. T Hom. Ω 100 (5.539.10 Erbse) (de Minerva)
πὰρ Διὶ πατρί· ἐκ δεξιῶν, ὥς φησι Πίνδαρος,

πῦρ πνέοντος ἅτε κεραυνοῦ
ἄγχιστα δεξιὰν κατὰ χεῖρα πατρός

ἵζεαι.

cf. Plut. *qu. conv.* 1.2.4.617C διαρρήδην δ' ὁ Πίνδαρος
λέγει· πῦρ πνέοντος ἅ τε κεραυνοῦ ἄγχιστα ἡμένη.
Aristid. *or.* 2.6 (2.305 Keil) Πίνδαρος δ' αὖ φησι δεξιὰν
κατὰ χεῖρα τοῦ πατρὸς αὐτὴν καθεζομένην τὰς ἐντο-
λὰς τοῖς θεοῖς ἀποδέχεσθαι.

392

141 Didymus the Blind, *On the Trinity*. "Even the pagans say":

> god, who accomplishes all things for mortals,
> also plants loveliness in song

143 Plutarch, *On Superstition*. "It is the common lot of men not to succeed continually in all things, (as Pindar says of the gods)":

> for they, without sickness or old age
> and unacquainted with toils, having escaped
> the deep-roaring passage of Acheron

146 Scholion on *Iliad* 24.100 ("of Athena 'beside father Zeus'"). "On the right hand, as Pindar says:

> who nearest the fire-breathing thunderbolt
> at the right hand of your father

you sit."

Plutarch, *Table-Talk*. "And Pindar says explicitly (of Athena), 'she, sitting nearest the fire-breathing thunderbolt.'" Aristides, *Oration* 37 (*Hymn to Athena*). "Again Pindar says that she sits at the right hand of her father and receives his orders for the gods."

PINDAR

148 Athen. epit. 1.40.22B Πίνδαρος τὸν Ἀπόλλωνα ὀρχηστὴν καλεῖ·

ὀρχήστ᾽ ἀγλαΐας ἀνάσσων, εὐρυφάρετρ᾽ Ἄπολλον

150 Eustath. *Il.* 9.45 καὶ Πίνδαρος . . . λέγει·

μαντεύεο, Μοῖσα, προφατεύσω δ᾽ ἐγώ.

151 Eustath. *Il.* 9.40 οὗ (sc. Ὁμήρου) ἀνάπαλιν Πίνδαρος ποιεῖ ἐν τῷ Μοῦσα ἀνέηκέ με, ἤγουν ἀνέπεισεν. οὐ γὰρ αὐτὸς Μοῦσαν, ἐκείνη δὲ αὐτὸν ἀνέπεισεν et 179.14 ἀνέηκέ με ἡ Μοῦσα.

Μοῖσ᾽ ἀνέηκέ με

152 *Epim. Hom.* Cram. *Anecd. Ox.* 1.285.19 Πίνδαρος·

μελισσοτεύκτων κηρίων ἐμὰ γλυκερώτερος ὀμφά

153 Plut. *Is. Osir.* 35.365A ὅτι δ᾽ οὐ μόνον τοῦ οἴνου Διόνυσον ἀλλὰ καὶ πάσης ὑγρᾶς φύσεως Ἕλληνες ἡγοῦνται κύριον καὶ ἀρχηγόν, ἀρκεῖ Πίνδαρος μάρτυς εἶναι λέγων·

δενδρέων δὲ νομὸν Διώνυσος πολυγαθὴς αὐξάνοι, ἁγνὸν φέγγος ὀπώρας

FRAGMENT 148

148 Athenaeus, *Scholars at Dinner.* "Pindar calls Apollo a dancer":

> dancer ruling over the celebration, Apollo of the
>   broad quiver

150 Eustathius, *Commentary on Iliad* 1.1. "And Pindar says":

> Give me an oracle, Muse, and I shall be your prophet.

151 The same. "Pindar reverses Homer's order (Μῆνιν ἄειδε, θεά) in his

> the Muse urged me

that is, incited me, for he did not incite the Muse, but she him."

152 *Homeric Parsings.* "Pindar (says)":

> my voice is sweeter than bee-built honeycombs

153 Plutarch, *On Isis and Osiris.* "That the Greeks consider Dionysus to be lord and master not only of wine but of all liquid nature, Pindar is a sufficient witness when he says":

> may Dionysus, bringer of joy, foster the grove of trees,
> the holy light[8] at summer's end

[8] It is not clear whether "the holy light" is in apposition to Dionysus or the grove.

155 Athen. 5.18.191F (de Aegyptiis) καθήμενοι μὲν γὰρ
ἐδείπνουν τροφῇ τῇ λιτοτάτῃ καὶ ὑγιεινοτάτῃ χρώμε-
νοι καὶ οἴνῳ τοσούτῳ ὅσος ἱκανὸς ἂν γένοιτο πρὸς
εὐθυμίαν, ἣν ὁ Πίνδαρος αἰτεῖται παρὰ τοῦ Διός·

τί ἔρδων φίλος σοί τε, καρτερόβρεντα
Κρονίδα, φίλος δὲ Μοίσαις,
Εὐθυμίᾳ τε μέλων εἴην, τοῦτ᾽ αἴτημί σε

156 Paus. 3.25.2 τραφῆναι μὲν δὴ τὸν Σιληνὸν ἐν τῇ
Μαλέᾳ δηλοῖ καὶ τάδε ἐξ ᾄσματος Πινδάρου·

ὁ ζαμενὴς δ᾽ ὁ χοροιτύπος,
ὃν Μαλέας ὄρος ἔθρεψε, Ναΐδος ἀκοίτας
Σιληνός

2 Μαλέας ὄρος Wilamowitz: μαλέγορος codd.

157 Schol. Aristoph. *Nub.* 223 τί με καλεῖς, ὦ ᾽φήμερε·
. . . περιέθηκεν οὖν αὐτῷ φωνὴν τὴν τοῦ παρὰ Πινδάρῳ
Σειληνοῦ. ὁ γάρ τοι Πίνδαρος διαλεγόμενον παράγων
τὸν Σειληνὸν τῷ Ὀλύμπῳ τοιούτους αὐτῷ περιέθηκε
λόγους·

ὦ τάλας ἐφάμερε, νήπια βάζεις
χρήματά μοι διακομπέων

1 νήπια Kuster: νήπιε codd.

155 Athenaeus, *Scholars at Dinner.* "For (the Egyptians) used to sit and dine, eating the plainest and most healthful food and drinking just enough wine to provide that good cheer, which Pindar requests from Zeus":

> What may I do to be dear to you, mighty-thundering
> son of Cronus, and dear to the Muses
> and pleasing to Good Cheer—this I ask of you.

156 Pausanias, *Description of Greece.* "These verses from Pindar's poem make clear that Silenus was raised in Malea":

> the ecstatic dancer with beating feet,
> whom the mountain of Malea[9] raised, the husband of
>   a Naiad,
> Silenus

[9] On the southeastern tip of the Peloponnesus.

157 Scholion on Aristophanes, *Clouds* 223. ("Why are you calling me, ephemeral creature?") ". . . he has given him (i.e. Socrates) the phrase of Silenus in Pindar, for when Pindar portrays Silenus talking to Olympus,[10] he puts such words in his mouth."

> O wretched creature of the day, you babble nonsense
> when boasting to me of money.

[10] The heavenly musician.

159 Dion. Hal. *de or. ant.* 2 (1.4.20 Usener-Radermacher)
ἀλλὰ γὰρ οὐ μόνον

  ἀνδρῶν δικαίων Χρόνος σωτὴρ ἄριστος

κατὰ Πίνδαρον, ἀλλὰ καὶ τεχνῶν . . . καὶ παντὸς
ἄλλου σπουδαίου χρήματος.

160 Stob. *ecl.* 4.58.2 (5.1142 Wachsmuth-Henze) Πιν-
δάρου·

  θανόντων δὲ καὶ φίλοι προδόται

  λόγοι post καὶ del. Bergk

166 Athen. 11.51.476B Πίνδαρος μὲν ἐπὶ τῶν Κενταύ-
ρων λέγων·

  ⟨ἀνδρ⟩οδάμαν⟨τα⟩ δ᾽ ἐπεὶ Φῆρες δάεν
  ῥιπὰν μελιαδέος οἴνου,
  ἐσσυμένως ἀπὸ μὲν λευκὸν γάλα χερσὶ τραπεζᾶν
  ὤθεον, αὐτόματοι δ᾽ ἐξ ἀργυρέων κεράτων
5 πίνοντες ἐπλάζοντο . . .

  1 ⟨ἀνδρ⟩οδάμαν⟨τα⟩ suppl. Casaubonus, Boeckh

168b Athen. 10.1.411C Ἴων . . . παρὰ Πινδάρου δὲ
τοῦτ᾽ εἴληφεν εἰπόντος·

159 Dionysius of Halicarnassus, *On the Ancient Orators.*
"Yet not only

for just men Time is the best savior

according to Pindar, but for the arts . . . and every other
serious endeavor."

160 Stobaeus, *Anthology* (*The Memory of Most Men
Quickly Vanishes After Death*). "Pindar's"

even friends betray those who have died

166 Athenaeus, *Scholars at Dinner.* "In speaking of the
Centaurs, Pindar (says)":

When the Pheres[11] came to know the man-subduing
blast of honey-sweet wine,
they quickly pushed the white milk away from the
tables
with their hands and, spontaneously drinking
from the silver drinking-horns, began to lose their   5
senses.

[11] Centaurs; the scene is at the wedding of Peirithoös and
Hippodameia.

168b Athenaeus, *Scholars at Dinner.* "Ion[12] has taken
this (i.e. his portrayal of Heracles' gluttony) from Pindar,
who said":

[12] Ion of Chios (c. 490–421), a tragic poet; the depiction of
Heracles was in his *Omphale.*

"διὰ βοῶν
θερμὰ πρὸς ἀνθρακιὰν
στέψαν πυρὶ δεῖπνον
σώματα· καὶ τότ' ἐγὼ
5   σαρκῶν τ' ἐνοπὰν ⟨∪∪?⟩ ἠδ' ὀ-
στέων στεναγμὸν βαρύν·
ἦν διακρῖναι ἰδόντα πολλὸς ἐν καιρῷ χρόνος"

1 διὰ βοῶν Boeckh: διαβοῶν codd.
2 πρὸς Schroeder: δ' εἰς codd.
3 δεῖπνον Lehnus: δ' ὑπνόων τε codd.: δ' ὤπτων Snell
5 ⟨ἴδον⟩ Schroeder: ⟨κλύον⟩ Snell

169a P. Oxy. 2450 (26, 1961), vv. 6–62. Plat. *Gorg*. 484B
δοκεῖ δέ μοι καὶ Πίνδαρος ἅπερ ἐγὼ λέγω ἐνδείκνυ-
σθαι ἐν τῷ ᾄσματι, ἐν ᾧ λέγει ὅτι νόμος—ἀθανάτων·
οὗτος δὲ δή, φησίν, ἄγει—ἀπριάτας ... ἠλάσατο τὰς
βοῦς. cf. *Leg*. 4.714E–715A. schol. Aristid. *or*. 2.226
(3.408 Dindorf) (Ἡρακλῆς) τὰς τοῦ Γηρυόνου βόας
οὔτε αἰτήσας οὔτε πριάμενος ἤλασεν. schol. Pind. *Nem*.
9.35a, vv. 1–4.

A´   Νόμος ὁ πάντων βασιλεύς
    θνατῶν τε καὶ ἀθανάτων
    ἄγει δικαιῶν τὸ βιαιότατον
    ὑπερτάτᾳ χειρί. τεκμαίρομαι

3 δικαιῶν τὸ βιαιότατον schol. Pind., Aristid.: βιαιῶν τὸ
δικαιότατον Plat. *Gorg*. 484B: δικαιοῦντα τὸ βιαιότατον Plat.
Leg. 715A

> "They put two
warm bodies of oxen
around the embers, and began roasting
the carcasses. Then I (heard?)
the cry of flesh and the 5
>   loud groaning of bones;
There was a long time on that occasion to see and
>   distinguish it."

169a An Oxyrhynchus papyrus (1st–early 2nd cent. A.D.) gives parts of vv. 6–62. Plato, *Gorgias*. "And it seems to me that Pindar demonstrates just what I am saying in the poem where he says (vv. 1–2), and then continues (vv. 3–6) . . . when he drove off the cattle without paying for them." Scholion on Aristides, *Oration 2* (*In Defense of Oratory*). "He (sc. Heracles) drove off Geryon's cattle without asking or paying for them." For accounts of this labor of Heracles, see Diod. Sic. 4.15.3 and Apollodorus 2.5.8. From the time of Herodotus (cf. 3.38.4) the opening of this poem has been quoted in support of various contradictory positions and what exactly Pindar means by νόμος ("law," "custom") remains disputed.

Law, the king of all,   Str. 1
of mortals and immortals,
guides them as it justifies the utmost violence
with a sovereign hand. I bring as witness

401

5 ἔργοισιν Ἡρακλέος·
   ἐπεὶ Γηρυόνα βόας
   Κυκλώπειον ἐπὶ πρόθυρον Εὐρυσθέος
   ἀνατεί τε] καὶ ἀπριάτας ἔλασεν,
   -??] Διομήδεος ἵππους
10 -? μ]όναρχον Κ[ι]κόνων
      παρὰ] Βιστονίδι λίμνᾳ
   χαλκοθώρ]ακος Ἐνναλίου
   ∪∪-] ἔκπαγλον υἱόν

   ∪∪∪] . ιαντα μέγαν
15 - οὐ κό]ρῳ ἀλλ' ἀρετᾷ.
   κρέσσον γ]ὰρ ἁρπαζομένων τεθνάμεν
   × χρη]μάτων ἢ κακὸν ἔμμεναι.
   --]εσελθὼν μέγα
   ∪- ν]υκτὶ βίας ὁδόν
20   ]ρε{ν}, λαβὼν δ' ἔν[α] φῶ[τ]α πεδά σ . [ ]

   8 suppl. Mette, Page
   10–15 suppl. Lobel
   16 suppl. Page, Lobel
   17 suppl. Lobel: πρὸ χρη]μάτων Page
   20 πεδάσα[ις] Snell: πεδά[ρ]σιον Lobel

FRAGMENT 169a

the deeds of Heracles,   5
for he drove Geryon's cattle
to the Cyclopean portal of Eurystheus[13]
without punishment or payment,
        Diomedes' mares
. . . monarch of the Cicones[14]   10
    by the Bistonian lake,[15]
the awesome son
of Enyalius[16] with the bronze breastplate.

            great   Ant. 1
. . . not with excess, but with virtue.[17]   15
For it is better to die when possessions
are being seized than to be a coward.
    having entered the great (palace?)
. . . at night the way of force
            having taken one man[18] . . .   20

[13] In Mycenae, according to Apollodorus 2.5.8.

[14] Diomedes is normally called king of the Bistones; the Cicones were a neighboring Thracian tribe to the east (cf. Hdt. 7.110 and Strabo 7 *fr.* 44).

[15] Along the southern coast of Thrace.

[16] A title of Ares. According to Apollodorus 2.5.8, Eurystheus was the son of Ares and Cyrene.

[17] The schol. *ad loc.* gives οὐκ ἐπὶ ὕβρει, ἀλλ' ἀρετῆς ἕνεκα. τὸ γὰρ [τὰ ἑαυτοῦ μὴ προ]ίεσθαι ἀνδρείου (ἐστίν) [ ] ἀλλ' οὐχ ὑβριστ[οῦ. Ἡρα]κλῆς δ(ὲ) ἠδ[ί]κει [ἀφελό]μενος (suppl. Lobel). "Not with violence, but by virtue. For not disregarding one's possessions is the action of a brave man, not of a violent one. And Heracles was wrong to take (them) away."

[18] Evidently one of the grooms (cf. Apollodorus 2.5.8); according to Diodorus 2.15.3, it was Diomedes himself.

φά[τναις] ἐν λιθίναις βάλ[∪–∪∪–
ἵππο[ι   ]ένạν φρέ[ν ∪––
καί μ[ιν   ] . ζον. ταχέως
   δ' ἀράβη[σε] δια[λ]εύκων
25 ὀστέ[ων] δοῦπος ἐ[ρ]<ε>ικομένων.
ὁ δ' ἄφ[αρ π]λεκτόν τε χαλκόν

ὑπερη[. .] . ε τραπεζαν
προβάτων ἀλυσιωτόν
δι' ἑρκ[έ]ων, τεῖρε δὲ στερεῶ⟨ς⟩
30 ἄλλαν [μ]ὲν σκέλος, ἄλλαν δὲ πᾶχ[υν,
τὰν δὲ πρυμνὸν κεφαλᾶς
ὀδ[ὰ]ξ α[ὐ]χένα φέροισαν.
. ρ . μι̣[ ] δ' ὅμως ε[ ]σ' ὑπα . [.|] . θυ . [ ]με
πικρο[τά]ṭạṇ ḳλάγεν ἀγγε[λία]ν
35 ζαμενε[   ]τυρανν[   ]
ποι]κίλ̣ω[ν ἐ̣]κ λεχέω[ν ἀπέ]δ{ε}ιλ[ος
     ]ν καθε . [   ]ς ῥά . [
     ] . ιον κακ[   ]
     ] . οṿ ἔ[   ]
    (inter 39 et 40 quot vv. desint incertum)
40 . νατ[   ]ν . [

Β΄ ἔμολε̣[.]αι παῖδα[∪–   ]
Ἡρακλ[έ]ος εξα . [.] . [.]ν̣ [ ]
τεταγμένον τουτά . [. . . .]εκατ . [

21–48 suppl. Lobel

404

he threw him into the stone mangers . . .
the mares . . . mind(s)
and him . . . quickly
   sounded forth the cracking
of solid-white bones being broken.   25
And he immediately . . . the chain

with bronze links . . . the manger(s)   Ep. 1
of the horses[19]
through the stalls, and he soundly thrashed
one mare carrying a leg in its teeth,   30
another a forearm,
and another the lower neck of the head.[20]
        nevertheless . . .
he shouted out the most bitter news
raging . . . tyrant . . .   35
without shoes from the elaborate bed[21]

  .   .   .   .   .   .
  .   .   .   .   .   .
    39
    40

he came . . . the child . . .   Str. 2
of Heracles . . .
having been ordained . . .

[19] Actually "table(s) of the cattle." Schol. *ad loc.* "meaning manger"; cf. Eustath. *Il.* 877.55 (*ad* 11.680): "Pindar . . . calls the mares of Diomedes 'cattle' and their manger a 'table for cattle.'"
[20] Lobel takes πρυμνόν as a noun in apposition to αὐχένα, "neck, butt of the head."   [21] It is uncertain how many lines may be missing between 39 and 40.

"Ηρας ἐφετμαῖς· Σθενέλο[ι]ό μιν
45   υἱὸς κέ[λ]ευσε‹ν› μόνον
ἄνευ συ[μμ]αχίας ἴμεν.
καὶ Ἰόλαο[ς ἐ]ν ἑπταπύλοισι μένω[ν τε
Θήβαις] Ἀμφιτρύωνί τε σᾶμα χέω[ν
    −??∪   ]μιᾷ δ᾽ ἐπὶ θήκᾳ
50   ]ν καλλικέρας
    ]άδις, οὕς οἱ
    ]ου στρατὸς οὐκ ἀέκ[ων
(restant frustula vv. 53–62)

47 τε suppl. Snell

172 Schol. Eur. *Andr.* 796 οἱ μὲν πλείους Τελαμῶνά
φασι συστρατεῦσαι τῷ Ἡρακλεῖ ἐπὶ τὴν Ἴλιον, ὁ δὲ
Πίνδαρος καὶ Πηλέα, παρ᾽ οὗ ἔοικε τὴν ἱστορίαν
Εὐριπίδης λαβεῖν· λέγει δὲ ὁ Πίνδαρος οὕτως·

Πηλέος ἀντιθέου
μόχθοις νεότας ἐπέλαμψεν
μυρίοις· πρῶτον μὲν Ἀλκμήνας σὺν υἱῷ
Τρώιον ἃμ πεδίον,
5   καὶ μετὰ ζωστῆρας Ἀμαζόνος ἦλθεν,
καὶ τὸν Ἰάσονος εὔδοξον πλόον ἐκτελέσαις
εἷλε Μήδειαν ἐν Κόλχων δόμοις.

2 μόχθοις νεότας Bergk: μόχοι νεωτάτοις M: μόχθοιν
νεώτατ᾽ A

on the orders of Hera. The son of Sthlenelus[22]
commanded him to go alone,   45
without any allies.
And Iolaus, remaining in seven-gated
Thebes and erecting a tomb for Amphitryon[23]
       upon one tomb
          . . . with beautiful horns   50
           whom
     army that was not unwilling

[22] Eurystheus.
[23] Pindar says (*Pyth.* 9.80–82) that after cutting off Eurystheus' head, Iolaus was buried in Amphitryon's tomb.

172 Scholion on Euripides, *Andromache* 796. "The majority say that Telamon fought with Heracles against Troy, but Pindar includes Peleus, from whom it seems that Euripides took the story. Pindar says the following":

The youth of god-like Peleus
shone forth with countless
toils. He went first with Alcmene's son
to the Trojan plain,
and then in pursuit of the Amazon's belt,   5
and, after completing Jason's famous voyage,
he seized Medea in the home of the Colchians.

179 Schol. Pind. *Nem.* 7.116 τὸ ποίημα ὑφάσματι παρέοικεν, ὡς καὶ αὐτὸς ἐν ἄλλοις·

. . . ὑφαίνω δ' Ἀμυθαονίδαισιν ποικίλον
ἄνδημα

180 Clem. Alex. *strom.* 1.10.49.1 (2.32 Stählin) Πινδάρου . . . γράφοντος·

μὴ πρὸς ἅπαντας ἀναρρῆξαι τὸν ἀχρεῖον λόγον·
ἔσθ' ὅτε πιστόταται σιγᾶς ὁδοί·
κέντρον δὲ μάχας ὁ κρατιστεύων λόγος

1 ἀχρεῖον Boeckh: ἀρχαῖον Clemens
2 πιστόταται . . . ὁδοί Bergk: πιστόταταις . . . ὁδοῖς Clemens: πιστοτάτα . . . ὁδός Sylburg

182 Aristid. *or.* 34.5 (2.238 Keil) καὶ πάλιν (Πίνδαρος) ὁρμηθεὶς ἐκ τῶν περὶ τῆς Ἐριφύλης λόγων·

ὢ πόποι, οἷ' ἀπατᾶται φροντὶς ἐπαμερίων
οὐκ ἰδυῖα

183 Strabo 9.5.5 Πίνδαρος μνησθεὶς τοῦ Φοίνικος·

ὃς Δολόπων ἄγαγε θρασὺν ὅμιλον σφενδονᾶσαι
ἱπποδάμων Δαναῶν βέλεσι πρόσφορον

179 Scholion on *Nem.* 7.79. "He compares his poem to weaving, as he himself (says) in other places":

> . . . I am weaving an elaborate headband
> for the sons of Amythaon[24]

24 Son of Cretheus (cf. *Pyth.* 4.126).

180 Clement of Alexandria, *Miscellanies*. "As Pindar writes":

> Do not blurt out a useless word in front of everybody;
> there is a time when the ways of silence are surest,
> whereas an overpowering word is a spur to battle.

182 Aristides, *Oration* 34 (*Against Those Who Burlesque The Mysteries*). "And again, taking off from what he says about Eriphyle, Pindar (exclaims)":

> Alas, how the mind of men who live day by day is misled
> when it does not know . . .

183 Strabo, *Geography of Greece*. "After mentioning Phoenix, Pindar continues":

> who led the host of the Dolopes,[25] bold at slinging,
> an aid to the weapons of the horse-taming Danaans

25 A Thessalian mountain tribe near Mt. Pindus. Cf. Hom. *Il.* 9.484 and Hdt. 7.132.

PINDAR

187 Plut. *qu. conv.* 2.10.1.643D τὰ δὲ Πινδαρικὰ (sc. συμπόσια) βελτίω δήπουθεν, ἐν οἷς

ἥρωες αἰδοίαν ἐμείγνυντ᾿ ἀμφὶ τράπεζαν θαμά

θαμά Stephanus: θ᾿ ἅμά codd.

τῷ κοινωνεῖν ἁπάντων ἀλλήλοις.

188 Strabo 14.1.28 λέγει δὲ Πίνδαρος καὶ Πολύμνα-στόν τινα τῶν περὶ τὴν μουσικὴν ἐλλογίμων·

φθέγμα μὲν πάγκοινον ἔγνω-
κας Πολυμνάστου Κολοφωνίου ἀνδρός

191 Schol. Pind. *Pyth.* 2.128b τοιοῦτόν ἐστι καὶ τὸ ἑτέρωθι λεγόμενον·

Αἰολεὺς ἔβαινε Δωρίαν κέλευθον ὕμνων

193 *vit. Pind. Ambr.* (1.2.18 Drachmann) καὶ γὰρ (Πίν-δαρος) ἐν τῇ τῶν Πυθίων ἑορτῇ ἐγεννήθη, ὡς αὐτός φησι·

πενταετηρὶς ἑορτά
βουπομπός, ἐν ᾇ πρῶτον εὐ-
νάσθην ἀγαπατὸς ὑπὸ σπαργάνοις

410

187 Plutarch, *Table-Talk*. "Pindar's banquets are certainly better, in which

the heroes often mingled around the venerable table

to share everything with each other."

188 Strabo, *Geography of Greece*. "Pindar speaks of a certain Polymnastus among those famous for music":

you recognize the well-known song
    of Polymnastus,[26] the man from Colophon

[26] A choral composer (c. 650 B.C.).

191 Scholion on *Pyth*. 2.69. "He says something similar elsewhere":

the Aeolian was traveling the Dorian road of hymns

193 *The Ambrosian Life of Pindar*. "For Pindar was born during the Pythian festival, as he himself says":

the four-year festival
with its procession of oxen, during which I was first
    put to bed as a beloved child in swaddling clothes

194   ⟨ΘΗΒΑΙΟΣ⟩

Aristid. *or.* 28.57 (2.159 Keil) ἄκουε δὴ καὶ ἑτέρων·

κεκρότηται χρυσέα κρηπὶς ἱεραῖσιν ἀοιδαῖς·
εἶα τειχίζωμεν ἤδη ποικίλον
κόσμον αὐδάεντα λόγων

2 εἶα Bergk: εια A^{ac}: οἶα codd.

Ἡράκλεις, ταυτὶ μὲν οὐδὲ παντάπασιν ἀναίτια τοῖς
ῥήμασιν, ἀλλ᾽ ὅμως καὶ ἐπὶ τούτοις σεμνύνεται ὡς
οὐδὲν ἀτιμοτέροις τοῦ νέκταρος καί φησιν ὅτι οὗτος
μέντοι ὁ τῶν λόγων κόσμος

καὶ πολυκλείταν περ ἐοῖσαν ὅμως
5   Θήβαν ἔτι μᾶλλον ἐπασκήσει θεῶν
καὶ κατ᾽ ἀνθρώπων ἀγυιάς

ὥσπερ οὐκ ἀρκοῦν, εἰ κατὰ ἀνθρώπους μόνον, ἀλλὰ
καὶ τοὺς θεοὺς ἔτι μειζόνως τιμήσοντας δι᾽ ἐκεῖνον τὴν
τῶν Θηβαίων πόλιν εἰς τὸ λοιπόν.

195 Schol. Pind. *Pyth.* 4.25b εἰώθασι δὲ οὗτοι συμπλέ-
κειν τὰ τῶν χωρῶν ἢ πόλεων καὶ τὰ τῶν ἡρωΐδων
ὀνόματα διακοινοποιοῦντες, οἷον·

⊗   Εὐάρματε χρυσοχίτων ἱερώτατον
ἄγαλμα, Θήβα.

194   FOR THE THEBANS

Aristides, *Oration* 28 (*Concerning a Passing Remark*).
"Listen to some more of Pindar":

A golden foundation has been wrought for holy songs.
Come, let us now construct an elaborate
adornment that speaks words . . .

Heracles! These words are in no way flawless, but never-
theless he prides himself on their being no less worthy than
nectar, and he says that his adornment of words

will, although it is very famous,
exalt Thebes even more   5
throughout the dwelling places of gods and men.

As if it were not enough for it to be famous among men, but
that the gods too would honor the city of the Thebans even
more in the future because of him!"

195 Scholion on *Pyth.* 4.14. "They customarily mix the
names of places or cities with those of their eponymous
heroines and use them interchangeably, as

Thebe of the fine chariot and golden chiton,
holiest adornment.

PINDAR

τὸ μὲν γὰρ εὐάρματε τῆς πόλεως, τὸ δὲ χρυσοχίτων
τῆς ἡρωίδος.

198a Chrysipp. π. ἀποφατικῶν *fr.* 180.2 (2.53 von
Arnim) ἀληθὲς ἐ[λέχθη ὅπερ] λεχθείη ἂν οὕτως·

οὔτοι με ξένον
οὐδ' ἀδαήμονα Μοισᾶν ἐπαίδευσαν κλυταί
Θῆβαι

198b Athen. 2.15.41E καὶ Πίνδαρος·

μελιγαθὲς ἀμβρόσιον ὕδωρ
Τιλφώσσας ἀπὸ καλλικράνου

κρήνη δ' ἐν Βοιωτίᾳ ἡ Τιλφῶσσα· ἀφ' ἧς Ἀριστοφά-
νης (=Ar. Boeotus) φησὶ Τειρεσίαν πιόντα διὰ γήρας
οὐχ ὑπομείναντα τὴν ψυχρότητα ἀποθανεῖν. cf. Strabo
9.2.27 Πίνδαρος δὲ καὶ Κηφισσίδα καλεῖ ταύτην (sc.
Κωπαΐδα; cf. *Pyth.* 12.27)· παρατίθησι γοῦν τὴν Τιλ-
φῶσσαν κρήνην ὑπὸ τῷ Τιλφωσσίῳ ὄρει ῥέουσαν
πλησίον Ἁλιάρτου καὶ Ἀλαλκομενῶν, ἐν ᾗ τὸ Τειρε-
σίου μνῆμα· αὐτοῦ δὲ καὶ τὸ τοῦ Τιλ[φωσσίου Ἀπόλ-
λω]νος ἱερόν.

199 Plut. *vit. Lycurg.* 21.3 (περὶ τῶν Λακεδαιμονίων)
Πίνδαρος δέ φησιν·

ἔνθα βουλαὶ γερόντων

414

The epithet 'of the fine chariot' belongs to the city, '(of the) golden chiton' to the heroine."

198a Chrysippus, *On Negation*. "Truly spoken would be that which is said thus":

> glorious Thebes taught me
> to be no stranger to nor ignorant of
> the Muses

198b Athenaeus, *Scholars at Dinner*. "And Pindar (says):

> delightful as honey, ambrosial water
> from the beautiful spring of Tilphossa.

Tilphossa is a spring in Boeotia, from which Aristophanes of Boeotia says Teiresias drank and died because his old age could not stand the cold."[27]

[27] Strabo, *Geography of Greece* 9.2.27 reports that Pindar located the spring near Lake Copaïs, where it flowed at the foot of Mt. Tilphossius near Haliartus and Alalcomenae, near which was Teiresias' tomb as well as the temple of Apollo Tilphossius.

199 Plutarch, *Life of Lycurgus*. "About the Lacedaemonians Pindar says":

> there the counsels of elders

καὶ νέων ἀνδρῶν ἀριστεύοισιν αἰχμαί,
καὶ χοροὶ καὶ Μοῖσα καὶ Ἀγλαΐα

201 Strabo 17.1.19 καὶ Μένδης, ὅπου τὸν Πᾶνα τιμῶσι
καὶ τῶν ζῴων τράγον· ὡς δὲ Πίνδαρός φησιν, οἱ
τράγοι ἐνταῦθα γυναιξὶ μίγνυνται·

Αἰγυπτίαν Μένδητα, πὰρ κρημνὸν θαλάσσας
ἔσχατον Νείλου κέρας, αἰγιβάται
ὅθι τράγοι γυναιξὶ μίσγονται

1–3 om. Strabo codd. EF

cf. Aristid. *or.* 36.112 (2.298 Keil) αὐτίκα Πινδάρῳ πε-
ποίηται, ὅσπερ μάλιστ᾿ ἀληθείας ἀντέχεσθαι δοκεῖ
τῶν ποιητῶν περὶ τὰς ἱστορίας, καὶ οὐ πόρρωθεν, ἀλλ᾿
ἐξ αὐτῶν τῶν τόπων καὶ οὗτος ὁ ἔλεγχος· φησὶ γὰρ·
Αἰγυπτίαν—θαλάσσας· καίτοι οὔτε κρημνός ἐστιν
οὐδεὶς ἐκεῖ οὔτε θάλαττα προσηχεῖ, ἀλλ᾿ ἐν πεδίῳ
πολλῷ.

203 Zenob. 3.23 τὸν ἵππον ὁ Σκύθης· ἐπὶ τῶν κρύφα
τινὸς ἐφιεμένων, φανερῶς δὲ ἀπωθουμένων καὶ δια-
πτυόντων αὐτὸ ἡ παροιμία εἴρηται· μαρτυρεῖ δὲ καὶ
Πίνδαρος λέγων·

ἄνδρες θήν τινες ἀκκιζόμενοι

1 ἄνδρες θήν Schroeder: ἀνδρεθάν codd. | Σκύθαι post ἀκ-
κιζόμενοι del. Schroeder

416

and the young men's spears prevail,
and choruses, the Muse, and Splendor[28]

[28] Aglaia, one of the Graces (cf. *Ol.* 14.13).

201 Strabo, *Geography of Greece*. "And Mendes, where
they worship Pan and, among animals, the he-goat; as
Pindar says, the goats there mate with women":

. . . Egyptian Mendes,[29] by the bank of the sea,
the end of the Nile's branch, where goat-mounting
he-goats mate with women.[30]

[29] On the south side of Lake Tanaïs along an eastern branch of
the Nile. Aristides, *Oration* 36 (*The Egyptian Discourse*) credits
Pindar with accuracy in most matters, but criticizes his descrip-
tion of Mendes as lying by the bank of the sea, when it is inland on
a plain.

[30] Herodotus 2.46 says that in the Egyptian language both the
he-goat and Pan are called Mendes. Aelian, *On the Characteris-
tics of Animals* 7.19, in discussing the lasciviousness of he-goats,
mentions Pindar's apparent astonishment at their mating with
women.

203 Zenobius, *Proverbs*. "The proverb 'like a Scythian
with a horse' applies to those who secretly long for some-
thing which they openly reject and scorn. Pindar confirms
it when he says":

In truth, some men pretend

PINDAR

νεκρὸν ἵππον στυγέοι-

σι λόγῳ κείμενον ἐν φάει, κρυφᾷ δέ
σκολιαῖς γένυσσιν ἀνδέροντι πόδας ἠδὲ κεφαλάν

2 κείμενον Wilamowitz: κτάμενον codd. | φάει Heyne: φασί
codd.

205 Stob. *ecl.* 3.11.18 (3.432 Wachsmuth-Henze) Πινδά-
ρου·

Ἀρχὰ μεγάλας ἀρετᾶς,
ὤνασσ᾽ Ἀλάθεια, μὴ πταίσῃς ἐμάν
σύνθεσιν τραχεῖ ποτὶ ψεύδει

207 Plut. *consol. Apollon.* 6.104A ἀνθρώπων γὰρ ὄντως
θνητὰ μὲν καὶ ἐφήμερα . . . πάνθ᾽ ἁπλῶς τὰ κατὰ τὸν
βίον, ἅπερ "οὐκ ἔστι φυγεῖν βροτὸν οὐδ᾽ ὑπαλύξαι"
(Hom. Μ 327) τὸ παράπαν, ἀλλὰ (ὥς φησι Πίνδαρος)·

Ταρτάρου πυθμένα †πτίξεις ἀφανοῦς
σφυρηλάτοις ἀνάγκαις

1 πυθμένα πτίξεις pg, Planudes: πυθμένα πιέζεις Zbv:
πυθμὴν πιέζει σ᾽ D: ποθ᾽ ἥξεις Wilamowitz

209 Stob. *ecl.* 2.1.21 (2.7 Wachsmuth-Henze) Πινδάρου·
τοὺς φυσιολογοῦντας ἔφη Πίνδαρος·

ἀτελῆ σοφίας καρπὸν δρέπ(ειν)

418

in their speech to hate the dead horse
    lying in the open, but secretly
with crooked jaws strip the skin from hooves and head.

205 Stobaeus, *Anthology* (*On Truth*). "By Pindar":

Starting point for great achievement,
Queen Truth, do not make my good faith
stumble against rough falsehood.

207 Plutarch, *Letter of Consolation to Apollonius.* "For truly all things in men's lives are mortal and transient, which 'no mortal may flee or avoid' (*Il.* 12.327) at all, but, as Pindar says":

you will . . . the depths of invisible Tartarus
by hammer-forged compulsions

209 Stobaeus, *Anthology* (*On the Gods and Natural Philosophy Concerning the Heavens and the Universe*). "Natural philosophers were said by Pindar"

to cull the unripe fruit of wisdom

PINDAR

210 Plut. *de cohib. ira* 8.457B χαλεπώτατοι δὲ (κατὰ Πίνδαρον)

> ἄγαν φιλοτιμίαν μνώμενοι ἐν πόλεσιν ἄνδρες·
> ἱστᾶσιν ἄλγος ἐμφανές

2 ἱστᾶσιν CX³S²: ἢ στάσιν plerique

211 Plut. *de ser. num. vind.* 19.562A ἄχρις ἂν ἐκχυθεῖσα (sc. κακία) τοῖς πάθεσιν ἐμφανὴς γένηται (ὥς φησι Πίνδαρος)·

> κακόφρονά τ᾽ ἄμφαν(εν) πραπίδων καρπόν

ἄμφαν(εν) Schroeder: ἀμφανῆ codd.: ἀμφάνη Ruhnken

212 Plut. *de inim. util.* 10.91E πᾶσα φύσις ἀνθρώπου φέρει φιλονικίαν καὶ ζηλοτυπίαν καὶ φθόνον (ὥς φησι Πίνδαρος),

> κενεοφρόνων ἑταῖρον ἀνδρῶν

213 Maxim. Tyr. 12.1 (145.13 Hobein) σὺ μέν, ὦ Πίνδαρε, ἀμφισβητεῖς πρὸς ἑαυτὸν περὶ ἀπάτης καὶ δίκης, παραβάλλων χρυσὸν χαλκῷ;

> πότερον δίκᾳ τεῖχος ὕψιον
> ἢ σκολιαῖς ἀπάταις ἀναβαίνει
> ἐπιχθόνιον γένος ἀνδρῶν,
> δίχα μοι νόος ἀτρέκειαν εἰπεῖν

420

210 Plutarch, *On the Control of Anger.* "But worst of all (according to Pindar) are"

> men in cities too eager for ambition;
> they cause manifest grief

211 Plutarch, *On the Delays of Divine Vengeance.* "Until vice pours forth and becomes manifest in the passions, as Pindar says":

> it revealed the malicious fruit of the mind

212 The same, *How to Profit by One's Enemies.* "All human nature produces rivalry, jealousy, and envy, which Pindar calls the"

> companion of empty-minded men

213 Maximus of Tyre, *Philosophical Lectures.* "Do you, O Pindar, dispute with yourself over deception and justice, comparing gold to bronze?"

> Whether the earthly race of men
> scales the higher wall through justice
> or by crooked deceit
> my mind is divided in telling precisely.

214 Plat. *Rep.* 1.331A τῷ δὲ μηδὲν ἑαυτῷ ἄδικον συν-
ειδότι ἡδεῖα ἐλπὶς ἀεὶ πάρεστι καὶ ἀγαθὴ γηροτρόφος,
ὡς καὶ Πίνδαρος λέγει. χαριέντως γάρ τοι, ὦ Σώκρα-
τες, τοῦτ᾽ ἐκεῖνος εἶπεν, ὅτι ὃς ἂν δικαίως καὶ ὁσίως
τὸν βίον διαγάγῃ,

γλυκεῖά οἱ καρδίαν
ἀτάλλοισα γηροτρόφος συναορεῖ
Ἐλπίς, ἃ μάλιστα θνατῶν πολύστροφον γνώ-
μαν κυβερνᾷ

215ab   [ΘΗΒΑΙΟΙΣ?]

215a P. Oxy. 2448 (26, 1961). cf. P. Oxy. 2449 (26, 1961)
Πίνδ]αρός φη[σιν | πατρί]δ᾽ ἀρχαία[ν | χ]αίταν παρ-
θέν[ου | το]ῦτο δὲ διθυρα[μβῶδες (suppl. Lobel).

.] . [. . .] . [. . . .] . . [
ἄλλα δ᾽ ἄλλοισιν νόμιμα, σφετέραν
      δ᾽ αἰνεῖ δίκαν ἀνδρῶν ἕκαστος.
γάιον, ὦ τάν, μή με κερτόμ[ει γόνον.
5 ἔστι μοι
πατρίδ᾽ ἀρχαίαν κτενὶ Πιερίδ[ων
ὥ]στε χαίταν παρθένου ξανθ[α ∪–(–)?
.]ν[. .]εν γάρ, Ἄπολλον[
      (restant frustula vv. 9–13)

4 suppl. Snell
6-7 suppl. Lobel

FRAGMENT 214

214 Plato, *Republic.* "Ever attendant upon the man who is conscious of no wrong deed is 'sweet hope,' that 'good nurse of old age,' as Pindar says. For beautifully, O Socrates, did he say that whoever lives his life justly and piously,"

> with him lives sweet Hope,
> heart-fostering nurse of old age,
> which most of all steers mortals'
>   much-veering judgment

215ab   FOR THE THEBANS(?)

215a A papyrus (late 2nd–early 3d cent. A.D.)

> .   .   .   .   .   .
> Customs vary among men, and each man
>   praises his own way.
> Do not, good sir, criticize me for my earthly birth.
> I can . . .   5
> my ancient homeland with the comb of the Pierians
> like a maiden's blond hair[31]
> . . . because, Apollo, . . .

[31] A scholion on the papyrus, as restored by Lobel, appears to comment on vv. 6–7: "Pindar says 'ancient homeland, hair of a maiden'; this is dithyrambic."

PINDAR

215b P. Oxy. 2448 (26, 1961)

(restant frustula vv. 1–6)

7 . . . .]ναιγιν χθόν', ἁ[. . . . . χ]άριν
ἀμ]φέπων χρυ[σο]π[λόκοις εὔδ]οξα Μοίσαις[
νέ]μομαι παρὰ [   ]

10 Παρ]νασσίδι [. .] . ọ[. . . . . . . ἀκρο]τόμοι[ς]
πέ]τραισι Κịρρα[   ] . . . ν
πεδίων
. . .] . . ν εὐκάρπ[ου χθον]ὸς ὀ[μ]φαλόν· οὔθ' ἵπ[-
ποισι]ν ἀγαλλόμ[ενος
(restant frustula vv. 14–19)

8–13 suppl. Lobel et Snell

217 Clem. Alex. *paedag.* 3.72.1 (1.275 Stählin) Πίνδαρος·

γλυκύ τι κλεπτόμενον μέλημα Κύπριδος

220 Plut. *qu. conv.* 7.5.3.705F αἱ δὲ (sc. τοῦ Μουσείου ἢ
θεάτρου ἡδοναὶ) παντὸς ὀψοποιοῦ καὶ μυρεψοῦ δριμύ-
τερα καὶ ποικιλώτερα φάρμακα ⟨τὰ⟩ τῶν μελῶν καὶ
τῶν ῥυθμῶν καταχεόμεναι τούτοις ἄγουσιν ἡμᾶς καὶ
διαφθείρουσιν, αὐτῶν τρόπον τινὰ καταμαρτυροῦντας·
τῶνδε γὰρ οὔτε—μεταλλακτόν, ὡς Πίνδαρος ἔφη, τῶν
ἐπὶ ταῖς τραπέζαις, ὅσσ' ἀγλαὰ—φέρουσιν.

οὔτε τι μεμπτόν
οὔτ' ὢν μεταλλακτόν, ⟨... ?⟩ ὅσσ' ἀγλαὰ χθών
πόντου τε ῥιπαὶ φέροισιν

424

215b Same papyrus

> land . . . charm   7
> tending, famous, for the golden-tressed Muses
> I live beside . . .
> Parnassian . . . sheer   10
> rocks (of?) Cirrha . . . of plains
>   navel of the fruitful earth; and not
>   glorying in horses

217 Clement of Alexandria, *The Schoolmaster.* "Pindar (says)":

> a sweet thing is Cypris'[32] concern when stolen[33]

[32] Aphrodite's.
[33] Or *concealed.*

220 Plutarch, *Table-Talk.* "The pleasures of poetry and the theater capture and corrupt us by their profusion of charms consisting of melody and rhythm, charms more pungent and varied than those of any cook or perfumer, which in a way testify against themselves. Of all the things on the tables, as Pindar says,"

> not to be blamed
> nor changed is anything . . . all that the splendid earth
> and waves of the sea produce

---

2 μεταλλακτόν Amyot, Heyne: μεταλλάττων vel μετάλλαττον codd.

PINDAR

221 Sext. Emp. *hyp. Pyrrh.* 1.86 (1.23 Mutschmann) ὁ μὲν γὰρ Πίνδαρός φησιν·

<‒∪> ἀελλοπόδων μέν τιν' εὐφραίνοισιν ἵππων
τιμαὶ καὶ στέφανοι,
τοὺς δ' ἐν πολυχρύσοις θαλάμοις βιοτά·
τέρπεται δὲ καί τις ἐπ' οἶδμ' ἅλιον
5 ναῒ θοᾷ †διαστείβων

222 Schol. Pind. *Pyth.* 4.410c ἄφθιτον δὲ αὐτὸ (sc. τὸ κῶας) εἶπε καθὸ χρυσοῦν ἦν· ὁ δὲ χρυσὸς ἄφθαρτος· καὶ ἡ Σαπφὼ <lacunam statuerunt Schneider et Boeckh> ὅτι

Διὸς παῖς ὁ χρυσός·
κεῖνον οὐ σῆς οὐδὲ κὶς δάπτει,
βροτέαν †φρένα κράτιστον φρενῶν

quae verba Pindari non Sapphus esse ostendit Plut. ap. Proclum ad Hes. *op.* 430 (p. 149.4 Pertusi) τὸ δὲ ἄσηπτον ἐδήλωσεν εἰπὼν ἀκιώτατον· ὁ δὲ Πλούταρχος (*fr.* 65 Sandbach) ἐξηγήσατο τὴν αἰτίαν λέγων εἶναί τι θηρίδιον, ὃ καλεῖται κίς, διεσθίον τὰ ξύλα· τοῦτο καὶ Πίνδαρον οὕτω καλεῖν περὶ τοῦ χρυσοῦ λέγοντα· κεῖνον οὐ σῆς, οὐ κὶς δάμναται, ὡς ἄσηπτον.

225 Schol. Pind. *Ol.* 2.42e πρὸ τῶν ἀγαθῶν τοῖς ἀνθρώποις τὰ κακά· ὅπερ καὶ ἐν ἑτέρῳ (-ροις v.l.) φησίν·

426

221 Sextus Empiricus, *Outlines of Pyrrhonism*. "For Pindar says":

> . . . honors and crowns won by horses
> with storm-swift hooves delight one man,
> living in halls rich with gold cheers others,
> and many a man enjoys crossing over the sea-swell
> in a swift ship   5

222 Scholion on *Pyth*. 4.230. "He called the fleece immortal because it was of gold, for gold is incorruptible. And Sappho[34] . . . that"

> Gold is the child of Zeus;
> neither moth nor weevil eats it
> (the strongest . . . of mortal minds)[35]

[34] Plutarch (*fr*. 65) quotes a variation of the second verse as Pindar's, not Sappho's.

[35] The last line is hopelessly corrupt. As emended by Valckenaer and Boeckh it reads, δάμναται δὲ βροτέαν φρένα κάρτιστον κτεάνων ("but it, mightiest of possessions, overpowers the mortal mind").

225 Scholion on *Ol*. 2.23. "Before good things come bad ones to men, just what he says in another poem":

PINDAR

ὁπόταν θεὸς ἀνδρὶ χάρμα πέμψῃ,
πάρος μέλαιναν καρδίαν ἐστυφέλιξεν

2 πάρος Nauck: προ(σ)μελαιναν codd.

226 Aristid. *or.* 34.5 (2.238 Keil) Πλάτων καὶ Πίνδαρος
πολλαχῇ μὲν καὶ ἄλλῃ σοφοί, καὶ δὴ καὶ κατὰ τόνδε
τὸν λόγον οὐχ ἥκιστα, ὁ μὲν οὑτωσὶ λέγων·

οὔτις ἑκὼν κακὸν εὕρετο

227 Clem. Alex. *strom.* 4.7.49.1 (2.270 Stählin) καὶ ὁ
Πίνδαρος·

... νέων δὲ μέριμναι σὺν πόνοις εἱλισσόμεναι
δόξαν εὑρίσκοντι· λάμπει δὲ χρόνῳ
ἔργα μετ᾽ αἰθέρ᾽ ‹ἀερ›θέντα

3 Boeckh αἰθέρ᾽ ‹ἀερ›θέντα: αἰθέρα λαμπευθέντα codd.

228 Plut. *an seni* 1.783B εἰρημένον εὖ καὶ πιθανῶς ὑπ᾽
αὐτοῦ (sc. Πινδάρου)·

τιθεμένων ἀγώνων πρόφασις
... ἀρετὰν ἐς αἰπὺν ἔβαλε σκότον

229 Schol. Pind. *Ol.* 8.92 καὶ ἀλλαχοῦ·

νικώμενοι γὰρ ἄνδρες ἀγρυξίᾳ δέδενται·
οὐ φίλων ἐναντίον ἐλθεῖν

2 οὐ BEQ: καὶ NV: καὶ οὐδὲ C

428

whenever a god sends joy to a man,
he first strikes his heart with gloom

226 Aristides, *Oration* 34 (*Against Those Who Burlesque the Mysteries*). "Plato and Pindar are wise in many respects, but not least of all in the following regard; Pindar says this":

no one willingly wins evil

227 Clement of Alexandria, *Miscellanies*. "And Pindar (says)":

. . . the ambitions of the young, when exercised with
toil,
gain fame. And in time deeds shine forth,
lifted up to heaven

228 Plutarch, *Whether an Old Man Should Engage in Public Affairs*. "A thing said well and convincingly by Pindar":

when contests are instituted, excuse
. . . casts excellence into sheer darkness

229 Scholion on *Ol.* 8.69. "And elsewhere":

for in defeat men are bound in silence;
(they cannot) come before their friends

PINDAR

231 Schol. Pind. *Nem.* 7.87 ὅλως ἀποδέχεται ὁ Πίνδαρος τὴν μετὰ συνέσεως τόλμαν·

τόλμα τέ μιν ζαμενὴς καὶ σύνεσις πρόσκοπος
ἐσάωσεν

τέ μιν Beck: τὲ μὲν B: τὲ D

232 Plut. *vit. Marcell.* 29.5 ἀλλὰ γὰρ (κατὰ Πίνδαρον)

τὸ πεπρωμένον οὐ πῦρ, οὐ σιδάρεον σχήσει
τεῖχος

233 Clem. Alex. *paedag.* 3.12.92.4 (1.286 Stählin) (κατὰ Πίνδαρον)

πιστὸν δ᾽ ἀπίστοις οὐδέν

234 Plut. *de tranq. an.* 13.472C

<–∪> ὑφ᾽ ἅρμασιν ἵππος,
ἐν δ᾽ ἀρότρῳ βοῦς· παρὰ ναῦν δ᾽ ἰθύει τάχιστα
δελφίς,
κάπρῳ δὲ βουλεύοντα φόνον κύνα χρή
τλάθυμον ἐξευρεῖν <∪. . .

1 ὑφ᾽ Plut. 451D: ἐν Plut. 472C

Plut. *de virt. mor.* 12.451D ὑφ᾽ ἅρμασι γὰρ ἵππος, ὥς φησι Πίνδαρος.

430

231 Scholion on *Nem.* 7.59. "Pindar wholly endorses courage with understanding":

furious audacity and prescient intelligence
    saved him

232 Plutarch, *Life of Marcellus.* "But (as Pindar says)":

what is fated neither fire nor wall of steel can hold
    back

233 Clement of Alexandria, *Pedagogy.* "As Pindar says":

nothing is believable to the unbelieving[36]

[36] Or *nothing is trustworthy to the distrustful.*

234 Plutarch, *On Tranquillity of Mind.*

. . . horse yoked to chariot,
ox to plow; the dolphin speeds most swiftly by a ship;
but he who plans to slay a boar must seek out
a tenacious dog . . .

APPENDIX

GENEALOGIES

The descendants of Hagesimachus (*Nem.* 6)
(a possible reconstruction after C. Carey,
"Prosopographica Pindarica,"
Classical Quarterly 39 [1989] 6–9)

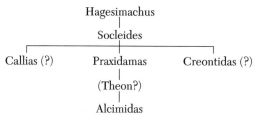

The line of Aeoladas (*Parth.* 2)
(reconstruction of L. Lehnus, "Pindaro: il *Dafneforico
per Agasicle*," *Bulletin of the Institute of Classical
Studies* 31 [1984] 85)

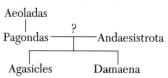

INDEX OF PROPER NAMES

References are to lines in the Greek text

Abas, grandfather of Adrastus, king of Argos, *Pyth.* 8.55; *Dith.* 1.9

Abderus, son of Poseidon, eponymous hero of Abdera, *Pae.* 2.1, 2.104

Acastus, son of Pelias, husband of Hippolyta, king of Iolcus, *Nem.* 4.57, 5.30

Achaeans, early Greeks, *Nem.* 7.64, 10.47; *Isth.* 1.31, 1.58; *Pae.* 6.85

Acharnae, a deme of Athens, *Nem.* 2.16

Acheloös, river in Acarnania, *fr.* 70.1

Acheron, river of the under-world, *Pyth.* 11.21; *Nem.* 4.85; *fr.* 143.3

Achilles, son of Peleus and Thetis, father of Neoptolemus, raised by Chiron, fought at Troy, *Ol.* 2.79, 9.71, 10.19; *Pyth.* 8.100; *Nem.* 3.43, 4.49, 6.50b, 7.27,

8.30; *Isth.* 8.48, 8.55a. *See* Peleus

Acragas, city on south coast of Sicily, *Ol.* 2.6, 2.91, 3.2; *Pyth.* 6.6; *Isth.* 2.17; river running through Acragas, *Pyth.* 12.3

Acron, father of Psaumis of Camarina, *Ol.* 5.8

Actor, father of Menoetius, grandfather of Patroclus, *Ol.* 9.69

Admetus, son of Pheres, cousin of Jason, *Pyth.* 4.126

Adrastus, son of Talaus, brother of Eriphyle, king of Argos and Sicyon, leader of the Seven against Thebes, founded athletic festivals at Nemea and Sicyon, *Ol.* 2.45, 6.13; *Pyth.* 8.51; *Nem.* 8.51, 9.9, 10.12, 10.28; *Isth.* 4.26, 7.10

Aeacidae, descendants of Aeacus (including Peleus, Telamon, Achilles, Ajax, and Neoptolemus) prominent in

INDEX

441

INDEX

Eirene (Εἰρήνα). *See* Peace

Elatus: (1) father of Aepytus, king of Phaesana in Arcadia, *Ol.* 6.33; (2) father of Ischys, *Pyth.* 3.31

Electran Gates, at Thebes, *Isth.* 4.61

Eleithyia, goddess of childbirth, *Ol.* 6.42; *Pyth.* 3.9; *Nem.* 7.1; *Pae.* 12.17

Eleusis, city near Athens, site of sanctuary of Demeter and of games honoring her, *Ol.* 9.99, 13.110; *Isth.* 1.57

Elis, the district around Olympia, *Ol.* 1.78, 9.7, 10.33; Elean, *Isth.* 2.24. *See* Epeians

Emmenidae, clan of Theron and Xenocrates of Acragas, *Ol.* 3.38; *Pyth.* 6.5

Endais, daughter of Chiron, wife of Aeacus, mother of Peleus and Telamon, *Nem.* 5.12

Enyalius, a name of Ares, *Ol.* 13.106; *Nem.* 9.37; *Isth.* 6.54; *Dith.* 2.16; *fr.* 169a.12

Epaphus, son of Zeus and Io, father of Libya, *Pyth.* 4.14; *Nem.* 10.5

Epeians, ancient inhabitants of Elis, *Ol.* 9.58, 10.35

Epharmostus, of Opus, victor in wrestling at Olympia, *Ol.* 9.4, 9.87

Ephialtes, gigantic son of Poseidon and Iphimedeia, brother of Otus, *Pyth.* 4.89

Ephyra, capital of Thesprotia, a district in Epirus, *Nem.* 7.37

Ephyraeans, inhabitants of Ephyra (later called Crannon) in Thessaly, *Pyth.* 10.55

Epidaurus, city in the Argolid, site of games honoring Asclepius, *Nem.* 3.84, 5.52; *Isth.* 8.68

Epigoni, descendants of the Seven against Thebes, *Pyth.* 8.42

Epimetheus (Hindsight), brother of Prometheus (Foresight), *Pyth.* 5.27

Epizephyrian Locrians. *See* Locri

Eratidae, clan of Rhodes, *Ol.* 7.93

Erechtheus, legendary king of Athens, *Pyth.* 7.10; *Isth.* 2.19

Ergoteles, son of Philanor, of Himera, victor in dolichos at Olympia, *Ol.* 12.18

Eriboas (Loud-Shouter), epithet of Dionysus, *fr.* 75.10

Eriboea, wife of Telamon, mother of Ajax, *Isth.* 6.45

Eriphyle, sister of Adrastus, wife of Amphiaraus, *Nem.* 9.16

Eritimus, son (or grandson) of Terpsias of Corinth, *Ol.* 13.42

Erytus, son of Hermes, brother of Echion, Argonaut, *Pyth.* 4.179

Ethiopian, *Ol.* 2.83; Ethiopians,

INDEX

Geryon (Geryones), king in
Spain whose cattle, guarded
by a three-headed dog, were
stolen by Heracles, *Isth.* 1.13;
fr. 81.2, 169a.6

Giants, children of Gaea, slain
by Heracles and the gods at
Phlegra, *Pyth.* 8.17; *Nem.*
1.67, 7.90. *See* Alcyoneus;
Porphyrion

Glaucus, son (or grandson) of
Bellerophon, of Lycia, Trojan
ally, *Ol.* 13.60

Good Cheer (Εὐθυμία), *fr.*
155.3

Gorgons, the three daughters of
Phorcus (Euralye, Medusa,
and Stheno), *Pyth.* 12.7; *Dith.*
1.5; specifically of Medusa,
Ol. 13.63; *Pyth.* 10.46; *Nem.*
10.4. *See* Euryale; Medusa;
Phorcus

Graces (Χάριτες), the three
daughters of Zeus and
Eurynome (Aglaia,
Euphrosyne, and Thalia),
goddesses of loveliness and
pleasure, worshipped espe-
cially at Orchomenus, *Ol.*
2.50, 4.9, 9.27, 14.4, 14.8;
Pyth. 2.42, 5.45, 6.2, 8.21,
9.3, 9.89a, 12.26; *Nem.* 4.7,
5.54, 6.37, 9.54, 10.1, 10.38;
Isth. 5.21, 6.63, 8.16a; *Pae.*
4.13, 6.3, 7.10, 12.7; *fr.* 95.4.
See Aglaia; Charis;
Euphrosyne; Thalia

Gray-Eyed Goddess. *See*
Athena

Great Mother (Rhea, Cybele),
Pyth. 3.78; *Dith.* 2.9; *fr.* 95.3

Hades, brother of Zeus, hus-
band of Persephone, god of
the underworld, *Ol.* 8.72,
9.33, 10.92; *Pyth.* 3.11; *Nem.*
7.31, 10.67; *Isth.* 1.68, 6.15;
synonymous with the under-
world, *Pyth.* 4.44, 5.96

Haemones, early inhabitants of
Thessaly, *Nem.* 4.56

Hagesias, son of Sostratus, of
Syracuse and Stymphalus,
victor in mule race at Olym-
pia, *Ol.* 6.12, 6.77, 6.98

Hagesidamus: (1) son of
Archestratus, of Western
Locri, victor in boys' boxing
at Olympia, *Ol.* 10.18, 10.92,
11.12; (2) father of Chromius
of Syracuse, *Nem.* 1.29, 9.42

Hagesilas, father of Theoxenus
of Tenedos, *fr.* 123.15

Hagesimachus, great-great-
grandfather of Alcimidas of
Aegina, *Nem.* 6.22

Halirothius, father of Samus of
Mantinea, *Ol.* 10.70

Harmonia, daughter of Ares
and Aphrodite, wife of
Cadmus, mother of Semele
and Ino, *Pyth.* 3.91, 11.7;
Dith. 2.27; *fr.* 29.6

Hebe (Goddess of Youth),
daughter of Hera, wife of the
deified Heracles, *Ol.* 6.58;
Pyth. 9.109; *Nem.* 1.71, 7.4,
10.18; *Isth.* 4.59

451

INDEX

daughter of Justice, *Ol.* 4.16;
Pyth. 8.1; *fr.* 109.2; (2) Eirene
(Εἰρήνα), daughter of
Themis, *Ol.* 13.7. *See also*
Horae; Justice; Order

Pegasus, winged horse arising
from the dead body of
Medusa, tamed by
Bellerophon, *Ol.* 13.64; *Isth.*
7.44

Pelasgian, from Pelasgiotis in
Thessaly, *fr.* 107a.1

Peleus, son of Aeacus and
Endais, brother of Telamon,
husband of Thetis, father of
Achilles, *Ol.* 2.78; *Pyth.* 3.87,
8.100; *Nem.* 3.33, 4.56, 5.26;
Isth. 6.25, 8.38; *fr.* 172.1; his
son Achilles, *Pyth.* 6.23; *Pae.*
6.99

Pelias, son of Poseidon and
Tyro, father of Acastus, king
of Iolcus, *Pyth.* 4.71, 4.94,
4.109, 4.134, 4.156, 4.250;
Nem. 4.60

Pelinna, city in Thessaly, *Pyth.*
10.4

Pelion, mountain of Magnesia
in Thessaly, *Pyth.* 2.45, 3.4,
9.5; *Nem.* 4.54, 5.22

Pellana, city in Achaea, site of
games, *Ol.* 7.86, 9.98, 13.109;
Nem. 10.44

Pelops, son of Tantalus, hus-
band of Hippodameia, king
of Pisa, *Ol.* 1.24, 1.95, 3.23,
5.9, 9.9, 10.24; *Nem.* 2.21,
8.12

Peneius, river in Thessaly, *Pyth.*
9.16, 10.56

Pergamia (Troy), *Isth.* 6.31

Pergamum (Troy), *Ol.* 8.42; *Pae.*
6.96

Periclymenus: (1) son of
Neleus, of Pylos, Argonaut,
Pyth. 4.175; (2) son of Posei-
don, defender of Thebes
against the Seven, *Nem.* 9.26

Persephone, daughter of
Demeter, queen of the un-
derworld, *Ol.* 14.21; *Pyth.*
12.2; *Nem.* 1.14; *Isth.* 8.55; *fr.*
133.1

Perseus, son of Zeus and
Danaë, slayer of Medusa,
Pyth. 10.31, 12.11; *Nem.*
10.4; *Isth.* 5.33

Persuasion (Πειθώ), of sexual
attraction, *Pyth.* 4.219, 9.39a;
fr. 122.2, 123.14

Phaesana, city of Arcadia on the
Alpheus, *Ol.* 6.34

Phalaris, tyrant of Acragas,
Pyth. 1.96

Phasis, river of Colchis, *Pyth.*
4.211; *Isth.* 2.41

Pherenicus (Victory-Bringer),
Hieron's horse, *Ol.* 1.18;
Pyth. 3.74

Pheres (Beasts), another name
for Centaurs, *fr.* 166.1

Pheres, son of Cretheus, uncle
of Jason, *Pyth.* 4.125

Philanor, father of Ergoteles of
Himera, *Ol.* 12.13

Philoctetes, son of Poeas, ar-

INDEX

Polydeuces, son of Zeus and Leda, half-brother of Castor, *Pyth.* 11.62; *Nem.* 10.50, 10.59, 10.68; *Isth.* 5.33

Polymnastus: (1) father of Battus of Cyrene, *Pyth.* 4.59; (2) son of Meles, of Colophon, 7th-cent. choral poet, *fr.* 188.2

Polyneices, son of Oedipus, father of Thersandrus, *Ol.* 2.43

Polytimidas, relative of Alcimidas of Aegina, *Nem.* 6.62

Porphyrion, king of the Giants, killed by Apollo, *Pyth.* 8.12

Poseidon, son of Cronus, husband of Amphitrite, patron of the Isthmian games, *Ol.* 1.26, 1.75, 5.21, 6.29, 6.58, 8.31, 9.31, 10.26, 13.5, 13.40; *Pyth.* 4.45; *Nem.* 5.37, 6.41; *Isth.* 1.32, 2.14, 4.54b, 8.27; *Pae.* 2.2, 2.41, 15.3; Earthholder (Γαιάοχος), *Ol.* 1.25, 13.81; *Pyth.* 4.33; *Isth.* 7.38; Earthshaker (Ἐννοσίδας), *Pyth.* 4.33, 4.173; *Pae.* 4.41; Earthshaker (Ἐλελίχθων), *Pyth.* 6.50; Horsetamer (Δαμαῖος), *Ol.* 13.69; of the Fine Trident (Εὐτρίαινα), *Ol.* 1.73; of the Rock (Πετραῖος), *Pyth.* 4.138; of the Sea, *Pyth.* 4.204; of the Splendid Trident (Ἀγλαοτρίαινα), *Ol.* 1.40; Wielder of the Trident

(Ὀρσοτρίαινα), *Ol.* 8.48; *Nem.* 4.86; *Pae.* 9.47

Praxidamas, grandfather of Alcimidas of Aegina, *Nem.* 6.15

Priam, king of Troy, killed by Neoptolemus, *Pyth.* 1.54, 11.19; *Nem.* 7.35; *Pae.* 6.113

Proetus, son of Abas, king of Argos, *Nem.* 10.41

Prophasis (Excuse), daughter of Epimetheus (Hindsight), *Pyth.* 5.28

Protesilas (Protesilaus), king of Phylaca in Thessaly, in whose honor games were held, *Isth.* 1.58

Protogeneia, daughter of Pyrrha and Deucalion and, apparently, also daughter of Opus of Elis, mother by Zeus of Opus, eponymous hero of Locrian Opus, *Ol.* 9.41

Psalychiadae, a clan of Aegina, *Isth.* 6.63

Psamatheia, daughter of Nereus, mother by Aeacus of Phocus, *Nem.* 5.13

Psaumis, son of Acron, of Camarina, victor in chariot and mule races at Olympia, *Ol.* 4.10, 5.3, 5.23

Ptoeodorus, father of Thessalus, grandfather of Xenophon of Corinth, *Ol.* 13.41

Ptoïon, mountain in Boeotia, site of a sanctuary of Apollo, *fr.* 51b.2

460

INDEX

463

INDEX

Therapna, town near Sparta, home of Castor and Polydeuces, *Pyth.* 11.63; *Nem.* 10.56; *Isth.* 1.31

Theron, son of Aenesidamus, brother of Xenocrates, uncle of Thrasybulus, tyrant of Acragas, *Ol.* 2.5, 2.95, 3.3, 3.39, 3.43

Thersandrus (Thersander), son of Polyneices, ancestor of Theron of Acragas, *Ol.* 2.43

Thessalus, son of Ptoeodorus, father of Xenophon of Corinth, *Ol.* 13.35

Thessaly, region of northern Greece, *Pyth.* 10.2; Thessalians, *Pyth.* 10.70

Thetis, daughter of Nereus, wife of Peleus, mother of Achilles, *Ol.* 9.76; *Pyth.* 3.92, 3.101; *Nem.* 3.35, 4.50, 5.25; *Isth.* 8.27, 8.47; *Pae.* 6.84

Thorax, of Thessaly, commissioned *Pyth.* 10 for Hippocleas, *Pyth.* 10.64

Thracian, of the area between Macedonia and the Black Sea, *Pyth.* 4.205; *Pae.* 2.25

Thrasybulus, son of Xenocrates, of Acragas, *Pyth.* 6.15, 6.44; *Isth.* 2.1, 2.31; *fr.* 124.1

Thrasyclus, relative of Theaeus of Argos, *Nem.* 10.39

Thrasydaeus, son of Pythonicus, of Thebes, victor in boys' stadion at Delphi, *Pyth.* 11.13, 11.44

Thronia, a Naiad, mother by Poseidon of Abderus, *Pae.* 2.1

Thyone, another name for Semele, *Pyth.* 3.99

Tilphossa, a spring, site of Apollo's shrine, *fr.* 198b.2

Timasarchus, son of Timocritus, of Aegina, victor in wrestling at Nemea, *Nem.* 4.10, 4.78

Time (Χρόνος), *Ol.* 2.17, 10.55; *fr.* 33.2, 159

Timocritus, deceased father of Timasarchus of Aegina, *Nem.* 4.13

Timodemidae, clan of Aegina, *Nem.* 2.18

Timodemus, son of Timonoös, of Acharnae, victor in pancratium at Nemea, *Nem.* 2.14, 2.24

Timonoös, father of Timodemus of Acharnae, *Nem.* 2.10

Timosthenes, elder brother of Alcimedon of Aegina, *Ol.* 8.15

Tiryns, city in the Argolid, home of Eurystheus, Heracles, Tlapolemus, *Ol.* 7.29, 10.68; Tirynthians, *Ol.* 7.78, 10.31; *Isth.* 6.28

Titans, children of Uranus and Gaea, subdued by Zeus but later released, *Pyth.* 4.291

Tityus, son of Zeus and Elara, tried to rape Leto, killed by Artemis, *Pyth.* 4.46, 4.90

Tlapolemus, son of Heracles and Astydameia, of Tiryns,

MAPS

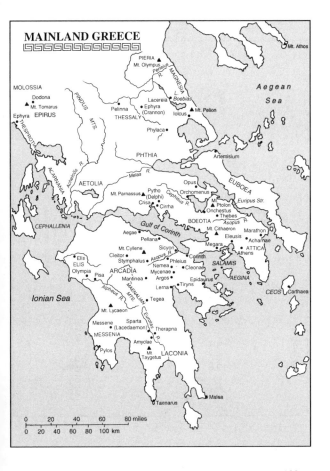

MAINLAND GREECE

Mt. Athos

PIERIA
Mt. Olympus ▲
Peneius R.

MAGNESIA

Aegean Sea

MOLOSSIA
Dodona •
▲ Mt. Tomarus

PINDUS MTS.

Lacereia •
Ephyra •
(Crannon)
L. *Boebias*

Pelinna •
THESSALY

Iolcus •
▲ Mt. Pelion

Ephyra •
EPIRUS

THESPROTIA

Phylaca •

Achelous R.

PHTHIA

Artemisium

ACARNANIA

AETOLIA
Melas R.

Opus
Orchomenus •
Cephisus R.

EUBOEA

Mt. Parnassus ▲
Pytho
(Delphi)
Crisa •
• Cirrha

Mt. Ptolon ▲
• Onchestus
• Thebes
Asopus R.

Euripus Str.

BOEOTIA

CEPHALLENIA

Gulf of Corinth

Aegae •
Pellana •

Mt. Cithaeron ▲

Marathon •
Eleusis •
• Acharnae
ATTICA
• Athens

Mt. Cyllene ▲
Cleitor •
Stymphalus •

Sicyon •
Asopus R.
• Phleius

Corinth •

Megara •

SALAMIS

• Elis
ELIS
Olympia •
Pisa •

ARCADIA

Nemea •
Mycenae •
Argos •
Mantinea •
Cleonae •

Epidaurus •
• Tiryns
Lerna •

AEGINA

Ionian Sea

Alpheus R.

MAENALIAN MTS.

▲ Mt. Lycaeon

• Tegea

CEOS Carthaea

Messene •
MESSENIA

Sparta •
(Lacedaemon)
Eurotas R.
• Therapna

Amyclae •
LACONIA

Pylos •

Mt. Taygetus ▲

Taenarus ▲

• Malea

0   20   40   60   80 miles
0 20 40 60 80 100 km

469

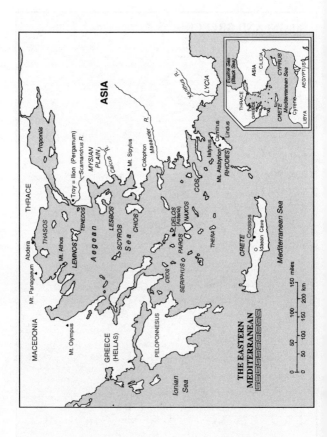

THE EASTERN MEDITERRANEAN

MACEDONIA
Mt. Olympus
GREECE (HELLAS)
PELOPONNESUS
Ionian Sea

THRACE
Mt. Panagaeum
Abdera
THASOS
Mt. Athos
LEMNOS
TENEDOS
Aegean Sea
SCYROS
LESBOS
CHIOS
CEOS
SERIPHUS
PAROS
DELOS (Asteria)
NAXOS
THERA
CRETE
Cnossos
Idaean Cave
Mediterranean Sea

ASIA
Proponis
Troy = Ilion (Pergamum)
Scamandrus R.
MYSIAN PLAIN
Caicus R.
Mt. Sipylus
Colophon
Maeander R.
COS
Xanthus R.
LYCIA
Mt. Atabyrion
Camirus
Ialysus
Lindus
RHODES

Euxine Sea (Black Sea)
ASIA
CILICIA
CYPRUS
THRACE
GREECE
CRETE
Mediterranean Sea
Cyrene
LIBYA
AEGYPTUS

0   50   100   150 miles
0   50 100 150 200 km

470